CIPS Study Matters

Level 5

Advanced Diploma in Purchasing and Supply

Risk Management and Supply Chain Vulnerability

Second Edition

Neil Cowan
Corporate control, governance, audit
and risk management consultant

THE
CHARTERED INSTITUTE OF
PURCHASING & SUPPLY®

Published by

The Chartered Institute of Purchasing and Supply
Easton House, Easton on the Hill, Stamford, Lincolnshire PE9 3NZ
Tel: +44 (0) 1780 756 777
Fax: +44 (0) 1780 751 610
Email: info@cips.org
Website: http://www.cips.org

First published July 2006
Second edition published June 2009

While every effort has been made to ensure that references to websites
are correct at time of going to press, the world wide web is a constantly
changing environment and CIPS cannot accept any responsibility for any
changes to addresses.

CIPS acknowledges product, service and company names referred to in this
publication, many of which are trade names, service marks, trademarks or
registered trademarks.

CIPS, The Chartered Institute of Purchasing & Supply and its logo are all
trademarks of the Chartered Institute of Purchasing & Supply.

The right of Neil Cowan to be identified as author of this work has been
asserted by him in accordance with the Copyright, Designs and Patents
Act 1988, in force or as amended from time to time.

Instructional design and publishing project management by Wordhouse Ltd,
Reading, UK

Content management system, instructional editing and pre-press by Echelon
Learning Ltd, London, UK

Index prepared by Indexing Specialists (UK) Ltd, Hove, UK

ISBN 978-1-86124-183-2

Contents

Introduction

This course book has been designed to assist you in studying for the CIPS Risk Management and Supply Chain Vulnerability unit in the Level 5 Advanced Diploma in Purchasing and Supply. The book covers all topics in the official CIPS unit content document, as illustrated in the table beginning on page xi.

The traditional idea that risk is the preserve only of actuaries, insurers and lenders no longer prevails. The ability to identify and evaluate strategic and operational risks is now an integral part of the management task and is central to ensuring the future well-being of all organisations.

The most effective approach to risk management is to involve staff at all levels in the risk assessment process. Education and training in risk should reflect the organisation's risk appetite and the enthusiasm for initiating and maintaining an effective approach to risk management should start at the top and permeate the entire organisation. When risk awareness becomes part of the organisational culture, every employee becomes a risk manager, rather than risk becoming segregated as a separate operational function.

How to use this book

The course book will take you step by step through the unit content in a series of carefully planned 'study sessions' and provide you with learning activities, self-assessment questions and revision questions to help you master the subject matter. The guide should help you organise and carry out your studies in a methodical, logical and effective way, but if you have your own study preferences you will find it a flexible resource too.

Before you begin using this course book, make sure you are familiar with any advice provided by CIPS on such things as study skills, revision techniques or support and how to handle formal assessments.

If you are on a taught course, it will be up to your tutor to explain how to use the book – when to read the study sessions, when to tackle the activities and questions, and so on.

If you are on a self-study course, or studying independently, you can use the course book in the following way:

- Scan the whole book to get a feel for the nature and content of the subject matter.
- Plan your overall study schedule so that you allow enough time to complete all 20 study sessions well before your examinations – in other words, leaving plenty of time for revision.

- For each session, set aside enough time for reading the text, tackling all the learning activities and self-assessment questions, and the revision question at the end of the session, and for the suggested further reading. Guidance on roughly how long you should set aside for studying each session is given at the beginning of the session.

Now let's take a look at the structure and content of the individual study sessions.

Overview of the study sessions

The course book breaks the content down into 20 sessions, which vary from three to six or seven hours' duration each. However, we are not advising you to study for this sort of time without a break! The sessions are simply a convenient way of breaking the syllabus into manageable chunks. Most people would try to study one or two sessions a week, taking one or two breaks within each session. You will quickly find out what suits you best.

Each session begins with a brief **introduction** which sets out the areas of the syllabus being covered and explains, if necessary, how the session fits in with the topics that come before and after.

After the introduction there is a statement of the **session learning objectives**. The objectives are designed to help you understand exactly what you should be able to do after you've studied the session. You might find it helpful to tick them off as you progress through the session. You will also find them useful during revision. There is one session learning objective for each numbered subsection of the session.

After this, there is a brief section reproducing the learning objectives and indicative content from the official **unit content document**. This will help you to understand exactly which part of the syllabus you are studying in the current session.

Following this, there are **prior knowledge** and **resources** sections if necessary. These will let you know if there are any topics you need to be familiar with before tackling each particular session, or any special resources you might need, such as a calculator or graph paper.

Then the main part of the study session begins, with the first of the numbered main subsections. At regular intervals in each study session, we have provided you with **learning activities**, which are designed to get you actively involved in the learning process. You should always try to complete the activities – usually on a separate sheet of your own paper – before reading on. You will learn much more effectively if you are actively involved in doing something as you study, rather than just passively reading the text in front of you. The feedback or answers to the activities are provided at the end of the session. Do not be tempted to skip the activity.

We also provide a number of **self-assessment questions** in each study session. These are to help you to decide for yourself whether or not you have achieved the learning objectives set out at the beginning of the session. As with the activities, you should always tackle them   usually on a separate sheet of paper. Don't be tempted to skip them. The feedback or answers are again at the end of the session. If you still do not understand a topic having attempted the self-assessment question, always try to re-read the relevant passages in the textbook readings or session, or follow the advice on further reading at the end of the session. If this still doesn't work, you should contact the CIPS Membership and Qualification Advice team.

For most of the learning activities and self-assessment questions you will need to use separate sheets of paper for your answers or responses. Some of the activities or questions require you to complete a table or form, in which case you could write your response in the course book itself, or photocopy the page.

At the end of the session are three final sections.

The first is the **summary**. Use it to remind yourself or check off what you have just studied, or later on during revision.

Then follows the **suggested further reading** section. This section, if it appears, contains recommendations for further reading which you can follow up if you would like to read alternative treatments of the topics. If for any reason you are having difficulty understanding the course book on a particular topic, try one of the alternative treatments recommended. If you are keen to read around and beyond the syllabus, to help you pick up extra points in the examination for example, you may like to try some of the additional readings recommended. If this section does not appear at the end of a session, it usually means that further reading for the session topics is not necessary.

At the end of the session we direct you to a **revision question**, which you will find in a separate section at the end of the course book. Feedback on the questions is also given.

Reading lists

CIPS produces an official reading list, which recommends essential and desirable texts for augmenting your studies. This reading list is available on the CIPS website or from the CIPS Bookshop. This course book is one of the essential texts for this unit. In this section we describe the main characteristics of the other essential text for this unit, which you are strongly urged to buy and use throughout your course.

The other essential text is:

The Complete Guide to Business Risk Management, 2nd edition, by Kit Sadgrove, published by Gower in 2005.

This book has a wide scope and gives a comprehensive coverage of risk management. It progresses from the need for effective risk management to the consideration of both strategic and operational risk and covers all the topics required by the CIPS syllabus. Chapters are well introduced and the text is clear and easy to read. There are many useful links to relevant websites and appropriate further reading is also well signposted.

Various operational areas are covered in terms of management's response to risk in each area – purchasing has its own dedicated chapter – and there is clear differentiation between threats and hazards, their impact and probability. The importance of risk standards is considered in relation to the proliferation of other standards and legal requirements which organisations must take heed of. Practice in both public and private sectors is taken account of but, if there is any criticism to be levelled at the book, it is in the lack of detail of the means by which mitigating strategies can be developed. Mitigating and controlling risks is covered but there is insufficient detail as to how these can be applied in practice. Similarly, the role of control frameworks and models as a powerful means for mitigating risks is not given appropriate significance.

Second edition amendments

The main changes introduced in this second edition relate to the area of negotiation, which is crucial in the context of risk management and supply chain vulnerability. In this course book candidates will be afforded the opportunity to learn about the use of sound negotiation approaches and techniques to help ensure better business value by reducing risk and vulnerability. Statements of practice and business intelligence considerations are also introduced in this edition.

Unit content coverage

In this section we reproduce the whole of the official CIPS unit content document for this unit. The overall unit characteristics and statements of practice for the unit are given first. Then, in the table that follows, the learning objectives and indicative content are given in the left hand column. In the right hand column are the study sessions in which you will find coverage of the various topics.

Unit characteristics

This unit is designed to enable students to undertake risk analysis and a variety of risk assessments relating to different aspects of purchasing and supply and to implement a range of appropriate risk management tools and techniques.

Students will use a variety of risk assessment tools and techniques designed to provide a detailed analysis of supply chain situations, including legal, corporate social responsibility (CSR), ethical, health and safety, financial, international, innovation and a variety of other potential risk scenarios. The scope covers both the proactive identification and avoidance of risk, as well as provision for post-event recovery initiatives.

By the end of the unit students should be able to:

- demonstrate a good knowledge and understanding of risk awareness and an effective approach to risk management
- apply a variety of tools and techniques, in a diverse range of contexts, to proactively establish the level of risk presented and to recommend ways of avoiding, mitigating or managing those risks.

Statements of practice

On completion of this unit, students will be able to:

- Analyse the nature and scope of risks for the organisation
- Assess the sources of risks and the likely impact of those risks upon the organisation
- Plan and implement an appropriate risk management process in order to protect the organisation's interests
- Explain how supplier appraisals, pre-qualification of suppliers and contract monitoring can help to mitigate risks
- Evaluate systems for testing risks and monitoring them accordingly
- Apply risk management principles to various purchasing and supply management scenarios
- Evaluate the application of a range of techniques to mitigate risk proactively and to reduce the consequential losses in the instance of a risk event occurring

- Explain how the use of sound negotiation approaches and techniques help to ensure better business value by reducing risk and vulnerability.

Learning objectives and indicative content

1.0 Understanding the nature of risk in purchasing and supply (Weighting 25%)

1.1 Define the terminology used in risk assessment and management.

Study session 1

- Definition of risk with use of examples
- How risk has a direct impact on an organisation's success and how risk can be directly related to cost
- Key terms: hazard, risk, risk event, exposure, loss - direct, indirect and consequential - mitigation, avoidance, assessment, management, force majeure and acts of God
- The differences between risk, vulnerability, exposure and loss, as well as understanding the range of management actions available
- What is meant by a risk appetite and use of practical examples to show how this is applied

1.2 Distinguish between direct physical loss (eg disrupted supply) and indirect consequential loss (eg reputation).

Study session 1

- Key types of loss that may occur: financial, reputational, environmental, health, safety, welfare and lost opportunities

1.3 Analyse potential sources of risk to organisations of both internal and external origin.

Study session 2

- Internal and external hazards and risks
- Range of risks that might occur within the workplace
- Analysis of external environment factors using the PESTLE tool
- The likely impact on the organisation and its appetite for risk
- Basic quantification methods for measuring

1.4 Analyse and explain the use of segmentation and business tools to reduce supply chain vulnerability.

Study session 2

- Segmentation tools to help assess and manage supply chain risk appropriately (eg Kraljic, Boston, Pareto, KPIs, Spider web or appropriate alternatives)
- How you would take a different approach to purchasing from a critical or bottleneck market to that of a leveraged or acquisition market
- Management of different products or services within an organisational portfolio
- Definition of supply chain vulnerability, supply failure and supplier failure
- How to map a typical supply chain and identify potential sources of supply vulnerability
- The potential impact of supply and supplier failure
- Range of mitigating activities that a purchaser could use when looking to protect against supply or supplier failure

1.5 Distinguish between strategic, operational and project-based areas of risk.

Study session 3

- Examples of how to define risk at the strategic, operational and/or project-based level
- Range of risk mitigation methods at each level
- How risk can be bounded and also how, if unmanaged, it can have knock-on consequential impacts on other areas of an organisation

1.6 Evaluate the role of an organisation's stakeholders in risk management.   Study session 4
- The roles and responsibilities of an organisation's risk function in relation to other functional areas
- The impact of a risk event at the functional level
- The benefits of a cross-functional team when assessing, preventing and minimising risk
- The role of purchasing to mitigate against potential losses to the whole organisation from risk events
- The merits of taking a consistent approach across the organisation to the assessment of risk

1.7 Evaluate how effective risk management can have positive benefits for organisations.   Study session 5
- Reduction in levels of threat
- Reduced exposure to uncertainty
- Higher risk opportunities being successfully pursued or mitigated
- Successful anticipation of shocks or other risk events
- Crises being avoided or mitigated
- Successful application of contingency or business continuity plans
- Disaster recovery planning and implementation
- Limited or no reputational or public relations damage
- Securing supply and mitigation of supply chain vulnerability
- Improved decision and policy making
- Increased customer and stakeholder satisfaction
- Improved organisational co-ordination with service and delivery partners

1.8 Assess risks involved with using technology.   Study session 2
- Reliance on technology
- Security
- Hackers
- Fraud
- Storing of vital documents and materials

2.0 Risk management processes and structures (Weighting 25%)
2.1 Develop a risk management strategy.   Study session 6
- Example of an appropriate supply chain risk policy
- How to define objectives and content for a risk management strategy
- How an organisation's appetite for risk may affect the risk policy
- The purpose of a risk management strategy and a risk management framework

- The key components of a risk management strategy
- The key implications of the Turnbull report

2.2 Formulate an effective risk management process in the context
of an organisation's strategic objectives and a dynamic external
environment.   Study session 7

- Key stages of a risk management process; risk identification,
risk analysis, risk evaluation, risk treatment and risk
reporting
- Methods for identifying, assessing and quantifying risks
- Classification of risk within the organisational context
- A risk report and the role of a board risk committee
- How identified risks should be monitored and reviewed

2.3 Evaluate the probability of a risk occurring in particular
circumstances, the possible consequences and the potential
range of mitigating actions required.   Study session 7

- Definition of probability in relation to the occurrence of a
risk event
- How the likelihood of a risk occurrence will affect the
approach to risk management
- Application of the use of historic statistical data in
predicting the likelihood of future risk occurrences
- Identification of a range of operational risks and a
probability assigned to each one
- Prioritisation of key risks with explanation as to how
resources might be allocated appropriately to mitigate such
risks

2.4 Analyse the resources required for effective risk management
and for building a risk aware culture within organisations.   Study session 8

- Responsibility of everyone in an organisation
- Definition of risk awareness and the benefits of awareness
- Description of an appropriate communication programme
to promote risk awareness
- How different functions can work together to reduce risk
- Promotion of a risk awareness culture among key elements
of the supplier base
- How suppliers can assist in the promotion of risk awareness

2.5 Propose ways in which third party supplier resources are used to
reduce risk and mitigate losses during a risk event.   Study session 9

- Range of supply solutions for mitigating losses in the
aftermath of a risk event: insurance, loss adjusting,
alternative accommodation, disaster recovery plus
restoration and recovery services
- Appropriate methods of purchasing and paying for disaster
recovery services both during a risk event and in the normal
run of business
- Incentives to retain specialist services at times of national
disaster, including flood and hurricane damage

2.6 Develop an appropriate risk register for the purchasing and
supply function.   Study session 8

- Definition of a risk register and the benefits of having one
- Outline of key components of a risk register
- The process of maintaining and reviewing a risk register

- What is meant by a contingency plan?
- The key components of a business continuity plan (BCP) and disaster recovery plan and how such plans are put into practice
- Key contingency measures used by a BCP: telephone cascades, emergency and fire wardens, use of IT systems to help co-ordinate activities, use of alternative accommodation and back-up information technology systems
- The benefits of business continuity planning from an operational, financial and reputational perspective

3.4 Analyse specific key risks and exposures in purchasing and supply and identify appropriate mitigating actions.
- Contractual failure, consequential loss and provision for remedies
- Supplier insolvency, monitoring and guarantees
- Quality failure, non-conformity and corrective action
- Project failure, project planning principles and corrective action
- Security of supply, contingency planning, stock holding and alternative sources of supply
- Technology failure, impact on supply, use of back-up systems and disaster recovery
- Security, theft and damage
- Fraud, accounting and payment exposures, conflicts of interest, purchasing ethics and codes of conduct
- Product liability, reputational damage, consumer confidence

3.5 Formulate sound and appropriate negotiation strategies to reduce future contract risk and supply chain vulnerability to enhance long-term business value.
- Key steps in negotiation planning for success
- Strategic approach and negotiation techniques
- Good practice methodology
- Tactics and standpoints
- Behaviours of successful negotiators
- Contractual issues and remedies
- Dispute resolution alternatives

Study session 1
Introduction, terminology and definitions

Introduction

Ordinary, everyday life means taking risks. Mostly this is done subconsciously – dodging traffic while crossing a road, running rather than walking up a moving escalator or speeding in a restricted area – and it's the same in business. Risk taking is the very lifeblood of commerce. *No risk, no reward.* Entrepreneurial risk is at the foundation of enterprise. Without risk there can be little prospect of profit or financial return. The trick is to understand the risk, assess the possible outcomes and manage them effectively.

It is a fact that people working in the management of supply chains are faced with every type of uncertainty in every single aspect of their job. It is said that nothing is certain but death and taxes. It is likely that supply chain managers and procurement staff will be dealing with risks and uncertainties every day of their working life. Only the alert and intelligent supply chain professional will recognise that these vulnerabilities need to be managed in order to protect their organisation from the damage and losses that these uncertainties may create.

'There is no way you can succeed in business by playing safe. It is always less risky to take risks.'
Hans Rausing of Tetrapak, quoted in *The Universe of Risk* by Pamela Shimell

Session learning objectives

After completing this session you should be able to:

1.1 Give examples of the definitions and meanings of the key words and phrases used in risk management.
1.2 Recognise some of the risks that an organisation faces in the modern world.
1.3 Describe the risk cycle.
1.4 Describe the role of a risk manager.

Unit content coverage

This study session covers the following topics from the official CIPS unit content document:

Learning objectives

1.1 Define the terminology used in risk assessment and management.
   • Definition of risk with use of examples
   • How risk has a direct impact on an organisation's success and how risk can be directly related to cost
   • Key terms: hazard, risk, risk event, exposure, loss – direct, indirect and consequential – mitigation, avoidance, assessment, management, force majeure and acts of God

- The differences between risk, vulnerability, exposure and loss, as well as understanding the range of management actions available
- What is meant by a risk appetite and use of practical examples to show how this is applied

1.2 Distinguish between direct physical loss (eg disrupted supply) and indirect consequential loss (eg reputation).
- Key types of loss that may occur: financial, reputational, environmental, health, safety, welfare and lost opportunities

Resources

You will need to gain access to two people, preferably colleagues, who have experience of managing risk and who will be happy to discuss this with you. You also need to become familiar with websites which deal with the management of risk, for example, the Institute of Risk Management http://www.theirm.org.

Timing

You should set aside about 2.75 hours to read and complete this session, including learning activities, self-assessment questions, the suggested further reading (if any) and the revision question.

1.1 Definitions and terms used in risk management

Learning activity 1.1

Jill is a safety equipment buyer who needs to decide upon which of several suppliers she should use for the supply of some safety equipment for her engineers. She places an order with Jones plc because their equipment has the lowest purchase price. Once the equipment is being used, Jill goes to visit the engineers to see how they are using the equipment. She is surprised to see that some of the engineers are refusing to use it and others are using it incorrectly. She tells them to carry on as best they can and she will contact the suppliers to arrange some training. She then arranges a training programme with the supplier.

Task: Jill thought that she was saving money by taking the cheapest option but the fact that the equipment is not being used or not used properly means that there is a risk that any saving will be wasted. There is also a risk of additional expenditure and that the engineers will suffer injury if there is an accident. What steps should Jill have taken prior to or during the procurement process to reduce or avoid these risks?

Feedback on page 11

Hazard

This is a source of potential harm or damage. In industrial terms it is a problem or difficulty caused by deviation from the design intent.

Risk, hazard and uncertainty

Let us start by defining the term **risk**. It is a word that is used frequently enough, but may be confused with other words such as hazard or uncertainty. A risk, in fact, is any event which may prevent or impair the achievement of objectives.

In the business sense we need to recognise that risk is not the same as hazard or uncertainty. For example, if we are managing outdoor events such as horse racing or garden parties or cricket matches, we might determine that bad weather in the form of heavy rain or high winds is a hazard. We also know that these hazards can cause losses and damage.

None of us can accurately foretell how every future event will turn out. We are unsure of whether adverse conditions will prevail. **Uncertainty** is a situation in which we know that an event might happen but we have no information about the probability of its occurring. There is no certainty that the event will, in fact, ever occur but, in risk management terms, we can attempt to make the assumptions about uncertainty stronger by measuring the probability of an event actually happening. In life and in business we are facing uncertainty all the time, but we must still make decisions and take actions in order to achieve our objectives.

In order to change an uncertainty into a measurable event, we need to apply some form of quantification to the likelihood that a certain hazard will occur at a certain point in the future and any possible impact that may result. For example, we might discover through research that, in a certain part of the United Kingdom in June, it rains on average on 6 of the 30 days of that month. We can then say that there is a 20% risk of rain in that place in June (6 divided by 30, expressed as a percentage). So instead of being uncertain about the hazard of it raining in that place, we have converted the uncertainty into a probability. We now know the likelihood of the hazard occurring and with further research into the probability of rain causing damage or injury, we can work out the likely consequences of that event.

We often use phrases such as 'it's possible' when referring to something which may or may not happen. A possibility is something that is capable of happening or being done but may not actually happen. Probability takes a possibility to a firmer state and it is the probability of an event occurring that we attempt to quantify when we look at managing risks. When we talk about risk, we mean the measurement of the likelihood, often also referred to as the probability, of a hazard or other event occurring and the potential effect it may have in monetary or other terms, also referred to as the impact.

According to the Institute of Risk Management (IRM), risk is 'the combination of the probability of an event and its consequences' (ISO/IEC Guide 73). A good international definition is that provided by the Australia/New Zealand Risk Standard 4360 which states that risk management is: 'The culture, processes and structures that are directed towards the effective management of potential opportunities and adverse effects.'

Exposure

This is simply the impact on the business of a hazard occurring. Exposure can be seen in foreign currency dealings. The exposure can be in the form of transaction exposure, translation exposure or economic exposure. **Transaction exposure** is simply the damage that may be brought about as a result of taking decisions on a single piece of business or transaction. For example, if we decide to make a one-off purchase from a foreign supplier, then we are exposing ourselves to potential losses resulting from the value fluctuations of the currency to be used to pay for the goods or services. The loss is related purely to this one transaction but frequent or continuous losses of this nature could be serious enough to affect the value of assets, equity or earnings.

Economic exposure occurs when the decisions taken by the business will have an impact on an organisation's cash flows, earnings or foreign and other investments which results in a change in the organisation's financial value as a business.

Losses

Loss or damage is often converted into financial figures in order to have a constant to allow measurement and prioritisation. Loss represents the impact of the hazard being suffered. Opportunity cost can be a loss. If we invest our resources in Project A rather than Project B, then the opportunity cost will be represented by any additional benefits that may have been gained by taking Project B. This is clearly a loss and needs to be set against any gains derived from Project A.

Loss can be described as consequential, direct and indirect. **Direct loss** is a loss which occurs as a direct consequence of the hazard. If I lose my wallet or purse containing £50 in cash, then my direct loss equates to £50 plus the cost of a replacement wallet or purse. An **indirect loss** would occur if, during the process of a burglary, the burglar destroys some invoices that were awaiting payment, resulting in an inability to collect the amounts due. In the case of our lost purse or wallet, the **consequential loss** would occur if we missed our train as a result of reporting the loss to the police. We may have to buy a more expensive ticket or even pay for a hotel room and catch the first train tomorrow morning. All of these costs are consequential losses.

Risk management is 'the process whereby organisations methodically address the risks attaching to their activities with the goal of achieving sustained benefit within each activity and across the portfolio of all activities' (IRM 2003). The key elements of risk management are risk identification and risk treatment. Effective risk management recognises, first, that if there is no risk there is no reward and, second, that there are two aspects of risk: *downside* risk and *upside* risk. In other words, by carrying out good risk management, not only will the risks and vulnerabilities be recognised and managed but the opportunities will be recognised also. The risk management process will tease out new ideas, new approaches to business and even new business opportunities while identifying and evaluating current business risks.

Risk identification is the process of ensuring that all of those things that need to be considered are included in our investigations. One of the problems here is that the risks to be identified may be limited by our own experience.

On our first visit to Western Australia, we may take along the sun cream and the insect repellent, but if we are ignorant of the existence of red-back spiders, together with the likely consequences of meeting one, then we may be totally under-prepared for a visit to that area.

Risk identification is a vital stage and demands that we consider a wide range of resources to assist us in identifying all of the things that could happen in order that we can move on to the analysis of the risk and a decision as to how to deal with the risk. This can be achieved by involving a number of other people who may have a different perspective on the issue under consideration. We also need to consider how risks can change with time. A view taken a year ago may be totally inappropriate today because of changing internal or external influences in our business environment.

Risk evaluation

This is used 'to make decisions about the significance of risks to an organisation and whether each specific risk should be accepted or treated' (IRM).

Risk appetite

This refers to the propensity of the organisation or individual to accept a certain amount of risk. We all know people who feel the need to follow the same route to work each morning, or who never try different food or who always visit the same holiday resort each year. These people have a low risk appetite. Other people will take chances; they may gamble on horse racing; they may allow staff to learn by making mistakes; they may hope that bad service will not drive customers away. These people have a high risk appetite.

Risk appetite usually has a basis in the culture of the person or organisation dealing with the risk. Gerd Hofstede's book *Culture and Organisations* is very good at defining which countries have a high or low appetite for risk. Although this may be dangerous in stereotyping nationalities, it can be a starting point for understanding risk appetite, especially when dealing in the international business environment. Of course risk appetite will also be based upon experience. Usually, once we have taken a risk which has resulted in loss or damage or failure, we are less likely to repeat the event. Hopefully we learn from experience. **Risk aversion** refers to the attitude that we should minimise the taking of risk and the possibilities of loss while **risk enthusiasm** recognises risks and evaluates them with an eye to the opportunities which may be presented.

Risk strategy should complement other corporate strategies and be related to the objectives flowing from all other corporate activities. Like other strategies, the risk management strategy has to be translated from a high-level 'vision' or overview to a policy and procedure which can be utilised throughout the organisation. Options for a risk strategy revolve around the key words *avoid, reduce, minimise, mitigate, share* and *accept*. From these, the generic strategies that have been developed are referred to as the '4Ts' – simply because each strategy begins with the letter T. The strategies are:

- Treat
- Tolerate

- Transfer
- Terminate.

Treating means to manage the risk actively and thereby recognising the probability of it occurring and the effect it may have on the organisation. Treating the risk will rarely reduce it to zero, despite any mitigating action we may take; it will simply bring the risk down to levels which are deemed to be acceptable (the risk remaining after being managed as much as is possible is termed **residual risk**).

Tolerating a risk means that a risk has been recognised and has either been managed down to acceptable levels or that, in the first place, the risk is so remote or minor a possibility that it is not worth the time, money or effort involved in doing something about it.

Transferring a risk means that, once the risk has been identified, it is resolved by giving it to someone else to manage. Insurance is a good example of risk transfer and outsourcing may achieve a similar result. **Part transfer** may also occur as a means of treating a risk and means sharing part of the risk with a third party, as might occur in a joint venture, for example.

Terminating a risk means that, having recognised a risk, whatever action may be taken to manage it, it is simply too risky to continue – or perhaps too expensive to manage – in relation to the rewards which might be available.

Establishing a strategy in order to achieve objectives is an expected activity at the level of the board or governing body of an organisation. However, enterprise-wide risk management involves not just the board but all operations and all staff. Everyone becomes involved in recognising and managing the risks which are evident at all levels and each member of the organisation becomes a stakeholder in delivering the best solution. Managing risk becomes embedded in the organisation.

Whichever strategy is adopted for managing risks, it remains the responsibility of each organisation to ensure that it is carried out effectively. Bear in mind that if, for example, insurance is chosen as a means of transferring a particular risk, it is not the insurance company but the contracting organisation which needs to make sure that the cover chosen is correct for the particular risk and is of sufficient value.

A simple illustration of risk strategy is the old joke about two men being chased by a polar bear. The basis of the joke is that we don't need to run faster than the polar bear, as long as we run faster than the other man who will be caught by the bear first. Other ways of dealing with the polar bear would be to share the risk, perhaps by attacking the bear together, or perhaps to share the responsibility of distracting it by catching another animal which will attract the bear and satisfy its hunger. Similarly, terminating a risk can be clearly illustrated by considering a company that may be involved in using animals for research. At some point in time, it may become too expensive and too dangerous to continue and termination becomes the realistic alternative.

Risk mitigation comprises all of those actions that can help to prevent the risk occurring or to reduce the impact or costs of such risks. Risk mitigation will lead to a more secure business environment, or even a safer working environment if we apply it to health and safety issues. In terms of quality, the implementation of total quality management (TQM) and quality assurance (QA) techniques and procedures is a way of mitigating the risk of a substandard product or service. By building quality into a product, service or process, we are clearly reducing the chances that something will go wrong and lead to loss, damage or injury.

We will deal with sources of risk in later chapters but many contracts identify a range of risks which may be treated as not only uninsurable but non-transferable. These are often known as **acts of God** or **forces majeures**. These phrases are intended to encompass all of those events which are beyond our power to control. In 2005, Hurricanes Katrina and Rita caused huge devastation across the southern states of the United States of America. Many businesses would have been dependent on the port of New Orleans for the importing or exporting of products. The flooding and damage caused by the hurricanes would have made it impossible for businesses to carry out their contractual obligations and they would have invoked their force majeure clauses to avoid claims for damage from the other parties to their contracts. From a legal point of view, there could easily be occasions when it is reasonable to expect the parties to foresee certain circumstances and a court may actually overrule a force majeure clause in such circumstance. In the case of New Orleans, it seems that the chances of such damage occurring were actually predictable, and in that case the courts may decide that organisations suffering damage should have made contingency arrangement to avoid suffering the losses.

Self-assessment question 1.1

1 Define risk.
2 Define risk management.
3 State the main components of an approach to risk strategy.
4 Define risk averse.

Feedback on page 11

1.2 Sources of general business risk

Learning activity 1.2

Discuss with at least two of your managers their perceptions of the risks faced by your organisation. You might discover that Finance and Safety will give you two very different approaches.

Feedback on page 11

Every area of an organisation is faced with daily risks and the organisation itself is faced with a range of risks in the external business environment.

Barings Bank was always faced with the risk that one of its traders would lose more money than that trader earned for the bank, but the implementation of training and control measures is intended to remove this risk. Barings had been in business since 1762, so it was well aware of the risks that it faced in a changing world. Over the centuries it was very successful and during that time the bank had implemented a number of control measures to restrict any possible losses. Unfortunately, it had allowed its control procedures to lapse and, as a result, a single trader managed to lose $1.4 billion by speculating on the Singapore International Monetary Exchange. This caused the bank to collapse. Barings collapsed as a result of not dealing appropriately with the risk of weak management and controls.

Nike suffered huge damage to its reputation in the early 1990s when television reports in the UK and the USA drew attention to some of the practices being carried out in the factories of businesses in the Far East that were supplying Nike. Nike was under the impression that it had implemented controls throughout its supply chain that avoided the possibility of such unethical practices taking place. Sadly, these were not working properly and the resulting revelations in the media led to a fall in the company's share price and sales. There were demonstrations by protesters and Nike's reputation was severely damaged, such that it has taken years of costly promotional work and the implementation of new supply chain controls to start to improve Nike's reputation and recover the loss in the share price that occurred at that time. Here, Nike was subject to the risks that can occur upstream in the supply chain.

In a natural fermentation business such as citric acid or penicillin, the production process entails a strict regime of feeding and growth of the organisms, to ensure optimum health and the maximum production of the end product. The organisms need to be maintained at the correct temperature, with correct oxygen levels and the correct dosage of nutrients. Factories making these products are heavily dependent upon steady supplies of materials and electricity for stirring the huge vessels containing the broth in which the organisms grow. A natural event such as a lightning strike that disables the electricity supply will trigger the emergency generators, but it would be impossible to generate enough electricity to maintain all of the vessels and their associated equipment. As a result, the factory will go into fail-safe mode. All of the product will be lost and the producers will incur huge penalties for disposing of the waste broth. Worse than this is the fact that the whole cycle will have to be started all over again and, for example with penicillin, it can take 28 days from sowing the seed to harvesting the penicillin, so 28 days of sales are lost, as well as all of the overhead recovery. All in all, the costs of one simple lightning strike in the wrong place at the wrong time can cause millions of pounds worth of additional costs. This demonstrates the risk of a natural phenomenon affecting the business.

As you can see from these examples, the cost of a risk actually materialising can be out of all proportion to the cost of taking action at an early stage to avoid, eliminate or minimise the risk. In Nike's case, the cost of putting a little more care into the management of their suppliers would have been tiny, but the cost of having their reputation damaged was enormous. Barings could easily have avoided their problems with some more management control, yet the huge losses they had sustained effectively put them out of existence after being rescued and then subsumed into ING bank. For the fermentation business, the contingency of providing sufficient backup generators to allow the factory to keep going despite a loss of mains power is simply not practicable, as processes like this would probably require in excess of 10 megawatts of electricity at any time.

So there are different sorts of risk. There is financial risk, reputational risk, and there are also risks such as in the health and safety area. As we mentioned in the opening statement, taking no risk is a risk in itself because we may be denying ourselves an opportunity – the upside of risk management. If we put our money under the bed, so as to avoid the risk of being robbed in the street, we will lose the opportunity to earn interest on that money. If we refuse to trial a new supplier, we may be missing out on the opportunity to use a supply chain that could bring massive advantages to our organisation.

1.3   The risk cycle

Risk management is an ongoing process. The cycle is continuous and never ends. It is not a one-off, occasional exercise. Risks change; new risks occur and existing risks may change in nature as a result of mitigation or other effects. Information technology (IT) can greatly assist the collection and management of risk data and is an essential tool at each stage of the risk cycle. Managing risk should be an integral part of the broader management function which periodically sets and reviews strategy, goals and targets and fine-tunes the underlying operational processes.

The risk cycle is composed of several key elements:

- Correctly identifying the most important risks
- Understanding the nature of the risks – their impact and probability
- Implementing the strategies which will manage the risks
- Identifying the organisational level at which the risk must be managed
- Identifying who can influence the risk outcome and how that should be undertaken
- Monitoring and reviewing the relevant processes.

The cycle involves the identification and documenting of the risks at all levels in an organisation which may have an impact on achieving objectives, then assessing and classifying the risks prior to assessing the consequences which may be suffered if they were to come to pass. At the evaluation stage some kind of modelling or simulation process may be undertaken to assist in making good decisions about the probability and impact of any one risk or a collection of risks. Mitigation strategies then have to be worked out along with the usual management tasks of finding and allocating resources and assigning responsibilities. The final part of the risk cycle is to put in place monitoring and reviewing procedures. Without these, performance of the risk management system will not be known and anomalies may be allowed to go unchecked.

1

1.4 The risk manager

Many organisations employ a risk manager. Organisations in the banking and the financial services sector may well employ specialist managers to deal with complex issues of credit risk and actuarial risk. In most organisations, the term does not mean that the management of all the organisation's risks is undertaken by one individual, rather that the risk manager is tasked by the board to ensure that risk management processes are in place and operating effectively throughout the whole of the organisation. The risk manager would therefore be expected to maintain central records of the activities in all departments or functions and to ensure that management is constantly updating and reviewing its risk management processes.

Consolidation of all risk registers, standard approaches to methodologies, the testing and implementation of software to facilitate risk assessment – all of these would be expected to be within the purview of the risk manager. The risk manager should also be seen as the organisation's 'risk champion', a manager delegated to spread enthusiasm for risk management, to be aware of current developments in this area and to be available to train others in techniques and processes.

Self-assessment question 1.2

Give details of a total of ten risks that your organisation or department currently faces, of which five should be supply chain related.

Feedback on page 12

Revision question

Now try the revision question for this session on page 355.

Summary

This has been a brief introduction to the concept and language of risk and risk management. It should already be clear that this can be a very complex subject that will need the application of a number of well-structured mechanisms to ensure that the correct decisions are made in the face of any risk. The failure to deal appropriately with risk can be seen in the case studies in section 1.2, with the resulting loss of business, loss of jobs or even loss of life.

Fortunately, the management of risk is not something new and we can take advantage of the work that has been carried out for many years in the finance, banking, insurance and safety sectors. This will assist us in the identification and treatment of those many risks that we are likely to encounter when managing the supply chain.

Suggested further reading

Mullins (1996), chapters 9 and 20.

You could read the relevant sections of Sadgrove (2005) and also look at HM Treasury (2001) and internet articles on Marconi, Barings and Railtrack.

Feedback on learning activities and self-assessment questions

Feedback on learning activity 1.1

Usually it is inappropriate to make a decision on price alone. Jill should have worked with the engineers as well as her health-and-safety experts to identify what risks were involved in the choice of equipment. Having defined the risks, Jill can then evaluate or analyse the impact of these. Once she has this information, she can work with her managers to decide upon how to treat the risk and to more effectively consider other prices on offer. In the case of safety, we may bring in a principle such as ALARP (as low as reasonably practicable) where we recognise that there are always some risks that need to be accepted. Jill can then mitigate the risk of non-acceptance by the engineers, by involving them in training, trials and contributing to the final decision.

Feedback on self-assessment question 1.1

Risk is the combination of the probability of an event occurring and its consequences if it does occur.

Risk management is the process whereby organisations methodically address the risks attaching to their activities with the goal of achieving sustained benefit within each activity and across the portfolio of all activities.

Risk strategy comprises treating, transferring, tolerating or terminating risks so that the organisation benefits from the recognition of potential vulnerabilities or opportunities. While a high-level strategy may be established at board level, all operations should benefit from the application of enterprise-wide risk management.

Risk averse is the description used for individuals or organisations who do not like to be exposed to risks and are unwilling to take risks even when, by so doing, a reward may be obtained. Enthusiasm for risk is the opposite end of the scale from risk averse and is typified by entrepreneurs for whom risk taking is a way of life.

Feedback on learning activity 1.2

Hopefully, you will have heard that there are a great number of risks faced by an organisation in many of its departments or functions. In addition to business risk and reputational risk, there is the risk of physical injury, leading to the risk of court action, the loss of staff and the loss of reputation. In the environmental sector, there is a risk of exceeding the limits agreed with the Environment Agency, whether this be the emitting of vapours to the atmosphere or the discharge of waste waters into rivers. This can lead to fines, orders to cease work and again a loss of reputation which could have an impact on any plans to develop the business. In the worst cases, the directors could also face the ultimate sanction of a jail sentence.

Feedback on self-assessment question 1.2

You could raise issues such as the following: loss of reputation; business discontinuity; inability to attract good staff; fines and other penalties; imprisonment; seizure of assets; loss of customers; breakdown of supply route; non-availability of scarce materials; surge in prices; ban on importation; piracy; computer failure, and many more.

Sources of risk: internal or external

2

Introduction

The hazards that are faced by people working in supply chain management will emanate from a wide variety of sources. We shall investigate those sources in this study session, recognising that not only are we faced with the impact of global issues, but also by elements of our own personality and from our own immediate surroundings, both human and physical. We need to consider that all of these issues are in a constant state of flux and changes may occur with frightening speed and frequency. Identifying the source of these hazards is, of course, the first stage in dealing with them, so as to minimise the negative impact on our business and on ourselves.

'We must learn to welcome change and innovation as vigorously as we have fought it in the past ... assess each and every action in light of its contribution to an increased corporate capacity for change.'
Tom Peters in *Thriving on Chaos*

Session learning objectives

After completing this session you should be able to:

2.1 Distinguish between strategic, operational and project risk in terms of internal and external hazards and risks.
2.2 Define some internal sources of risk, in particular, operational and project risk and reliance on IT.
2.3 Define some external sources of risk including IT exposure to hackers and virus attacks.
2.4 Explain the purpose of segmentation and describe some tools commonly used to categorise or segment stocks, suppliers, and so on.
2.5 Assess the vulnerability and criticality within supply chains.
2.6 Assess the risks involved in using technology.

Unit content coverage

This study session covers the following topics from the official CIPS unit content document:

Learning objectives

1.3 Analyse potential sources of risk to organisations of both internal and external origin.
 • Internal and external hazards and risks
 • Range of risks that might occur within the workplace
 • Analysis of external environment factors using the PESTLE tool
 • The likely impact on the organisation and its appetite for risk
 • Basic quantification methods for measuring
1.4 Analyse and explain the use of segmentation and business tools to reduce supply chain vulnerability.

- Segmentation tools to help assess and manage supply chain risk appropriately (eg Kraljic, Boston, Pareto, KPIs, Spider web or appropriate alternatives)
- How you would take a different approach to purchasing from a critical or bottleneck market to that of a leveraged or acquisition market
- Management of different products or services within an organisational portfolio
- Definition of supply chain vulnerability, supply failure and supplier failure
- How to map a typical supply chain and identify potential sources of supply vulnerability
- The potential impact of supply and supplier failure
- Range of mitigating activities that a purchaser could use when looking to protect against supply or supplier failure

1.8 Assess risks involved with using technology.
- Reliance on technology
- Security
- Hackers
- Fraud
- Storing of vital documents and materials

Prior knowledge

Study session 1

Timing

You should set aside about 6.75 hours to read and complete this session, including learning activities, self-assessment questions, the suggested further reading (if any) and the revision question.

2.1 Assessing the sources of risk

Risks may arise from sources both within the organisation and external to it. The risks themselves may be operational and unique to the particular industry or activity. They occur as a result of human behaviour or natural events, or because of market and competitive conditions. Physical and environmental risks may affect the continuity of business and the recovery from disasters. Non-compliance with laws or regulations both in the home environment and overseas could result in personal as well as organisational risks materialising.

Detailed consideration of strategy, operations and projects follows in a later study session but our understanding of the sources of potential risks can begin by considering risk **categories.** Whether arising internally or externally, the source of risks can be generally categorised into the eight main areas identified in the AS/NZS 4360 risk standard:

- commercial and legal relationships
- economic circumstances

- human behaviour
- natural events
- political circumstances
- technology and technical issues
- management activities and controls
- individual activities.

Categorising risk in this way shows that an organisation's strategy may pose the greatest risks if the board is not directing resources in an effective way to meet objectives or, indeed, that the objectives themselves are either no longer relevant or have become unattainable through a mix of circumstances. Operational risks occur in functions and processes which are designed to produce products and services related to the organisation's strategy. Projects tend to be complementary to operations, and are often one-off or unique activities with defined objectives which may be additional to normal programmes and plans. Operations and projects bring with them their own risks but, if the overriding strategy is faulty, then everything else becomes a waste of time, effort and money.

Returning again to the Barings Bank example, several of the categories listed above can be applied. Implementing control mechanisms, both internal control and external control, is one of the ways in which risks can be mitigated. These will both be dealt with in detail in later study sessions, but at this stage it is sufficient to realise that businesses often fail to implement the control mechanisms that would immediately highlight any irregular or illicit activity. Managements often fail to act in a clear and coherent manner and, in terms of human behaviour, the Barings Bank case has resulted in a number of psychologists attempting to develop schemes to identify potential 'rogue traders' as they are now called. The banking sector has itself developed a more stringent approach to internal control, perhaps not wholly as a result of Barings but hastened by it, not least to implement the basic control of separating activities between front and back office operations (the Basel Committee on Banking Supervision).

If there is no coherent investment strategy in information technology (IT) systems, such as a relational database management system and networks, or if business units are permitted to implement their own IT solutions, then data may be captured and processed by disparate systems and presented in different ways to those managers who read the reports. According to Waring and Glendon in *Managing Risk*, 'while adequate investment in state-of-the-art technology could well have saved Barings, the technology which existed made hiding the fraud easier because no paper was involved and no money actually changed hands' (Waring & Glendon, 1998).

The nature of some commercial work demands young, intelligent and enthusiastic people with a drive to win. This in itself is a high risk because these may be the very people who may try to circumvent controls to achieve a speedier or, in their view, 'better' result, or in other ways cut corners and perhaps, unknowingly, increase risk. It could even be that these are the people most likely to become 'rogue traders' or similar and it is essential that we employ managers capable of maintaining discipline and control in line with the organisation's accepted procedures.

2

Learning activity 2.1

Understand the principles of risk strategy and the means – particularly the use of IT in collecting and analysing data. Research the terms hazard and risk with a safety manager or safety representative, to discover their understanding of these terms. Contrast this with the views of a manager in your finance department on financial risk and compare how each is applied within your organisation.

Feedback on page 30

Creating risks ourselves

Although we have concentrated on the risks that were occurring in the Barings operation, we can usually find a host of hazards and risks in every department of every organisation. These may be external or internal in nature and we will discuss different internal and external risks later in this study session.

The hazards most commonly identified by auditors are the self-created ones.

Few of us operate at work in a manner that is safe from a health and safety point of view. Visit most offices and you may find:

- no ergonomic reviews of seating and computer monitor position
- cables and stationery lying across walkways
- files and boxes stored above head height on the top of cupboards
- operating procedures that are not enforced.

Sometimes the creation of risk results from our own personalities. There was once a buyer who was excellent in a crisis. She had spent years working in an unstructured environment where chaos was normal. She enjoyed the excitement of rushing around dealing with panic and then, at the last moment, she would manage to get the goods delivered just before the factory was forced to close. On investigation, it transpired that this lady became very bored by routine, which took away her opportunity to take the starring role. Over a period of time, her manager had implemented new working practices that removed the sources of the panics. As a result, this lady would leave things to the last moment and allow or even encourage the crises to develop. The risk to the business was immense.

It should be clear that the sources of risk are many and varied and may not always stem from the obvious suspect. This is why we need to apply rigorous investigations to risk management to ensure that we can identify the root causes of the hazard. Without dealing with the root cause, the hazard will recur with all of its associated risks. In later study sessions we will be addressing a number of tools and techniques that will assist you in analysing the root causes of potential hazards.

Overconfidence can often exacerbate an existing risk or create a new one. Inner belief tells us that we can overcome a particular obstacle or achieve a particular objective when, if we were to be honest in our own self-analysis, it would be clear that we are being overoptimistic about our abilities. This overconfidence can often result in procedures being overturned or not followed to the letter because of our belief that 'we know better than the boss'. A risk which might have been identified and properly controlled may then materialise despite an effective approach to risk management. This is the worst type of risk, sometimes called a *silent risk* because it has gone unrecognised in the risk management process and can often wreak havoc when it materialises.

Self-assessment question 2.1

What differences are there between your approach to risk and the approach adopted by your safety representative? What things might you do differently now you have discussed risk with that person?

Feedback on page 30

2.2 External sources of risk

Whether we are aiming at personal life objectives or workplace goals and objectives, things that occur in the wider world are bound to affect our ability to succeed in their fulfilment. It is vital that we take notice of those possible effects to ensure that we and our employers achieve our objectives and retain the ability to fund our human and organisational needs.

Figure 2.1: The impact of external issues

External influences (figure 2.1) which could affect our approach to risk include infrastructure difficulties such as loss of strategic air and rail services, road closures, laws and regulations, both here and abroad, political crises, market interventions and acts of God.

These external sources of risk may occur to us as individuals, to our organisation and at many other stages, right up to global influences such as climatic phenomena and the spread of disease.

Sporting teams or holidaymakers take account of the weather. There is nothing they can do to stop it raining or snowing, but they can at least make contingency arrangements to avoid the most damaging effects. They will use different footwear or even change the makeup of the team to reduce the risk of defeat and increase the likelihood of success.

Learning activity 2.2

Talk to a senior manager and discover what they consider to be the three greatest external risks to the organisation.

Feedback on page 31

What we really need is some form of checklist or aide-memoire that will assist us in identifying those elements that may be outside of our direct control but which may cause us severe damage in some form.

The mechanism that is used most often is PESTLE (sometimes given as PESTEL). This is an acronym to help remind you to address six of the most important areas of risk that exist in our business environment (table 2.1).

Table 2.1 PESTLE matrix

P	Political	An example could be the differing approach to union power that could be adopted by left-wing governments. This can lead to a change in industrial relations and business confidence.
		Relationships between countries may also go sour, resulting in difficulties in maintaining a supply line to or from a country. Recent examples include Burma (Myanmar) and Zimbabwe
E	Economic	This could cover such issues as interest rates and their impact on spending patterns, house prices and disposable income
S	Social	This could be represented by the changing social tastes such as the trend away from carbohydrate consumption following the introduction of the Atkins diet
T	Technological	The move from surface post to email is a result of technological changes and the ability of individuals to adapt to that new technology, either through training or through peer pressure or necessity
L	Legal	The Sale of Goods Act or European Directives have both had a major effect on business
E	Environmental	Climatic change, geographical issues such as the melting of the Polar icecap or the drying up of the Aral Sea, or issues such as the reducing availability of sites for disposal, would all represent elements that may need to be considered under this heading

With the effects of extreme weather conditions as well as the impact of geographical changes, we should probably include another category. This could be C for climate or G for geography, though many people are happy to include these under E for environment.

Another way of looking at this situation can be seen in Saunders' model of environmental factors (figure 2.2), which shows how we are surrounded by all of these factors which are having an impact on our organisation:

Figure 2.2: Saunders' model of environmental factors

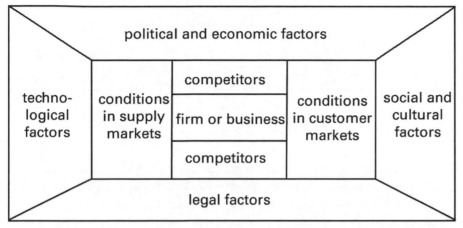

Source: Saunders (1997)

We could also use Michael Porter's five forces as detailed in his book *Competitive Strategy*. Porter recognised that there are a number of key influences upon an organisation and upon the market in which it operates.

It should be clear that our business environment can be severely affected by what others are doing. For example, if it is easy for new businesses to enter the marketplace, then we will always stand the risk of losing part of our market to those new entrants (figure 2.3). Similarly, there may be risks posed by the relative bargaining power of suppliers and buyers who can threaten to reduce their prices or remove their business respectively. Although this illustration was aimed at sales organisations, it can also be used as a model for purchasing and supply chain management.

Figure 2.3: Porter's forces driving industry competition

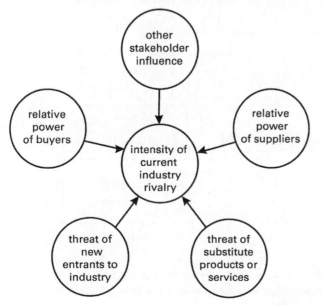

Source: adapted from Porter (1985)

2

Self-assessment question 2.2

Consider how your organisation could cope if there were no computing facilities for an extended period of time. List the risks of returning to a manual system.

Feedback on page 31

2.3 Internal sources of risk

The internal sources of risk usually centre on the staff within our organisation upon whom reliance is placed to implement the policies, procedures and systems designed to achieve objectives. Our human resources may often be described as 'our greatest asset' in company reports and in presentations to the stakeholders, yet it is surprising how often the staff are badly selected, badly trained and badly managed.

Within organisations, we are always somehow part of a team, striving to complete objectives as part of an organisational strategy. Yet, so often these teams simply don't work.

Why teams don't work

Spend a few minutes considering whether any of the problems in figure 2.4 exist within your own organisation and how you would deal with them.

Figure 2.4: Why teams don't work

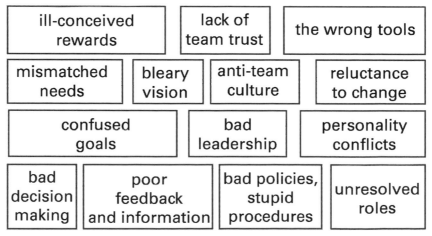

Source: adapted from Robbins & Finley (2000)

Most of these internal problems will derive from selection, training and or management issues and in a later session we will explore how they may appear at the strategic, operational and/or project-based levels.

Examples of internal problems

Corporate strategy and missions should be the guideline for all of the staff, who then will manage their departments, teams and workload to harmonise with the overall target. Yet, from the highest level, we find that the goals of the organisation may be in competition with personal or departmental goals.

If we accept that problems exist within our own organisation, it should also be clear that similar problems are likely to exist in every link of our supply chain. Untrained or malicious staff, bad drivers, inept managers, poor accountants and so on will all be internal sources of risk to their organisations, but the hazards that they create could also become a risk to the adequate functioning of the entire supply chain.

The role of human resources

It should be clear to you that functions such as human resources (HR) have a huge responsibility to ensure that selection and training are carried out properly, but they will be constrained by the capability of the line managers and the directors. In particular, a poorly performing HR function may result in weak selection techniques, minimal and uncoordinated training programmes and poor organisation structures. Each of these will have a knock-on, cumulative effect on the risk portfolio of the entire organisation.

The need for good communication

In communication (figure 2.5), there is always the risk that we will apply our own perceptions, language and interpretations to the message. This adds 'noise' to the message. When the message is then transmitted to the listener, the language plus noise may well create a totally different message to what was originally intended.

Figure 2.5: The communication process

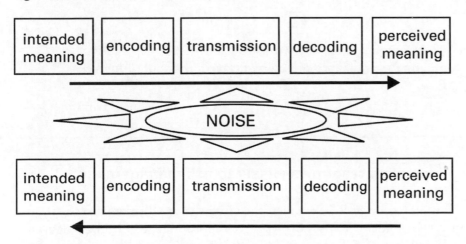

The problem could be cultural, educational or even religious in its source. Whichever way it has come about, we still need to identify it as a risk to the continued success of our supply chain and take appropriate action to deal with it in some way.

2

Communicating potential risks is a significant task for organisations and society in general. Good communication embodies an open and accountable approach to understanding and mitigating any of the unwanted events which may affect us as individuals or organisations. Conversely, poor communication, or even a deliberate false message, is ultimately counterproductive and constitutes in itself a key risk for most organisations.

A number of assessment tools can be used to identify any gaps in the knowledge and ability of individuals or departments or organisations as a whole. The Office of Government Commerce (OGC) has developed a whole range of these tools which can be seen on their website http://www.ogc.gov.uk. Alternatively you could consider using models such as those developed by the Forum for the Future which has a 'Public sector sustainable procurement assessment tool' available for downloading free of charge http://www.forumforthefuture.org.uk. There are also the EFQM models http://www.efqm.org.

Learning activity 2.3

Identify five occasions when a colleague may have caused a problem with a supplier. Consider such things as mistakenly (or otherwise) revealing information, losing an invoice, promising early settlement without agreeing it with the finance department, and so on.

Feedback on page 31

Now try this self-assessment question.

Self-assessment question 2.3

Produce a memo of about 200 words to your finance department, explaining the risks that are caused by delayed payment of invoices.

Feedback on page 31

2.4 Allocating resources wisely to risk management

Sun Tzu, in his *Art of War*, extolled the virtues of appropriate use of resources. 'A leader who uses his resources appropriate to the challenge at hand will win' and 'Do not tackle difficult problems with inadequate resources' aptly illustrate the importance of effective resource allocation.

As time and resource have become more precious in business so there has been an increasing interest in tools and techniques which can help us to prioritise the way in which resources can be allocated. Some of the better-known techniques are discussed briefly below.

The Boston grid

In 1970, the Boston Consulting Group came up with a simple matrix (figure 2.6) to segment a portfolio of products with different growth rates and different market shares.

Figure 2.6: The Boston Consulting Group matrix

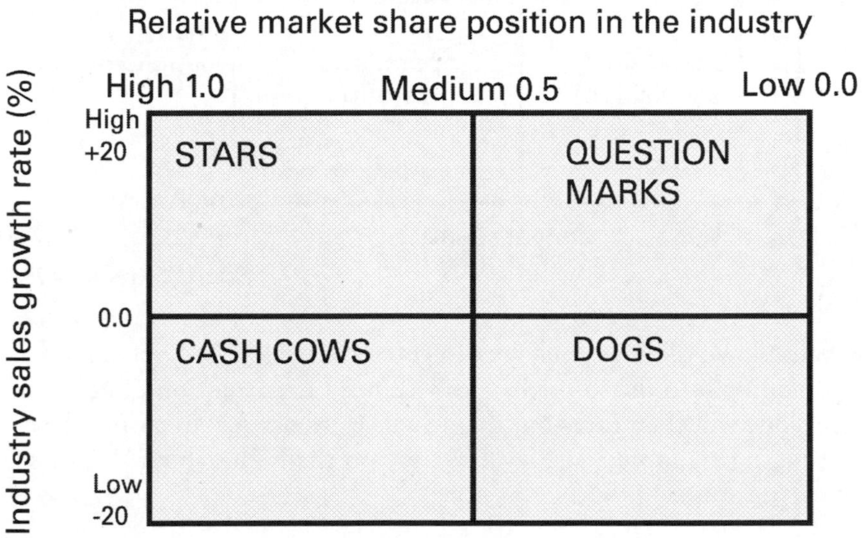

Relative market share position in the industry

	High 1.0	Medium 0.5	Low 0.0
High +20	STARS		QUESTION MARKS
0.0	CASH COWS		DOGS
Low -20			

Industry sales growth rate (%)

This helped businesses to understand how they should manage different products within their product portfolio so as to maximise the profit potential of each one. They could start to consider what resources to apply to which products so as to grow the business and obtain the best return.

Pareto's theory

In the 19th century, Vilfredo Pareto identified a form of segmentation with his 80/20 rule. He discovered that 80% of the wealth of a country would be held by 20% of the people. Pareto's theory can be applied equally well to most things in the business world, whether this be spend by supplier, items in inventory, contribution of ideas or supplier defects. Armed with the knowledge that just 20% of our suppliers account for 80% of our spend it becomes very easy to see how we should allocate our time in terms of supplier management. This theory is also sometimes referred to as the *80/20 principle* and/or '*the vital few and the trivial many*'.

Kraljic's matrix

In 1983 Peter Kraljic wrote a paper for the *Harvard Business Review* entitled 'Purchasing must become supply management', in which he stated the virtues of managing our portfolio of suppliers, by segmenting them by value and risk. Organisations like GlaxoSmithKline have been known to carry out such reviews on a regular basis to ensure that they are applying the correct level of resources to individual suppliers or product portfolios.

2

Figure 2.7: Kraljic's matrix

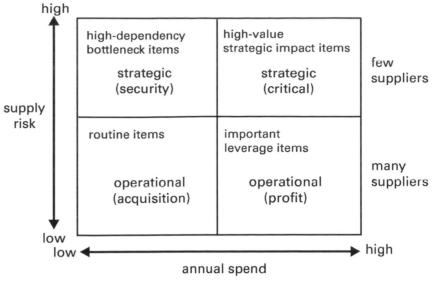

Source: Kraljic (1983)

The low-value/low-risk issues may be delegated to our lowest level of staff, while those falling into the top right area will need the attention of our best teams. Everyone will then carry out their own segmentation to ensure that they are spending an appropriate level of time on the high-value/risk issues among their portfolio.

Supplier perceptions

Segmentation tools can also be used to assess how our upstream supply chain views us as a customer. It is vital that we understand where we lie in their perceptions, as factors such as the risk of supply failure, late notification of problems or loss of credit terms may be influenced by how we fit into their customer portfolio. Only by carrying out the segmentation exercise can we decide how our suppliers view our business and what we need to do to ensure that we are positioned in one of the two top boxes in the supplier perceptions matrix (figure 2.8).

Figure 2.8: Supplier perceptions matrix

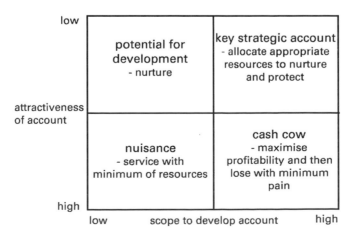

Learning activity 2.4

Select ten of your suppliers and identify where you would position them in Kraljic's matrix. Compare their position with the amount of resource used to manage each supplier.

Feedback on page 31

By using these tools, we may still be at risk by selecting the wrong scales to use on the matrices, but at least we are addressing the issues and we will highlight those areas of the greatest vulnerability. As with all hazards and risks, once we have identified them we can then proceed to their analysis and treatment.

Supply chain mapping

Process mapping entails identifying every single step, whether it be a service, a process, or a product. So within a supply chain there will be steps covering documentation, authorisation, data entry, data processing, reporting, packing, movement, inspection, consumption and recycling. Evaluation of each step can help identify the key risk areas and give us an indication of the resource input for each part of the chain.

Self-assessment question 2.4

Explain the steps that you would take to apply the 80/20 rule to your supplier base. Identify how this might help you to position suppliers more accurately using Kraljic's matrix.

Feedback on page 32

2.5 Assessing the vulnerability and criticality within supply chains

We need to remember that the supply chain encompasses the chain of events that links the initial creation and production of an item or service through to the consumption by the end consumer. This concept of a chain implies that the process moves from one link to the next in a logical fashion. In fact, this is not usually the case and each step in the supply chain may be fed by several more or less complex earlier steps. It may actually be better to think of the supply chain as a network, as there will be processes and data moving in many directions between many of the participating processes and players.

Learning activity 2.5

Select a supply chain with which you are familiar. Draw a diagram of that supply chain and identify an area of vulnerability in each link of that chain. Ensure you retain your work for future use.

Feedback on page 32

Procter & Gamble uses coconuts

Procter & Gamble wants to cut its reliance on crude oil to make surfactants. P&G has mapped its supply chains and recognised that the risk of continued price rises and inconsistent availability should be major causes of concern for its laundry detergents and shampoos business. The company is investing time and money in the development of products derived from palm kernel oil and coconut oil. As a result, P&G is investing in Indonesian plantations to develop growth techniques so that it can ensure the costs, supply and quality of sufficient raw materials. With consistent quality and supply, the company can then develop production and refining capability for the alcohol that is the product of those oils and which is the raw material for the surfactants.

Examples from military history

In military history, we can see very simple examples of supply chain vulnerability if we look back at various events in European wars. Napoleon's march into Russia and domination of that country was totally dependent upon a good flow of troops, artillery, food and all of the support services. The speed of movement of the troops to Moscow and beyond was so fast that the supply lines were strained to breaking point. This was partially caused by the decisions by the Russian generals to yield land and eventually to allow Moscow to be taken. Resistance would have slowed the advance and allowed the logistics to keep up with progress. Napoleon's troops were forced to turn back, resulting in the loss of the army due to starvation and cold.

Vulnerability in the USA

Over recent years, supply chains that have involved ports in the United States of America have displayed huge vulnerability to disruption. The tragedy of 9/11 led to substantial increases in the amount of security for goods and people passing through air- and seaports. Later we had the strike of dock workers that paralysed the whole of the west coast. More recently, we have had Hurricanes Katrina, Rita and Wilma which in 2005 destroyed much of the facilities along the Gulf of Mexico, damaging storage installations, shipping and shipping routes. For businesses importing or exporting through New Orleans, the costs and disruption must have been enormous.

Assessing the vulnerability

In the modern world, where information is more easily available than ever before, and where data processing capacity is greater than ever, there really should be no excuse for taking a cavalier attitude to risk within the supply chain.

The use of questionnaires, visits, audits, financial data, supply mapping and so on should certainly identify the main areas of risk. If we are visiting a foreign country we can consult the websites of the Foreign and Commonwealth Office (FCO) or the US State Department to find out about the risks that they have identified and precautions that might be needed.

Work on supply chain vulnerability at Cranfield

It is certainly worthwhile keeping up with developments and research being carried out at Cranfield School of Management. As early as 2001, the college was investigating supply chain vulnerability on behalf of the UK government and its conclusions at that time were as follows.

- Supply chain vulnerability is an important business issue.
- Little research has been undertaken into supply chain vulnerabilities.
- Awareness of the subject is poor.
- There is a need for a methodology for managing supply chain vulnerability.

Since that time, the Office of Government Commerce, the Institute of Risk Management and a number of other bodies have increased their focus on risk management in the supply chain, which has to start with an awareness of supply and supplier vulnerability. The tools and techniques that we will identify throughout this unit may not be new, but the encouragement, support and momentum that are being applied are greater than ever, as we search for ways of removing uncertainty in our organisations' progress and adding value to the stakeholders.

Self-assessment question 2.5

Read the following mini-case study and identify some of the issues that need to be addressed by the buyer, as a priority.

Jack is a new buyer who has the task of buying chemicals for the business. The range of chemicals includes small quantities of common salt, commodity solvents like acetone and thousands of tonnes of specialist chemicals which use old-fashioned arsenic chemistry. His suppliers include local salt processors and local merchants, as well as manufacturers in India and China.

Feedback on page 32

2.6 Technological risks

Technology is indeed a wonderful thing, as can be evidenced by people who have been rescued from certain death by the use of heat-seeking rescue equipment in earthquake rubble, or cardiopulmonary resuscitation equipment. New technology can sweep aside established practices and tested procedures in virtually all fields of endeavour from product design through robotic manufacture to real-time accounting. All of this brings new risks as well as new takes on existing risks.

We take it for granted that we can access telecommmunications, computers, television, gas, water and electricity 24 hours per day and seven days per week. It therefore comes as a major shock to us when our computer crashes or there is a power cut, or the normal mode of transportation is disrupted. Communication of information as well as security of information has brought with it a better appreciation of the risks inherent in the supply of utilities, vulnerabilities in communications networks and systems and the HR difficulties of ensuring that decision makers are also the people who understand the risks as well as the opportunities that come with technology in all its guises. E-commerce is commonplace in supply chain management but brings with it new risks and challenges while contributing to more effective and efficient purchasing practices.

This progress into the world of technology brings with it a number of risks, especially in the light of the possibility of terrorist activity or, as has been experienced in California for example, the regular loss of electricity. According to the British Standards Institution website:

'Information is the lifeblood of all organisations and can exist in many forms. It can be printed or written on paper, stored electronically, transmitted by mail or by electronic means, shown in films, or spoken in conversation. In today's competitive business environment, such information is constantly under threat from many sources. These can be internal, external, accidental, or malicious. With the increased use of new technology to store, transmit, and retrieve information, we have all opened ourselves up to increased numbers and types of threats.

'There is a need to establish a comprehensive Information Security Policy within all organisations. You need to ensure the confidentiality, integrity, and availability of both vital corporate information and customer information. The standard for Information Security Management System (ISMS) BS 7799, has fast become one of the world's established biggest sellers.'

ISO/IEC 17799 has been developed as a code of practice for information security management together with BS 7799-2:2002 as the specification for information security management.

Computer security

We also face issues with computer security, including:

- hackers
- fraud
- industrial espionage
- failure to validate changes
- transcription errors
- virus attacks

and other threats to our information communication systems which could easily temporarily halt the business, or even do it permanent damage, to the same extent that a catastrophic fire or natural disaster could do now or before the days of computers and electronic communication.

Learning activity 2.6

In the supply chain that you drew in learning activity 2.5, list the technological risks at each tier of the chain.

Feedback on page 33

In this activity you will have identified some of the technological risks that are faced at every link in the supply chain. It is vital that we also identify the root cause of these risks, so that we can eliminate that root cause. For example, one of the root causes may simply be a lack of responsiveness by board directors to technological change.

Now try this self-assessment question.

Self-assessment question 2.6

Identify five root causes of technological risk.

Feedback on page 33

Revision question

Now try the revision question for this session on page 355.

Summary

This study session has been devoted to helping you to assess the various sources of risk. It is clearly impossible to comprehensively identify all of the sources of risk unless we know where to search for them.

Risks can be:

- global
- international
- national
- regional
- local.

The PESTLE acronym can assist in interrogating some of the areas. These risks are threatening not just our own organisation but every link in our supply chain. If we follow the works of Michael Porter we will recognise that, on the whole, it is not individual businesses which compete with other individual businesses, but it is our supply chain that has to compete with other supply chains for a share of a limited business. If any link in our chain fails for any reason, then we can expect to lose advantage to our competitors.

2

In addition to the external forces working on our business, we need to pay due attention to the ways in which we select, train and manage our own staff, as here is possibly the greatest source of risk. If we are unable to manage our own workforce, the likelihood of ensuring success in our supply chain is low.

Suggested further reading

British Standards Institute (2005) *IT Security Techniques. Code of Practice. BS ISO/IEC 17799.*

Institute of Risk Management (2002) *The Risk Management Standard* http://www.thcirm.org.

Sadgrove, K (2005), chapters 3 and 14.

You could also read the relevant sections of Shimmell (2002).

Feedback on learning activities and self-assessment questions

Feedback on learning activity 2.1

Safety managers are very aware of the nature and range of hazards that exist in a normal working environment. For example, it is well known that where there is oxygen, some flammable material and a source of ignition all in the same place, then there is a risk of fire. Remove any one of these and the risk of fire is removed. The safety manager may raise the issues of ALARP (as low as reasonably possible) and SFAIRP (so far as is reasonably practical), which are terms used to rationalise the decision as to whether the risk justifies prevention, mitigation or removal and whether any residual risk is acceptable.

The finance department may use financial data as a means for measuring risk, for example the length of time debtors take to pay or the risk to positive cash flow of paying creditors too quickly. Treasury risks may be controlled by software 'flags', for example, which alert finance managers to the approach of breaches of banking covenants and the risk of incurring financial penalties. Projects may use software tools such as Project Manager™ or Prince.

The organisation as a whole may use standard software for identifying and evaluating risks in all its departments. Some software may be exclusively tailored for discrete activities but be capable of being integrated into an enterprise-wide database. You should have asked about the role of IT and the approach used by each manager you visited.

Feedback on self-assessment question 2.1

It is expected that you will have discovered that most safety managers and other risk managers will be trained to follow the process from risk identification through to risk treatment. You may have also discovered that different people have ascribed a variety of definitions and values to the words risk, hazard and mitigation. Hopefully, you will consider a more risk-averse approach to safety issues.

Feedback on learning activity 2.2

The risks likely to be identified will depend on which function the senior manager works in. In finance, cash flow or profitability might be mentioned. In project management the risks could be the availability of skills or the fickle nature of clients. In procurement, the risks mentioned could be commodity price volatility or the impact of war or terrorist activity on the supply chain. By discovering the perceived major risks in one's own organisation, it should be easier to apply some of the tools and techniques that we will address later, to treat the risk appropriately.

Feedback on self-assessment question 2.2

You should have correctly identified two relevant examples of each of the sections of PESTLE and should have given a clear explanation of how the selected risks will impact upon your organisation. Economic, for example, could include the inability to interact speedily within the organisation and thus lose early payment discount. Lack of computer data on stockholdings could result in increased interest charges as a result of overstocking and, thus, constitute an economic risk. Technological risks could include loss of competitive edge through inability to use e-commerce.

Risks in returning to a manual system include:

- lack of paper material
- excessive learning curve (time and training)
- cost of paper, printing, storage and so on.

Feedback on learning activity 2.3

There are so many occasions when we can create problems for ourselves, for our colleagues and for our organisations. It is expected that you will have no problem in identifying behaviour, comments or errors that contribute to problems with suppliers.

Feedback on self-assessment question 2.3

You should have mentioned that business survival is dependent on good cash flows. Failure to pay on time may cause the supplier to consider obtaining short-notice funding, which is usually expensive. The supplier may be unable to pay for raw materials and labour needed to maintain a continuous supply of good quality goods and services. Your supplier may stop supplies until payment is made and may withdraw credit facilities.

Feedback on learning activity 2.4

By aggregating the non-critical spend with fewer suppliers, the business with that supplier may move into the leverage or strategic quarters. The same effect can be achieved by outsourcing. It is possible that you will discover that a supplier who used to supply critical items or services of high value is only now supplying small quantities as a result of changes in technology and so on. Instead of spending large amounts of time with that supplier, it might be worthwhile relegating them to the care of lower-level staff or even delegating the purchasing authority directly to the user department.

Feedback on self-assessment question 2.4

You can apply the 80/20 principle to many aspects of your supplier base including:

- total spend with each supplier
- number of invoices submitted by each supplier
- number of deliveries from each supplier
- service failures or complaints logged against each supplier.

You can do this by, for example, gathering details of spend by supplier and then ranking suppliers in descending order of spend.

Note how a small number of suppliers may absorb a disproportionate amount of resource. For example, 80% of your suppliers account for 20% of your spend. A handful of suppliers will usually be responsible for most of the product or service quality failures that you suffer.

You should be able to understand each quartile of the Kraljic matrix and how it can focus the application of resources.

Feedback on learning activity 2.5

You should have identified a reasonably complex supply chain for a product or service used by your organisation.

- Work from the origin to the point of consumption.
- Include movement or transportation, inspection and authorisation, processing and packaging.
- Include channels for reverse logistics covering the need for rejects, reworks, refurbishment, returns and recycling.

Feedback on self-assessment question 2.5

- Identify the values and risks of each of the items in the purchase portfolio.
- Involve knowledgeable colleagues.
- Have discussions with his suppliers to gain further awareness of any issues that may need urgent attention.
- Map out the supply chain, identifying where the vulnerabilities may lie. The problems may include withdrawal from the market due to old technology and the dangers of working with poisons; interruption or delays in the supply chain due to the distances involved; the benefits and disadvantages of using agents and merchants.
- The selection of appropriate segmentation tools and techniques should also be mentioned.

Feedback on learning activity 2.6

- Identify the loss of data to the competition
- Computer breakdowns
- Loss of power
- Hacking
- Communication errors
- Calculation error
- Under-resourcing of implementation and maintenance programmes
- Inadequate skills applied to the change process
- Poor design
- Inadequate materials being used
- Lack of contingency plans for technology breakdown and similar issues.

Feedback on self-assessment question 2.6

You should have been able to identify many of the following:

- ignorance of technological change
- underfunding of research and development
- use of wrong sources of advice
- fear of change
- fixation with historic methods
- lack of training.

2

Sources of risk: strategic, operational and project based

3

Introduction

We discussed in study session 2 the sources of risk and how these can emanate from both inside and outside our organisation. In this chapter, we shall look in more detail and quote some modern examples of how the risks can be created through the selection and adoption of certain strategies, tactics and projects.

> 'If our forces are ten to the enemy's one, surround him; if five to one, attack him; if equally matched, we offer battle; if quite unequal in every way, we can flee from him.'
>
> **Sun Tzu**

Session learning objectives

After completing this session you should be able to:

3.1 Recognise the risks that may arise from the selection of a particular strategy.
3.2 Recognise the risks that may arise from specific tactics and operations.
3.3 Recognise the risks that may be specific to projects.

Unit content coverage

This study session covers the following topics from the official CIPS unit content document:

Learning objectives

1.5 Distinguish between strategic, operational and project-based areas of risk.
   • Examples of how to define risk at the strategic, operational and/or project-based level
   • Range of risk mitigation methods at each level
   • How risk can be bounded and also how, if unmanaged, it can have knock-on consequential impacts on other areas of an organisation

Prior knowledge

Study sessions 1 and 2.

Resources

Internet access.

Timing

You should set aside about 5 hours to read and complete this session, including learning activities, self-assessment questions, the suggested further reading (if any) and the revision question.

3

3.1 Risks at the strategic level of business

Formulation of strategy

During the creation and development of a new business, the founders will need to develop a business case that contains clear evidence of a strategy, indicating to potential investors and other sources of funds exactly what it is that the organisation is planning to do.

As time passes, the organisation will develop, so its strategy will usually need to change in line with those events which may occur in the marketplace in which it is operating. Major changes will happen to an organisation over time and it is vital that the strategy reflects any new conditions. Some organisations may undergo takeover, merger or acquisition of other businesses. Consider how government departments such as the Department of Environment, Food and Rural Affairs (DEFRA) or the Office of the Deputy Prime Minister (ODPM) have had to adapt to changes in their role and in the expectations of their stakeholders in recent years.

Possibly more extreme is a business such as Northumbrian Water, which has, in a relatively short period, moved from being a public sector utility, through privatisation, takeover by French parents, acquisition of other water companies and towards a future that could hold yet more changes.

An organisation's strategy represents its intentions for the future. It should be reflected in the mission and/or vision which then gives all of its management, staff and shareholders some guidance as to the likely future path that the organisation will follow. From this information, the directors and managers can select appropriate functional strategies and then select a range of tactics and operations that will help to achieve these.

The strategy will then dictate the funding needed to achieve the objectives, as well as the location(s), the need for human resources and any other resources and relationships.

Emergent or deliberate strategy

Various authors have investigated the application and selection of a wide range of strategies. Writers like Mintzberg have identified that, although, in a perfect world, organisations would be expected to set a deliberate strategy as part of a planned formal approach to directing and managing the business, patterns often develop in spite of the directors' intentions and this forces the strategy to emerge over time. It is possible that, when adopting the deliberate strategy, some of the facts were not available or considered and it is their later emergence that can cause adaptation of the strategy.

Once our strategy has been chosen, it should provide the context for all of the actions to be taken in each functional area. This should all seem quite straightforward. We have chosen our direction, we have turned it into a strategy and we have communicated it to our staff and other stakeholders. In theory we can now sit back and wait for the actions of our staff to bear fruit and take us in the chosen direction.

Sadly it does not always work that way and the strategy itself can lead to major problems.

3

Commercial risk

Commercial risk can come from a number of areas including volatile marketplaces or material costs, selection of supply chain partners, failure of businesses and underperformance in the supply chain. Lack of knowledge of new markets or products and poor board direction often serve to exacerbate these risks.

For example, Marconi had been operating since 1897, developing in a variety of business sectors, including radar, transport and marine, heavy electrical engineering, communications and instrumentation. In 1999, Marconi decided to focus on information systems and telecommunications. Its timing was disastrous, buying companies just before the hi-tech bubble burst and the company could not survive with its huge debt burden. The downturn started in the dot.com sector in early 2000 and spread rapidly to other hi-tech sectors. According to Amicus:

'despite the downturn, Marconi's Lord Simpson and John Mayo continued to issue wildly optimistic forecasts. When they subsequently issued profit warnings, their credibility sank to zero and Marconi shares went into freefall. At its zenith at the height of the telecoms business, Marconi was worth £34.5bn; and at its nadir it was valued at just over £50m. Now it is valued at just over £600m. Marconi's demise marks it out as one of Britain's most catastrophic corporate failures.'

Financial risk

Although we may be seeking to achieve profitability or at least management of a budget, it is often cash flow and capital funding that provide the greatest financial risks to an organisation.

For example, a company called IQ(BIO) working in human diagnostics could easily fund the first phase of its development and the business thrived and grew for two or three years. It was decided to expand the business into the veterinary area, at the same time as massively extending the product range and the markets that it would be serving. They were trying to achieve this with the same finance and funding as previously. A whole new business strategy had been chosen, but a new and relevant financial strategy was needed. This was not completed early enough and, as a result, the business, despite being highly successful, ran out of money and was forced to sell out to Boots Celltech.

Directional risk

This simply means that an organisation may select a direction that is the wrong one or, at least, it may turn out to be the wrong one. For example, a business may set out to dominate a market, by acquiring some competitors and driving others out of business by aggressive pricing techniques. However, as in the contract catering industry, there will always be new companies setting up, growing and then threatening the profitability of the dominant businesses. Dominating, acquiring and aggressive pricing can eventually wear down the first business which set out to be the dominator. Complacency may set in, or it may simply run out of the right type of staff to maintain strength and aggression and its original core competence may have been lost or at least changed as a result.

For example, Porter quotes in *Competitive Advantage* the example of Continental Illinois Bank. This bank had decided that it wanted to be the market leader. It certainly achieved its goal, but in order to succeed, it was forced into giving loans that other banks refused, and its client base of large corporations demanded much better terms, thus eroding the bank's profitability and return on capital. By selecting a strategy of market leadership, the bank had reduced its attractiveness to investors because of diminishing shareholder returns and totally changed its cost and client base by being forced into unfamiliar markets.

Environmental risk

This area of risk may encompass changes to environmental legislation such as the Waste Electronics and Electrical Equipment Act (WEEE) or it may pertain to changes in the climate. It could even cover such issues as where residential housing is built right up to a factory's perimeter, thus altering the factory's environmental awareness needs.

For example, a pharmaceutical business in Northeast England used to produce vast quantities of natural waste as part of the manufacturing process. This was disposed of into the sea and it was a good source of nutrient to fish. Unfortunately, due to tidal movement, there was a risk that the waste would contribute to increasing algal bloom, which can deprive the sea of oxygen and badly affect fish stocks, off the coast of Lincolnshire. The Environment Agency gained new powers that allowed it to enforce limits on the quantity of waste that could be dumped at sea. These new rules led the company to invest over £6 million in new waste treatment processes. In addition, they lost large quantities of product while the new equipment was being installed. Efficiency thereafter never reached the former levels. The business was unable to sustain the additional financial burden and eventually folded.

Acquisitional risk

Mergers and acquisitions are always a risky business, not just because of the financial implications, but also because of the need to harmonise the culture of the acquisition with the original business. The integration of IT systems has also proved to be a major stumbling block following many acquisitions. It was in no small part responsible for the problems that surfaced at Marconi and also at Morrissons following their takeover of Safeway.

For example, in the 7 February 2005 issue of *Fortune* magazine, Carol Loomis asked whether the famed merger that Carly Fiorina engineered between HP and Compaq produced value for HP's shareholders, and whether, nearly three years after the merger, HP was in shape to thrive in its brutally competitive world. In her view the answers were 'no' and 'doubtful'.

In the 14 September 2005 issue of *Boston.com Business*, David d'Alessandro discussed the Gillette merger with Procter & Gamble and suggested that Gillette suffered a good deal of criticism as a result of possibly being more concerned with the share price than the stakeholders. This claim was based upon a lack of information about local job losses and the impact upon the upstream supply chain. He also claimed that Gillette failed to come up with any assurances about jobs and community funding until the bad press forced them to do so.

This example highlights the risks of an acquisition which is based on one criterion, in this case, share price. A company's worth is dependent on its products, its people, its market and its ability to generate wealth from these factors. Remove one or more of the competitive advantages in these areas and trouble will follow. A drop in staff morale, disgruntled consumers and reputational difficulties mean threats to earnings, profitability and return on capital. Even the single objective of share price suffers and the lack of a consolidated approach to other common goals spells inevitable problems.

Managing and mitigating the strategic risk

It can be easy in hindsight to see how some of these strategies and decisions were doomed to failure. Lack of knowledge and understanding can be one of the causes, but it is more likely that the parties concerned were either badly advised or they simply failed to take the advice they were given. At the same time, they are operating in a dynamic environment where there are numbers of competing goals and influences which need to be identified and overcome.

During the battle of Waterloo in 1815, Napoleon knew that by disguising his intentions, his adversaries Wellington and Blücher would have great difficulty in preparing their countermeasures and that the resulting inaction would cause great confusion and stress. It was a sign of Napoleon's excellence in battlefield strategy, that he was able to exploit the situation to the full.

In business generally, we are faced not just with what is happening now, but also with what we perceive might be the future and how others might perceive it. The opportunity for confusion is immense. Gaining sufficient knowledge, conditioning others to accept your view of the future and then selecting a path that will lead to victory are all essential.

We also need to state that it is not just in the selection of the strategy that we are facing risks but also in the dissemination to all stakeholders. There is likely to be a variety of forms of communication which may lead to misunderstandings, misinterpretations and simple mistakes.

Organisational vision and mission

Many organisations have a high-level, 'big picture' view of what they are trying to achieve. This is often articulated as a brief but all-encompassing vision of the main strategic reason for the organisation's existence. The vision may be too brief or even too fanciful to make sense as a strategic value statement, so it is translated into a more meaningful and understandable format, usually known as the mission statement. This statement formalises the driving philosophy for the organisation and sets the standard for all that follows: detailed strategy, objectives, policies and procedures. Strategic direction should fulfil the vision of those at the top of the organisation but may also give an early indication of where there may be problems in achieving the vision and mission. 'To be the very best in our chosen field of operation' may be a laudable aspiration but immediately suggests those areas where future difficulties lie.

Risks are the unexpected and unwanted events which may prevent the achievement of objectives. Therefore, in the context of mission statements,

3

we should avoid if possible setting ourselves up for things that may be unachievable or may incur too many risks. Consider the following mission statements:

- International Red Cross (IRC) : 'To serve the most vulnerable.'
- Microsoft: 'We work to help people and businesses throughout the world to realise their full potential. This is our mission. Everything we do reflects this mission and the values that make it possible.'

The IRC has a laudable vision as stated but it is risky as it stands. Who are the most vulnerable? Vulnerable in what way? We may assume that the vulnerable are those suffering from lack of care and those in poverty but others are also vulnerable and, besides, poverty is a relative concept as is lack of care. This vision needs to be clarified in well-stated objectives in order to minimise the risks of non-achievement, loss of reputation and reduction in funding.

With Microsoft, again, the statement is laudable but is subjective. What is the measure for potential, for example, and more importantly, potential for what? It could be potential for criminal activity (although, it is hoped, it is not). What values contribute to the mission? Are these good values, bad values, generally accepted values or what? Once more, without a great deal of refinement, this mission statement presents all kinds of risks if it is seen not to have been fulfilled, a judgement which, itself, could only be subjective.

Learning activity 3.1

Go to http://www.communities.gov.uk and review the strategies and objectives of the Department of Communities and Local Government (DCLG). Give your views as to how these compare with a 'mission and vision'.

Feedback on page 47

We have considered risk in the context of discrete areas of strategy but we should remember that the management of risk can only take place within an organisational framework which is inclusive of all parts of the corporate infrastructure. Without this framework risks cannot be effectively discussed, communicated, compared and managed in a coherent way across the whole organisation. The key elements are:

- Clearly stated, coherent corporate risk policies and standards which include a definition of the types of risk which are unacceptable and raise risk awareness at all levels of the organisation.
- Suitable forums for discussion of risk – from the board downwards. This should include the formation of a board risk committee if deemed appropriate.
- Risk should be a feature of any management discussion of any uncertain circumstances including new initiatives of any kind and the implementation of significant projects.

- Responsibility for accepting risk and authority to manage risk should be clearly defined and assigned to key staff, ie establishment of risk 'ownership' and 'championing'.
- Suitable corporate risk programmes and procedures which take account of the organisational culture, management style and the level of risk management experience within the organisation.
- Implementing suitable systems and documentation of the risk management process including the reporting of significant risk experiences or events.
- Arrangements for monitoring and reviewing the risk management process including ensuring compliance with corporate risk policies and external regulation.
- Becoming a 'learning' organisation: using good and bad risk experiences to inform future decision making.

The tools and techniques which might be used at the strategic level of management of risk can be equally applied to operational risk. Assessing risks is not a 'one-off' activity but should be seen as a cycle – the *risk cycle* – and is an ongoing repetitive process. It should not stand alone or be seen as an additional element which may be omitted, but needs to be integrated with the broader management process which periodically sets and reviews strategy, goals and targets. There are several key aspects of the risk cycle:

- correctly identifying the most important risks
- understanding the nature of the risks – their impact and probability
- putting strategies in place to manage the risks
- identifying the organisational level at which the risk must be managed
- identifying who can influence the risk outcome and how that should be done.

These key areas involve the board and management in establishing the context for risk management and putting it into perspective before commencing the risk analysis and evaluation process which may apply at either the strategic or operational level.

The cycle involves identifying and documenting the risks at all levels which may impact on objectives, then assessing, quantifying and classifying the risks before undertaking an evaluation. At the evaluation stage some kind of modelling or simulation process may be carried out to assist in making informed decisions about the probability of the risk arising or to help in quantifying its possible impact. Mitigation and control strategies then have to be worked out along with the usual management tasks of allocating resources and assigning responsibilities. The final part of the cycle, but an inherent part of it, 'closes the loop' by putting in place monitoring and reviewing procedures.

Self-assessment question 3.1

What risks do you think might be posed by the following strategy (this is just part of the strategy published by the Department of Food Environment and Rural Affairs)?

(continued on next page)

3

Self-assessment question 3.1 *(continued)*

A more sustainable future for everyone – that's Defra's top priority.

Key areas include:

- To promote sustainable management and prudent use of natural resources domestically and internationally.
- To improve productivity in the least well-performing rural areas and to increase accessibility of services for rural people.

Feedback on page 47

3.2   Risks at the operational level

We will address operational risks in much greater detail from study session 11 onwards. This study session can be read as an introduction to what we mean by operations and how the risks that we face in this area can be managed appropriately.

The word **operations** can be used to cover every aspect of the production of a product, a process or a service. This may be the actual manufacture of a plate or a keyboard, using machinery or hand tools, or it could be the provision of a service such as advice or even entertainment in the production of a show or concert. Everything that is produced depends on a whole series of tasks, issues and decisions that are taken by many people who will make a contribution to the final delivery.

In the world of theatre, we may be paying to go and see a particular actor or playwright, but the operations that precede, support and follow up on the show are vast in number. We could mention the sound engineers, the security staff, box office, wardrobe staff, hair stylists and impresarios, to name just a few. Each of the steps in the operations that result in the production of such entertainment are fraught with risks, with the potential consequences of damage to the person, to reputations, finances and so on.

We can certainly link operational risk to strategic risk. The strategy may be fine. It may be appropriate to the business and achievable, but we need to ensure that the operations are capable of supporting the strategy. For example, the operations need to be sufficiently resourced with people, materials and money. The strategy needs to be correctly interpreted and translated into effective procedures and instructions, in order that the outcome of the operations matches the desired outcome from the strategy.

We then need to identify all of the operations that will be needed to deliver the desired outcome. This can often be achieved by developing a process map and identifying who and what will be involved at every step, in order to identify any risks and deal with them appropriately. We will discuss risk assessments in a later study session, but every operation does need to be assessed for any risks and these can then be prioritised for attention.

The sources of risk at the operational level may come from the same sources as at the strategic level. And we should continue to ask ourselves the same question: *what may happen to stop us achieving our objectives?* There may still be the external influences that we have identified by using the PESTLE analysis which was explained in study session 2. We could also use the

Ishikawa cause-and-effect diagram or 'fishbone diagram' (figure 3.1). This can allow us to drill down from a particular heading and identify areas that contain uncertainty which we can then analyse as risk. For information on how to use this useful tool, take a look at http://www.skymark.com/resources/tools/cause.asp.

Figure 3.1: Ishikawa's cause-and-effect diagram

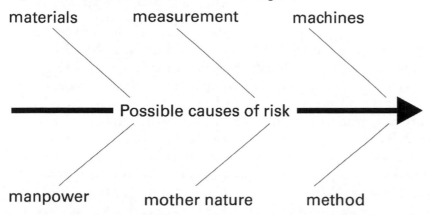

Mind-mapping is another simple tool which can be adapted to analysing steps in an operation and the decisions attached to the steps. This can aid a consideration of potential threats or hazards and the way in which these risks could be managed (see figure 3.2). Risk maps are also common tools used in this connection and are dealt with in detail in a later study session.

Figure 3.2: Mind map example on time management

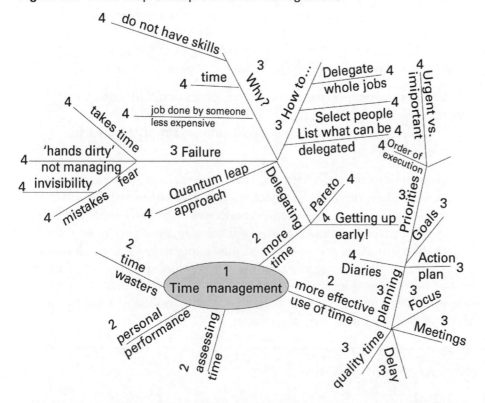

The Ishikawa fishbone and the mind-mapping techniques have been used here in the context of operational risk but are not exclusive to this level. Both these methods could be used with equal effect when considering risk assessment at the strategic level also.

Learning activity 3.2

Read the following mini case study and rank in descending order of priority the uncertainties and potential impacts that Corin seems to be facing. You may wish to use Ishikawa's fishbone or a mind map to help you identify some issues.

Corin Ivry has given up his job in a car factory and set up as a concert promoter for local rock bands. It has taken him some time to convince some new bands with a good local following to sign up with him and he is under pressure to arrange some concerts to maintain the momentum that those bands have created in the local area. Corin has booked a concert room located behind a large hotel on a major road for eight consecutive Saturdays and he has agreed to share the profits with the hotel instead of paying a fee. He has enlisted the support of some family members to assist with security, publicity and finance.

Feedback on page 47

Sometimes it is difficult to categorise risks into convenient slots such as 'strategic' or 'operational' and, as we have seen, some of the tools and techniques used may be the same. Operational risks in general terms are those we find in the functions and activities which every organisation undertakes in its day-to-day processes. In terms of the risk management process, it has cascaded down from the level of board and senior management to the level of front-line activity, that is, the level of *operations*. The Institute of Risk Management in its 2002 Risk Standard gives some examples of 'key drivers' in each category:

* Strategic risks include competition, customer demand, customer changes, industry changes.
* Operational risks include regulations, culture, supply chain and recruitment.

Risks relate to objectives. To identify, assess and manage the risks there must first be an understanding of the objectives that it is hoped will be achieved. We need to bear in mind, however, that effective risk management is not a guarantee of success: no matter how well we may anticipate risks and calculate their outcome, the unexpected may happen. Even the risk which remains after all our management action (the residual risk) may escalate over time and become problematic. Whether at strategic or operational level, risk management per se is just another item in the toolkit to assist in the achievement of organisational objectives.

Self-assessment question 3.2

Reread the case study and suggest some solutions to the risks that you have identified.

Feedback on page 48

3.3 Risks at the project level

Some organisations make their entire living from winning and completing projects. These businesses build up expertise in particular areas and use that expert knowledge to undertake discrete projects in other organisations. For most organisations, however, projects mean scenarios that are only likely to appear once in a while, have a finite time and have clear objectives of product, service or system improvement. Chapman & Ward quote Turner (1992) who defines a project as 'an endeavour in which human, material and financial resources are organised in a novel way, to undertake a unique scope of work of given specification'.

We are not just talking about building projects such as a new stadium. The building of a new telecommunications system; the introduction of new computers; the conversion of a warehouse into a block of flats; the outsourcing of a group of facilities such as cleaning, catering and so on; setting up a value analysis team to investigate a certain process; these are what we mean by projects. They usually have time limitations and it is the matching of lead times, with the availability of land, materials, knowledge, labour and/or finance which creates the greatest problems.

Issues of uncertainty will exist in the areas of budgets and estimates, design and logistics, objectives and priorities and relationships between all of the people and departments working on the project.

Project life cycle

The life cycle of a project is rife with opportunities for problems, which can be solved in a number of ways, but their resolution is almost certain to have an adverse impact on either the cost or the quality or the timeliness of a project, if not on all three. To achieve the right quality may affect the cost. To achieve the right cost, we may have to sacrifice punctuality. To achieve the right punctuality, we may have to sacrifice cost and quality.

Projects tend to undergo a series of stages which are known as the project life cycle. The following life cycle is based upon Chapman & Ward's example in *Project Risk Management:*

1   Conception – including clarification of idea and purpose.
2   Design – converting the concept and purpose into performance criteria.
3   Plan – develop how the design will be achieved with milestones, resource-based plans and activity timings.
4   Allocate – resources need to be applied to all of the stages.
5   Execute – this comprises the doing, the monitoring and the controlling.
6   Deliver – complete the objective to no less than the stated targets.
7   Review – what went right and what went wrong.
8   Support – ensure the project continues to deliver through ongoing maintenance, training and upgrades.

You may recall from study session 2 that mention was made of software availability which can assist with the management of projects. Go to http://www.p2launchpad.com to review details of the Prince project management tool. You will also find a template-driven project management aid at the Method123 website: http://www.projectsatwork.com.

3

Learning activity 3.3

Consider a recent project, preferably one you have been involved in. Identify ten risks that needed to be addressed. Assess the extent to which any available project management software could have assisted in the process.

Feedback on page 48

Most of us have heard of the problems in the project to build a new home for the Scottish Parliament in Edinburgh. The principal conclusions from the inquiry into why the project was late and over budget can be read on the Parliament's own website (http://www.scottish.parliament.jk/vli/holyrood/inquiry/sp205-18.htm). In summary, the 'fast track' procurement method entailed relatively high risk; the original budget figure of £40–50 million was never going to be sufficient; whenever quality and cost conflicted, quality was preferred; whenever early completion and cost conflicted, completion was preferred though no significant acceleration was achieved; the complexity of the architect's evolving design and its inevitable cost was not appreciated until too late; costs rose because the client wanted increases and changes or at least approved of them.

Self-assessment question 3.3

Select a project, draw up a project life cycle list as shown in Chapman & Ward's example above and identify the potential costs of failure at each stage.

Feedback on page 48

Revision question

Now try the revision question for this session on page 355.

Summary

We have considered in this study session the high-level approach to risk management referred to as *strategic risk* and discussed how this can cascade down the organisation to become *operational risk*. Although the two approaches are discrete there is a great deal of crossover between the two in terms of the understanding of principles and application of techniques. We have also discussed the fact that, at whatever level, risk management should be an integral part of management action on a continuous basis. It is not a 'fix and forget' solution but part of the need to manage effectively in order that strategy and objectives can be achieved.

Suggested further reading

You could read the relevant sections of Porter (2004) and

Chapman and Ward (2003).

3

Feedback on learning activities and self-assessment questions

Feedback on learning activity 3.1

A vision statement is often brief and to the point (for example, to be the best in our field) and flows from the broad vision which the board has of what the organisation wishes to achieve. The vision then translates into a broader mission statement which may contain specific aims and objectives. This encapsulates the expectations we should have from the vision for our organisation and its primary mission which is then perceived as objectives which, in turn, can be measured for achievement over time. You will find that the aims and objectives of this department appear as a series of 5-year plans with performance targets.

You might wish to compare the DCLG statements (and those of IRC and Microsoft) with your own organisation's vision and mission.

Feedback on self-assessment question 3.1

As was discovered by DEFRA's predecessor, MAFF, the world is a changing place and agriculture and environment are changing faster than most of us could ever have imagined. The risks of changes in diseases of animals, humans and crops, the potential impact of genetic modification (GM) and the growing population will all work against DEFRA's aims. At the same time, it needs to convince the Treasury of the need to allocate sufficient funds and human resources to achieve this, in the face of massive competition from other public sector areas such as the armed forces, healthcare and education. Similarly, there is a risk of a change of political direction, while changes in the World Trade Organization regarding the subsidies payable to farming are under review.

One of the major risks of this strategy is that it is very vague. There is no clear definition in the case of 'a more sustainable future for everyone'. Not only is it open to a range of interpretations but it is almost impossible to measure. DEFRA management may see little risk associated with this part of their strategy and it may also be impossible to achieve on the basis that DEFRA may struggle to obtain the resources or the control to be able to achieve this.

Feedback on learning activity 3.2

As with all scenarios like this, there is never enough information to make a truly informed decision about the risks. There are certainly many areas of uncertainty such as the potential audience, the price they will be prepared to pay for entrance, the amount they will spend on concessions and souvenirs, the suitability and experience of family members, the reliability of the band, together with lighting and sound. There is uncertainty about competing events, the quality of the publicity and Corin's own intentions here.

The consequences of failure will certainly affect Corin's finances and reputation, though he has shared some of the financial risk by paying a profit-related fee for the hire of the venue.

At this stage it is difficult to assess the scale of the risks, as we have no information about the probability of those uncertainties impacting upon the outcome of the events. However, even with these constraints we can make some assumptions – as long as we state them. Probably Corin would have based his decision upon knowledge of the marketplace, the customer base and their propensity to attend his promotions in preference to competing attractions. His decision should also have been made with clear understanding of the possible outcomes resulting from a number of combinations of events.

Feedback on self-assessment question 3.2

To identify the risks after the decision has been taken is not the preferred sequence. Corin should have assessed the risks he faced at the early stages of his career change but, by discovering the facts at this late stage, it may still allow us to affect the outcome in the following ways: stepping up publicity; negotiating contingency arrangements with additional entertainers; building in additional security; negotiations with police; charging concession stalls a fixed fee; consulting with other promoters; identifying backup sound and lighting engineers and supplies; timing the event to avoid clashing with other events; laying on additional public transport; using professional security firms; taking out insurance.

Feedback on learning activity 3.3

The risks to be identified may include budget over/underrun; missed deadlines; injuries; loss of earnings; loss of reputation; failure of suppliers' performance; supply chain breakdown; design errors; obsolescence; change of need; discovery of new information; change of personnel; incompetent workers; lack of training; no aftersales support; relationship breakdown; litigation.

There will be many more that could be identified and use of software such as Prince (or Prince 2) assists in formalising critical points, decision impacts and time or money difficulties.

Feedback on self-assessment question 3.3

The answers here will depend on the example that you choose. Some of the answers used in the learning activity will be acceptable here, such as loss of earnings, cost of litigation, damages, loss of profits, need to repeat work, cost of retraining, learning curve costs for new personnel, costs of public enquiry, cost of safety review (eg HAZOPS; discussed in study session 12).

The stakeholders' influence

Introduction

Stakeholders are those people or groups who have a vested interest in what an organisation does. In other words, what happens in the organisation will affect them in some way. These people and groups can have a major input to the success or failure of the business, as they may block our plans or remove their support. Not only is it imperative that we identify who are the stakeholders, but we must also ensure that we are dealing with each of them in a manner that is appropriate to their level of potential influence.

'Participation is the process by which stakeholders influence and share control over priority setting, policy making, resource allocations, and/ or programme implementation. There is no blueprint for participation...' The World Bank's *Poverty Reduction Strategy*

Session learning objectives

After completing this session you should be able to:

4.1 Identify the stakeholders in an organisation.
4.2 Evaluate the role of a private sector organisation's stakeholders in risk management.
4.3 Evaluate the role of a public sector organisation's stakeholders in risk management.
4.4 Evaluate the needs and desires of the key stakeholders in a public limited company (plc).
4.5 Understand factors influencing stakeholder satisfaction and the impact that purchasing may have on these factors.

Unit content coverage

This study session covers the following topics from the official CIPS unit content document:

Learning objective

1.6 Evaluate the role of an organisation's stakeholders in risk management.
  • The roles and responsibilities of an organisation's risk function in relation to other functional areas
  • The impact of a risk event at the functional level
  • The benefits of a cross-functional team when assessing, preventing and minimising risk
  • The role of purchasing to mitigate against potential losses to the whole organisation from risk events
  • The merits of taking a consistent approach across the organisation to the assessment of risk

Prior knowledge

Study sessions 1, 2 and 3.

Resources

Internet access.

Timing

You should set aside about 6 hours to read and complete this session, including learning activities, self-assessment questions, the suggested further reading (if any) and the revision question.

4.1 Identifying the stakeholders in an organisation

Learning activity 4.1

List the external and internal stakeholders in both a public and a private sector organisation of your choice.

Feedback on page 64

Who and what are stakeholders? Why should they be interested in the way in which organisations manage risks?

The Organization for Economic Cooperation and Development (OECD) has laid down five principles of good corporate governance. More about OECD and its role in governance will be found at http://www.oecd.org but, at this stage, all we need consider is the principle which deals with the role of stakeholders. In essence, this principle identifies the stakeholder community as being shareholders and employees but extending to all who may have an interest in the operations of the organisation. The principle goes on to call for cooperation between organisations and stakeholders in the creation of wealth, jobs and the sustainability of financially sound enterprises. Stakeholders, then, can be almost anyone with an interest in the operation and outcomes from organisations in both public and private sectors of activity.

Stakeholders can be as diverse as investors in a plc and all employees in any organisation. They can be taxpayers, contributing to both local and central government revenue raising – in that taxpayers clearly have an interest in the way in which tax revenues are spent – and they can be close neighbours to a factory complex whose emissions policy can directly affect all who live near the factory. All of these groups have a close interest in the way risks are managed in virtually all organisations because any or all may be affected by risk decisions which ultimately affect outcomes.

You can see from the above that stakeholders may be inside the organisation, an **internal stakeholder**, or outside the organisation, an **external stakeholder**. If you can imagine an organisation to have a ring or circle drawn around its structure, then within that circle are the internal stakeholders. These include the owners, directors or governing body and staff at all levels – their jobs and salaries depend upon the organisation continuing and prospering. Outside the circle are the external stakeholders – individuals or bodies who have a financial, environmental or other interest in the way the organisation is performing. They are also dependent on the way management performs its task: suppliers need to be sure of continuity – for payment as well as their own future business – pension funds need to safeguard their members' rights and returns while legal and environmental compliance avoids potential reputational damage and, perhaps, loss of customers.

Internal stakeholders

Possibly the best place to start is to look at ownership. In a private business, the most important stakeholders are the people who own the business, namely the shareholders. These people have invested their money in the business on the basis that they will be expecting a financial return on their investment. They may be private individuals; they may be directors of the business who have taken a stake in the business either by investing their own savings or through part of their remuneration package. Shareholders can move their funds out of the business and invest elsewhere, in a business that they think is more likely to generate the desired returns.

In a public sector organisation, ownership will be in the hands of the state. Theoretically this means all citizens, whether taxpayers or not, own the organisation and it should be accountable to them. In this sense we are all captive stakeholders (or to be precise, 'customers') because there is often no credible alternative supply. Voters are the internal stakeholders in the large strategic services such as defence and health through our stake in public ownership and we can affect strategic decisions by voting in a particular way at parliamentary elections. If we are registered in local tax areas, whether we are exempt from tax or not, we have a stake in the way in which the local council operates and spends money. We can affect the business of the council by attending meetings, by lobbying councillors and by voting them out of office if they fail to achieve the desired outcomes.

In all sectors, we have stakeholders in the form of employees. The success or failure of the business will affect their safety and security of employment, their take-home pay and the way in which they are treated at work. Most organisations will also have a large number of dependent workers, contractors and suppliers.

External stakeholders

External to the organisation are a large number of stakeholders, not the least of whom will be the customers and suppliers.

When Northumberland's last deep coal mine was shut in January 2005, 340 direct jobs were lost, but the impact is much greater on the local community that serviced those 340 jobs. Builders, electricians, cleaners, contractors, suppliers of materials and parts, and even the catering companies have been affected and the knock-on effect cannot yet be accurately judged. The disposable income in the region will fall and takings in pubs, clubs, shops and travel agencies will also drop, as soon as the redundancy payments are spent.

- Stakeholders may also include neighbours who live near our premises or who may be impacted by the traffic, noise and dirt created by delivery vehicles and staff.
- Organisational stakeholders include HM Revenue & Customs who has a vested interest in the taxes and duties that we need to pay.
- The Environment Agency has a responsibility to ensure that we are remaining within our emissions limits.
- Other government departments will be interested from the point of view of employee rights, equal opportunities, union activity and so on.
- The local council will have a stake in the business rates that are to be paid as well as the impact upon the community for schooling, policing, roads and waste disposal. Planning permission and building regulations authorities will also come under the council's auspices.

Stakeholder analysis

Developing a strategy and selecting the tactics and operations to be used in achieving the desired outcomes demands that we answer the question 'what are we trying to achieve?' In order to develop an appropriate answer, we need to have a clear view of who the stakeholders are, in order that we can take account of all of the key concerns. Failing to deal with these at the outset is likely to lead to much greater problems when they arise and need later treatment.

The Civil Contingencies Secretariat in the Cabinet Office has addressed this issue and they suggest that we ask ourselves the following questions:

- What are the potential issues?
- Who will be affected by the risk and the consequences of any management decision?
- Which parties or individuals have knowledge and expertise which may be useful to inform any discussion or both?
- Which parties or individuals have expressed an interest in this particular, or a similar type, of risk problem?
- Which stakeholders will be prepared to listen to and respect different viewpoints, and be prepared to negotiate?

Specific stakeholders might include different medical or education professions, charities and campaigning groups, various government departments and agencies, certain businesses, local authorities, and so on. Many issues have strong international or European stakeholders.

So, first, list all stakeholders:

- own department (including ministers)
- government departments
- public sector
- private sector, including professional associations

- non-governmental organisations, charities, pressure groups, victims' groups
- international stakeholders (for example, export markets)
- the general public, particularly diverse groups who might otherwise be excluded from public policy.

Once we have identified the stakeholders, we can start to identify not just their level of interest but also the degree of influence that they may be able to exert on the organisation and its decisions.

A simple way of segmenting the stakeholders according to interest and influence would be a simple 2 by 2 matrix as shown in figure 4.1.

Figure 4.1: Stakeholder analysis matrix

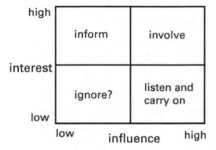

Here, you simply rank the stakeholder based upon the two parameters of how interested the stakeholder is in your business and what degree of influence they can exert over any decision. You can then identify how to prioritise your resources and apply appropriate techniques to those stakeholders depending upon where they fall in the matrix.

Self-assessment question 4.1

Draft a report of 250–300 words that proposes how best to ensure a favourable attitude from two key stakeholders that you have mentioned in learning activity 4.1 above.

Feedback on page 64

4.2 The role of a private sector organisation's stakeholders in risk management

Learning activity 4.2

Identify the potential contribution to risk management that can be made by stakeholders in a private sector organisation.

Feedback on page 65

We have earlier mentioned that the stakeholders in a private sector organisation will be likely to include the owners, staff, suppliers and customers as well as the external stakeholders such as government departments, local councils, contractors, suppliers, customers and neighbours.

The role of these people and organisations will, of course, depend upon their interest and degree of influence. For example, a small businessman working from home and making a small living will hardly ever attract the interest of HM Revenue & Customs, other than an occasional telephone check on VAT and tax issues. However, that businessman may be affecting his neighbours by the number of people visiting the house, including delivery vehicles. In this case the businessman stands a risk that the neighbours will seek some form of redress against him for using his residence for business. Other stakeholders may be his insurance company and bank. The success or otherwise of the business and the amount of business equipment may start to interest his insurance company and bank, as they may insist that he takes additional steps to protect their investment, or their policies.

Within a larger organisation, there will be functional divisions probably with managers heading each function. In an ideal world, we would expect these managers to deal with risk in the same way that they are legally obliged to deal with health and safety. In other words, they should not only be responsible for their own risks but also any other issues that may cause risks to others.

If we force the managers and their staff into functional silos, however, and if we force them to compete with other functions for resources, funding and kudos, then it is quite likely that we will firstly reduce the likelihood that they will highlight any risks that appear in another function and secondly that they will refuse to listen to any suggestions and recommendations for dealing with risk that emanate from another function. Organisations should, in fact, strive for an enterprise-wide approach to risk management in order to both provide assurance that all key risks are recognised and achieve best value for money from the use of resources.

The shareholders

The shareholders make a major contribution as to whether a business takes a risk-averse approach. In autumn 2005, the Edinburgh football club, Heart of Midlothian has gone through a very turbulent period. Even though the club is top of the Scottish Premiership and is unbeaten after playing 25% of its games, the major shareholder, Lithuanian Vladimir Romanov, seems to have decided that this is still not good enough and he wants to take a much bolder approach to how the business is run. The manager, George Burley, was forced out, the chief executive was sacked and the chairman has resigned in sympathy. It will be interesting to see how Hearts progress from this point on.

In 2003, GlaxoSmithKline suffered a humiliating shareholder revolt over plans to raise the chairman's pay to include a £22 million 'golden parachute' should he lose his job. The company had clearly failed to assess correctly the strength of feeling among the major shareholders (typically pension fund managers and other financial institutions) over very high levels of executive pay. As a result it failed to assess the risk of a very public shareholder revolt and the damage to management credibility that this would cause.

The board of directors

The primary role of the board is to manage a company on behalf of the shareholders in order to achieve the company's aims, strategies and objectives. In a public limited company, the board is accountable to the shareholders for its actions and its performance but, as we have seen in considering the wider stakeholder community, consequences arising from company operations affect many more people than shareholders alone. The board has a key responsibility to assess risks at the highest level of the organisation and to ensure that the risk management process is in place and operating effectively throughout each part of the organisation. Directors depend upon re-election by shareholders at company annual general meetings, so effective performance is a significant factor in their continuing in their roles. Thus, directors need to ensure that any direction given is in harmony with corporate strategy but also that it is communicated in such a way that misinterpretation is kept to a minimum. At the same time they must involve all appropriate stakeholders in order to be aware of stakeholder needs and adjust the strategy accordingly. By doing this, they are minimising the risk of later costly adjustment and they are ensuring that the risk of failure to achieve objectives is minimised. At the same time, they need to recognise feedback from the managers about resource needs. Failure to resource the work adequately and to build contingency arrangements and plans will surely increase the risk of failure.

The role of boards and directors of companies – and their equivalent in the public sector – has been subject to much scrutiny over recent decades, not least because of major corporate scandals over the years such as WorldCom, Enron and Parmalat. In the UK this has resulted in a spotlight being turned on to the way companies are directed and controlled; the way, in fact, that they are governed. While the UK has avoided legislation in this area, referred to as *corporate governance,* much has been put in place in terms of voluntary codes of practice. For companies, this is the Combined Code of the London Stock Exchange (usually referred to as the Combined Code). In terms of our understanding the role of the board of directors in managing risks, this Code is a key ingredient since one of its provisions (C.2.1) requires, among other things, that the board:

'… should conduct … a review … of all material controls, including financial, operational and compliance controls and risk management systems.'

Control will be dealt with in depth in a later study session, but for more information on the Combined Code see the website http://www.fsa.gov.uk.

Management

Managers have the role of taking their direction from the board and converting it into practicable tactics and operations that again are in harmony with the overriding strategies of the organisation. They have the responsibility of informing the directors to allow correct decisions to be made regarding strategy and future plans. At the same time they should be involving their staff, as well as their colleagues in other functions, in the decision-making process.

The risks of failure to achieve objectives, failure to operate safely, failure to identify key stakeholders or major risks, can, of course, be mitigated through training as well as the provision of the right tools for the job. Understanding the business environment in which they work is a vital element and with this knowledge they can interpret the likely risks from various courses of action. Using good deductive techniques, the management can then ensure that the route most likely to achieve the targets can be selected, with risk levels appropriate to the culture and risk appetite of the business.

Many businesses expect their managers to take on more than just their functional roles. As we develop multiskilled managers, they are expected to take on their share of other areas such as quality, safety and risk. After all, it is only the larger organisations who can afford to have quality managers, safety managers and risk managers in full-time posts. Even in large organisations where these specialists exist, they usually perform an advisory and compliance role. It is up to the line manager to ensure safety, quality and so on in their part of the business.

Staff

The staff still have responsibilities. They should be informing management of issues regarding health and safety, potential quality improvement, as well as the need for skills enhancement or personal development. Their role is also to communicate needs in a clear, concise and timely manner to other contributors, such as service providers, suppliers and contractors.

Suppliers and customers

The contribution that these parties can make to the management of risk within an organisation is immense, but their contribution does depend upon there being good communication links. In other words, we have got to be prepared to seek the feedback, to listen to it and to deal with it appropriately. After all, it is our suppliers and customers who should know more about their marketplaces, their needs and wants than we do. We can then use their knowledge and the opportunity for early warning of any changes that may be taking place, to adjust our position and again mitigate the new and emerging risks to our organisation.

The communication can be facilitated by employing and facilitating professional purchasing and sales staff whose role would be to gather and analyse the information and produce advice for management and the board, to ensure that correct adjustments are made to financing, positioning and policy.

Risk events that might be spotted by the purchasing team could include:

- the financial instability of a company in the supply chain
- the impact of weather conditions on a supply route
- the opportunity for lower tariffs resulting from a reciprocal trade agreement
- the effect of new environmental legislation on costs of disposal.

Auditors

Auditors could be grouped within the division of service providers, but I think it is necessary to consider them as a separate stakeholder and contributor to risk management. One could say that the sheer necessity to have an auditor visit the business from time to time is a check on some of the less wholesome practices that might take place in an organisation. Knowing that they are soon to arrive will often put the firm into a frenzy of activity, correcting and cleaning data and locating missing files. The auditors' arrival and response (and their departure) will be eagerly awaited, as we certainly need to be given a clean bill of health. More important is any advice they may be able to give us on where we might be facing risk, where our weaknesses are and what we can do about these. Their vested interest is in doing a proper job and avoiding any later adverse publicity regarding a failure to identify fraud or mismanagement.

The external auditor role has been affected by the Combined Code referred to above in that the auditors will wish to ensure that the company has complied with the requirements of the Code and reported accordingly in the public domain. In this respect, the auditors will wish to ensure that risk management and control processes are in place as required by the Code.

Internal auditors have a key role to play in risk management also. The in-house team plans its activities around the company's risk assessment and provides assurance on the quality and efficacy of mitigating strategies, including internal control. In most listed companies and large organisations the internal auditors report to the board and audit committee, thus providing an excellent in-house assurance and early warning system.

Self-assessment question 4.2

Draft a short report that details the potential costs of failing to correctly manage the key stakeholders in a manufacturing company.

Feedback on page 65

4.3 The role of a public sector organisation's stakeholders in risk management

Learning activity 4.3

Identify the potential contribution to risk management that can be made by stakeholders in a public sector organisation.

Feedback on page 65

The public sector comprises all of those organisations which are not controlled by individuals, voluntary organisations or private companies. This includes national government with departments such as DTI, DEFRA and so on; local government in the form of county, city, borough and town councils, and government-owned businesses such as Royal Mail. There are also the agencies such as the Prescription Pricing Agency, HM Revenue & Customs, the Environment Agency, and so on. In addition, there are the other organisations which operate on behalf of the public such as the UK Atomic Energy Authority, Transport for London, and Network Rail.

Clearly all of these bodies have stakeholders in the form of boards, management, staff, suppliers and customers or end users in one form or another.

The main difference is in the management and ultimate accountability of these organisations. The strategy for public sector organisations may be driven by public need but may also be heavily influenced by political direction or expediency. Funding may come from a variety of sources, particularly through innovations such as the Private Finance Initiative and public-private joint ventures. The risks which have to be managed in these organisations, and the way they are managed, can vary, sometimes significantly, from those in the private sector. For some public provision – defence or policing are good examples – termination is a risk strategy that could not be contemplated and there is no real alternative provision in these areas. Whatever the risks, although clearly they can be mitigated, there is no alternative but for the government to provide the armed forces. Ultimately, accountability for public services is to the citizen. Even for arms-length organisations such as agencies and quangos (quasi-governmental bodies), the ballot box provides the sanction which, in the private sector, would be the withdrawal of funding and support from the financial markets and shareholders.

The way in which the public sector organisations will be run will to some extent depend upon the political persuasion of the party in power as well as the extent of their majority at any time. With a small majority, the government is much more likely to adopt conciliatory measures in the way that it delivers its public services, in order to protect the goodwill of the voters. We have seen this happening over many years in France, where the majority of any party has been small. With a large majority, the government can force through changes, in the knowledge that, in the short term, the measures are disliked by the electorate. However, the risks to its tenure are not high, so the government knows that these measures may contribute to longer-term performance improvement with the consequent favourable effect on the polls.

The foregoing applies to the ministers themselves, but of course, the civil servants in the UK are independent of the political system. Their role is to act on behalf of citizens and to persuade ministers towards this end.

Citizens and taxpayers

Some citizens may be exempt from paying central or local taxes for a number of very good reasons. All citizens in the correct age groups are enfranchised, however, and can contribute by attending council meetings, lobbying councillors or members of parliament and generally making the decision makers aware of their requirements and preferences.

Review bodies

In recent years, the contribution of purchasing in the achievement of best value in the public sector has gained a raised profile. Following the work of Byatt with regard to improvements in the way local councils spend their money, we have had the report from Sir Peter Gershon highlighting the potential contribution that can be achieved through the application of professional procurement practice, not just in the reduction of total spend, but in the better provisioning and support to front-line services.

The **Audit Commission** has a mission statement that says

> 'Our mission is to be a driving force in the improvement of public services. We promote good practice and help those responsible for public services to achieve better outcomes for citizens, with a focus on those people who need public services most.'

The Commission has a vested interest in ensuring that certain public sector bodies obtain best value for money, as that is their mission. By working with the Office of Government Commerce (OGC), councils and other public bodies in the areas of health, housing, criminal justice and fire and rescue, the Audit Commission can not only assist these bodies in identifying areas of risk, but it will also make its findings public so that other councils and public bodies can learn from its findings.

The **National Audit Office** 'audits the accounts of all central government departments and agencies as well as a wide range of other public bodies and reports to Parliament on the economy, efficiency and effectiveness with which they have used public money'.

Support organisations

The **Office of Government Commerce** (OGC)

> 'works with public sector organisations to help them improve their efficiency, gain better value for money from their commercial activities and deliver improved success from programmes and projects. Our priorities are to support the delivery of:
> * the public sector's £21.5bn annual efficiency gains by 2007/08
> * £3bn saving by 2007/08 in central government procurement
> * improvement in the success rate of mission critical projects.'

It does this by developing tools training to assist all public sector employees to do their job better. This includes a high degree of risk management, in order to achieve their testing objectives. The tools are predominantly aimed at managing procurement more wisely, closely linked to the findings in the Gershon reports.

The **National Health Service Purchasing and Supplies Agency (PASA)**
is another body set up to support practitioners in the delivery of best value service. The role of the Agency is:

> 'to act as a centre of expertise, knowledge and excellence in purchasing and supply matters for the health service. As an integral part of the Department of Health, the NHS Purchasing and Supply Agency is

4

in a key position to advise on policy and the strategic direction of procurement, and its impact on developing healthcare, across the NHS. Intended to function not just as an advisory and coordinating body but also an active participant in the ongoing modernisation of purchasing and supply in the health service, the agency contracts on a national basis for products and services which are strategically critical to the NHS. It also acts in cases where aggregated purchasing power will yield greater economic savings than those achieved by contracting on a local or regional basis.'

So again, PASA has a role that compels it to assist the NHS in the delivery of its goals, which entails the management of risks throughout the supply chain. This may bring very special needs when there are occasions such as the SARS outbreak, the threats of terrorists using anthrax, and now the possibility of avian flu.

Treasury advice

HM Treasury issues advice and information to public sector bodies on matters of corporate governance and risk management. This data takes account of the essential differences between private sector and public sector bodies while promoting the principles of sound governance and the effective management of risks. The advice has included a statement on internal control and guidance on the strategic overview of risk. For more information see the website http://www.hm-treasury.gov.uk.

Self-assessment question 4.3

Draft a report that details the potential costs of failing to identify the key stakeholders in a local council.

Feedback on page 65

4.4 Factors influencing stakeholder satisfaction and the impact that purchasing can have

Learning activity 4.4

Produce questionnaires that might be issued to stakeholders – one for internal and one for external stakeholders – in order to clarify how a supply chain manager can satisfy their needs and desires. Identify which sections may be particularly relevant to specific stakeholder groups.

Feedback on page 66

In order to identify the factors that influence stakeholder satisfaction, we again need to consider which stakeholders we are talking about.

As we mentioned earlier, if an education authority were chosen, then the stakeholders would include students, parents, employers, government, local government, suppliers, teachers, feeder schools and education links at the next level up, as well as the taxpayer. Let us deal with each of these briefly in a matrix format, in table 4.1, which is not intended as an exhaustive list.

Table 4.1 Stakeholder listing for a school or education authority

Stakeholder	Satisfied by	Purchasing impact
Student	Quality of education	Through spending the available money wisely, the governors and headteachers should be able to allocate more of the money to teaching aids, decor maintenance, special provisions such as sports, music.
	Pass rates	
	Working environment	
Parent	Reputation	
	Pass rates	Purchasing involvement in the design of any new or refurbished facilities may also allow the use of supplier expertise in bringing in lower total life cycle costs.
	Special provisions	
Local employer	Quality of job applicants	
Government	Conformance to targets	Using the purchasing power of consortia and the principles of virtual inventory, we can also use other non-monetary resources more effectively.
	Lack of complaints	
Local government	Compliance issues	
	Lack of complaints	Pass rates may not change, as these are dependent upon many other external factors, but the quality of life at the school should improve which should then reduce the number of problems which can sap resources very quickly.
Teachers	Quality of support	
	Pay rates	
	Promotion prospects	
	Pass rates	
	Working environment	
Schools up- and downstream	Quality of education	
	Dealing with special needs	
Taxpayer	Reputation	
	Lack of complaints	
	Value for money	

Self-assessment question 4.4

Compare the needs and desires of various stakeholder groups that may impact upon the supply chain and identify any areas that may be potentially in conflict.

Feedback on page 66

4.5 Evaluate the needs and desires of stakeholders

Learning activity 4.5

Imagine that you want to build a major extension to your factory or offices. You will be leading the briefing sessions. Produce some notes detailing how these sessions will be managed to get the most positive reactions from your stakeholders.

Feedback on page 66

According to the Centre for Academic Practice:

> 'Needs analysis is closely linked with evaluation and dissemination. It is the crucial diagnostic part of an effective evaluation. The purpose of evaluation is to offer a means to investigate, provide evidence, learn, share and make judgements about what we do and how we do it. There are inevitably links with feedback gathered from dissemination activities, as you may engage with stakeholders who can inform the choices you make in your development. A needs analysis is the starting point for defining the criteria against which judgements about success can be made. ... Some of the areas your needs analysis should address may be determined by your stakeholders.'

Table 4.2 is an extract from a user needs analysis from a University of Westminster report on a road user charging survey.

Table 4.2 Stakeholder needs analysis

Policy objectives (relate these objectives to transport measures)	Transport service providers and operators		
	PT operators and taxi companies	Freight and delivery	Emergency services
Environment/health			
To reduce noise			
To improve local air quality			
To reduce greenhouse gases			
To encourage physical fitness			
Safety			
To reduce accidents	S		P
To improve security	P		P
Economy			
To reduce congestion	P	P	S
To raise revenue	P		
Accessibility			
To reduce severance			P
To improve access	P	P	P

Source: adapted from Kocak (2004)

P, primary interest to support stakeholder groups

S, secondary interest to support stakeholder groups

In the same way, many businesses use a tool known as quality function deployment (or house of quality) to identify the features of a product or service and how these may impact upon customer satisfaction.

As part of the quality assurance processes within an organisation, it is worthwhile specifying that this sort of tool should be used on every development and before every change. From a design point of view, we are talking about the implementation of value engineering and value analysis techniques which have been around since they were developed by LD Miles in the 1950s.

In its *Risk and Value Management Procurement Guide*, the Office of Government Commerce (OGC) recommends value management 'to identify stakeholder needs, objectives and priorities'. They say that value management '… enables stakeholders to define and achieve their needs through facilitated workshops that encourage participation, teamworking and end-user buy-in'.

Many people think that this is just about reducing total cost, when in fact, as Gershon states, it is more to do with delivering the required services in such as way as to liberate more funds to front-line services. By addressing stakeholder needs at the earliest stage of financial commitment, we can obtain:

- a clear and precise specification of stakeholder requirements
- the opportunity to gather facts about alternatives
- the possibility to include creative and novel approaches to service delivery
- achievement of value for money
- high service levels
- lean supply lines
- improved teamworking
- more harmony with existing customers
- a platform for continued future performance improvements.

Self-assessment question 4.5

List the stakeholders from the above activity and identify two issues that need to be addressed for each of them.

Feedback on page 66

Revision question

Now try the revision question for this session on page 355.

Summary

We have identified in this study session that the stakeholders are many and varied and their wants and needs will also be varied. Unless we clearly determine who the stakeholders are and what are their needs it is impossible to identify where there may be conflicting demands or where tradeoffs need to be applied.

Influencing the stakeholders is an important part of maintaining progress, so that the war can be won before the fighting starts. This can only come about as a result of gaining sufficient knowledge to take the right approach.

Suggested further reading

You could read the relevant sections of Krause (1995) and Cowan (2004).

Office of Government Commerce (2002) *Management of Risk: Guidance for Practitioners*. http://www.ogc.gov.uk sections 4.4 and L9.

Office of Government Commerce (2003) *Risk and Value Management* http://www.ogc.gov.uk.

Research the following websites:

http://www.mindtools.com/stress/pp/StakeholderManagement.htm

http://www.sustainability.com/sa-services/stakeholder-engagement.asp

http://www.ukresilience.info/home.htm.

Feedback on learning activities and self-assessment questions

Feedback on learning activity 4.1

The list of stakeholders will of course depend upon the organisation selected. If an education authority were chosen, then the stakeholders would include students, parents, employers, government, local government, suppliers and teachers, feeder schools and education links at the next level up, as well as the taxpayer.

For a private sector business, you should have mentioned shareholders, managers, employees, suppliers and customers, local authorities and governmental organisations.

Feedback on self-assessment question 4.1

To start with this must be in a report format, starting with an introduction and ending with a summary or conclusion. It should be broken into small chunks with headings and subheadings. The report should give a balanced approach considering advantages and disadvantages, and should give clear recommendations for action. Ideally, you should have included issues concerning:

- understanding stakeholder need
- identifying the key drivers
- consideration of tradeoffs

- persuasion and involvement techniques
- using the right communication channel as well as the right message.

Feedback on learning activity 4.2

You should have drawn a matrix listing perhaps four or five stakeholders with two examples of contribution such as:

- accuracy of forecasting
- flows of information
- early warning of changing needs
- technical information
- information about competitors
- changes to legislation
- improved relationships
- clear targets.

Feedback on self-assessment question 4.2

It's a short report so it just needs a few notes under a number of headings. Also again, a matrix could suffice, listing four or five stakeholders, followed by the risks that might need to be managed and the costs that will accrue from failure to manage. An example could be for shareholders where we risk losing their investment, there may be a cost in making their investment more attractive through higher dividends, better corporate social responsibility, or more free benefits.

For the staff, the costs could be more training, better working conditions, more effective management and similar.

Feedback on learning activity 4.3

The answers to this are really in the text. The main issue here is the way in which public sector officials can identify the risks internally by consulting with their own staff and externally by consulting customers and end users. It is only when the risks are identified that we can progress to their proper analysis and management. At the overview level, much like directors of a plc, civil servants should be working on behalf of the public to soften the political element of government policy through identifying the risks to the minister, to the budget and to the government as a whole. In terms of service delivery, the views of users as well as staff point the way to seeking the views of the wider stakeholder community in as much as their perception of risks can assist the body in its overall approach to risk management.

Feedback on self-assessment question 4.3

This report needs a few headings detailing the key stakeholders, ie local citizens, taxpayers and service users, the councillors and the staff, and some notes below each heading. The costs can be those related to exceeding budget (short-term loans, government caps, loss of services); protests by taxpayers and the resources needed to manage these; failure to collect the council tax and the need to borrow the money or sell off assets; failure to control the staff through management, training and so on can lead to loss of good workers, poor procurement practices, fraud and loss of reputation due to bad publicity.

Feedback on learning activity 4.4

This is a very open activity but you should use questionnaires wisely and avoid any bias. Open questions should be asked and the respondent should be encouraged to express their views. You must state for which stakeholders the questionnaires are intended, ie internal or external, and the questions must be relevant.

Feedback on self-assessment question 4.4

It is expected that you will try and assess the tradeoffs necessary in satisfying the various stakeholders and demonstrate how different stakeholders will demand different combinations of the five rights (place, time, quality, quantity, cost).

Feedback on learning activity 4.5

You need to first identify the stakeholders and their specific needs. It is worthwhile analysing these needs to identify which are incompatible with the corporate objectives. It may be possible to supplant some needs by the concession of other previously unidentified needs and desires. The notes should certainly not minimise the needs or patronise the stakeholders, while at the same time highlighting the benefits of the plan and the contribution it will make to the overall community.

Feedback on self-assessment question 4.5

This should be a very short exercise as it has basically been addressed repeatedly during this study session.

The outcomes of successful risk management

Introduction

This session will help you to identify the positive benefits that can be derived by reducing your organisation's exposure to uncertainty.

'Men occasionally stumble over the truth, but most of them pick themselves up and hurry off as if nothing ever happened.'

Sir Winston Churchill (1874–1965)

5

Session learning objectives

After completing this session you should be able to:

5.1 Allocate appropriate resources to deal with the more important risks and threats.

5.2 Recognise how good risk management leads to increased confidence both within the organisation and in all parts of the supply chain.

5.3 Assess the value of contingency planning (business continuity planning) and disaster recovery plans.

5.4 Prepare for situations where the organisation's reputation may be at risk.

5.5 Predict the impact of changes in the business environment on your supply chain.

5.6 Give examples of the benefits that can be derived from improved organisational coordination with service and delivery partners.

Unit content coverage

This study session covers the following topics from the official CIPS unit content document:

Learning objective

1.7 Evaluate how effective risk management can have positive benefits for organisations.
- Reduction in levels of threat
- Reduced exposure to uncertainty
- Higher risk opportunities being successfully pursued or mitigated
- Successful anticipation of shocks or other risk events
- Crises being avoided or mitigated
- Successful application of contingency or business continuity plans
- Disaster recovery planning and implementation
- Limited or no reputational or public relations damage
- Securing supply and mitigation of supply chain vulnerability
- Improved decision and policy making
- Increased customer and stakeholder satisfaction
- Improved organisational co-ordination with service and delivery partners

Prior knowledge

Study sessions 1, 2, 3 and 4, and some awareness of quality assurance (QA) and total quality management (TQM).

Resources

Internet access.

Timing

You should set aside about 6 hours to read and complete this session, including learning activities, self-assessment questions, the suggested further reading (if any) and the revision question.

5.1   The allocation of resources to risk management

Learning activity 5.1

Select a sporting team or a business team. Identify six risks that your chosen team will have to face over the next six months. Prioritise these risks using segmentation tools such as those discussed in section 2.4.

Feedback on page 77

Sun Tzu, in the book *The Art of War*, exhorts his readers to 'know your enemy'. It is important for an organisation to understand its own strengths and weaknesses as well as those of all of the forces mentioned in Porter's Five Forces diagram figure 2.3 discussed earlier.

Only when you know the relative strengths and weaknesses and relate these to your organisation's goals and mission, can you start to determine where best to allocate the resources available to you. This assessment will also assist in determining whether additional resources may be needed at various points, how long they will be needed for and what will be the likely cost.

If you have ever been involved on a capital project or a new product launch, you will be familiar with the stages of defining risk, and assessing the resource needs at various points in the project.

It is important not just to identify the people needed and where they should be placed, but also any equipment, materials and services that those people may need to do their job.

Some businesses will set up risk teams and will not move forwards until a complete risk analysis has been completed. Other organisations will adopt a cavalier approach and try to deal with the risks as they occur.

5

There is another way. In 1940, Winston Churchill was appointed Prime Minister of Great Britain, at a time when the country was at war with Germany.

Germany was equipped with a larger army, a bigger navy and a substantially greater air force, complete with all the necessary personnel, materials and support services. Churchill asked his war cabinet to state their weaknesses and strengths. There was much competition between the armed forces representatives for the allocation of factory space, materials and skilled staff, but it was clear that no real assessment had been carried out on the priorities involved. Churchill made his decision. He decided to acquire land, requisition materials and labour, and build factories all over the country. At that time he was unaware of what would need to be made in all of the factories and yards, but the assessments could be carried out while the land was being cleared and foundations were being laid. So, by allocating resources to the basic needs, the work could start immediately with the refinements coming later when proper consideration had been given to the true needs of the situation.

By allocating resources to proper assessment of the threat, we can actually reduce the risk. We will understand the threat better and marshal our forces in a more appropriate manner. Consider also that organisations often utilise a SWOT analysis as an early step in assessing the current state of a department, function or the whole business at a point in time. Analysing the strengths, weaknesses, opportunities and threats can assist later assessment of specific risks.

Self-assessment question 5.1

By reallocating resources from areas of strength, you may increase the areas of risk. Explain how you would deal with this problem.

Feedback on page 78

5.2 How good risk management leads to increased confidence

Learning activity 5.2

Discuss with your finance manager some of the successful decisions that have been made recently in respect of risk mitigation strategy.

Feedback on page 78

Quality assurance is all about the good management of risk in the supply chain. Providing we have understood and correctly identified what is required of us by the customer, we are able to specify the quality required. Quality, after all, is another way of expressing 'fit for the purpose'. It is then incumbent upon us to ensure that our supply chain can provide this fitness for purpose. We could apply traditional techniques and check everything that comes to us from our suppliers, but it is much more cost effective and time efficient to assure the quality as far upstream as possible.

By building in quality assurance techniques at our suppliers and at their suppliers, we are much more likely to get what we require right first time. If we know that the tests are all being carried out, that there is a quality management system in place and working, then we can redeploy our resources away from quality control (QC) or inspection tasks to more value-adding processes. After all, QC adds no value. It simply detects defects. If, however, we have developed a system that will not produce defects, then there should be no need for QC downstream, apart from occasional random sampling to ensure that the QA is working correctly.

Synpac Pharmaceuticals used to purchase corrugated cases from SCA Packaging in Langar, for packing their end-of-line bulk powders via powder chute. On arrival, the pallets of lay-flat boxes were broken down and samples were removed. Immediately there was a risk of damage as the integrity of the pallet was broken. The samples were taken up to the laboratories where they were erected and dimensions were checked against the specification. At the same time the board quality, adhesives, closure facility, markings and coatings were scientifically assessed. Occasionally problems were discovered and the whole consignment would be returned to SCA as a reject.

At Synpac, every box was erected by hand by the operator on the powder chute. Part of his job was to check the closure facility, the gluing and the dimensions. Similarly, SCA had inspectors checking all of these things before the goods were despatched. It became clear that the QC laboratory checks were duplicating other checks and were unnecessary as they had 100% inspection at the powder chute, where the operator simply put any rejects to one side for subsequent claim against SCA. Supplier audits had proved also that SCA had excellent systems and procedures. Synpac were able to strip out a complete process, as a result of confidence in supplier quality assurance, backed up by operator discipline. At the same time, they removed risks caused by breaking up the pallet of cases, slowing down the flow of materials and adding to the total lead time.

The greater trust that was being placed by Synpac on SCA was reciprocated in closer relationships and a more responsive attitude to co-development of improved processes and innovations in the packaging.

This is a good example of a risk not only being identified but of a mitigation strategy being put in place. The original risk of poor quality pallets was controlled by product sample and additionally by laboratory test. Supplier audits added to the confidence level which Synpac could enjoy. This was a clear case of over-control and the opportunity side of risk management came into play by recognising duplication of effort along with the upside benefits of maintaining the required quality while realising cost savings.

Self-assessment question 5.2

List six things that need to be regularly checked when dealing with a new supplier, but which can be eliminated or reduced as soon as consistent quality is assured.

Feedback on page 78

5.3 Disaster recovery and business continuity plans

Learning activity 5.3

Consider a scenario at work, where a critical service is unavailable for days or weeks. Evaluate the costs of that service being unavailable.

Feedback on page 78

According to the British Computer Society (BCS) disaster recovery planning is:

'a business function that details the measures required to restore technical infrastructures and services following disruption or disaster. The key objective is to minimise the impact that such an event will have on the business.'

A well-considered disaster recovery plan is built around the specific requirements of an individual organisation, as well as the potential damage and degree of risk and exposure that their infrastructures are exposed to. The advantages of disaster recovery planning can include:

- an ability to maintain, or resume, trading
- safeguarding of reputation, brand and image
- reduction of downtime through the mitigation of disasters
- prevention of loss of customers due to inability to trade
- increase in confidence of stakeholders.

Business Link has done a lot of work to assist local business in the management of disaster recovery and business continuity as can be seen from the following extract from their website.

'Unplanned events can have a devastating effect on small businesses. Disasters such as fire, damage to stock, illness of key staff or IT system failure could all make it difficult or even impossible to carry out your normal day-to-day activities. At worst, this could see you losing important customers – and even going out of business altogether. With good planning you can take steps to minimise the potential impact of a disaster – and ideally prevent it happening in the first place.'

Go to http://www.businesslink.gov.uk/bdotg/action/ then carry out a further search by entering 'business continuity planning'. Subjects covered in the various guides on offer include:

- Why you need to plan for possible disasters
- Disasters that could affect your business
- Assess the possible impact of risks on your business
- Minimise the potential impact of disasters
- Plan how you'll deal with an emergency
- Test your business continuity plan
- Here's what I learned about contingency planning after a disaster.

Self-assessment question 5.3

Do some research into disaster recovery specialists, what they offer and what you think would be the limitations of such services.

Feedback on page 79

5.4 Managing reputational risk

Learning activity 5.4

Identify three situations where a well-known company has been exposed in the media and describe the impact on these companies' reputations as a result of the exposures made.

Feedback on page 79

Financial services companies have raised the profile of risk management and they regard reputational risk as the greatest threat to their market value, according to a new study by PricewaterhouseCoopers and the Economist Intelligence Unit (EIU).

Loss of reputation is one of the greatest threats to any organisation. Enron, Tyco, WorldCom, Coca Cola and its UK water bottling operation, Marconi and Equitable Life in Britain – all these demonstrate how quickly and how devastatingly things can go wrong.

In 1986 Sandoz suffered a major fire at one of its warehouses in Basel, Switzerland, which left a 60-km pollution slick in the River Rhine. Apart from the physical damage and insurance liability, Sandoz's shares fell 16%. In Pamela Shimell's *Universe of Risk*, Sandoz's head of corporate safety says:

'It was an accident that severely damaged the reputation of our company among the general public. It released emotions that surprised and dismayed us. The confidence of many residents in the Basel area had been shaken. In the long term, beneficial co-existence ... is impossible without the confidence and goodwill of the local population. Retaining this confidence is one of our main concerns.'

Reputation is something that needs to be built up over a period of time. Often, our individual or team reputation is based less upon positive elements like 'she produces good reports' or 'he runs his meetings effectively' than on the absence of negatives.

If we are investigating a hotel online using a feedback website such as tripadvisor.com, it is better to see a good number of reviews, even if some of them are negative, so that it is easier to make the decision as to how important the negatives are and what might be the impact on our stay at that hotel, should they be repeated. A hotel with no reviews might not mean that the hotel is poor, but we have no immediate information on which to make a decision.

Some hotels will manage the risk of not receiving reviews, by simplifying the contributions to the website. Clearly, those visitors who have booked online are the ones to impress, as they are the most likely to leave an online review.

Understanding customer needs, and ensuring that customers' expectations are met, will always generate a majority of good reviews leading to a better reputation and more business. At the same time, selecting good staff and educating them in the effect of negative feedback on our reputation are ways in which we can reduce the risk of reputational damage.

In the purchasing area, telling lies, revealing confidential information, being disrespectful and discourteous and generally operating adversarial relationships is a sure-fire way of damaging the organisation's reputation with the consequent risk of refusal to supply, loss of flexibility and innovation, and possibly higher prices. This type of behaviour would, of course, be unacceptable in any areas of the business, not only in purchasing.

Self-assessment question 5.4

What steps could you take as a buyer to protect your organisation's reputation?

Feedback on page 79

5.5 How the business environment impacts upon your supply chain

Learning activity 5.5

List some effects that changes in the business environment such as internet trading and legislation might have on your supply chain and consider the impact these could have on your business.

Feedback on page 79

In study session 2 we looked at PESTLE as a tool for identifying elements in the business environment which are outside our direct control but which still need to be managed in order to predict likely outcomes and deal with these in such a way as to reduce the impact on our business. Here are some further examples of the ways in which the supply chain can be affected.

Political

Any change in government in any country may bring a new party to power and, with that, changes in policies which could affect all manner of commercial enterprise from commodity pricing, taxation regime and labour policies to the raising (or lowering) of trade barriers. For example, the dispute between the European Union and the USA over the illegal tax concession allowed to US exporting businesses led the EU to apply $4 billion worth of sanctions on US goods. This would give the buyer of US produce a major headache as the application of ad hoc levies (properly known as countervailing duties) would not normally have been allowed for in the budget.

Economic

The increase in the interest rates in India during October 2005 could completely change the financial equation for those companies investing in elements of the supply chain in India, as the costs of operating there will increase. Similarly, increasing fuel prices and carbon emission penalties will have a significant effect on the business models of low-cost airlines.

Social

Demographic changes can affect customer buying habits and have knock-on effects on product categories and stock holdings. Several retailers have addressed the risk of alienating an older clientele which may dislike being served by a predominantly young staff. These organisations have begun to employ people from older age groups to avoid this risk materialising. Other societal changes such as the decline in heavy industry have meant that sources of some raw material once commonly available in home markets now have to be sourced from abroad where different risk profiles have to be considered. This particular change impacts also on population movements from areas of high unemployment to more prosperous areas and a concomitant effect on both demand and supply.

Technical

The impact of the internet on traditional trading methods provides a good example of technical change. Purchasing online has become a way of life for many people from ordering supermarket requirements to auctions such as eBay. The challenges can be considerable. In the music industry for instance, the threat posed to established retailers such as HMV by the ability to download direct from the internet has made traditional revenue streams vulnerable. Additional vulnerabilities include breaches of copyright and bypasses of the royalty payments system.

Environmental

Tomsk in Siberia is a major source of the chemical, formalin. Unfortunately roads around Tomsk are mostly built on bogs and are only passable by heavy freight when they are frozen solid. However, when trying to ship material out of Tomsk, it is worthwhile knowing that the port may be frozen solid for three months of the year.

Legal

The Doha round of the World Trade Organization negotiations will lead to new legislation in all parts of the world, reducing the subsidies payable to farmers and relaxing the tariff barriers on produce from less developed and developing countries (LDDCs) and least developed countries (LDCs). This will reduce the costs to buyers of agricultural products and open up new markets at competitive prices.

Self-assessment question 5.5

What contingency plans should you consider to alleviate the effects and impacts that you mentioned in the activity?

Feedback on page 79

5.6 Coordination with service and delivery partners

Learning activity 5.6

Identify who are your organisation's key service and delivery partners.

Feedback on page 80

If an organisation is approaching risk management in an effective manner, all of the suppliers and service providers will have been identified on the map of the supply chain. Using the usual segmentation tools or portfolio management tools, it should be relatively easy to ascribe a degree of risk and value to each supplier of goods and services.

Having done this and after prioritising the suppliers, we need to assess the relationship with each of these and the ways in which we communicate. Often, our communication flows are based upon historic assumptions and custom and practice. Sometimes it is useful to use these communities of practice, especially if they are working well. For example, if our junior buyer has an excellent working relationship and good communication flows with the supplier's contracts manager, then this community of practice is worth preserving and developing to facilitate greater flows of information.

Trying to reinvent the relationship could be very risky and could lose some of the advantage resulting from the obligational relationship that results from people who enjoy working with each other.

Many cleaning companies expect their area managers to control up to 20 clients at the same time. This means that each client's contracts manager or buyer is unlikely to have quality time with their service provider for more than 1/2 day per month. For a major contract where the key performance indicators need to be regularly reviewed, discussed and adjusted, this is simply insufficient and it is therefore unsurprising that so many firms are unhappy with their service provision.

Associated Site Services operates a cleaning business and can count many major retail chains among its customers, whom they have serviced satisfactorily for many years. The business was founded by Mr Brian Flood, who built his business success on the basis that customers and workforce need constant attention and direction. His attention to detail was legendary and probably stemmed from his military training. Brian ensured that he understood each client's needs and he moulded the service provision team appropriately, ensuring that the client was always delighted with the service.

Communication flows were facilitated by weekly visits and the on-site manager would ensure that he or she was positioned within the information flows that happened on each site. This meant that there was always early warning of any problems or changes and Brian had a team that was sufficiently agile to invoke contingency plans.

Coordination could also be considered in terms of segmentation such as the Kraljic matrix referred to in section 2.5. More time, effort and cost should certainly be put into those suppliers who fall into the category of key strategic suppliers as opposed to those of a routine nature. There will be fewer suppliers in the strategic supply area and a commensurate need to maintain close collaboration – beyond just a good relationship – with these suppliers. The need for this is clear. Failures of any kind in these suppliers are going to have an immediate effect on our business. Collaboration therefore means working with these suppliers in understanding their threats and helping to address them. Close working could include coordination of computing systems, limited access to confidential data, attendance as observers at supplier meetings, and exchange of market and other information.

This depth of working needs to be appropriately scaled as collaborations are considered in each segmentation area. For routine purchases, for example, there are likely to be many potential suppliers and the supply itself will not be of such importance that it could stop the business. Efforts in this category, although still important, can clearly be of a lesser nature than those required for the strategic suppliers.

Self-assessment question 5.6

Name some tactics that can improve the communication flows with those partners.

Feedback on page 80

Revision question

Now try the revision question for this session on page 355.

Summary

This chapter has been about understanding how important it is to facilitate good risk management techniques by using all of the resources at your disposal. Suppliers and service providers should be considered as part of our armoury and, by bringing their skills and techniques into the communication flows, we stand a much better chance of getting early warning, as well as gaining the opportunity to mobilise their resources to support our organisation when a threat appears.

Suggested further reading

Office of Government Commerce. *Management of Risk – Guidance for Practitioners* – http://www.ogc.gov.uk. Annex A

The Business Continuity Institute (2003) *Certification Standards for Business Continuity Professionals* http://www.thebci.org

Research the following websites:

http://www.neverfailgroup.com/

http://www.continuitycentral.com/feature0139.htm

http://www.eon-commerce.com/riskanalysis/disaster-recovery.htm

http://www.bcs.org/BCS/Information/Security/disaster.htm

Feedback on learning activities and self-assessment questions

Feedback on learning activity 5.1

You will be expected to identify a specific team and list some relevant risks. These might include:

- change of manager leading to different styles and goals
- loss of team members leading to gaps in knowledge
- increase in workload causing stress and mistakes
- change in business environment leading to short-termism
- loss of funding leading to cash flow crisis
- purchase prices soaring causing budget overspend
- loss of revenue (for example, from sponsors) resulting from bad press
- rising interest rates making capital projects unviable.

You should then make a list of the potential impact of the risks and put them in descending order of priority. Remember that some risks may not be immediately quantifiable in monetary terms; for example, a change of manager may have an immediate risk of fluctuating team performance on the field which may lead to a further potential risk of loss of revenue at the gate.

Feedback on self-assessment question 5.1

Some mention should be made of the need to define the extent of the risk at all points and then to only release resources from those areas that will not suffer from their withdrawal. Decisions need to be taken on the duration of their removal and the time frame within which the benefits of a change need to be achieved. Constant review needs to be made of the situation, so as to ensure that resources are brought back to protect any areas that are in danger of being lost.

Feedback on learning activity 5.2

This could lead to a large number of outcomes which may include:

- choice of bank – better advice on investment decisions
- selection of currency hedge – loss of money through currency volatility
- use of particular auditor – more approachable and helpful.

Other risks which might have been addressed include:

- discount rate to be used for capital appraisals
- selection of insurance partner
- degree of pressure to put on a good customer who is paying late
- allowing departmental budget increases in a volatile sales environment.

Feedback on self-assessment question 5.2

The following list is not intended to be exhaustive and you may come up with many more, provided that it is reasonable to reduce the frequency of checking over time:

- document accuracy
- compliance with promises
- quantity accuracy
- punctuality
- health and safety issues – driver use of protective equipment, and so on
- relationships with our staff
- punctuality of management information
- accuracy of management information.

Feedback on learning activity 5.3

You may consider the loss of the telephones or computers. Alternatively the heating or air conditioning could be mentioned. The costs are not just the direct ones of temporary replacement fans, heaters, and so on, but the disturbance to staff and the effect on the quality and quantity of their work. The inability to run production plans, issue purchase instructions and so on may delay the arrival of materials and services and impact upon an organisation's ability to service its customers.

Feedback on self-assessment question 5.3

You should simply make some notes on what is available from your research. The limitations will be linked to the competence of the selected partner, the organisation's willingness to invest appropriate funds, and their ability to identify all possible sources of disaster.

Feedback on learning activity 5.4

You could mention British Airways and its problems with Gate Gourmet; MSD and the problems with its Vioxx drug; Nike and its problems with low-cost country sourcing; Ratners jewellers following Gerald Ratner's comments about cheap jewellery; Newcastle United football club after the chairman's comments about exploiting the fans. The impact can be lower share price; loss of custom; loss of sponsorship; loss of confidence of the regulators.

Feedback on self-assessment question 5.4

You should have mentioned some of the following:

- professional approach to business
- application of total quality management techniques
- robust supplier appraisal techniques
- good code of ethics
- use of 360 degree appraisals
- adoption of rigorous health and safety practices
- dealing promptly with poor performance
- PR plan.

Feedback on learning activity 5.5

Business environment changes could include several issues which relate to a PESTLE analysis:

- Internet trading: change in business practice away from retail shops to online catalogue. Impacts include changes in staffing profile, stock and distribution changes and sales income policy.
- Utilities supply: government changes to market forces and plcs rather than state industry. Impacts include price competition and proliferation of suppliers.
- Working hours: EU Directives fix maximum hours and are subsumed into UK law and regulation. The impacts include limitations on hours that can be worked, different shift patterns and overtime working – all of which could affect administration, warehousing and distribution staff.

Feedback on self-assessment question 5.5

The answer here depends upon the issues raised. These could include:

- Using SWOT analyses to highlight vulnerabilities
- Introducing new technology to manage new trading approaches

- Establishing new staff recruiting requirements, for example computer literacy
- Being part of trade and professional associations to gain prior knowledge of potential business changes
- Maintaining watch over government policies
- Keeping up to date with overseas business patterns through trade links and government departments.

Feedback on learning activity 5.6

Strategic supply, that is, goods or services without which the business cannot continue, should have been identified as key issues. Whatever the organisation, the student should also consider banks, insurance companies, facilities management, and any outsourced service providers. The key strategic suppliers, however, are likely to be raw material and commodity suppliers or providers of bureau IT service without which the business cannot operate.

Feedback on self-assessment question 5.6

Tactics to be mentioned might include:

- regular meetings
- openness regarding plans and intentions
- working towards partnership arrangements
- issue newsletters
- regular two-way visits and quality circles
- sharing market knowledge
- electronic data interchange
- development of extranet
- larger organisations may create the role of relationship manager
- harmonised ICT development.

Selecting and building the strategy

Introduction

Risk is an area that no organisation can afford to ignore. We need to link risk and the control of risk to our business objectives. The selection of appropriate policies, objectives and a risk management strategy are essential in the communication to all employees and stakeholders of what the board or management committee is trying to achieve. These policies can effectively add scope to our activities, in that they will define what are acceptable practices and what are unacceptable.

'The task ahead is to implement control over the wider aspects of business risk in such a way as to add value rather than merely go through a compliance exercise.'

Sir Brian Jenkins, Chairman Corporate Governance Group, Institute of Chartered Accountants

6

Session learning objectives

After completing this session you should be able to:

6.1 Demonstrate that you understand your organisation's risk management strategy and risk appetite.
6.2 Explain how the development of a corporate risk management strategy will impact upon HR issues.
6.3 Explain how the development of a corporate risk management strategy will impact upon all financial decisions.
6.4 Explain how the development of a corporate risk management strategy will affect the selection of supply chain strategies.

Unit content coverage

This study session covers the following topics from the official CIPS unit content document:

Statement of practice

Plan and implement an appropriate risk management process in order to protect the organisation's interests

Learning objectives

2.1 Develop a risk management strategy.
 • Example of an appropriate supply chain risk policy
 • How to define objectives and content for a risk management strategy
 • How an organisation's appetite for risk may affect the risk policy
 • The purpose of a risk management strategy and a risk management framework
 • The key components of a risk management strategy
 • The key implications of the Turnbull report

Prior knowledge

Study sessions 1 to 5.

Resources

Internet access.

Timing

You should set aside about 6.5 hours to read and complete this session, including learning activities, self-assessment questions, the suggested further reading (if any) and the revision question.

6.1   The risk strategy

Every organisation will have a different risk appetite and that appetite depends upon many factors. A long-established and staid organisation, perhaps in a traditional industry where its place seems to be assured and competition is not a worry, will typically be bureaucratic, slow to change and unwilling to take significant risks. This epitomises a risk-averse organisation and often the reasons are not hard to find: capital intensive, often with plant and equipment which is difficult to change or adapt quickly and with long payback periods. Sometimes these companies have key shareholders from older generations who are unwilling to accept change or, at the very least, are slow to change. Sometimes, also, these can be small to medium-size family businesses which, because of their ownership structure, maintain a staid but relatively secure approach, following a path which has seen moderate success for many years. On the other hand, an aggressive, well-led organisation with relatively 'flat' hierarchies, perhaps in an emerging market, will be willing to accept greater risk to win quicker and bigger rewards. Entrepreneurial organisations adopting new technologies quickly and with an adaptable internal culture typify the risk enthusiasts.

Large numbers of organisations will, of course, lie between these two extremes and examples of all three categories are not hard to find. Heavy industries, unable to adapt quickly enough to new technologies or changing consumer wants and needs, are often viewed as the dinosaurs now as compared with companies which have embraced and survived the dot.com revolution or those which have prospered by developing new products or new markets.

Shareholder expectations, fuelled by the comments of investment analysts and market pundits, can be the catalyst for changes in strategy. Coupled with changes in management, market expectations can transform some of the dinosaurs from risk-averse to at least moderately risk-enthusiastic by making assets work harder and by greater cost effectiveness. Conversely, many dot.com companies failed to survive because of poor management and early good returns quickly turned to large losses as a result of enthusiasm not being curbed by good business sense.

All of these actions change the risk profiles of an organisation, and, while bringing new opportunities, also raise the possibility of new risks.

The elements of risk strategy were explained in section 1.1 and were described as the 4Ts. One risk or a collection of risks will probably require a different approach from some others. In fact, approaching effective risk management means taking a holistic approach across the whole organisation. Whereas the strategy and policy ought to be driven from the top down, the risks themselves are best identified and evaluated from the bottom up. This means implementing a true enterprise-wide approach involving all people, functions and operations. In this way, the best treatment against a risk materialising can be put in place in line with the organisation's accepted approach to risk appetite. Techniques for facilitating enterprise-wide risk management are explored in later study sessions.

An essential early step in dealing with risk is to build a risk policy. This will identify the ways in which the potential threats can be reduced to a level that is compatible with the organisation's risk appetite. This is an essential task for the board or governing body of an organisation and, in the case of a UK listed company, will often be delegated to a board committee. In some cases there will be a specified risk committee, but where this does not exist, then listed companies are required to make this part of the Audit Committee's responsibility as part of the Combined Code requirements.

According to the OGC, the policy also contributes to:

- fewer surprises
- better service delivery
- more effective management of change
- more efficient use of resources
- better management through improved decision making
- reduced waste and fraud
- innovation
- management of contingent activities.

Consider the risk appetite and strategy for the following organisations:

GlaxoSmithKline (GSK)

- Mission: Our global quest is to improve the quality of human life by enabling people to do more, feel better and live longer.
- Our spirit: We undertake our quest with the enthusiasm of entrepreneurs, excited by the constant search for innovation. We value performance achieved with integrity. We will attain success as a world-class global leader with each and every one of our people contributing with passion and an unmatched sense of urgency.
- Strategic intent: We want to become the indisputable leader in our industry.

Shell (extract from 2004 Company Report)

- The Group's approach to internal control includes a number of general and specific risk management processes and policies.
- Within the essential framework provided by the Statement of General Business Principles, primary control mechanisms include strong

6

6

functional leadership, adequate resourcing by competent staff, and self-appraisal processes in combination with strict accountability for results.

- These mechanisms are underpinned by established Group policies, standards and guidance material that relate to particular types of risk, structured investment decision processes, timely and effective reporting systems and active performance monitoring.

Microsoft

- Our mission: At Microsoft, we work to help people and businesses throughout the world realise their full potential. This is our mission. Everything we do reflects this mission and the values that make it possible.

The risk policy to be adopted by each of these organisations has to take account of and be appropriate to the objectives of the organisation. What is right for GSK may well be totally inappropriate for Microsoft.

It can be the case that where the risk mitigation strategy emphasises control, then those organisations which are risk averse are, in fact, erring too much on the side of caution since they may not be taking a sufficiently robust attitude to the upside of risk identification, that is, opportunity. Consider, for example, the above statements made by Shell in the light of the problems experienced in 2004 when an overstatement of oil reserves shook the confidence of investors and had a considerable effect on the company's chairman – he was forced to stand down from his post. Will the Shell board be prepared ever to take anything other than a cool, calculated and, perhaps, ponderous approach to risk again? In the light of this kind of experience, probably not for a long time to come.

Learning activity 6.1

Investigate the risk management strategy of your own organisation. You should consider how the strategy compares with the OGC framework and seeks to address:

- legal requirements that the organisation has to meet
- the market demands of the sector within which it operates
- the requirements created by objectives and goals of the organisation
- the guidance given in the Turnbull report.

Feedback on page 93

A framework for managing risk

Most of the reference works give a very similar approach to the development of a risk management process and policy. These all indicate the need to start by building a framework covering the context of the business and how risks need to be managed.

A corporate framework for managing risk begins with a clearly stated and coherent risk policy, based on globally accepted standards and which includes the types of risks which are unacceptable to the organisation. There needs to be suitable forums set up where risks can be discussed in a meaningful manner and risk management should feature heavily in any management discussion of uncertain circumstances, new initiatives or any new projects. There needs to be clear responsibility for accepting risk and the authority to manage risk should be defined and assigned to key staff – this embodies *risk ownership* and *risk championing*. An effective framework should also cover the implementation of suitable systems for documenting risks and for the reporting of any significant risk events or experiences, thus providing for learning from experience. Finally, but certainly as important as anything else, there must be suitable monitoring and reviewing of the risk management system to provide assurance that it is operating as effectively as expected.

The framework is well illustrated by the OGC, which lists the following areas that need to be addressed:

- how risks are identified
- how information about probability and impact is obtained
- how risks are quantified
- how options to deal with them are identified
- how decisions on risk management are made
- how these decisions are implemented
- how actions are evaluated for their effectiveness
- how effective communication mechanisms are set up and supported
- how stakeholders are engaged on an ongoing basis.

All of this needs to be done within the context of the business sector in which the organisation is working and it must be closely linked to the appetite for risk of the organisation.

The Turnbull report

The Turnbull report is the abbreviated name given to guidance produced by a working group headed by Nigel Turnbull, executive director of Rank Group plc. It was produced in 1999 and provided by the Institute of Chartered Accountants to enable UK companies to implement the internal controls required by the Combined Code on Corporate Governance. The full title of the Turnbull report is *Internal Control: Guidance for Directors on the Combined Code* and is available for reading or download at http://www.continuitycentral.com/turnbull.htm.

The guidance is intended to:

- reflect sound business practice whereby internal control is embedded in the business processes by which a company pursues its objectives
- remain relevant over time in the continually evolving business environment
- enable each company to apply it in a manner which takes account of its particular circumstances.

The guidance emphasises the links between internal control and good risk management and requires directors to exercise judgement in reviewing how their organisation has implemented the requirements of the Code, relating to internal controls and the manner in which they manage the reporting of such controls to stakeholders.

The guidance stresses the need to adopt a risk-based approach to establishing a sound system of internal control. The effectiveness of these controls also needs to be reviewed to ensure that changes in the business environment are being accommodated in the policy. The controls should be incorporated by the organisation within its normal management and governance processes. It should not be treated as a separate exercise undertaken to meet regulatory requirements.

The Code states that a company's system of internal control has a key role in the management of risks that are significant to the fulfilment of its business objectives. A sound system of internal control contributes to safeguarding the shareholders' investment and the company's assets.

Internal control (as referred to in paragraph 20 of the Code) achieves the following:

- It facilitates the effectiveness and efficiency of operations.
- It helps ensure the reliability of internal and external reporting and assists compliance with laws and regulations.

Effective financial controls, including the maintenance of proper accounting records, are an important element of internal control. They help ensure that the organisation is not unnecessarily exposed to avoidable financial risks and that financial information used within the business and for publication is reliable.

They also contribute to the safeguarding of assets, including the prevention and detection of fraud.

The Appendix to the Code is definitely worth reading, as it highlights a number of questions that need to be asked and answered relating to assessing the effectiveness of the organisation's risk and control processes.

The Turnbull guidance was reviewed in 2005 by another committee headed by Douglas Flint on behalf of the Financial Reporting Council. Flint concluded that little change was necessary to the Turnbull guidance and, provided companies complied with the guidance, then internal control, as part of effective risk management, should be viewed as a key risk mitigation strategy.

Self-assessment question 6.1

Name some of elements that need to be addressed by the corporate risk management strategy.

Feedback on page 93

6.2 The impact of corporate risk strategy on human resources activity

Learning activity 6.2

Discuss with your HR manager how the corporate risk strategy, or any policies and procedures existing which, collectively, could constitute a strategic approach, affects the recruitment, retention, health and safety of key staff.

Feedback on page 94

6

The human resources function usually includes the following elements:

- recruitment
- training and development
- promotion and redeployment
- career planning
- pay and productivity issues
- retirements and redundancy
- staff welfare
- disciplinary action
- succession planning
- trades union negotiations.

The approach to each of these and their successful management will be affected by the corporate risk strategy.

To start with, it is possible that the organisation may have identified reputational issues as among the key drivers to business success. Such a decision will drive the HR function to ensure that job advertisements, media interaction and commercial relationships are of the highest quality and are integrated with promoting the organisation's key messages to its stakeholders (for example, a key phrase from the mission statement on all documentation). This in turn will drive the need to recruit HR staff who can maintain and manage such relationships.

On the other hand, a business may be cost driven. In this case, the risk of losing market share to lower-cost producers is paramount and human resources must all be geared to lowest total cost objectives. This might involve HR in rigorous management of its disciplinary processes as well as in the exploitation of the lower end of the labour market. On the other hand, HR might recognise that total costs can be reduced by ensuring that staff turnover is minimised, thus avoiding the need for retraining and all the costs associated with the learning curve.

A cavalier approach to risk management, possibly working on the principle that 'we will cross that bridge when we come to it', is likely to cause a lot more effort in the HR area, especially on issues such as negotiations with any trades union or staff committees.

Compare, for example, a management consulting company and a financial services call centre. Both probably experience high staff turnover. In the case of the consultancy, successful staff will be expected to move on relatively quickly and, in any case, the consultancy is geared to taking in new people to keep its approach and skill base fresh, high quality and innovative. For many consultancy firms former 'alumni' also very often become future 'clients'. For the call centre, high staff turnover will be accepted as a normal business issue. Staff are in stressful jobs, often involving shift working and working to short term targets. The majority will be relatively low-paid and will find motivation a problem.

While high staff turnover is a risk for both organisations, the strategic approach to the risk is vastly different in each case. In fact, for the consultancy, staff turnover has both *upside* and *downside* risk factors. The risk involved in losing highly motivated, knowledgeable and successful consultants is offset by the opportunity to recruit people with different skill sets, different ways of thinking and motivated by new challenges. New opportunities and new revenue streams are constantly being opened up. By contrast, the call centre mitigation strategy for the risk of losing staff may call for new ways of recruiting – even new labour markets, constant training for new entrants, concentration on more and more schemes to encourage staff retention and higher levels of supervision. All of this mounts up to a considerable on-cost and a disproportionate amount of management time and effort simply to maintain a reasonable level of service.

Baxter Healthcare's president once announced to a shareholder AGM that he was unconcerned with the high levels of staff turnover at junior management level. He argued that there were plenty more graduates coming from the major universities, and this would lead to greater innovation and improvement of shareholder returns.

Unfortunately for the company, the repercussions of such a statement were immense (Baxter quickly acquired a reputation as a 'hire-and-fire' organisation despite the fact that its HR policies remained unchanged and relatively 'paternalistic'). The HR function, however, started to find it very difficult to recruit the best staff, who perceived that they would be treated by the firm as disposable. The organisation was quickly forced to reconsider its overall corporate risk strategy.

Self-assessment question 6.2

Explain how your corporate risk management strategy will affect the training of existing staff.

Feedback on page 94

6.3 The impact of corporate risk strategy on finance activity

Learning activity 6.3

Discuss with your finance manager how the company's finance strategy affects the management of cash flow.

Feedback on page 94

One of the most complex challenges facing senior executives today is to manage the tradeoffs between improving the underlying economic value of their businesses over the long term and getting credit from the capital markets for their actions in the short term. In other words, to ensure the long-term success of the business while maximising the short-term returns to shareholders.

It is essential for organisations to define an integrated financial strategy which, as far as possible, meets the objectives which flow from the company's long-term goals. This means ensuring that sufficient wealth is generated to meet the medium- to long-term expectation of a sustainable business while ensuring that short-term gains meet shareholder and staff expectations of dividend and salary respectively. The role of the board in this respect is crucial. Boards which are continually involved in short-term problem solving or fire-fighting do not fulfil the need for forward thinking and the fine-tuning of strategy which is essential for business continuity and wealth generation. The role of the board in risk management is to look at a few – perhaps no more than ten – 'big picture' threats which could affect business survivability. One of these should certainly be the availability of sufficient finance to fund future aspirations.

Financial risks include liquidity (that is, the ability to convert assets into cash to meet short-term liabilities), interest rates, foreign exchange, credit and, of course, future funding. Any and all of these risks may be affected by the company's day-to-day operations, including purchasing. Sourcing products from overseas could entail foreign exchange risks as well as credit risk. Fluctuating interest rates affect timing of purchases as well as values of stockholding. New lines of business as well as projects will be affected by the way that future funding is approached in relation to the risks associated with uncertain future costs and returns.

The risk appetite of the organisation will be reflected in the way that these financial risks are mitigated. For example, extending periods of credit beyond industry norms may increase short-term sales but will increase the risk of cash flow difficulties because the cash realised from sales will take longer to materialise. Finance managers may need solutions such as extending payment dates with the company's own creditors or negotiating better overdraft terms with the company's bankers to offset the increase in sales. In terms of future operations, finance managers may cast their investment appraisal projections using either more or less favourable interest and discounted cash flow methods depending on the accepted risk appetite within the company. Later study sessions will look at investment appraisal and other tools and techniques which can assist in more effective risk management. However, the foregoing examples serve to emphasise the all-pervasive nature of finance within any organisation and also the absolute necessity for an integrated approach to the management of risk.

The management of financial risk within a business is also of key interest to the shareholders. They, after all, are the ultimate risk takers; if the business fails they lose the money they have invested. Important questions for shareholders will be:

- Does the information that I am receiving from the company accurately reflect the performance of the business?

- Am I being given accurate information about the risks that the company is taking on and are these commensurate with the returns that are likely to be achieved?
- Can I be sure that the scope for fraud, deception and accounting irregularities has been minimised?
- What controls are in place to ensure that my interests are protected?

In the early part of the new millennium there were a number of high-profile business failures in which investors were misled about the performance of the business. The best known were the American examples, Enron and Worldcom, although there have also been cases in Britain.

In the UK one of the responses designed to enhance stakeholder (including shareholder) confidence has been the implementation of the Combined Code referred to earlier and ancillary guidance such as the Turnbull report, the Higgs report on the role of non-executive directors, and the Smith report on the role of the Audit Committee (all accessible at http://www.fsa.gov.uk). The UK Code is voluntary in contrast to some other countries where regulations have the backing of the law, but, regardless, unscrupulous directors, investors seeking a 'fast buck' and companies which are set up with the intent to dupe the public will continue to find a place in the economy. Nonetheless, the rights of shareholders also come with responsibilities. One of these responsibilities should be to encourage boards which provide reasonable short-term returns while promoting longer-term gain and continuity of economic wealth within a reasonable ethical and socially responsible environment.

Strategic planning defines a sound competitive strategy, translates it into the right actions, and focuses efforts on the most important issues. A high-performing strategic planning process can create enormous value.

Interpreting the risk

So, our financial managers need to interpret the corporate risk strategy in such a way as to ensure that the organisation as a whole is able to derive the best value from its various functions. For example, if finance perceives that there is a need to retain cash for as long as possible, to protect its cash flows, then, as shown above, the result could be delayed payments to suppliers and consequent late deliveries. The supplies function may well point to the impact on reputation and total cost of such a practice, but it all needs to be put into the context of the business. Many organisations find themselves in the position where cash flow problems dictate that we have to choose between paying our staff or our suppliers. Failure to do the former will lead to immediate closure. Failure to do the latter will postpone the problem, and the costs may be minimal compared with those costs involved in correcting the cash flow, through the use of expensive overdraft facilities, short-term loans, and so on.

Decisions on currency and other risk areas

Similarly, the risk strategy will determine how finance may deal with foreign currency, commodity price volatility and other risks. Although there are many tools that can be used to mitigate these risks, as we shall see in later study sessions, the culture and risk appetite within the organisation may be such that all dealings have to be made in the home currency to minimise the potential losses, even though this may lead to missed opportunities.

Self-assessment question 6.3

Explain how your corporate risk management strategy (or policy and procedures) will affect the timely payment of suppliers.

Feedback on page 94

6.4 The impact of corporate risk strategy on supply chain management

Learning activity 6.4

Read your departmental objectives and identify how these are aligned to the corporate strategy. For example:

- How well do they support the corporate objectives?
- Are there any departmental objectives which appear to conflict with the corporate objectives?
- How measurable are the departmental objectives and how easy is it to tell whether departmental achievement is contributing to the overall success of the organisation?

Feedback on page 95

Over recent years a greater recognition has existed of the risks of failing to include supply chain risks within the corporate risk management strategy. In the manufacturing sector, decisions need to be taken on the degree of resistance of customers to delays in supply. We live in a world where most customers want their needs to be satisfied immediately. If the goods are not on the shelf, or able to be delivered within a few days, then we are likely to place our order elsewhere.

Continuity of supply

For supermarkets, the greatest risk may be the failure to provide a shopper with what they want. Sainsbury has had major problems in maintaining full shelves of produce and, as a result, shoppers have deserted Sainsbury to buy from supermarkets which maintain better stock. For Shell, rebel activity in Nigeria has put its continuity of supply at risk from that source. Its alternative, to continue to be demand-responsive while remaining competitive, is to use other sources, perhaps where Shell has less preferred contractor status, and to bear the additional costs incurred.

More and more companies wish to minimise their stockholdings and operate JIT (just in time) with their suppliers. This pushes the costs of maintaining stock further down the supply chain but brings with it the risk of a failure in supply continuity if the supplier is unable to deliver on time. The upstream effect of this will impact on our own ability to service customers effectively and also affect cash flow through delay or even loss of business.

Responsiveness to customer demand

Companies such as Dell have built their business on agility, yet they still offer an immense number of options on their computers, most of which can be delivered, assembled and ready for use within days.

Because of this, our supply chains need to be more agile than ever before and the risk of failing to manage this appropriately is represented by the loss of competitive advantage, leading eventually to the failure of our business.

Cost management

In the service sector, we may perceive that the greatest risk is represented by the costs of staff and service delivery infrastructure. If our competitors can provide the service cheaper, then we will soon lose a large number of our customers. Just consider the changes in the banking sector over recent years. Loyalty to a particular bank can no longer be taken for granted in the most competitive areas of mortgage and personal lending. Many customers will simply move their business to whichever provider offers the best interest rates and service. This has, in turn, driven service sector firms to use low-cost countries for the provision of support services such as call centres. Such outsourcing and offshoring is growing at the rate of 9.7% per year, according to a recent report by the Gartner Group. The risk of losing customers who may be disaffected by the principle of offshoring is accepted as being less than the risk of losing customers to cheaper competition, but the strategy does need to include the regular review of such practices.

Outsourcing

The corporate risk strategy should involve some degree of portfolio management, which will rank the supply chains based upon their relative risk and value. Having done this, we are better able to identify those areas that are the best candidates for outsourcing, namely low-risk and low-value work that is not perceived to be one of our core competences.

Dutch financial services group ABN Amro recently signed a monumental $2.4 bn IT outsourcing initiative, which divided up the tasks across a portfolio of discrete contracts. The reason for this was that the organisation was not prepared to risk relying on a single provider to service all its needs.

Self-assessment question 6.4

List some factors that might cause you to consider altering your strategy for dealing with risks in the supply chain.

Feedback on page 95

Revision question

Now try the revision question for this session on page 355.

Summary

We have stressed the importance of setting a strategy for risk and ensuring that the strategy is communicated and implemented by means of a framework throughout the whole organisation. The need to identify and evaluate risks in the areas of finance and HR emphasises the fact that vulnerabilities in these matters can have both immediate and long-term effects on any company. The behaviour of people will determine the extent to which risk management is taken seriously and contributes to corporate health and, without sound financial bases, the business will soon be in trouble. Supply chain strategy must integrate with the overall corporate strategy and the particular risks in this area are, again, extremely important. Without effective risk management in this area, the business will have difficulty in meeting its objectives.

Suggested further reading

Institute of Chartered Accountants in England and Wales (1999).

Institute of Risk Management (2002).

Office of Government Commerce (2005).

Sadgrove (2005), chapter 3.

You could also read the relevant sections of Shimmell (2002).

Feedback on learning activities and self-assessment questions

Feedback on learning activity 6.1

You should have been able to identify the following issues:

- How the strategy is developed to comply with legislation and who is responsible for doing this, together with keeping it under review.
- How the strategy is appropriate to the business sector and does it follow the OGC points?
- The strategy should link in to the business mission and objectives, that is, the overall corporate strategy. Has the board ensured this is the case?
- Has the board reviewed application and compliance with the guidance in the Turnbull report? You should be able to see the results of this in the company's Annual Report.

Feedback on self-assessment question 6.1

This question is included to ensure that you have taken due notice of the elements involved in the OGC framework.

These are:

- corporate objectives and mission
- risk identification
- identify potential risk owners
- risk assessment
- risk analysis
- risk reporting
- risk appetite
- risk treatment
- review.

Feedback on learning activity 6.2

As demographic movements and economic change affect the supply and demand of the highest calibre staff, HR functions are finding it increasingly difficult to attract the right staff. People are no longer expecting a 'job for life' and are likely to be seeking jobs that give them a chance to use their skills and develop a career that will allow them to move on to higher paid jobs in 3–4 years' time. Issues like succession planning may be important, but the best staff are more interested in working for high-profile businesses with good support packages, not just in the area of remuneration, but also in the provision of modern resources, working conditions and flexible hours. A strategy that stifles innovation, that rewards stagnation and that implies huge amounts of bureaucracy is most likely going to repel the best candidates.

Feedback on self-assessment question 6.2

You should have mentioned the use of appraisal and objectives systems; the need for succession planning; the speed of technological development and the need to keep up with modern techniques. Exposure to external training courses will also allow networking, which may well help to identify new risks. For those businesses working in the fastest clockspeed sectors, the risk of falling behind the competition will be paramount and staff will need to be involved in a vigorous and dynamic training programme, structured to meet those corporate objectives.

Feedback on learning activity 6.3

This discussion should raise the issues of credit terms and how the business should strive to reduce terms to customers while extending credit with our suppliers. This will comply with corporate risk reduction, while formalising contractual terms. The finance manager will probably raise the issue of inaccurate budgeting and forecasting; the volatility of interest rates and their impact on cash flows as well as the need for contingency funds to cover unexpected cash outflows.

Feedback on self-assessment question 6.3

Many corporate risk strategies will recognise the dangers of poor budgeting and forecasting. At the same time they should also recognise the risk involved in paying suppliers late. This includes not just the reputational risk but the very real risk that suppliers will invoke late payment penalties. However, finance may be fixated on the cash flows. The easiest way for them to balance the flows is to hold back on supplier payments. This may be done in ignorance of the true costs of this practice. These costs may be the actual ones involved in tying up valuable resources in mending commercial relationships, as well as the occasional need to undergo a new sourcing exercise to replace a supplier who refuses to deal with us.

The corporate risk strategy should identify the risks involved in late payment and, depending upon the context, should disallow unilateral action by finance to delay payments.

Feedback on learning activity 6.4

It is expected that the departmental objectives will link closely into the overall corporate objectives of the organisation. For a public sector organisation, these will probably be linked to best value, beacon status, customer satisfaction, target performance levels, as well as conformance to legal issues and government initiatives.

For an organisation such as Microsoft, whose mission statement includes 'helping people and organisations realize their full potential', one would expect the purchasing department's objectives to include elements of improved commercial and ethical relationships, partnering, early supplier involvement, principles of fair trading and so on since the mission statement also calls for 'the values that make the Mission possible'.

In other words, it should become clear that the functional objectives link closely to the corporate strategy.

Feedback on self-assessment question 6.4

You could raise a large number of issues, many of which would fall into the PESTLE area:

- Political – a change of government or a war may affect continuity of supplies or the cost of goods, causing a change to the supply chain relationships, negotiation style, and so on.
- Environmental – The building of a school or residential housing close to your factory may demand the review of the methods and timing of bulk deliveries of raw materials.
- Social – changes in what is ethically acceptable, such as sweatshop labour and so on, may determine the need for upstream controls and compliance with the Ethical Trading Initiative.
- Technological – implementation of e-commerce and access by third parties to confidential data.
- Economic – the effect of EC Directives and new UK regulations in a particular industry sector; also the impact of international standards.
- Legal – money laundering legislation, for example, needs to be taken into consideration when agreeing contract payment methods.

6

Study session 7
Identifying appropriate processes

Introduction

In the previous study session we identified the overall framework of the risk management strategy. We now need to address the individual elements of this and identify some tools that can assist us in ensuring that all risks are identified and appropriate action can be taken, once we have this knowledge. We must bear in mind that it is virtually impossible to reduce a risk to zero while maintaining reasonable cost and effort, other than by terminating the activity which has given rise to the potential threat. However, analysing and evaluating risk before any mitigating action is taken identifies the existence of **inherent** risk (often referred to as gross risk). The mitigating action taken minimises the possible effects of a risk to an acceptable level, thus arriving at a **residual** risk (often referred to as retained or net risk). The effective application of risk management processes occurs in reducing gross risk to net risk and is achieved by taking subjective (or intuitive) approaches or objective (often labelled quantitative) approaches to identify and evaluate the potential risks. In summary:

- What could go wrong (identification of risk)?
- How likely is it to happen (probability)?
- What might be the cost or consequence (impact)?
- Who is responsible for the process?
- When and how will monitoring and review occur?

'Take calculated risks. That is quite different from being rash.'
George S. Patton, US general (1885–1945)

Session learning objectives

After completing this session you should be able to:

7.1 Summarise some risk identification methods.
7.2 Show how risks can be analysed.
7.3 Evaluate the impact of risks upon the organisation.
7.4 Make the right decision on how to treat the risk.
7.5 Gather feedback on potential problems.
7.6 Link the various stages into a risk management process.

Unit content coverage

Learning objectives

2.2 Formulate an effective risk management process in the context of an organisation's strategic objectives and a dynamic external environment.
- Key stages of a risk management process; risk identification, risk analysis, risk evaluation, risk treatment and risk reporting
- Methods for identifying, assessing and quantifying risks
- Classification of risk within the organisational context

7

- A risk report and the role of a board risk committee
- How identified risks should be monitored and reviewed

2.3 Evaluate the probability of a risk occurring in particular circumstances, the possible consequences and the potential range of mitigating actions required.

- Definition of probability in relation to the occurrence of a risk event
- How the likelihood of a risk occurrence will affect the approach to risk management
- Application of the use of historic statistical data in predicting the likelihood of future risk occurrences
- Identification of a range of operational risks and a probability assigned to each one
- Prioritisation of key risks with explanation as to how resources might be allocated appropriately to mitigate such risks

Prior knowledge

Study sessions 1 to 6.

Resources

Internet access.

Timing

You should set aside about 6 hours to read and complete this session, including learning activities, self-assessment questions, the suggested further reading (if any) and the revision question.

7.1 Identifying risks

Learning activity 7.1

Use an Ishikawa cause-and-effect (or fishbone) diagram (figure 7.1) to identify some potential risks in contracting with a new supplier.

Figure 7.1: Fishbone diagram

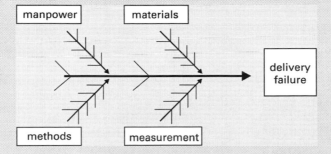

Feedback on page 112

The process of identifying risk needs to be done in a methodical and logical manner, to ensure that the correct decision can be made as to how we treat each risk.

The IRM *Risk Management Standard* lists the following as examples of risk identification techniques:

- brainstorming
- questionnaires
- business studies which look at each business process and describe both the internal processes and the external factors which can influence those processes
- industry benchmarking
- scenario analysis
- risk assessment workshops
- incident investigation
- auditing and inspection
- hazard and operability studies.

To this can be added some of the techniques that are regularly used for total quality management and other tools such as decision tree analysis and a refined version of brainstorming known as Delphi analysis. Decision tree analysis was developed from the mind-mapping technique referred to in an earlier study session and is an excellent tool in assisting in choosing between several possible courses of action. Decision trees can assist in achieving a balanced picture of the risks and returns associated with each possible course of action. Good examples of costed decisions using this method are available at http://www.mindtools.com. Delphi analysis works effectively in group situations by allowing anonymous submission of ideas so that there is no fear of ridicule such as might occur in a straightforward brainstorming session. A higher expectation of full group participation may therefore be expected. Additionally, the Six Sigma process has a defined step that insists upon identification of the issues prior to measurement and analysis.

Brainstorming can be carried out in a more structured manner using processes such as Ishikawa's cause-and-effect (or fishbone) diagram.

This tool starts by encouraging us to consider category headings. Then we drill down to subheadings within each category, in an attempt to identify every possible root cause of a risk. For example in 'manpower' the high-level risks might be the high cost and lack of supply of suitable staff. Below that could be identification of poor training so that existing staff are not being made ready for promotion or it could be that staff are available but there is poor communication – not all staff having access to the company intranet, for example, therefore not being aware of suitable vacancies. Each main heading then has to be treated in this same way. Six Sigma adds another raft of techniques including such elements as the 'critical to quality' (CTQ) tree, the data collection and the calculation of common versus special causes. More can be discovered on the Six Sigma techniques through a number of books by George Eckes and a visit to the Six Sigma website (http://www.isixsigma.com) will give access to a wealth of data including techniques and publications from balanced scorecard to Pareto analysis. As we identify each risk, the next step is to register it in the form of a risk register with as many details as are relevant. This will then allow later classification, analysis and treatment of the risk.

A risk register provides an easy but effective means for tracking risks once they have been identified. It is a simple template document that records each risk, its status in terms of impact and probability and then indicating the controlling action taken, or required to be taken, together with a record of monitoring and review having taken place. The risk register may be maintained at departmental or functional level and can be consolidated at senior management level for the whole organisation. Use of spreadsheets or other standard software simplifies the use and maintenance of registers and makes it easy, once they are compiled, for all staff to be kept aware of the current status of risks in the organisation.

A simple risk register with headings relating to the HR function is illustrated at table 7.1.

Table 7.1 Simple risk register

Risk	Controls and actions	Reviewed by
1.1 Lack of succession planning	Personal development plans for managers	Annually by HR director
1.2 Injury at work, eg RSI	Training and education	Line managers and HR managers
	Supervisory review	
	Annual report on completion of training	

More complex registers will include headings like the risk related to an objective, its impact, probability, the control or mitigation strategy, the action proposed and the named individual or group responsible for managing the risk. Risk registers are covered in more detail in study session 8.

Self-assessment question 7.1

Develop a list which ranks the risks you identified in the above learning activity in terms of the impact they might have on your organisation and the probability that the risks might actually occur. Simply use high (H), medium (M) or low (L) for both rankings.

Feedback on page 113

7.2 Risk analysis

Learning activity 7.2

Take the risks identified in learning activity 7.1 above and analyse the root causes of those risks to the organisation.

Feedback on page 113

Once we have recorded all of the risks, we need to decide how to deal with them. Risk analysis may be undertaken using qualitative techniques or quantitative techniques. Qualitative, or subjective, techniques are usually based on an individual's perception of risk which is shaped by numerous influences including experiences, psychological factors, cultural factors and social factors. In other words, an individual's judgement is brought to bear. Quantitative techniques, or objective techniques, use statistical analyses which aid the measurement of risks and rely on the thesis that risks are readily quantifiable as long as appropriate numerical values can be assigned to the probability of a risk event occurring and its impact on the organisation. Both methods are aimed at the same objective: getting as good an idea as possible of the scale and exposure of the threats which the organisation may face.

Qualitative methods are often used first in risk analysis to obtain a general indication of the risk issues which may be faced and will certainly be used when numerical data is insufficient or too difficult to obtain. These methods use simple descriptors, generally 'high', 'medium' and 'low', which are assigned to the probability of a risk occurring and then the impact it may have on the organisation. Quantitative methods, on the other hand, appear to take the subjectivity out of risk assessment and can rank risks by using a single rating comprising the financial value of a risk multiplied by a weighted probability factor. Some examples will follow our discussion of probability in section 7.3.

The terms 'upside risk' and 'downside risk' were explained earlier but, briefly, refer to the threats and vulnerabilities as *downside* and new opportunities as *upside*. According to the IRM *Risk Management Standard*, the following list covers a good range of methods and techniques that can be used as appropriate:

Upside risk

- market survey
- prospecting
- test marketing
- research and development
- business impact analysis.

Downside risk

- threat analysis
- fault tree analysis
- failure modes and effects analysis (FMEA).

Both

- dependency modelling
- SWOT analysis
- event tree analysis
- business continuity planning
- PESTLE analysis
- real option modelling
- statistical inference.

Risk maps (see example at figure 7.2) are a method of illustrating the complementary nature of impact and probability in a simple, easy-to-understand way. The map is a pictorial representation of the risks which have been identified and then plotted against the *x* and *y* axes of a graph. The map concentrates the attention on those risks most in need of management action and is complementary to the risk register referred to in section 7.1. The map is an easy-to-use tool, often used in risk workshops or risk self-assessment groups, which can be template-based, easily stored and accessed on networks and intranet sites and can be used and understood by staff at all levels.

Figure 7.2: Risk map

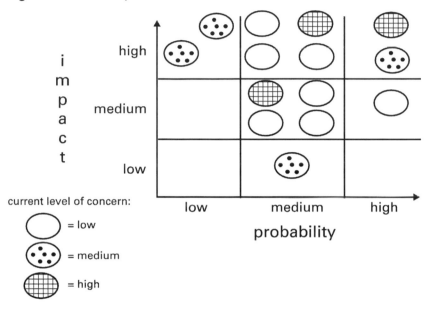

Further information on the appropriate application and method of various risk management techniques can be seen in the OGC *Guidance to Practitioners* Annex H.

However, it should be recognised that the whole analysis phase is totally dependent upon the accurate collection of data. A recognised method of doing this is to set up a series of risk workshops based on risk self-assessment, usually referred to as control and risk self-assessment (CRSA) because the complementary nature of risk and control is a fundamental driver of effective risk management. CRSA is fully explained in section 7.5.

Probability

So, having collected the data, we need to define the probability of the occurrence of each predicted event. In other words, how likely is it that the event may happen? Is the time frame in which it may happen appropriate and of concern? Statistical analysis can assist when large volumes of data need to be considered and this is often the case in assessing the data collected in relation to risk management.

Briefly, statistical methods can provide a means of achieving an understanding of large volumes of data by selecting samples of that data which will represent all of the data set, referred to as a population. A random sample of the population could be either biased or simply be unrepresentative but, by using statistical methods, the confidence level that the sample is, indeed, representative can be increased. The higher the confidence level then the more reliable can be the conclusions drawn from the sample. Statistical methods require an understanding of distribution theory and of standard deviations. Basically, this means the measure of how much any population varies, or is dispersed, around the mean of that population (the mean, or average, is calculated by finding the sum of all the items in a population and then dividing that figure by the number of items). Standard deviations measure dispersion around the mean and provide an indication of how accurately the mean represents all the items in a set of data.

Standard deviations are associated with the normal distribution of a population and are commonly represented as a bell curve as shown in figure 7.3.

Figure 7.3: Bell curve

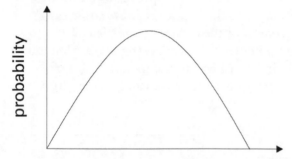

What we are trying to achieve by using a statistical method is a means for improving the accuracy of any subjective judgement of an event occurring such as a high, medium or low probability. Applying statistics helps to fine-tune all the data that has been collected and needs to be considered when assessing the probability of a risk materialising.

We consider in detail various qualitative and quantitative techniques which can be applied to risk management in study session 10 but, at this stage, suffice to know that probabilities in decision making, particularly in a commercial undertaking, are closely tied to the expected value of particular outcomes. Whenever alternatives are to be selected in a risky or uncertain decision process, evaluation can be done by using expected value techniques. Simply put, once we have decided the probability of a particular outcome actually occurring, a value can be placed on each alternative by multiplying each by the probability of its occurrence. The highest expected value then gives either the best opportunity or the worst risk outcome. Much of this can be achieved using the decision tree analysis referred to earlier in this study session and can be seen by visiting the MindTools website http://www.mindtools.com.

The calculations for EV (expected value) and their use in pay-off tables can get quite complicated. For more detailed technical information, students may wish to refer to John Schuyler's *Risk and Decision Analysis in Projects*.

At a simpler level, we can simply look at probability from a notional level. On a scale of 1 to 10 with 10 being certain, we can estimate the likelihood of Manchester United winning the English Premiership. Although this may be a naive way of estimating the likelihood of an event, if we put the same question to a number of people we may be able to exclude any prejudice or bias. In the same way, we can ask a number of banks for their perception of the likelihood of a specific exchange rate occurring at a certain point in the future. Again we shall receive a number of differing forecasts and we can use this simple information to estimate the probability of specific rates occurring. A more causal approach would, of course, be to analyse the drivers of exchange rate volatility and carry out a probability analysis of each of those drivers.

Software tools to simplify any protracted calculation or application of complicated methodologies are easily available, for example Risk Analyser [www.add.ins.com], and many organisations build their own methods by applying in-house spreadsheets with as much or as little data as is deemed necessary.

This can often be simply to plot historical data on a spreadsheet and use spreadsheet tools to project that data into the future. However, this can be too simplistic, as it takes no account of the drivers of the historical events. We also need to decide on whether the future extrapolation should be carried out in an exponential, linear or logarithmic manner. Linear regression, for example, explained in study session 10, can assist in this deliberation.

Self-assessment question 7.2

List six methods you could use to analyse risks.

Feedback on page 113

7.3   Evaluating the impact of risks

Learning activity 7.3

Take the risks identified in learning activity 7.1 above and evaluate the impact of those risks on the organisation.

Feedback on page 113

The impact of a risk on the business is usually converted into terms of cost and time or other resources. Even the impact on quality can usually be broken down to these factors as in the labour-hours needed for rework and recall, the costs of failure and so on. These costs need to be defined in terms appropriate to the activity under consideration.

The OGC *Guide for Practitioners* (see Annex D of the Guide) recommends that a five-level scale be applied to each of the impacts being addressed on a scale of very low impact (say £0 to £25,000 in cost) to very high (say a delay of three months or more for schedule impact). These examples could be applied to the risk map illustrated above at figure 7.2 in terms of the impact axis.

The only difficulty with using such a simplistic tool is in selecting appropriate scales for the axes. By plotting each of the risks onto such a grid, we are able to concentrate on those that fall into the top right box. The biggest worry here is that failure to deal with a low/low risk may increase the likelihood of a low/high risk. For example, petty thieving may be seen as a low/low problem that can be dealt with over time. However, if the thieves happen to steal safety equipment, then it is possible that the likelihood of a catastrophic incident may be raised dramatically.

By using the five-level scale referred to above for a number of impact areas, we can operate in a manner similar to failure modes and effects analysis (FMEA), where the factors being measured are multiplied to give a final score. For example in the severity dimension, danger of death would score 10, whereas negligible would be scored at 1. Death as an outcome or impact is a good illustration of those risks or hazards which should never be allowed to happen and raises the concept of the tolerability of risks. We have already considered an organisation's risk appetite, but the philosophy of risk tolerability involves the determination of whether a risk is

- so great as to be unacceptable
- so small that no further precautions are necessary
- somewhere in between the two extremes.

Thus, if a risk falls between the unacceptable and the unlikely then there should be a process to take into account the benefits of taking avoiding action. This then brings into play the performance of a cost–benefit analysis to assess the pay-off between reducing the risk of a particular outcome and the cost of achieving this reduction. Cost–benefit analysis is widely used by organisations such as local councils and the Highways Agency before investing in road improvement schemes which are designed to reduce road traffic accidents.

The impact of a risk materialising may be calculated using various methods or assessed by using judgement alone. Whichever technique is used, the important fact is to evaluate the possible consequences if the risk were to materialise, in a way which helps the organisation to take informed management decisions. Effort and cost incurred in managing a risk which could have only a negligible outcome is clearly a waste of resources.

Categories of possible impact include:

- loss of revenue
- loss of shareholder value
- costs and penalties
- reputation
- environmental damage
- quality failure
- health and safety issues
- legal issues
- production and distribution issues.

7

These impacts can be furthered classified into catastrophic, serious, minor and insignificant as illustrated in Sadgrove (2005: 29). Nonetheless, we have to bear in mind the correlation between likelihood and impact; each should be judged in relation to each other and not in isolation. Only then do we obtain a real holistic view of the possible outcomes of risks arising.

Self-assessment question 7.3

List six sources of information that would help you evaluate the impact of risks.

Feedback on page 113

7.4 Treating the risk

Learning activity 7.4

Take the risks identified in learning activity 7.1 above and identify three alternative actions for each risk identified.

Feedback on page 114

According to the IRM *Risk Management Standard*, risk treatment is the process of selecting and implementing measures to modify risk.

However, although this implies that risk treatment is limited to risk control and mitigation, we need to understand that it also encompasses risk avoidance, risk transfer, risk financing (insurance); in other words, a comprehensive risk strategy.

Sadgrove (2005) includes the following as strategies for treating risk and are alternative terms for the 4Ts strategy referred to in an earlier study session:

* avoid
* minimise
* spread
* accept.

The way in which we treat the risk should depend on the context and the impact. The whole concept of risk management is to have as much information as possible to hand in order that the most effective decisions to mitigate risk can be taken. In other words, we need to carry out comprehensive identification, measurement and analysis before we can possibly be in a position to select the correct way of treating the risk.

At the racecourse, we may like the look of that grey horse, but unless we have studied the conditions, the jockey, the form of the horse and a number of other issues, we are highly unlikely to have taken a betting decision on anything other than intuition.

Avoidance

Avoiding a risk entirely may mean considering one of the 4T strategies – termination. Potential risk factors and outcomes may be judged to be so great that the only safe course of action is to terminate that line of business or that activity. We must also remember that by avoiding the risk, we may also be avoiding any benefits that can accrue from treating the risk in another way. If Marie Curie had considered it too risky to play around with chemicals, she might never have discovered radium and the techniques for extracting it. By the same token, even when extremely risky, some activities simply cannot be terminated. Governments, for example, know that sending armies into trouble spots is highly risky but they do not normally have the option of terminating the work of their armed forces.

Minimise

We can minimise the risk of suffering from adverse weather conditions by carrying a raincoat, umbrella, scarf, wellington boots, sunglasses and so on. However there is a cost of doing this, not the least of which is the possibility of leaving behind some of this equipment.

Spread

Many buyers spread the risk of supply failure by using more than one supplier. There is a risk here that the business that is awarded to each of the suppliers is below a level that can justify volume discounts, top quality service and so on.

Accept

By failing to do our revision or background reading we are accepting the risk that we will fail in the exams, yet, unfortunately, this may still be the most appropriate action when we are faced with all of the competing demands of family and work.

Self-assessment question 7.4

Under what circumstances would you do nothing, even though risks had been identified?

Feedback on page 114

7.5 Gathering and dealing with feedback on risks

One of the most important elements to be considered in risk management is the ongoing review of risks. As time passes, we should be gathering more information that might change our view on the appropriate treatment for any risk.

For example, a near-miss or an accident will change the probability of the recurrence of the risk. The fact that there has been no fatal road traffic accident on our street means that the county council cannot justify implementing traffic calming measures. However, as soon as an accident occurs with associated injuries, then the council will need to review the position. On a road approaching the Northumberland town of Morpeth, it took two fatal accidents before anti-slip surfaces and crash barriers were applied. Note that the term 'near miss' is applied in risk management terms to an event which did result in a risk materialising which had not been properly forecast. An example of a near miss would be when flooding occurs in an area where you did not identify this as a potential risk. Some flooding does subsequently happen but there is no damage to your property or equipment. Near misses in this sense should be used to inform the risk management learning process.

Many organisations attempt to delineate near-miss incidents into common cause or special cause variation. An Ishikawa cause-and-effect diagram may be used which identifies six major sources of variation – manning, machinery, materials, mother nature, measurement and method. When there is no undue influence from any of these six, then the variation is called common cause. When one or more of these components have an undue influence on the outcome, special cause variation results. The important thing is to understand the actions that are taken by your organisation to learn from these incidents: is there a system which feeds back into training, for example; does the near-miss cause a new risk to be identified and evaluated; and is there an effective communication system which makes sure that the right people are told about an incident?

Learning activity 7.5

Discover what happens in your organisation when an accident or near-miss form is filled in.

Feedback on page 114

Risk registers

A risk register should be designed to identify all risks together with the results of analysis and evaluation. The register, together with a simple example, was referred to earlier and should be added to whenever a new risk is identified. Regular reviews should be carried out to re-evaluate the risks and the desired treatment thereof.

For another example of a risk register see Annex L of the *Guidance for Practitioners.*

Appraisals

Appraisal systems are usually designed to identity strengths, weaknesses, opportunities and threats (a SWOT analysis) in achieving objectives and targets. In the process of personal or supplier appraisals, risks will be identified which should be added to the risk register.

Statistical process control (SPC)

Ongoing collection of data under SPC techniques can be used to identify any processes that are heading out of control or towards an unacceptable level of variance from target. Trend and tracking data should be marked to generate alarms, so that the risk of continuing variations can be reconsidered and corrective action taken.

Control and risk self-assessment (CRSA)

Collecting risk data, ensuring every significant area of operation is covered, making risk awareness part of the collective mindset, taking the right action, monitoring and reviewing risk management processes – all of these are the activities which lead to sleepless nights for board members if they are not undertaken effectively. CRSA is a methodology which can not only help the board help itself but ensure that the entire organisation is more risk-aware and ensure that everyone plays a part in managing significant risks at every organisational level.

CRSA relies on high-level commitment to ensure that the resources are made available to allow it to happen, effective facilitation and willing participation on the part of all the workforce. The process is characterised by being a systematic and participative approach to the identification, categorisation and assessment of both the risks which may prevent the achievement of objectives *and* the controls which are put in place to mitigate these risks. It works from a base of workshops designed to include work groups close to particular processes or functions and, therefore, those most aware of the threats and hazards involved in the day-to-day work which they undertake. Although the board and senior managers may see the risks to the strategy and goals of the organisation, it is at the grassroots level that significant operational risks will be identified.

CRSA workshops can claim direct benefits such as contributing to improved staff morale by engendering a feeling of empowerment. Staff views are not only actively solicited – they are acted upon. The workshops are also likely to be the place where new opportunities emerge as a result of operational risks being considered at activity level. Run properly, workshops will promote better understanding of the purpose behind managing risks and implementing control – too often, workers see control but are unaware of the reasons behind the imposition of control. The workshops also clarify responsibility and accountability for risk identification and mitigation: while management is responsible for these activities, CRSA pushes ownership and awareness down throughout the organisation, making everyone more aware and involved.

The outputs from a CRSA workshop should include a list which that particular group has identified of the risks it sees in its area, together with ideas for appropriate actions to manage these risks. Once the lists have been refined at varying management levels, the risks can be incorporated into the consolidated risk register. The risk register should allocate specific responsibility for one or more of these risks to named directors or senior managers who then have ultimate accountability for ensuring that the appropriate mitigating actions are taken.

There is a great deal of time and effort involved in running CRSA in the proper manner. Much streamlining can be achieved by using appropriate software and by ensuring that workshops are run by experienced facilitators. A further benefit it can achieve for boards is its use in complying with the Combined Code. The Code requires that the board should annually, as a minimum, disclose 'that there is an ongoing process for identifying, evaluating and managing the significant risks faced by the company'. This has to be reported upon in the annual Statement on Internal Control required for UK listed companies and the CRSA process can go a long way to helping to meet this requirement.

CRSA is expensive in terms of time, manpower and opportunity cost but decreases dramatically as each progressive review is undertaken. The time taken to amend the list of risks after this has been done for the first time reduces both as expertise increases and as the risks themselves remain relatively constant. Given the additional benefits available from this methodology, the initial expense appears to be more than worthwhile.

Auditing

An organisation's internal audit function may well undertake reviews of the risk management system in addition to basing its own process around the organisation's assessment of risk. Internal audit may carry out these audits as part of its annual or other programme and will report to the audit committee and the board on its findings. Internal auditing is part of the assurance process which the board seeks in order to ensure compliance with the Combined Code or other regulatory requirement but, more importantly, to ensure that its own objectives and goals are being achieved. Internal auditors will examine the inter-relation of objectives (at whatever level is appropriate), risks and controls. Where control is felt to be ineffective, they will usually also recommend control solutions.

Internal audits may be carried out by departments or functions themselves with the objective of assuring departmental management that risk and other processes are being undertaken as expected. Staff from the departments themselves may be used for these audits but care should be taken that the objectives of these audits are clear and that the results are put to good use.

Monitoring and review

The risk management process is not a one-off, do-it-and-forget-it activity. To get the best results, it is essential that the identification and evaluation of risks is subject to continual review to ensure that new risks are identified quickly and current risks remain as previously assessed. Similarly, monitoring should be done on an ongoing basis to provide evidence that mitigation is working to the extent expected. Responsibility for monitoring and review should be placed firmly with the appropriate level of management.

Self-assessment question 7.5

List some events that might need to be reported during the delivery or goods-receiving phase, noting some controls which relate to the risks.

Feedback on page 114

7.6 Linking the stages into a risk management process

Learning activity 7.6

Obtain your own organisation's risk manual and review the contents. Identify the means for monitoring and updating its contents.

Feedback on page 115

Risk management manual

Ward recommends the use of a risk management manual, possibly based on the intranet, containing all of the tools and guidelines as to how to treat each risk in an appropriate manner. The manual would contain such things as:

- guiding principles
- corporate philosophy
- objectives
- capabilities and practices
- regulatory requirements
- roles and responsibilities
- sources of risk checklists
- standard documents for risk management.

Further valuable information can be found on the UK Resilience website http://www.ukresilience.info/risk/.

It is also recommended that students investigate the CRAMM software package (CCTA Risk Analysis and Management Method – the Central Computer and Telecommunications Agency first developed this approach manually in the 1980s and software was created subsequently) which assists in the attainment of BS 7799 (ISO 17799), the information security management standard. Further information and walkthrough CDs may be available at http://www.insight.co.uk.

It is also recommended that organisations carry out a risk management health check and there is a wealth of information on how this can be achieved in Annex B of the OGC's *Guidance for Practitioners*.

Self-assessment question 7.6

You have been asked by the head of the purchasing department to review and update the department's risk management manual. State the main steps you would take to undertake this task.

Feedback on page 115

Revision question

Now try the revision question for this session on page 356.

Summary

We have covered a great deal of ground though not a lot of detail in this study session, and it is essential that you carry out some background research to enable you to understand the application of some of the principles that have been mentioned here. The sections of this study session have covered the core of risk management – identifying, analysing and managing risks together with the important issues of ensuring that the whole organisation is being communicated with effectively in order to understand the approach to risk adopted by the organisation. The importance of manuals and procedures has been stressed together with the need to keep processes and procedures under review and up to date. The use of quantitative assessment methods will be addressed in another module, but an awareness of how to use probability theory in practical situations is vital, as you may be expected to show how probability is used in the parts of the examination.

Suggested further reading

Institute of Risk Management (2002).

Office of Government Commerce (2005).

You could also read the relevant sections of Eckes (2000) and Schuyler (2001).

Feedback on learning activities and self-assessment questions

Feedback on learning activity 7.1

You should draw out the diagram following the example in the text. Some of the elements that may contribute to the risk are as follows:

- untested ability to deliver to time and quality
- lack of e-commerce experience
- poor customer liaison
- contract terms not complied with.

These should form the main categories. Drilling down could include:

- contact with other customers: learn their experience of supplier
- IT training in client system as related to e-supply
- training in customer services
- application of contract sanctions.

Feedback on self-assessment question 7.1

Sources of risk in your list could include: impact on old supplier (L); loss of confidential information (H); cost of relationship (H); communication issues (M); language and specification issues (M); dilution of leverage (L); learning curve issues (L); confidence (M); internal relationships (L); cost of additional QC (M); set-up costs (M).

The list should have ranked H risks at the top, M below those and L beneath them.

Feedback on learning activity 7.2

The key words here are 'root causes'. It is very easy to look at the immediate cause of a problem or hazard occurring. It takes a lot more effort to work backwards and identify the root cause. The best way to achieve this is to drill down to each decision point and assess the alternatives which might have been available. Using a decision tree analysis or mind-mapping technique may assist this and the reason for rejection of each possible solution may become clearer.

Often the driver will turn out to be lack of direction; lack of finance; poor communication. Most safety investigations, for example, usually end up with these as the root causes.

Feedback on self-assessment question 7.2

The list might include risk maps, variance analysis, probability ranking, benchmarking, impact analysis, radar charting, cause and effect diagrams, cost–benefit analysis, trade-off analysis, probability/decision trees, expected value, Monte Carlo simulation, checklists and registers, workshops and brainstorming sessions.

Feedback on learning activity 7.3

You should use a defined scale, possibly a 1–10 scale, or a very high to very low scale, for each of the risks. Having done this, you could simply plot each risk onto a risk map.

Feedback on self-assessment question 7.3

You may mention some of the following:

- Historical information – what was the outcome elsewhere when the event occurred?

7

- Forecasting tools – what is the likely outcome of a particular event?
- Costing information
- Customer perceptions – what is important to the customer?
- Health & Safety Executive can predict the cost of time lost through injury
- Volatility analysis on currencies and commodity prices
- Climatic information
- Opportunity cost information.

Feedback on learning activity 7.4

This should be done by considering the alternatives of accept (and minimise), spread (share or transfer), avoid (terminate if possible) and minimise all the risks identified.

Feedback on self-assessment question 7.4

The student may mention any scenarios where the likelihood or impact is low, or where the available resources need to be focused on issues of greater importance. Using the analyses which you have now completed throughout this study session as learning activities and questions, compare your results with the situation in your own organisation. Where there are differences, can you see why there are differences? It could be, for example, that your particular industry has a different perspective on some risk areas because of the nature of the business.

Feedback on learning activity 7.5

Hopefully, investigations will be carried out by independent managers using the root cause analysis techniques and their findings will be added to the risk register to be dealt with according to the risk management strategy. Review any technique which is used by your organisation such as the Ishikawa diagram and consider how well the result of a near-miss has been used to update the risk management process.

Feedback on self-assessment question 7.5

You might mention some of the following:

- delivery driver not wearing protective equipment: issue and enforcement of goggles
- failure to observe speed limits: driver training courses
- missing or erroneous documents: delivery rejected
- incorrect or damaged packaging: delivery rejected, and so on
- comments from driver about traffic problems
- lack of space to offload or put goods away
- purchase order information incorrect or missing
- hazard information
- spills and breakages
- damage to delivery vehicle
- weight or number discrepancies.

Feedback on learning activity 7.6

You should have found that the risk manual is widely available in hard copy and on the company's intranet. There should be information on the corporate strategy for risk, procedures for undertaking identification and evaluation of risks, information on responsibilities for carrying out the processes and a system for monitoring and reviewing the manual and the risk management activities. A procedure should be in place for tracking changes to the manual and for documenting the procedure which ensures that all staff are communicated with effectively in terms of risk management and the risk manual.

Feedback on self-assessment question 7.6

Your review should follow the framework of a 'health check' followed by a reworking of the manual into the main sections suggested in learning activity 7.6. You should also ensure that the departmental manual accords with corporate strategy and matches in with the corporate manual. This will include:

- principles
- objectives
- procedures relevant to purchasing
- risk register examples
- standard documents and templates
- regulatory requirements
- responsibilities and authorities
- monitor and review procedures.

7

Resources for a risk-aware culture

Introduction

Most organisations have learned that all staff and contractors must understand the responsibilities for health and safety and for quality. The Health & Safety Executive (HSE) state in their leaflet *Your health, your safety: A guide for workers* that:

> 'You must take care of your own health and safety and that of people who may be affected by what you do (or do not do).'

In other words, we must all apply appropriate resources to make our working environment safe and, although management may have the ultimate responsibility to encourage and facilitate this, we cannot shirk our individual responsibilities.

Similarly, from a quality point of view, the *Guide to Good Manufacturing Practice* (GMP) included in *Rules Governing Medicinal Products in the European Community* states that:

> 'all personnel should be aware of the principles of GMP ... and have specific duties and adequate authority to carry out their responsibilities.'

This means that we are each responsible for contributing to the quality of the goods and/or services produced by our organisation. In the same way, we need to assess and allocate appropriate resources and responsibilities to ensure that there is a clearly defined ownership of risk across the organisation.

The management of risk can be most effective when it takes place within an organisational framework that is inclusive of all parts of the corporate infrastructure. Without this framework, risks cannot be properly discussed, communicated, compared and managed in a coherent way. Risk awareness is therefore everyone's responsibility – from boardroom to shopfloor. Generally, this defines the difference between a 'silo' approach to the assessment of risk – where departments or business units manage risk separately and independently – and the enterprise-wide risk management (ERM) approach, where there is an integrated approach of divisions, departments, units and, of course, people.

'Tradition has it that business teams organise themselves into boxes. Unfortunately, we then behave as though we are shut in one.'
Richard Russill in *Purchasing Power* (1997)

8

Session learning objectives

After completing this session you should be able to:

8.1 Identify appropriate resources.
8.2 Demonstrate methods of raising risk awareness.
8.3 Summarise the value of using risk registers.
8.4 Propose ways of monitoring risk and reacting appropriately to changes in the risk parameters.

Unit content coverage

This study session covers the following topics from the official CIPS unit content document:

Learning objectives

2.4 Analyse the resources required for effective risk management and for building a risk aware culture within organisations.
  • Responsibility of everyone in an organisation
  • Definition of risk awareness and the benefits of awareness
  • Description of an appropriate communication programme to promote risk awareness
  • How different functions can work together to reduce risk
  • Promotion of a risk awareness culture among key elements of the supplier base
  • How suppliers can assist in the promotion of risk awareness

2.6 Develop an appropriate risk register for the purchasing and supply function.
  • Definition of a risk register and the benefits of having one
  • Outline of key components of a risk register
  • The process of maintaining and reviewing a risk register
  • Design of a basic risk register for the purchasing and supply function
  • Procedures for monitoring and managing the key risks identified

Prior knowledge

Study sessions 1 to 7.

Resources

Internet access.

Timing

You should set aside about 4.5 hours to read and complete this session, including learning activities, self-assessment questions, the suggested further reading (if any) and the revision question.

8.1 Identify the appropriate resources to develop effective risk management

Learning activity 8.1

Select a meeting, supplier visit or negotiation that you have had recently. Try and list the time that you spent preparing for that event. Can you

(continued on next page)

Learning activity 8.1 *(continued)*

cost this time? Did it represent good value for money? Because of the time you spent, did you have more or less time available for another task? On reflection, what additional resources might have helped you to achieve a better outcome?

Feedback on page 127

The resources that should be applied to the identification and analysis of risk should be appropriate to the business sector in which the business is operating and the organisation's own risk appetite. Similarly, if the organisation is in a monopoly position, or, alternatively, is a not-for-profit organisation, the risks that it faces will be very different to those faced by an organisation which is in a fiercely competitive market.

In the short term, a business may be advised to concentrate on carrying out its core competence, because, if it diverts vital resource to non-core elements such as risk management, it may be the cause of its own downfall. Conversely, the very fact of ignoring good risk management could result in that downfall anyway.

It is rare for there to be sufficient time and money available to deal correctly with every situation, reviewing all of the possible risks of every decision, so again we need to consider segmenting those decisions and ranking them in order of importance, with the most important decisions getting the lion's share of the resources available.

However, a lean approach to risk management can be adopted, through using or augmenting existing processes to give automatic identification and analysis.

The role of the board

The Combined Code places the responsibility for managing risks squarely on to the board of directors. Whereas the board may delegate work to its committees, ultimate responsibility for all corporate decisions and outcomes lies with the board collectively. If there is no risk committee then the audit committee will assume responsibility for risk and control as stated in the Combined Code and subsequent guidance for audit committees (Turnbull Report 1999; Smith Report 2003). The Turnbull Report also states: 'The board should annually review its scope of work, authority and resources.' Clearly, it is the board which sets the 'tone at the top' and is the main driver for setting corporate culture, including enthusiasm for risk management and for providing the necessary funding to carry out this and other activities.

The attitude of the board towards effective risk management will permeate the whole organisation. If directors are seen to be taking risk management seriously then this will be reflected by the way in which all employees approach identifying and evaluating the risks in each area of operation. The time and effort spent by the board on risk matters will be seen by all staff as an encouragement for them to do likewise.

The board is the responsible body for ensuring that risk management is effective throughout the entire organisation. It follows, therefore, that it is the board which should make sure that the risk culture embraced by the whole organisation reflects the board's risk appetite and that adequate resources are put into the risk management framework. Resourcing all corporate activities is a key board function. Adequate resources for implementing the board's risk management requirements is a significant part of that overall function.

Managers and staff

Managers implement board policies in order to achieve the organisation's strategy and objectives. In simple terms, each manager will be responsible for achieving output and outcomes in a particular area at a cost which will allow the appropriate margin to be achieved. Within the forecasting and budgeting for these achievements to be realised, managers will allow for the implementation of the organisation's agreed risk management framework. The particular methods used to identify and evaluate risks will reflect on the costs which will have to be included in the budgeting process. The effectiveness with which staff implement the risk management procedure will feed into the actual costs incurred and reflect ultimately on the profit or loss achieved. As to whether 'risk management' is a separate line of cost or whether it is an 'add-on' to other activities is an operational decision for every organisation to make depending on its financial management ethos.

Managing by walking about

In *In Search of Excellence,* Tom Peters and Robert Waterman introduced a management technique called MBWA, an acronym for 'managing by wandering around' or 'managing by walking about'. It's a style that is the ideal description of many of the best leadership styles. By showing staff that you are interested in how resources are being used by looking at what is going on out in the offices or in the warehouse or on the shopfloor and by asking questions, it is possible to infect the staff with enthusiasm and inquisitiveness. Not only should this improve relationships between managers and staff, but it can facilitate the identification of risks at a minimal cost and help to maintain the organisation's risk culture.

Human resources

The HR function can contribute to the risk awareness not just in the induction and training of staff, but also in the rigorous development of disciplinary processes and in supporting management in the application of these. Under McGregor's theory X, we might see workers as inherently lazy, avoiding responsibility and requiring coercion and control. In such a scenario, the application of strong discipline may be needed in order to convince the workforce that they need to address risks properly.

On the other hand, under McGregor's theory Y, we need to have managers who can cultivate the atmosphere of goodwill and the situation where staff are seeking additional responsibility, to foster a more analytical approach to risk. This may be achieved by adding a risk category to each employee's objectives and discussing risk management in personal appraisals.

Project risk

We have defined projects earlier in our studies but, in considering risk resourcing, it needs to be borne in mind that the nature of the project

8

will define the particular risks which may arise. Risk identification and evaluation must, therefore, be part and parcel of project management just as it should form part of mainstream management approaches. It follows that adequate resources for this part of project management need to be as adequate as any other. In *Project Risk Management*, Chapman and Ward state that every source of uncertainty must have a manager and an owner and, by implication, someone responsible for resources. Failure to do so may result from a failure to identify the risks early enough in the project life cycle.

The owners of the risk may not just be employees, but also contractors, subcontractors, customers and other stakeholders.

Part of the rationale clarifying the ownership of various risks is to verify the feasibility of responses and their effects. Chapman and Ward say that:

'client-initiated redesign is a response that may invalidate all allocations of risk to a contractor, with knock-on cost implications that are orders of magnitude greater than the cost of the redesign itself.'

All of this helps to emphasise that adequate resourcing of the risk assessment process is vital to achieving good project outcomes.

8

Self-assessment question 8.1

List the resources that might be needed by a small café to mitigate the risks which may prevent ensuring that all customers are satisfied with their lunch.

Feedback on page 127

8.2 Methods of raising risk awareness

Learning activity 8.2

Reflect on your induction on joining your current or a previous employer. To what extent were you advised of the safety risks that you faced and did you get any instruction on the company's approach to risk management and ethics?

Feedback on page 128

Let us start by considering the term 'risk awareness'. In an earlier session, we mentioned that, when travelling abroad, we may be ignorant of the risks that face us, such as the redbacked spiders, the rip tides and the box jellyfish that are all waiting to harm us in parts of Australia. Many tourists don't even know where they are going. They step on a plane in the UK and step off in an exotic location, without really knowing anything about the geography, politics and hazards to be faced in that area.

In 2000 the HSE set up a risk education programme of work to identify and influence the degree to which risk management techniques are taught in schools and other educational establishments, including universities where undergraduate courses lead to entry into safety-critical professions such as engineering and design.

One of the outcomes of the research work was the creation of health and safety awareness officers (HSAOs). The overall role of HSAOs is to undertake proactive work, which promotes the benefits of health and safety and increases HSE's interaction with duty holders, stakeholders and others, by:

- acting as the main contact with small firms
- providing advice and guidance
- gathering and maintaining intelligence on workplaces
- carrying out and assisting with centrally-driven programme and project working
- developing partnerships with stakeholders.

This is the sort of attitude that needs to be adopted in all organisations, with regard to the management of risk and the raising of awareness among staff and contractors. In fact, organisations should aim to make risk management an embedded part of the culture and structure, a normal part of doing business.

Embedding risk management simply entails making risk awareness part of every employee's activity and responsibility to the extent that it ceases to be an 'add-on' and becomes a normal part of everyday working life. Embedding risk management into every business process provides the best added-value to the organisation's operations; it also represents one of the best ways of recognising risk as opportunity. The more that risk identification and evaluation becomes an integral part of the organisation's ethos, the more likely it will be that new opportunities will emerge for undertaking new or improved business activities.

The GMP guide recommends regular internal review and assessment of risks.

The Australian Government has also addressed risk awareness and is trying to convince businesses to be aware of how risk can positively influence business success in overseas markets. They have developed a free self-assessment which will enable businesses to become sensitised to generic risk issues as well as those unique factors specific to a number of Australia's export markets. It is a preliminary step towards understanding what issues a business will be likely to face, and whether further assistance is needed.

Control Risk Group (CRG), in conjunction with Austrade, has created a series of questions, the results of which are designed to assist in identifying risk factors associated with doing business overseas. They state that all

Australian enterprises, large or small, listed or private, should be aware of the fundamental risk issues when entering various markets around the world.

Please see http://www.austrade.gov.au for further information.

The OGC states:

> 'Making staff aware of risks can help to identify and reduce them. Assigning "ownership" of high risks to the appropriate managers delegates the responsibility for monitoring and controlling them. This can be particularly effective if the risk often materialises, for example, theft.'

The Risk Management Standard states:

> 'Risk management should be embedded within the organisation. It should be highlighted in induction and all other training and development as well as within operational processes.'

Methods to raise risk awareness

So we have seen that some major organisations recognise the need to raise risk awareness. The methods that we should consider building in to our risk management process include:

- training from induction onwards
- self-assessment (CRSA) or health checks (see OGC Guide Annex B)
- external and internal audit
- cross-functional review teams and quality circles
- risk registers
- broad network of contacts
- rewarding and publicising successful risk identification
- changes in responsibilities to dispel complacency.

Most of the above list is to be applied internally, but our supply base should also be used to develop our protection against risk. The first hurdle to be overcome is in convincing our suppliers that we are prepared to listen to their comments about risks in the supply chain. Then we should move on to the development of targets that can be developed within service level agreements. These targets can drive all of the issues listed above upwards through the supply chain, in the same way as we drive supplier quality assurance. By building good risk awareness upstream we are effectively building a series of buffer zones between the hazard and our business.

Self-assessment question 8.2

List ten safety hazards that exist in your working environment. How would you ensure that a new starter would be aware of these hazards?

Feedback on page 128

8.3   Using risk registers

Learning activity 8.3

Have a look at the risk register at http://www.dh.gov.uk/
assetRoot/04/06/21/09/04062109.pdf and make some notes regarding the
value to that organisation of using such a register.

Feedback on page 128

Project managers and the insurance industry have understood the use of
risk registers for a long time – they have been used to list and assess risks
at early stages in projects and, for the insurers, to document assumptions
about risk and risk judgement. Now, the risk register is an integral part of an
organisation's approach to assessing and evaluating risks. The register acts as
a vehicle for capturing all the assessments and decisions made in respect of
all of those risks which have been identified.

Many methods for risk identification and evaluation may be used and some
have been discussed in earlier sessions, for example CRSA. A risk register
follows the identification and evaluation work and documents the results
in a formal manner. The risk register or log may also be used separately at
the beginning of a project or process review to record project risks. It is an
important component of an organisation's risk management framework.

The register, once established, should be reviewed and amended as existing
risks are regraded in the light of the effectiveness of the mitigation strategy,
and new risks are identified.

Risk registers are usually compiled to accord with organisational objectives.
This is in line with the concept that a risk only occurs when there is a
known objective and the risk is any event which may prevent that objective
being achieved. The register will include the control or other mitigating
action which it has been decided to implement, as the example at table 8.1
illustrates.

Table 8.1 Risk register, strategic objective...

Risk	Impact	Probability	Control	Action	Owner

Table 8.2 in Chapter 8 of the OGC *Guide for Practitioners* gives a substantial
listing of the types of entry that can be recorded in a risk register.

There is plenty of software as well as 'boilerplate' templates available to assist
in building risk registers and an example of a template is available at the
following website:

http://www.dfes.gov.uk/ppm/uploads/docs/Risks%20-%20Risk%20Register
%20blank%20template%20May%202004.xls.

Self-assessment question 8.3

What elements would appear in a risk register for the purchasing and supply department?

Feedback on page 129

8.4 Monitoring risk and dealing with change

Learning activity 8.4

Imagine that you have booked a foreign holiday for next month in an area affected by the 2004 tsunami. How would you ensure that any risks have not increased in probability since you booked the holiday?

Feedback on page 129

8

We have already discussed the resourcing of risk management. In fact, the biggest resource requirement is for time: time to get the process going, time for staff to be involved in workshops, time for monitoring and review. In the main, this is an indirect cost but can be considerable in terms of lost production or additional staffing costs to provide for cover when staff attend workshops or focus groups. Consultants may be brought in to establish the process (disadvantages here, of course, of lack of detailed organisational knowledge) but, at some stage, ownership must pass to the organisation itself. The problem then is not the startup cost and effort, but the ability to monitor the success of the system and to review it for continued relevance.

Are the risks recorded in the register still the key risks? Are controls and actions actually working as expected? Are senior management and the board getting periodic reports? It could be argued that if we cannot answer these questions then the system is probably not working, and all the time and effort used in setting it up has been wasted. If we have been successful with our education and training, our staff should now be alert to the need to maintain vigilance on all of those risks that may affect not just their own tasks but the organisation in general. We will have built a system of risk registers possibly based on the intranet and/or extranet operating in our organisation and possibly applying to particular supply chains.

If the organisation has a risk manager on its staff then much of the system monitoring will be done by that individual or function. However, the role of the risk manager is to ensure that there is a system in place and to advise on system quality, standard and compliance rather than to implement the practices and procedures which flow from the system. Besides, it is operational managers themselves who have the detailed knowledge of objectives and risks in their areas and it is they who are the risk 'experts' in the relevant operations. Nonetheless, the risk manager can be a key element in ensuring that monitoring and reviewing does take place and can often be the catalyst for disseminating information collected centrally from data networks to help the appropriate managers.

Also, if we have knowledge management software within the business, we should be gathering all sorts of data about changes that may affect our business decisions. This data may emanate from meetings, from the press cuttings service, from online data flows such as those provided by the banks and Reuters as well as from reviews, appraisals and visits.

Another way of monitoring risk and dealing with change can be the use of fire drills, simulated disaster and suchlike. By simulating a worst-case scenario, which may be a computer crash, a gas leakage or an explosion, it is possible to observe whether there are any risks that exist and for which the control mechanisms are inadequate. Observers are placed in strategic positions so that a full review can take place, identifying any weaknesses which could heighten the risk of physical damage or financial loss. Whereas simulations are generally a means for ensuring that response is adequate, they can also be a means for highlighting omissions and new risks. These changes can then be dealt with by amendments to the risk management system.

Monitoring is often forgotten when we consider how successful systems have been in achieving their objectives. Yet without monitoring, there can be no understanding of continual improvement. If the first indication of a system fault is when something goes wrong, this is certainly too late. In terms of risk management, if a key risk materialises because the control has not worked and there has been no monitoring, the result could be catastrophic. Similarly, whenever there is a change in the operating conditions, we need to consider the impact of such a change on our exposure to risk. Good change management processes will ensure that these risks are addressed before the change is made.

Self-assessment question 8.4

Take the elements that you identified in self-assessment question 8.3 above. For each element, identify one thing that could change the probability that it would occur. What methods would you use to gain early warning of that change?

Feedback on page 129

Revision question

Now try the revision question for this session on page 356.

Summary

This study session has addressed the need to ensure that we should be dealing with risk in a similar way to the way in which we address quality. It is the responsibility of everyone and the more action we can take in advance of an adverse situation, the less likely it is that our business will be damaged by the impact. Enabling all links in the supply chain to make a contribution to the agile management of changing situations is vital. However, it all needs to be based upon a solid information management base and the foundation of this is the risk register that receives contributions from all quarters and undergoes regular reviews. These reviews may bring about changes in direction as well as in the balance of resources that are allocated to projects and processes across the organisation.

Suggested further reading

Institute of Risk Management (2002) *The Risk Management Standard* http://www.theirem.org.

Lock, D (2003) *Project Management*. Aldershot, UK: Gower Publishing Ltd; chapter 24.

Office of Government Commerce. *Management of Risk – Guidance for Practitioners* http://www.ogc.gov.uk.

Sadgrove, K (2005) *The Complete Guide to Business Risk Management*. Aldershot, UK: Gower Publishing Ltd; chapter 18.

Feedback on learning activities and self-assessment questions

Feedback on learning activity 8.1

The point of this activity is to consider the responsibility that we have for allocating appropriate resources to a particular issue. In this case, failure to prepare, failure to understand the issues, failure to gather measurements and analysis of the data may all lead to a less than acceptable outcome. By delegating the work, by setting up data capture systems and report writing systems, we can remove some of the waste from the process but still have the information needed to achieve an adequate negotiation or meeting. By involving others who are adequately briefed, we can share some of the workload. If we had afforded that extra day of training, then we may also save ourselves time in the long run, by avoiding the mistakes that we keep making. Balanced against this is the need to prioritise our workload, but also to remember that delaying a non-critical item today may turn it into a critical item next week.

Feedback on self-assessment question 8.1

You may include some of the following:

- time and inclination to ask the customers during and after their meal; opportunity cost of this time leading to delay in serving other customers
- the facility to record this feedback
- review and feedback on food returning to the kitchen

- provision of feedback forms or a comments book
- time to allow scanning of the tables for customers requiring attention
- the provision of small free extras (a *digestif* with post-meal coffee, biscotti with a cappuccino, newspapers or magazines)
- a waiting area
- prompt and efficient tills/billing machinery; cost of updating machinery
- illustrations of the meals to condition expectations
- tokens of loyalty (remembering their preference, money-off tokens, etc); on-cost of this promotion
- additional costs, direct or indirect, of the mitigation actions.

Feedback on learning activity 8.2

Modern business is generally getting better at inducting new staff into the business. There should certainly be a checklist to ensure that new staff are made aware at the earliest opportunity of the risks not just to person and property but also to the business. Training in fire safety, use of personal protective equipment and the ergonomic application of office equipment is fine, but the induction phase is also an invaluable opportunity to raise issues of reputation, transparency, opportunities for feedback and/or whistle-blowing. Ideally, the firm will show staff how to report an accident or a near-miss, how to use safety equipment and how to operate in a safe manner.

Feedback on self-assessment question 8.2

You may include the following:

- cables – tripping hazard
- computer keyboards – hazard of repetitive strain injury
- stationery stores – hazard of lifting and handling injury
- drinks machines – burns, and spills leading to slipping hazard
- filing cabinets – tipping hazard
- chairs – potential source of back pain
- practical jokes – leading to injury
- computer monitors – source of eyestrain
- photocopiers – potential source of ozone gas
- microwave – source of microwave leakage.

One of the best ways to induct a new starter into these areas is to get the person involved with the safety representative for the area and to attend some of the internal safety audits.

Feedback on learning activity 8.3

The student should identify the benefits of maintaining a dynamic register or log of all risks, in particular mentioning that this register enables frequent reviews of up-to-date information. This will allow decisions to be based upon current data and allows for prioritisation and allocation of resources to be updated according to the current context in which an organisation finds itself.

Feedback on self-assessment question 8.3

You should have mentioned some of those headings listed in the OGC *Guidance for Practitioners* as they apply to risks, such as:

- quality failure
- supply chain breakdown
- price variances
- lead time extensions
- non-availability of raw materials
- fraud
- staff absence
- computer breakdown
- communication breakdown.

Feedback on learning activity 8.4

Sources of information should include:

- news media for the country being visited
- the BBC
- the Foreign & Commonwealth Office
- the US State Department
- Financial Times or banks' currency charts
- weather maps
- the embassy or high commission for the country to be visited
- the airline on which you are planning to travel
- travel agents
- Department of Health (guidance to travellers abroad)

And you should have considered the information available and how this might impact on your plans.

Feedback on self-assessment question 8.4

Your answer needs to be in context to the elements chosen. Methods for early warning should certainly include a good network of contacts, data flows, and possibly early warning indicators such as can be delivered by tracking an upstream material – for example, a buyer of vinyl gloves can track the price and availability of naphtha, as an indicator of later impact on the cost and availability of plasticiser for the gloves.

8

Sharing risk throughout the supply chain

Introduction

One of the ways in which we can treat risk is to share it and, sometimes, even transfer it. This study session will address the issue of sharing and transferring risks especially throughout the supply chain.

'We must develop simple systems that encourage participation and understanding by everyone and that support initiative-taking on the front line.'

Tom Peters in *Thriving on Chaos*

Session learning objectives

After completing this session you should be able to:

9.1 Identify appropriate third parties to assist in the mitigation of risk.
9.2 Recognise methods of deciding upon appropriate insurance.
9.3 Demonstrate how upstream supply chain partners can contribute to risk sharing.
9.4 Demonstrate how downstream supply chain partners can contribute to risk sharing.

Unit content coverage

This study session covers the following topics from the official CIPS unit content document:

Learning objectives

2.5 Propose ways in which third party supplier resources are used to reduce risk and mitigate losses during a risk event.
   • Range of supply solutions for mitigating losses in the aftermath of a risk event: insurance, loss adjusting, alternative accommodation, disaster recovery plus restoration and recovery services
   • Appropriate methods of purchasing and paying for disaster recovery services both during a risk event and in the normal run of business
   • Incentives to retain specialist services at times of national disaster, including flood and hurricane damage
2.7 Evaluate insurance as a financial means of risk protection.
   • The insurance service including the role of the broker and the insurer
   • How insurers use the re-insurance market to spread their risk
   • The key stages to resolve a claims event
   • Definition of captive or self-insurance with description of its practical application
   • The merits of an organisation self-insuring and the types of risk that this might include
   • The relative merits of captive self-insurance

Prior knowledge

Study sessions 1 to 8.

Resources

Internet access.

Timing

You should set aside about 6 hours to read and complete this session, including learning activities, self-assessment questions, the suggested further reading (if any) and the revision question.

9.1   Using third parties to assist in the mitigation of risk

When we consider mitigation of risk, insurance is traditionally the first thing we think of. Insurance has been around for a long time and is an essential consideration in an organisation's risk strategy. Insurance is usually thought of as a risk transfer strategy – giving the risk to someone else to manage – rather than the sharing of a risk. In fact, insurance can reduce the financial impact of an unwanted event but cannot address the underlying risks which may be occurring because of poor management, employee disregard of procedures or external hazards and threats. Transferring and/or sharing a risk is an appropriate strategy under particular circumstances but the strategy does not relieve management of the responsibility and the accountability for the underlying activity or operation. For example, you can take out car insurance but, as the car owner, you are accountable for what happens when you are driving the car.

The history of insurance

With the development of the industrial revolution, it became clear that further expansion of enterprises depended on capital – money that would be risked for the profit it offered. For those risk takers, insurance provided a guarantee that all would not be lost through error, bad judgement or bad luck.

The early merchants in Italy and England who financed voyages to gather silks and spices knew the dangers their ships would face. Pirates, poor navigation and storms all threatened their investment. But an early form of marine insurance was created in Italy in 1063 to counteract these dangers. Under the Amalfi Sea Code any merchant whose ship was lost was reimbursed from a pool of money to which all members contributed. In 1574, Elizabeth I granted permission for the establishment of a Chamber of Insurance to register all insurance transactions in London. By 1688 Lloyd's coffee shop on Tower Street was a thriving marine insurance centre where merchants, bankers, seafarers and underwriters came together to do business. This meant that businessmen and merchants were free to expand their activities in the knowledge that one loss at sea would not bankrupt them.

In addition to marine insurance, the insurance industry was built on the serious risk of fire, and in particular following the Great Fire of London in 1666, when much of the city was destroyed.

Placing insurance in context by considering the foregoing brief history illustrates the kind of 'comfort factor' which occurs when a risk is transferred or shared. The strategy gives us the opportunity of getting on with our core business, secure in the knowledge that at least part of a possible consequence will be shared by another party.

Learning activity 9.1

Investigate and identify the various types of business insurance that are available. You can research this by using the internet and/or talking to an insurance broker.

Feedback on page 143

9

The insurance supply chain

The insurance market is too complex to be covered here, but it is important to recognise that there is a chain of organisations which facilitate the provision of insurance.

An organisation may deal with its insurance requirements directly with an insurance company or the chain may start with the **broker** who, as the agent of the insured or reinsured, negotiates the contract with the insurer or reinsurer.

The **insurer** will usually be one of the large organisations such as RSA, Admiral, Norwich Union, and so on. These insurers may pay commissions to the broker in recognition of having the business placed with them and these payments form a significant part of the broker's income. The insurer will then lay off that risk across the insurance market ('underwriting' the risk) or through reinsurance.

Reinsurance is an insurance of an insurance. In other words, the main insurer (the principal) contracts with other insurance providers to cover some of the risk and, by so doing, the principal spreads the risk exposure. This exposure could be to a single large loss or to an accumulation of smaller losses.

All parties to an insurance must act under the principle of **uberrimae fidei** or in the utmost good faith. This implies that parties will do nothing to increase the risk and that any issues that may be of significance to the parties must be communicated without delay. It is the same with your car insurance. In the event that you are caught for speeding, you are supposed to declare this to your insurance company as evidence of *uberrimae fidei*. Failure to do so may invalidate your insurance.

Self-insurance

In recent years, however, financial pressures and rapidly escalating insurance premiums have meant that large organisations, and some smaller ones, are choosing not to take out insurance. They are still faced with the same risk profile costs following a catastrophe or other significant loss but choose to treat that risk by building up an internal insurance 'fund'.

Self-insurance means establishing reserves for future losses instead of purchasing insurance. It can also entail accepting a proportionately large excess on claims in return for reduced upfront insurance costs – the reserve fund bearing the cost of the excesses if incurred. The decision to self-insure often arises because insurance premiums become too large or significant an expense or because there are no insurers available to take a particular class of business. Hand in hand with this decision must go the belief that the organisation is capable of good risk management practice and that reasonable transfers of money go into the self-insurance fund.

For those who don't self-insure, the obvious recourse is to tap existing cash reserves, provided you are lucky enough to have them. However, if the money is there, it should already be working for you and may be inaccessible in the short term, when you need it most. If this is the case, or if your organisation doesn't hold a significant ready reserve of cash, then it will need to look to its bank or other funding agencies to extend borrowing facilities, at a high cost to the company, to see it through the immediate crisis.

Captive insurance

With this form of alternative insurance, large corporations or industry associations form stand-alone insurance companies to insure their own risks, thereby substantially reducing their insurance premiums and gaining a significant measure of control over types of risks to be covered. There may also be significant tax advantages to be gained from the formation and operation of captive insurance companies, particularly offshore.

Pooling

Pooling is an alternative risk transfer strategy that combines elements of self-insurance and risk transfer. This strategy is used to finance insurance liabilities. Pools are designed by and for their members, who share similar risk profiles and an interest in long-term stability of insurance costs, derived from spread of risk and aggressive loss control and claims strategies.

In the 1970s and the 1980s, the insurance industry often looked upon public entities as undesirable clients. Counties, cities and education authorities had generally not embraced effective risk management philosophies, and had yet to discover the benefits of loss control best practices. In recent years, market conditions have again pushed public entities toward the pooling model. Court rulings on environmental liability, weakening governmental immunity and terrorism issues have led to wildly fluctuating insurance expenses from year to year for public entities and the need to consider pooling along with a more professional approach to risk management. In fact, by the turn of the new century, local government in particular had moved away from pooling to setting up individual self-insurance funds. This was due to the perception of achieving better value for money without the need to rely on other bodies, some of which might not have shared the same objectives and ideals of the local authority.

Hedging

A hedge is an investment that is taken out specifically to reduce or cancel out the risk in another investment. Hedging (as in the expression 'hedging your bets') is designed to minimise exposure to a risk while still allowing the opportunity to profit from an investment. A good example is foreign exchange risk. When an overseas order is placed in a currency other than our own, exchange rate fluctuations between order, delivery and invoicing can easily cut into the margins which might have been expected. As the party at risk of this volatility, we would wish to insure against the worst effects of margin erosion and we would do so by buying a hedging instrument through a bank or in the market.

Self-assessment question 9.1

What factors would you consider when selecting an insurance company or insurance broker?

Feedback on page 143

9

9.2 Selecting appropriate insurance

Learning activity 9.2

Assuming that you have limited personal finances available, identify which items of household equipment you might decide not to insure and list your reasons.

Feedback on page 143

So, the decision as to whether or not to insure, and for how much and against what damages, is very much dependent upon the context.

In some cases, we may have to take out insurance, because it is part of our contract with our customers. They may have insisted that we maintain alternative supply lines or spare parts, or insurance to cover these. Some training companies insist that freelance trainers take out professional indemnity insurance to protect them against later claims from the client that bad advice was given by the trainer.

Many contracts provide for substantial public liability and other clauses to be included in order to provide principals with indemnity against various risks which might arise during the currency of the contract. The contract itself, if large enough, will contain liquidated damages clauses which the contractor will want to cover by means of bank guarantee or insurance. Appropriate insurance, therefore, depends upon several things. Not least of these is the nature of the business being transacted and the level of cover being sought.

Disaster recovery

Adequate disaster recovery and business continuity planning is now accepted as a basic requirement for virtually every organisation and business of any size. It is widely acknowledged that a detailed disaster recovery or business continuity plan should not only exist, but should be current and have been tested. It should reflect the real and ongoing needs of the business activity or function.

Awareness of disaster recovery and business continuity as an approach which embraces all organisational activities is changing the market, and there is a sea change under way from business continuity planning having been just an option to it becoming essential to business survival. The bottom line is that no matter what size the business or the perception of invincibility to disaster, there needs to be an additional layer of protection to the business. Since the 1980s, disaster recovery has morphed into being just one component of business continuity, with the mindset moving from reactive to proactive, and including much more than just information technology.

Belinda Wilson, executive director of Business Continuity Services, has said that IT security and business continuity are the highest priorities for business professionals, which will result in spending of up to $155 billion worldwide on such products and services in 2006.

It is clear that IT managers must radically change their thinking about risks. They should not just worry about the next major event, such as we experienced at the millennium and after 9/11. They should be much more concerned about their organisational reputation, brand protection and corporate image. These intangible costs have become significantly more important than tangible costs. Natural disasters still need to be taken into consideration, but we also need to be prepared for man-made risks such as viruses and worms in our computers, employee theft and loss of intellectual property.

Organisations in both the private and public sectors need to develop a thorough understanding of what constitutes a business continuity plan in order to mitigate risks with both internal and external issues that can damage the organisation.

The implementation of disaster recovery and business continuity solutions has changed the way CEOs and IT managers do business, and this shift is becoming more visible. It is incumbent on businesses to have a thorough understanding of what makes a comprehensive business continuity plan, to help mitigate risks with both internal and external issues that can affect the business.

IT pervades even the smallest of businesses these days so it's not surprising that for many years disaster recovery was synonymous with hot or cold startups for the IT department or sharing facilities with other sites or companies. That is not the be all and end all of disaster recovery. Consider the need for new buildings if you are a school and your building has suffered an arson attack; where do all the pupils go when they turn up on the first morning after the fire?

So disaster recovery is not something that we just talk about. We need to do something about it. In 2005, Aardman (the company responsible for Wallace and Gromit and other animation products) suffered a huge fire destroying many of the props, files and designs. However, many key elements had been duplicated and were either being stored in separate locations or were on display around the country at a number of sites. So the damage caused by the fire was mitigated to some extent by intelligent consideration of distributing the significant assets.

Some businesses make sure that they have an exact duplicate of their computer systems available to run within say 30 minutes of a disaster. The cost of this is huge, but the cost of losing the system for longer may be even greater. Like so many things, it's a matter of cost–benefit analysis.

We will look at contingency planning in more detail in study session 20.

Self-assessment question 9.2

Explain the concept of self-insurance and identify some occasions when self-insurance would be appropriate.

Feedback on page 143

9.3 Sharing the risk with the upstream supply chain

Learning activity 9.3

Consider the product liability risks of a product or service that your organisation provides. Try to understand whether any of that risk can reasonably be allocated upstream by, for example, a completely different approach such as a joint venture. Alternatively, consider if a claim for damages could be made against a supplier's insurance in a normal trading arrangement.

Feedback on page 144

The idea that we, as organisations, are not working in isolation is still relatively recent. It was really only with the introduction of Michael Porter's concepts of the value chain and Kraljic's concept that purchasing must become supply chain management that we really started considering the value that can be contributed by our 'partners' in the supply chain. The vertical integration principles (buying out the competition and merging it with own operations) that prevailed in many industries during the nineteenth and early twentieth centuries are no longer valid in the modern business world. We are increasingly dependent on our suppliers and their suppliers for the creation of value that we provide to our customers.

Adding value is not all that suppliers do. Suppliers add risk, but, additionally, if managed correctly they can share risk or act as a buffer against risk.

Outsourcing

Outsourcing is the practice of getting a supplier to do something that you used to do yourself. It involves the transfer of all the assets (people and capital) that enabled you to carry out the process in-house. In this respect it means handing over your complete capability to perform a particular task to someone else. Activities which might be appropriate to outsource need to be identified and assessed by considering:

- the core competencies of the organisation in relation to its current and future plans and strategies – core competencies should normally be kept in-house
- the extent to which there are well-developed supply markets capable of providing outsourced support services.

Outsourcing has become popular in some fields such as IT, logistics and distribution services, payroll services, facilities management and catering. There are many organisations which now exist specifically to provide these services to customers on an outsourced basis.

Outsourcing can have real benefits, not just in allowing a business to focus on its core, but also in identifying efficiencies and improvements in the process. In 2004 it was stated that outsourcing large parts of its production process had boosted shoemaker Clarks' profits by 16%. Clarks had moved its production to low-cost labour markets, retaining administration and some distribution elements of its business in the UK. Profits rose 16% on only a 1% rise in turnover. However, organisations often make fundamental errors when outsourcing.

Firms should concentrate their outsourcing activities on those elements of their business that are of lower value and risk. They should not retain groups of products and services that are non-critical as it is usually these groups of purchases and assets which can be outsourced most successfully and at least total cost. Strategically critical assets or activities should not be outsourced, such as IBM did with its PC operating system and microprocessor to Microsoft and Intel respectively in the 1980s.

Often, managers do not sufficiently understand the risks that can come with outsourcing. Lock-in is particularly prevalent and covers the following issues:

- The problems and difficulties of detaching from an outsourced contractor.
- The difficulty of in-sourcing (bringing an activity back in-house).

- The loss of leverage in the particular marketplace of the outsourced service.
- The potential loss of transferred staff who gain promotion and take their knowledge with them.

Managers need to be trained in avoiding these mistakes. One way of improving the rate of success is to involve more user functions in the selection of the outsourcing partner and the service level agreements that ensue. By setting up milestones and review points, we can better understand how relationships and performance are changing over time. We also need to ensure that there is sufficient opportunity to terminate the contract when appropriate without large compensation sums.

It needs to be fully understood, also, that there can be no transfer or outsourcing of accountability. The principal (the buying organisation) remains responsible for service or market provision to its own customers. It cannot rely on blaming the outsourced supplier when things go wrong. The end-user customer will blame the principal if and when failure occurs and will certainly not be interested in seeking redress from an arms-length third party.

Joint ventures

Creating a joint venture with a partner or partners to achieve an objective which may be too risky to be contemplated by one enterprise is a means of transferring or sharing risk. The joint venture may also come about because of pragmatic business decisions in connection with tendering for a contract, part of which cannot be undertaken by the main tenderer as a result of lack of expertise or lack of resources. Good examples exist in oil exploration where joint ventures are common between several partners in order to share risks (and rewards) but also to make use of particular specialisms such as deep-water ocean drilling skills.

Consignment stock, vendor-managed inventory and virtual inventory

The concept of having your suppliers take responsibility for stock is another way of sharing the risk. In the event that your premises burn down, then, provided the stock is serviced from the suppliers' warehouses, the burden of the disaster is reduced. The financial risk of carrying excess stock is shifted in this case to the supplier although there remains the residual risk to the supplier's premises of fire or other disaster. Similarly, by sharing inventory with other, local businesses, or sister companies in the form of virtual inventory (that is, available to you in electronic form but not physically held by you), the impact of a single disaster will be lessened. The benefits of e-commerce clearly apply to these arrangements although, again, a residual risks remains of IT failure or security breach.

Early warning

By sharing information electronically (or otherwise) and involving our suppliers at various tiers in the risk management process, we can ensure that, in the event that a change is about to happen, we will have the best chance of gaining early warning, which can allow us to take evasive action. This

9

may entail buying up quantities of material that are likely to go short or increase in price. We can also pass this information on to our customers to protect them from any volatility on the supply side.

Contracts

It is important that all purchasing professionals understand that the contract document is a vital component in defining how risk and reward are to be allocated between buyer and supplier. In this context buyers need to be aware that there will be some risks that the supplier will see as part of the normal course of doing business. The cost of covering these risks will be included within the supplier's normal pricing and they are unlikely to argue too strongly against accepting these risks. Asking suppliers to take on risks which they are not well placed to accept can result in protracted and difficult negotiations and/or higher prices.

A sound understanding by the buyer of the product or service they are purchasing, along with good negotiating practice backed up with clear and unambiguous contracts, can assist in an appropriate division of risk between the parties. Purchasing power and security of delivery over reasonable time periods can assist in assuring supply by attaining preferred customer status for products from your main suppliers. Good purchasing practice usually dictates, however, that alternative sources are always nurtured and maintained as a hedge against the risk of supply shortages. Locking in price changes at agreed rates (say, inflation plus a small percentage) in contract terms assists in managing the risk of unexpected price hikes as does fixed-price term contracting – thus passing the risk of short-term price increases to the supplier.

Self-assessment question 9.3

Which types of insurance would you insist on your suppliers having? Would this be different if your supplier were a sole trader?

Feedback on page 144

9.4   Sharing risk in the downstream supply chain

Learning activity 9.4

First, list the steps in the downstream supply chain, right through to the end user of the goods or services, for a large retail supermarket chain. Then identify what steps are taken by those downstream customers to ensure that the end user gets the appropriate quality of product or service. What strategies can be used to manage the risks at each point in the chain in terms of product not-fit-for-purpose or other potential customer liability?

Feedback on page 144

We have considered the ways in which our supplier can take some of the risk. There is no reason why our customers cannot also take some of that burden.

The old adage that 'the customer is always right' is not true. The customer is often wrong and the information that they provide can often be unreliable. This also applies internally to organisations, where, for example, our sales and marketing forecasts that are given to the production department are simply not accurate enough.

One way of getting customers, whether internal or external, to share the risk is to develop a two-way service agreement, often referred to as a service level agreement (SLA). It could be something as simple as:

- correct and complete purchase requisitions will be converted into purchase orders within 24 hours, or
- orders received by 4 pm will be dispatched the same day, or
- the use of retrospective rebates which come into play on actual deliveries and obviates the need to rely upon the customer's unreliable statements of likely usage.

The first two are simple examples of a service being offered between two or more departments internally. Sanctions will almost certainly form part of an SLA so that if the promised level of service does not materialise then there is a means for recompense for the internal customer. This could be re-performance at no extra cost, so there is a reasonable incentive for the risk of poor performance to be avoided. Risk sharing of this nature between internal customers does have the effect of sharpening performance and gives the workforce a closer relationship with 'customers' than they might otherwise have.

The third example illustrates the way that some financial and production risks can be passed to customers in the form of well-crafted sales agreements backed up by good contract terms. Retrospective discounts pass the incentive, ie the reward, to the customer to perform to the agreed level by gaining benefit only when that performance is actually achieved or surpassed. The risk of overproduction is avoided where it has been based on front-end discounts for quantity which is never realised. Pricing can be based on the actual volumes delivered rather than on spurious volumes set by the customer prior to delivery only in the hope of higher discount for all purchases, whatever their level.

Sharing the risk is especially applicable when decisions are being made to spend money on capital equipment to satisfy customer demand. For example, the customer may demand a design change to a plastic component. This may involve us in acquiring a new moulding tool costing, say, £100,000. We need to make sure that the payback for that capital outlay is covered, not just by using the appropriate investment appraisal techniques, but also by contractual obligations on our customer, for example volume of product that will be taken and when, together with contract price guarantees.

The risks in each part of the supply chain depend on the way we do business and with whom. We could be dealing with multiple levels of supplier to achieve one output of service or product which will reach one class or more of customer. We need to recognise that different strategies will be applied depending on the differing risks in these relationships and on our ability to make good contractual agreements. Insurance is not the only strategy which can be employed when a risk is identified. Other strategies may be equally – or more – relevant.

Self-assessment question 9.4

What steps can you as a buyer take, to ensure that downstream customers do not increase the risks of product or service failure through their actions and inactions?

Feedback on page 144

Revision question

Now try the revision question for this session on page 356.

Summary

This study session has skirted briefly around the principles of insurance and the sharing of risk. Where possible it is advised that you discuss with your own finance and business managers how your organisation shares risk and what further contribution could possibly be made in the supply chain.

Decisions on sharing the risk and on the types of insurance to be taken out should be based upon good analytical techniques and need to be reviewed on a regular basis, taking into account any changes in the business environment or changes in knowledge.

Suggested further reading

The following websites can be researched for relevant information to add to the reading you have done for this study session:

http://www.telegraph.co.uk/money/main.jhtml?xml=/money/exclusions/businessinsurance/bioutline.xml

http://www.businesslink.gov.uk/bdotg/action/layer?topicId=1074298750&tc=000KW011242672

http://www.som.cranfield.ac.uk/som/research/centres/lscm/downloads/Vulnerability_report.pdf

http://www.intelligententerprise.com/040101/701infosc1_2.jhtml

http://www.startinbusiness.co.uk/flowchart/8flowchart_ins.htm

Feedback on learning activities and self-assessment questions

Feedback on learning activity 9.1

You should have come up with a variety of areas that can be covered with insurance including:

- loss of profits
- business continuity
- fire and theft
- public liability
- professional indemnity
- employer's liability
- goods in transit.

You could also have accessed the Business Link website: this has a useful summary of different types of business insurance.

Feedback on self-assessment question 9.1

You would be expected to mention all of the usual sourcing criteria, such as Carter's ten Cs (commitment, cost, control, cash, capacity, and so on). There also needs to be some mention of specific competence, for example any specialism (sector, perhaps, as in maritime or personal accident) of the broker or insurance company and the impact of the insurance supply chain on that competence. Aggregating different types of insurance will bring about increased negotiation leverage, but it may dilute the specific competencies that may be needed for critical and unusual processes such as robotic control of a manufacturing process.

Feedback on learning activity 9.2

You should have considered carrying out a risk evaluation exercise on a few pieces of equipment. For example, we may consider the number of times they are switched on and off, the temperature that they are exposed to, the amount of maintenance needed, and the criticality of supply. For example, if the kettle breaks, my exposure and impact are low, as I have other ways of obtaining a hot beverage. However, the failure of the central heating boiler on the coldest day may be considered as unacceptable and a fast response time may be imperative.

Feedback on self-assessment question 9.2

Self-insurance was explained in section 9.1, but here you are meant to apply some logical thought as to when it might be used. You may have mentioned the following:

When the insurance premiums are very high; when the costs of failure are low; when the impact and/or likelihood of occurrence is low. This is a situation when you might use an impact assessment grid.

You should clearly explain that self-insurance is a positive approach that is not simply an avoidance of insurance but a structured and planned

9

approach that allocates money to an internal fund to provide cover for events which may happen and for which external insurance would otherwise be sought. You should be able to point out that, without insurance or self-insurance, the only other recourse is to existing company funds (should they be available). Use of these funds could easily limit current operations by draining working capital and lead to difficult if not impossible trading.

Feedback on learning activity 9.3

Liabilities occur when things go wrong. It is good management, therefore, to consider potential liabilities before they become reality. Thus, what risk strategies could be employed in offsetting potential liabilities? Risk share or transfer should immediately come to mind. Insurance is a suitable transferring strategy although you, as provider of the product, are the first call for any claim – what you are transferring is the financial cost of meeting a claim. In that sense a claim is not being made directly against your insurers. In considering a joint venture or partnering approach, you might have considered making an agreement with a different company for the design and supply of the product. By doing that, and assuming effective partnering agreements, you have transferred the liability to the production company.

Feedback on self-assessment question 9.3

You should have mentioned most of the insurances listed in learning activity 9.1, though the insurance to be taken will depend upon the context. For example, the purchase of one day of training from a small provider is hardly likely to justify that provider spending £6,000 on professional indemnity insurance. Similarly, in the shipping of goods, you may decide to select an Incoterm that excludes insurance, as you may be able to purchase the insurance at a more competitive rate.

Feedback on learning activity 9.4

The answer here will depend on the numbers of intermediate supply chain partners, such as wholesalers, for whom you are the customer. The consumer buying his or her weekly shopping is your end user customer. You should benefit from understanding how their sales and marketing functions deal with such issues, how service level agreements can work and how product liability works between intermediate supply chain members. Also, consider what indemnity is needed for the end user retail customer who will make you the first point of claim if the product fails to satisfy. There should be recognition that any obligations and indemnities incurred downstream should ideally be pushed upstream through back-to-back agreements.

Feedback on self-assessment question 9.4

There is certainly a need to ensure that our sales and marketing functions are not agreeing to customers' demands without considering the potential impact on the business. The costs of achieving such demand may be far in excess of the value derived and may even result from a misinterpretation of customer needs by our salesperson. Highlighting the costs of such insurance and asking questions as to the true value of the demand is one way, but a better way of hearing the voice of the customer is to have clear dialogue involving supplier and customer.

Similarly, achievement of customer needs and demands may be dependent on such things as early and accurate forecasts, prompt notification of changes, clear specifications and service level agreements. These can all be mirrored in our agreements with our suppliers.

For your own further information you may wish to consider the issues raised by the mis-selling of endowments and pensions. Look at the Financial Services Authority website http://www.fsa.gov.uk to see some of the ways in which customers may seek redress if they feel wronged.

9

9

Tactics and tools for risk identification and analysis

Introduction

In this study session we need to look at some of the tools and tactics that can help us to recognise risks that face us, and which can then be analysed and assessed and appropriately treated. It is usual for risk management processes to be based largely on qualitative judgements in the early stages of identification and structuring. Later on, in the choosing and evaluating phase, we are more likely to use deductive processes, arrived at by reasoning and quantitative measures.

'Practitioners, consultants and academics should not recommend tools and techniques unless they have a proper understanding of the likely impact in particular contingent circumstances.'
Andrew Cox in *Strategic Procurement Management*

Session learning objectives

After completing this session you should be able to:

10.1 Apply some tools for the qualitative identification and analysis of risk.
10.2 Apply some tools for the quantitative identification and analysis of risk.
10.3 Identify the resources that would need to be in place in order to facilitate the tactics and tools mentioned.
10.4 Calculate the impact using specific tools.

Unit content coverage

This study session covers the following topics from the official CIPS unit content document:

Learning objectives

2.8 Identify and apply a range of qualitative and quantitative risk identification and analysis techniques to ensure better decision quality in reviewing alternatives for a superior project outcome.
  • Scenario analysis and planning
  • Auditing
  • Decision tree analysis
  • Fault tree analysis
  • Dependency modelling
  • External environment analysis
  • Assumption
  • Identification frameworks

Prior knowledge

Study sessions 1 to 9.

Resources

Internet access.

Timing

You should set aside about 6 hours to read and complete this session, including learning activities, self-assessment questions, the suggested further reading (if any) and the revision question.

10.1 Tools for qualitative identification of risk

Learning activity 10.1

Analyse the following mini-case study and list some of the qualitative decisions that are being made and some of the risks that these may cause.

Roberts Kelly (RK) is a company that has been in business for 30 years delivering a range of services to purchasing departments across the North of England. These services have included sourcing, training, cost reduction exercises, sale of obsolete goods and the recruitment and induction of new staff. RK employs a total of 12 staff. The original partners have now retired and the new board of three directors (John, Mike and Anne) needs to make some decisions about the future direction and shape of the business.

They have already decided that they want to concentrate on public sector work, due to the decline of the UK manufacturing industry. John has substantial experience of the catering industry and has proposed that the firm use this as a focus for their attention, possibly extending into areas of facilities management. Anne has a background in HR and Mike is an accountant.

Following a brainstorming session, they agree that, in order to meet their profit targets for the next three years, turnover needs to be a minimum of £3 million per year. To achieve this, they will concentrate on major government bodies and councils, with no customer yielding less than £100,000 of business per year. They will concentrate on selling support, advice and training in any area that could be classified under the heading of facilities management. The sales staff will be converted to commission-only contracts and the staff responsible for training and support will have their contracts adapted to performance-related pay, as an incentive to achieve the targets. They state that the business will operate in a manner that is as environmentally friendly and ethically responsible as possible.

Feedback on page 159

According to http://www.wikipedia.org/:

- Qualitative analysis uses subjective judgement in evaluating issues such as management expertise, cyclicality of industry, strength of research and development, and labour relations.

- In the social sciences, 'qualitative research' is an umbrella term used to describe various non-quantitative research methods or approaches. For many researchers qualitative methods are simply exploratory methods used chiefly to generate hypotheses for quantitative testing.

In effect, the underlying issue of qualitative analysis is the main driver of the way in which organisations approach risk management and decision making. As human beings, we tend towards inductive thought processes. For example, when faced with a problem we are likely to think of a possible solution and only when that idea fails to solve the problem do we seek alternative possibilities.

In the same way, when faced with a problem, our directors may well come up with solutions based upon their own experience or culture, in an inductive or intuitive manner based on this experience, rather than considering all of the possibilities in a deductive way. This statement is not criticising the process as, in many cases, there is simply not the time or other resource to carry out a comprehensive deduction process.

Subjective analysis

Qualitative, or subjective, methods are often used first in risk analysis to obtain a general indication of the risk issues to be faced and their possible outcomes. The method is often used, also, where numerical data is insufficient, inadequate or simply too costly to collect. Qualitative analysis uses words as descriptors for impact and probability, generally in three bandings: high, medium and low. Once a risk has been identified, judgement is used to rate risks relative to each other. Thus a risk may be judged to have a high impact but a low probability. Combinations of high, low and medium descriptions can then be shown either in matrix form or listed by rank in a risk register.

The IRM Risk Standard provides guidance on these subjective descriptors and can be viewed by visiting the IRM website http://www.irm.

Risk mapping

An ideal way of illustrating the high, medium and low descriptors in relation to impact and probability is to use the risk mapping technique already shown in an earlier study session. More impact can be achieved by using 'traffic light' colouring for the risks at various levels: a risk which is mapped as high impact and high probability would appear in red, while a low/low risk would be green.

Scenario analysis

Scenario analysis is a technique which demands the visualised achievement of high goals and provides a viable pathway to achieving them. It creates a 'can-do' mindset, changing how people think, plan and behave in order to achieve high goals. UK athletes such as Lynford Christie and Colin Jackson have laid some of their success at the door of scenario analysis, in that they would imagine how every element of the race would go right up to passing the finishing line first.

10

149

Auditing

We will address audits in more detail in study session 19, but suffice it to say that the auditing of a process or supply chain may review the quantitative data in compliance, variances, accuracy of data and so on, but all of that data is then interpreted in a qualitative way.

SWOT and PESTLE

Please refer back to coverage of these methods in study session 2.

Self-assessment question 10.1

If you were working with the company in learning activity 10.1 above, which qualitative tools would you advise that they use and why would you recommend these?

Feedback on page 159

10.2 Tools for quantitative identification of risk

According to http://www.wikipedia.org/:

- Quantitative research is the numerical representation and manipulation of observations for the purpose of describing and explaining the phenomena that those observations reflect. It is used in a wide variety of natural and social sciences, including physics, biology, psychology, sociology and geology.

Quantitative research begins with the collection of statistics, based on real data, observations or questionnaires. In the field of health, for example, researchers might measure and study the relationship between dietary intake and measurable physiological effects such as weight loss. Opinion surveys are a form of qualitative research that is converted into a quantitative form by the allocation of scores to the responses. In the field of climate science, researchers compile and compare statistics such as temperature or atmospheric concentrations of carbon dioxide as quantitative data.

The effectiveness of quantitative analysis is driven by the quality of the data collected, the type of analysis used and the conclusions drawn from the results of the analysis. This last point is most important to remember in that no matter the level of complexity and sophistication of the tools employed in quantitative risk analysis, the results will be applied by fallible human brains.

John Schuyler says in *Risk and Decision Analysis in Projects*:

> 'We all rely daily upon our intuition and the purpose [of quantitative assessment] is not to replace intuition. Rather the quantitative methods will bolster our intuition.'

10

A simple quantitative method

An easy-to-use-and-understand hybrid analysis uses a nine-square basic risk matrix as shown in table 10.3. A subjective analysis using high, medium and low ratings is given weighting values. However, this only translates the grid into a non-arithmetic representation which catches the eye, with the highest number indicating the risk which needs the most management attention.

Table 10.3

4	7	9
HL	HM	HH
2	5	8
ML	MM	MH
1	3	6
LL	LM	LH

We can refine this by giving the factors of impact and likelihood joint ratings of 3 for high and 1 for low. Applying this to the data in table 10.3 results in the illustration at table 10.4.

Table 10.4

$1 \times 3 = 3$	$2 \times 3 = 6$	$3 \times 3 = 9$
$1 \times 2 = 2$	$2 \times 2 = 4$	$3 \times 2 = 6$
$1 \times 1 = 1$	$2 \times 1 = 2$	$3 \times 1 = 3$

There remains a great deal of subjectivity in this method but it begins to point us down the road of understanding *how* quantitative methods can help us to refine our judgemental approach to risk analysis.

Decision trees

Making good decisions based on the best available information helps us to approach risk assessment in the best possible way. We referred to mind maps earlier in our studies and decision trees are an extension of the basic mind-map theory. Wikipedia defines a decision tree as a graph of decisions and their possible consequences (including resource costs and risks) used to create a plan to reach a goal. They help you to choose between several courses of action, and provide a highly effective structure within which you can lay out options and investigate the possible outcomes of choosing those options. They also help you to form a balanced picture of the risks and rewards associated with each possible course of action.

http://www.mindtools.com has the following information on how to draw a decision tree:

'You start a decision tree with a decision that you need to make. Draw a small square to represent this towards the left of a large piece of paper. From this box draw out lines towards the right for each possible solution, and write that solution along the line. Keep the lines apart as far as possible so that you can expand your thoughts.

10

At the end of each line, consider the results. If the result of taking that decision is uncertain, draw a small circle. If the result is another decision that you need to make, draw another square. Squares represent decisions, and circles represent uncertain outcomes. Write the decision or factor above the square or circle. If you have completed the solution at the end of the line, just leave it blank.

Starting from the new decision squares on your diagram, draw out lines representing the options that you could select. From the circles draw lines representing possible outcomes. Again make a brief note on the line saying what it means. Keep on doing this until you have drawn out as many of the possible outcomes and decisions as you can see leading on from the original decisions.'

(Copyright: Mind Tools)

Any technique which can improve our decisions in connection with managing risk is helpful and decision trees have a part to play. They can now be swiftly implemented using software such as that provided by Mind Tools. Go to http://www.mindtools.com where, among other things, you will find a graphic example of a decision tree used to develop a new product or consolidate an existing situation. The expected value of the possible decisions (we referred to expected value in study session 7) are calculated using figures for probability and the value of outcomes, thus resulting in a value for each possible decision for comparison purposes.

Fault tree analysis

Similar to the decision tree analysis, fault tree analysis is a graphical technique that provides a systematic description of the combinations of possible occurrences in a system, which can result in an undesirable outcome. This method can combine hardware failures and human failures and is often used in continuous process industries in relation to system safety where a fault could have disastrous consequences. Like decision trees, fault trees can provide an effective structure within which the user can lay out options and investigate possible outcomes of each choice of action. Please see the following website for a graphical illustration of a fault tree: http://www.iee.org/Policy/Areas/Health/hsb26c.pdf.

Network analysis

Techniques in this area are commonly used in project planning and control but, in terms of risk management, they may be applied as a means for ensuring that decision making is well based and may provide a documented means for management to review project risks. The most common network analysis techniques are critical path analysis (CPA) and programme and evaluation review technique (PERT).

Hazard and operability analysis (HAZOP)

This technique, although mainly qualitative, can be given added value by the use of additional tools such as a Pareto analysis to give more quantitative-oriented results. HAZOP uses a systematic process which can highlight possible deviations from normal, thereby illustrating that safeguards are in place or indicating where they should be in place. Used mostly as a systems-level risk assessment technique, it is applied primarily to continuous process systems but can also be used in environmental procedures reviews.

Dependency modelling (DM)

This uses goal-oriented logic to help build realistic business models. DM highlights the business dependencies from the corporate goals down through to the technology delivering those goals. The strength of DM is that it allows organisations to identify single points of failure, not just in items of equipment but also where people, processes and external influences such as competitors affect business operations. The models use data relating to the probability of failure and the costs of failure should it occur. By identifying the critical interdependencies between people, systems, processes or technology, DM can show you how your organisation is exposed to risk, the effects of that vulnerability and indicate which countermeasures will prove most effective. Companies such as Cool Waters offer DM as part of their business continuity planning support.

Learning activity 10.2

Reread the case study in learning activity 10.1 above and list some quantitative tactics and tools that could be used to analyse and evaluate the risks that you identified. Use the information in the annexes of the OGC *Guide for Practitioners* to help you.

Feedback on page 160

Now you could attempt self-assessment question 10.2 below.

Self-assessment question 10.2

Compare the advantages and disadvantages of the tools and tactics that you used in the learning activity.

Feedback on page 161

10.3 Allocation of resources to the use of risk analysis tools

You should now read or reread Chapter 3 of Sadgrove's *Complete Guide to Business Risk Management*, as it covers the following issues:

- the allocation of responsibilities
- the use of consultants
- the development of an openness culture
- the setting of budgets (and provision of funds).

There is also useful information in Chapter 2 of the OGC's *Guidance for Practitioners*.

10

Learning activity 10.3

Draft a report of 300–400 words to the organisation in the case study in learning activity 10.1 above with your recommendations and rationale for the resources that would be needed to apply the tools and so on appropriately.

Feedback on page 162

Now you could attempt self-assessment question 10.3 below.

Self-assessment question 10.3

Conduct a risk profile on the case study in learning activity 10.1 above using the impact assessment grid (figure 10.1).

Figure 10.1: Impact assessment grid

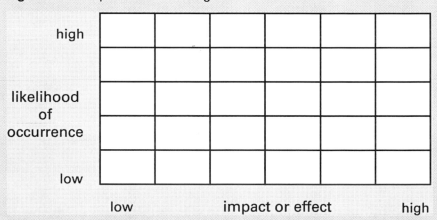

Feedback on page 162

10.4 Calculating the impact

To calculate the impact of a potential risk, we need to use probability tools and arrive at the 'expected value'. If we look at dice, for example, we would expect the outcome of 600 rolls of a single die or dice to yield 100 ones, 100 twos and so on. This could be described in the formula {(100 × 1) + (100 × 2) + (100 × 3) + (100 × 4) + (100 × 5) + (100 × 6)} divided by 600

$$= 100(1 + 2 + 3 + 4 + 5 + 6) / 600 = 21/6 = 3.5$$

So the expected value of rolling the die or dice 600 times is 3.5, which is interesting as it is not even a number on the die!

Expected value

For risk analysis and evaluation purposes, probabilities in decision making are closely related to the expected values of particular outcomes. If we can place values on the various alternative decisions that can be reached, then multiply them by the probability of their actually occurring, the highest expected value would signal the best alternative in quantitative terms and indicate the highest value risk areas. In terms of risk, this could be used to identify those risks which require the closest management attention and action and could also be used to consider contingent liabilities when decisions are being made about prospective clients' future prospects.

Ratio analysis

Applying ratios to financial data can give information which will assist in assessing how a prospective supplier company – or potential customer – is placed to meet short- and medium-term commitments. This can assist us in assessing which suppliers can work with us in terms of the prices we can negotiate and their being in business long enough to ensure our required period of supply. Similarly, we can make judgements on the risk which potential and existing customers pose in terms of ability to pay. Ratios can tell us how a company has fared over recent times and provide a guide for future performance.

Typical ratios which can be easily calculated include:

Gross profit %

Gross profit/sales × 100

Return on capital employed %

Profit before tax and interest/capital, reserves and long-term liabilities × 100

Acid test

Current assets (excluding stock) : current liabilities (ratio of 1 : 1 indicates that liabilities are exactly covered by assets)

Debtor collection

Trade debtors/sales × 365 (length of time being taken to pay)

Gearing

The relationship between a company's debt and equity shareholders funds. Gearing is usually expressed as a percentage and is calculated by dividing the company's debt by its equity. Companies with high levels of debt tend to be more risky.

Linear regression

This is a graphical mathematical analysis which can forecast the behaviour of a variable based on historical data. The method requires two sets of data, each dependent on the other. It could be profit and turnover, comparing companies in the same industry or, in risk terms, it could be insured loss experience in relation to turnover and this would allow us to forecast the expectation of loss in relation to different levels of turnover using a 'line of best fit' as shown in figure 10.3. Table 10.6 tabulates profit and turnover data for a number of fictitious companies. Figure 10.2 shows the scatter diagram and figure 10.3 shows the line of best fit which can be used to project forecasted values.

Table 10.6

Company	Turnover (£m)	Profit (£m)
A	21	13
B	27	19
C	33	24
D	29	24
E	23	21
F	30	19
G	16	7
H	20	15
I	18	10
J	13	8

Figure 10.2: Scatter diagram

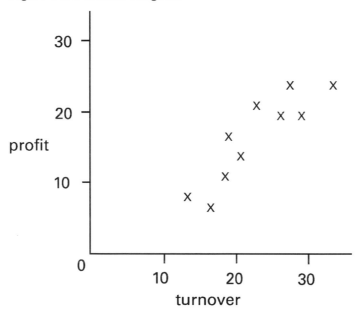

Figure 10.3: Line of best fit

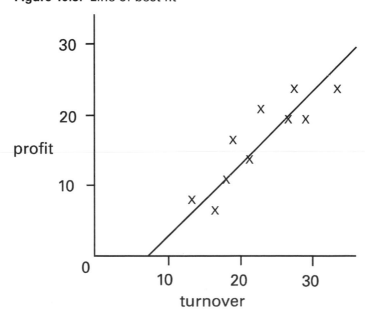

The profit in relation to turnover is not relevant here; the figures used in this example are for illustrative purposes only to show how the correlation works and how this technique can work in risk management terms. Regression analysis has many uses other than the application used here. In agriculture, for example, we could use the graph to establish a link between rainfall and crop yield.

Value at risk

Value at risk (VaR) is a category of market risk measures which rely on complex mathematical relationships which can provide a value of portfolio holdings for which an understanding of risk outcome can be inferred. Suitable software is easily available for this complex issue and one source is http://www.contingencyanalysis.com. Figure 10.4 illustrates the three inputs required for this analysis: the input – portfolio data and historical market data; the processes – mapping and inference procedures and transformation procedure; output – a VaR metric – the measure of VaR value.

Figure 10.4: VaR measure

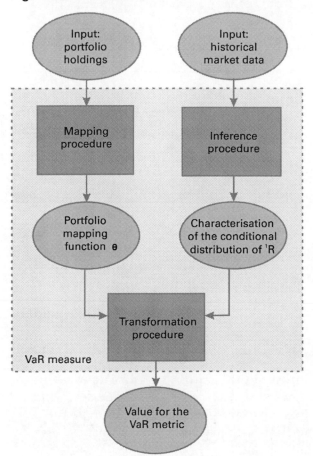

Source: riskglossary.com

VaR can be enhanced by using the Monte Carlo method which, although introducing a standard error, is a more effective transformation procedure which analyses large volumes of variable data while producing relatively simple and understandable results. The Monte Carlo method is extremely complex and is best used and understood by investigating its application to the assessment of financial market risk. Figure 10.5 gives an example of a Monte Carlo analyser applied to several variables using different calculations and providing one composite graphic. For further information go to http://www.mbrm.com.

Figure 10.5: MBRM Multi-asset Monte Carlo analyser

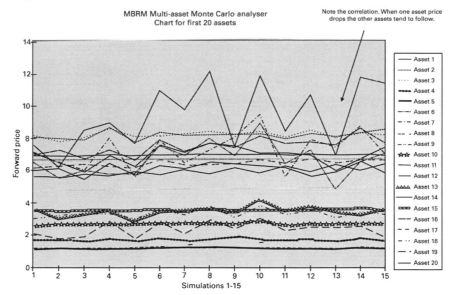

Source: Adapted from www.mbrm.com with permission.

Learning activity 10.4

Select something that you buy at work on a regular basis. Identify ten hazards to that supply – defects, wrong quantity, error, missing documents, damage in transit, breakdown, lateness, un-forecast demand and so on.

Try and attribute a probability of each of those hazards occurring and make notes on your reasoning for that figure.

Feedback on page 163

Now you could attempt self-assessment question 10.4 below.

Self-assessment question 10.4

Now consider the potential impact of the hazards that were addressed in learning activity 10.4 above. The worst-case scenario would be death and personal injury. Other outcomes might include adverse exposure in the national press, damage to reputation with key customers or financial loss due to scrap, rework or warranty claims.

Calculate the costs of these outcomes; estimate the likelihood of them happening and plot this on an impact assessment grid such as figure 10.1.

Feedback on page 163

Revision question

Now try the revision question for this session on page 356.

Summary

This session has addressed some of the ways in which risk can be approached and how we need to take care to balance the qualitative or judgemental decisions with the quantitative or data-based information.

Suggested further reading

You could read the relevant sections of Eckes (2000), Sadgrove (2005) and Schuyler (2001).

Office of Government Commerce (2005).

Feedback on learning activities and self-assessment questions

Feedback on learning activity 10.1

You should mention some of the following qualitative decisions and risks (table 10.1):

Table 10.1

Qualitative decisions	Additional risks
Concentration on public sector	Possibility of saturated market; lower returns; more difficult to break into; more demanding of resources in the tender process
Focus on facilities management	Catering skills may not carry across to other functions; possibility of saturated market; low profitability; labour intensive
Profit targets	Possibly unrealistic and driven by desire rather than rational and empirical (relating to the facts) decisions
Turnover targets	Driven by profit targets which may have unsound foundations
Size of customer business	Unsupported by context; figures all based on profit targets
Selling of support, training and advice	No indication of market for such services; no voice of the customer; no awareness of how to pitch the sale let alone how to cost it; ignorance of what advice is needed; the required knowledge may not be available within the team
Quality of delivery seems to be taken for granted	Failure to satisfy the customer may lose that customer or cost more money in re-delivering up to an acceptable standard
Staff will react favourably to performance-related pay	Loss of staff; loss of motivation if targets are perceived to be unachievable; employment tribunals; hard selling may switch off potential customers
Ethics and CSR	They may attract too much business; difficulty of measurement; need for trade-off against profit maximisation

Feedback on self-assessment question 10.1

Table 10.2

Qualitative tools	Rationale
Enlightened gambles	Directors and staff have knowledge and experience. These are part of a firm's competitive advantage. By encouraging the use of

(continued on next page)

10

Table 10.2 *(continued)*

Qualitative tools	Rationale
	enlightened gambles, the staff are given an opportunity to shine, or, if they are wrong, to gain valuable experience. Hunches and gut feelings are usually the result of years of knowledge and the development of intuition.
The voice of the customer	Listening to the customer is the only way to discover what is required and how needs can be satisfied. Remember Henry Ford, though, who suggested that if he had asked the customer what he wanted, he would have asked for a faster horse!
Shareholder value assessment	Shareholders may want more dividend and share value growth, but, as Nike found out when suffering adverse publicity, the shareholders were not prepared to suffer sloppy ethical practices in the supply chain.
Setting tolerances or allowable variances	Quality is fitness for purpose and perfection is unachievable. The degree of acceptable imperfection has to be set and cannot always be based upon quantitative assessment.
Reiteration of strategy following quantitative analysis	We may set out to have a holiday in paradise with a budget of £100. However, on discovering that flights and hotels would far exceed our budget, we may wish to revisit our strategy for the holiday.
Setting uncertainty acceptance levels	If we wait until all data is available, the time for decision making will be past. Deciding how much information is enough information is an important qualitative tactic.
Influence diagrams (see Chapman & Ward)	An *influence diagram* was originally a compact representation of a decision tree for a symmetric decision scenario. You are faced with a specific sequence of decisions and between each decision you observe a specific set of variables. An influence diagram is *solved* by computing a strategy yielding the highest expected utility.
Personal appraisals	Questioning, listening and watching skills can elicit responses and attitudes that would not be achievable in a questionnaire.
Relationship assessment	Although some relationship assessment tools may appear to be quantitative, such as the relationship continuum (a scale ranging from adversarial at one end to partnership at the other) and perceptions matrices (with attractiveness and value on the axes) and radar charts, the positioning and the selection of the scales can only be a purely qualitative decision.

Feedback on learning activity 10.2

Table 10.5

Qualitative decisions	Additional risks	Quantitative tools
Concentration on public sector	Possibility of saturated market; lower returns; more difficult to break into; more demanding of resources in the tender process	Market research
		Cost/benefit analysis; value analysis
		Sales call/conversion to order ratio
		Cost/benefit analysis
Focus on facilities management	Catering skills may not carry across to other functions; possibility of saturated market; low profitability; labour intensive	Skills analysis; gap analysis
		Market research

(continued on next page)

Table 10.5 *(continued)*

Qualitative decisions	Additional risks	Quantitative tools
		Cost/benefit analysis; value analysis
		Efficiency and yield probability analysis
Profit targets	Possibly unrealistic and driven by desire rather than rational and empirical (relating to the facts) decisions	Market research
		Target costing process
		Decision tree
		CRAMM software
		Process mapping
Turnover targets	Driven by profit targets which may have unsound foundations	Market research
		What-if modelling
Size of customer business	Unsupported by context; figures all based upon profit targets	Portfolio management (possibly Kraljic's value/risk matrix); return on investment figures; what-if modelling
Selling of support, training and advice	No indication of market for such services; no voice of the customer; no awareness of how to pitch the sale let alone how to cost it; ignorance of what advice is needed; the required knowledge may not be available within the team	Needs analysis
		Training needs analysis
		Skills analysis
Quality of delivery seems to be taken for granted	Failure to satisfy the customer may lose that customer or cost more money in re-delivering up to an acceptable standard	Radar charts
Staff will react favourably to performance-related pay	Loss of staff; loss of motivation if targets are perceived to be unachievable; employment tribunals; hard selling may switch off potential customers	Probability and impact grid
Ethics and CSR	They may attract too much business; difficulty of measurement; need for trade-off against profit maximisation	Probability and impact grid
		Benchmarking exercise

Feedback on self-assessment question 10.2

You should be able to recognise that some of the tools are easier, quicker and cheaper to access than others. The implementation of some new modelling software or the carrying out of extensive market research can be resource-intensive. On the other hand, much of the data may already exist within the firm's relational database (or within someone else's) and simply needs to be pulled together in the form of some graphically enhanced reports.

Collected data needs to be validated and the collection process needs to be objective.

To paraphrase what George Eckes says in *The Six Sigma Revolution,* there are three levels of mastery of any subject: memorising, interpretation of what has been memorised and assimilation or the ability to make sense of what you have interpreted.

The data that we are capturing during the quantitative analysis has to be gathered carefully in order to facilitate the correct interpretation and subsequent assimilation. Under Six Sigma we would develop a data collection plan that describes exactly where the data is to be sourced, what we are doing with it and how we are validating it.

Feedback on learning activity 10.3

First, your answer should be in report format with an introduction, a conclusion and a body that is broken up by headings and subheadings.

Clearly, Roberts Kelly (RK) is making decisions based upon the flimsiest reasoning. It may be worth starting by taking a step backwards and revisiting the definition of what it is we are supposed to be trying to achieve and what are the parameters for achieving this. There is nothing wrong with profit as a motive, but we need to address our short-, medium- and long-term objectives. Our profitability targets in the long run may be achieved by some method other than profit maximisation in the short run. We need to set up an information-gathering resource, either internally or externally, and we may need to fund information systems to facilitate the collation, validation and assimilation of this data. There is a need for market awareness and customer data. This can be obtained correctly only by using third parties with the appropriate expertise. Using internal staff on these duties runs the risk of diluting effort on current business, as well as the risk of clouding the outcomes with prejudice or bias from their subjective approach to the problem.

This will all entail the identification, negotiation, selection and monitoring of third parties who will provide these services for us.

There will need to be a detailed estimate of costs and timings and it should all be treated as a fully-fledged project with board-level support and encouragement, regular reviews and clearly defined outcomes.

Feedback on self-assessment question 10.3

You need to make an assessment on a scale of low to high as to what is the likelihood of the risk occurring and what would be the impact, positive or negative, on the organisation of that risk occurring. Your assessment grid (risk map) should have included at least these examples:

- Concentration on public sector – high impact, medium probability (market penetration in doubt, future revenue depends on this)

10

- Focus on facilities management – high impact, high probability (failure of all this effort affects future survival)
- Unrealistic profit targets – high impact, high probability (set in isolation, aspirations rather than targets)
- Unrealistic turnover targets – high impact, high probability (based on profit wanted rather than business case)
- Market for training activities – high impact, high probability (insufficient market research, market unknown).

Your own work should follow this pattern for other risks which you have identified.

Feedback on learning activity 10.4

You should be able to identify a number of hazards and discover the risk of each hazard occurring based upon your own particular experience.

Feedback on self-assessment question 10.4

You should have used your figures to create a grid or risk map which would show you those hazards which require most management attention: those with high impact and probability would need more attention than those with low impact and probability. Many risks will be 'medium/high' or 'medium/low'; these need to be carefully considered to ensure that the correct factors have been used to arrive at these forecasts. Poor consideration of impact and probability means that these risks will not be managed effectively and could have far-reaching effects on the organisation.

10

Supplier selection

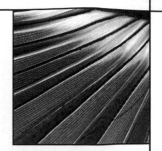

Aggressive purchasing methods can only be judged to be successful if suppliers stay in business while delivering the required product or service to time, cost and quality.

Introduction

Procurement risks fall into two main categories:

- external risk from selected suppliers going out of business, being unreliable in quality or slow in delivery
- internal risk from our own organisation's self-imposed procurement policies.

We can review our internal strategies, policies and procedures from time to time to ensure that best practice is being adhered to and that the best use of resources is being achieved. In terms of managing the external risks posed by our suppliers, we need to be sure that our supply strategy is appropriate and relevant and that our supplier selection procedures are adequate. Various techniques and methods are available to help in this regard and this session addresses a selection of these approaches.

Session learning objectives

After completing this session you should be able to:

11.1 Explain some supplier appraisal techniques that will assist in the identification of risks.
11.2 Propose supplier selection methods based upon solid risk management techniques.
11.3 Formulate some financial tests to evaluate a supplier's financial status.
11.4 Propose some contingency plans to enable early warning of changes in a supplier's financial position.

Unit content coverage

This study session covers the following topics from the official CIPS unit content document:

Learning objectives

3.1 Develop appropriate solutions to mitigate the inherent risks in the following issues:
- Supplier appraisal, selection and management
- Project failure (eg capital procurement – investment appraisal)
- International sourcing
- Implementation of new technologies
- Corporate social responsibility (CSR) including ethical, environmental and health and safety issues
- Public sector procurement

11

3.4 Analyse specific key risks and exposures in purchasing and supply and identify appropriate mitigating actions.
- Contractual failure, consequential loss and provision for remedies
- Supplier insolvency, monitoring and guarantees
- Quality failure, non-conformity and corrective action
- Project failure, project planning principles and corrective action
- Security of supply, contingency planning, stock holding and alternative sources of supply
- Technology failure, impact on supply, use of back-up systems and disaster recovery
- Security, theft and damage
- Fraud, accounting and payment exposures, conflicts of interest, purchasing ethics and codes of conduct
- Product liability, reputational damage, consumer confidence

Prior knowledge

Study sessions 1 to 10.

Resources

Internet access.

Timing

You should set aside about 4.5 hours to read and complete this session, including learning activities, self-assessment questions, the suggested further reading (if any) and the revision question.

11.1 Techniques for appraising potential suppliers

Learning activity 11.1

Select one of your most recently acquired suppliers. Investigate what appraisal techniques were applied. If there were none, try and list the techniques you think should have been used.

Feedback on page 178

The specification for the product or service which is required will be provided by our own line management together with an idea of the anticipated time line: new product manufacture commencement, for example, or the date for introduction of a new or improved stock item. The source of supply is our first consideration when approaching potential risks:

- Single source. There are several reasons why we may choose or be forced to choose a 'single source'. Some supplies, particularly some raw materials, may have only one or a few suppliers, even in a global market. Conversely, for some purchases there may be benefits to the buyer in single sourcing, regardless of numbers of suppliers. These can include saving administrative time and effort, better discounts for volume and greater power or 'leverage' with the supplier. In the first case, the risk for the buyer is the monopoly's ability to fix both price and volume, a risk which can only partially be mitigated by bulk purchase agreements and fixed-term pricing. In the second case, there is a risk of becoming overdependent on a single supplier. What happens if that supplier is taken over by one of our competitors, or if a serious fire at their factory stops all their production? What if they have a strike? Some of you will remember how the strike at Gate Gourmet, a single-source supplier to British Airways, more or less grounded the airline in 2005.

- Multiple source. Selecting more than one supplier effectively treats the risks associated with too great a reliance on one source of supply. Supply volumes can be spread between several suppliers thus maintaining an ability to switch quickly and easily if one supplier runs into any kind of difficulties. Prices can be more competitive because each supplier can be negotiated with in the knowledge of easily available alternative sources.

Wider risks in sourcing include particular risks in overseas supply and environmental issues such as pollution and land use.

Reputational risk can also be a major consideration when we are appraising potential suppliers. There are two main ways in which our reputation might be damaged by our suppliers:

- If suppliers fail to meet our standards of quality, timeliness and customer service this may affect our ability to meet our own customers' expectations. If we let our customers down they will go to our competitors. They are very unlikely to be sympathetic to the claim that it was all the fault of one of our suppliers.
- When buying overseas, particularly from third world or developing countries, we need to be aware that ethical and environmental issues are often accorded a much lower priority than they are in the developed countries. The fact that a company in, say, the Far East is using child labour at very low wage rates and in poor or even dangerous conditions may be the very reason that they can offer such competitive prices. The risk is that our customers may come to see us as exploiting a situation which is morally unacceptable. Sometimes such crises of conscience are prompted by the fear of widespread media interest in a 'good story'. The effects on companies using child labour, for example, reverberate not just on that company but beyond to tarnish the reputations of all the users of its products.

It should be remembered that many things can change in quite a short space of time in an organisation. Assessment of suppliers therefore is not a one-off exercise to be conducted before we start doing business with them. Assessments need to be updated on a regular basis. This means not only monitoring the ongoing performance of our key suppliers but also maintaining a close dialogue with them and, ideally, visiting them on a regular basis. Too many buyers expect their suppliers always to come to them because they are too busy to go out and meet their suppliers. However,

11

the benefits of going to your suppliers' sites and keeping your eyes and ears wide open while you are there cannot be overestimated.

Similarly, do talk to other suppliers. Word can go round quickly in any industry and you may find that some of your suppliers' competitors know more about them than you do. All this will supplement your own internal information plus, of course, the published information that you can obtain, such as the Annual Report and Accounts.

Customer audits of suppliers

Internal audits may well be carried out within potential supplier companies but will not be readily available since they are for internal consumption only. Even if they were available, their independence and reliability as a means for providing assurance to external users might be doubtful. Most suppliers should be amenable to allowing your own staff to review particular parts of their operations which may be important to you as a potential user of their product or service. Although this access may be strictly controlled, particularly if there are sensitive processes involving competitive advantage, most potential suppliers will allow this as a gesture of good faith and as a demonstration of their interest in winning the business. Service level agreements often include clauses which allow for audit access to the supplier's operations. If a key supplier to your organisation will not allow you access to their operations to carry out a supplier audit you need to ask yourself why this is and whether you should be considering doing business with them. Some organisations have a standard information pack that they send out to any business that approaches them about becoming a supplier. Often this contains an agreement that the buyer will have the right to carry out regular audits or inspections. This ensures that both parties are clear about the basic terms of any future relationship before discussions even begin.

It may be possible to use an independent organisation such as a trade body to carry out the audit as this could satisfy both parties as to the competence of the people undertaking the audit in addition to the independence and confidentiality which would be involved. Comments made by external auditors may also be useful and these are available in Annual Reports.

Questionnaires

Pre-contractual questionnaires are a common approach to supplier appraisal. Their aim is to provide the client company with sufficient information to assess the supplier's suitability to meet the client's requirements. Although in document form, it will typically first be used by emailing the supplier with a request for the form to be completed and returned as part of the pre-contract negotiating or tendering process. Full reliance should not be placed on the supplier's responses alone and a follow-up should be undertaken using the same or a slightly refined format, by the client's own staff on a visit to the supplier. This visit will also allow the client's staff to observe operations on the ground and to get a good 'feel' for the potential supplier's approach to business. The responses on this questionnaire should be used subsequently, if the supplier is successful, as part of the means for monitoring supply: did what they said on the questionnaire actually happen as stated?

11

Financial reviews

Getting as much financial information about a supplier as possible is a critical part of data gathering. Financial health will often be the deciding factor in the client's choice between one or more suppliers. Financial stability and sustainability of the supplier's business is a key issue in ensuring continuity and quality of supply. Lack of sufficient funding in the supplying organisation may lead to compromise on quality, poor labour availability, which may affect delivery on time and in the necessary volume, and inability to sustain both working capital and future investment, thus affecting production and sustainability. Possible bankruptcy or even short-term supply interruption is a key procurement risk for a client company and a financial review can assist in avoiding this potentially catastrophic outcome.

Using a range of financial ratios on available company reports and data provided in the public domain is a good starting point in appraising the viability of potential suppliers. Since the possibility of a supplier going out of business is a key risk, predicting possible bankruptcy is a good starting point. One of the models available to achieve this is the Springate model (developed by Gordon L. Springate; Sadgrove 2005) which uses four significant financial ratios as follows:

1   Working capital/total assets (A)
2   Net profit before interest and tax/total assets (B)
3   Net profit before tax/current liabilities (C)
4   Sales/total assets (D)

Calculate Z (the indicator of financial soundness) by applying weighting factors which were devised by Springate from data gathered by research of many companies over a considerable period of time.

$$Z = 1.03\,A + 3.07\,B + 0.66\,C + 0.4\,D$$

Using this formula, the higher the score the more financially sound the company, and if the Z score is less than 0.862, the company is classified as 'failed'. In appraising a potential supplier for sustainability, the higher the score, the more confidence we can have in the ability of the supplier to meet our purchasing requirements.

In study session 10 we looked at some common financial ratios which can be used in making assessments. Much more data is available on various websites and these can be researched to increase your knowledge in this area. Dun & Bradstreet, the well-known credit analyst firm, also provides a service which gives indicators for predicting company solvency (http://www.dnb.com).

Other assessments

Direct contact with potential suppliers, perhaps the most obvious means of appraisal, should occur through face-to-face contact with key personnel in the supplier company. These meetings can give the opportunity of gaining anecdotal information about the supplier company, its way of doing business, the quality of its people and its financial standing. Meetings

11

also give the client the opportunity for using judgement based on the relationships which can be built up.

In addition to company reports, audited accounts and auditors' reports should be scrutinised as another means of obtaining financial information.

Gaining an understanding of the potential supplier's approach to standard setting in its industry can also give valuable added information to the supplier selection decision. Industry awards and national awards can give a flavour of the supplier company's approach to quality, human resources investment and customer satisfaction. Investment in People awards, Queen's Awards to Industry, and so on, are all indicators of an organisation's culture and approach.

Enquiries could also be requested from your own bankers and the supplier company's bankers as to the creditworthiness of the supplier company. This would be done as a matter of course when undertaking due diligence – a term applied to undertaking audits of a prospective partner, takeover or merging company to ensure that expectations can actually be realised – and can be used in a limited application to potential suppliers.

Self-assessment question 11.1

Build a plan of action showing the appraisal techniques you would use for a prospective new supplier of security services.

Feedback on page 178

11.2 Relating supplier selection to risk management

Learning activity 11.2

Consider the different ways in which a contract can be awarded. Consult the OGC website and read the guidance therein.

Feedback on page 178

Risk management begins at board level. The board sets strategy and lays down the objectives which are required to be met. And, if the board takes the potential outcomes of risks arising seriously, it will ensure that risk management permeates the whole organisation and all its operations. It follows that there should be a strategy for procurement and that the board will be the prime mover in setting that strategy and ensuring that it fits with overall corporate strategy.

Managing the risks in the procurement process flows from the board's risk appetite and the process for selecting potential suppliers ought to reflect this approach. The key factor in all of this is to adopt research methods which will adequately survey the marketplace without ending up with a tranche of suppliers so large that refinement is time-consuming and expensive.

Procurement risk management means anticipating the threats and vulnerabilities which may occur in the buying and supply processes and minimising the chances of a risk arising that has not been anticipated and managed. This means we need to:

- set procurement objectives
- identify the risks which may prevent achievement of objectives
- evaluate these risks
- control the risks where appropriate.

Selecting suppliers to meet our objectives will include, first, ensuring that the procurement function is involved at the right time – ideally at the time when the requirement is being planned, ie before a product or service specification has even been drafted. Thereafter, the major risks concern ability to get delivery on time, to quality and to price and then that timely remedial action can be taken if things go wrong.

We have already considered how we can get the right supplier by using appraisal techniques. Now we need to add on the ways in which we can get the right suppliers with whom we can work to minimise the risks of our own objectives not being met.

The best approach is to ensure that our own procurement objectives are set first and these generally fit into the following categories:

- Is our own funding in place to meet procurement needs?
- Is our procurement strategy delegated effectively within our own organisation?
- Is there a supplier base of credible and legitimate companies?
- Can our own and our suppliers' legal/regulatory obligations be met?
- Can we assure compliance?

Establishing our own procurement needs by integrating service/product operational plans and budgets with financial planning and treasury operations can lead into a banding process for the awarding of contracts. By including individual managers' authority levels for the placing of contracts into these various cash levels, we can begin to have control over the risks of unsuitable staff making decisions which are inappropriate to their skill or knowledge level. Depending on the size of organisation, it could be, for example, that all contracts worth £1 million or more can only be let, or must at least be formally approved, by the board itself. Lesser values then cascade down the organisation to first line manager level. A similar scheme in reverse could apply to the choosing of suppliers. The purchasing department could set up suppliers in categories of product or service in levels of contract value for which they might be eligible. In this way we can manage the risk of (a) insufficient funding – or funding not available at the time it is needed, and (b) at the same time, qualifying suppliers who have sufficient financial standing to tender for our business at each appropriate level of our spend.

11

Large organisations will almost always have a procurement specialism operating as a purchasing department or similar. Smaller organisations may make buying part of a line manager's responsibility. The risk of not having sufficient specialist knowledge of purchasing and the time to devote just to that task is the greatest risk under these circumstances. This may often be manifested by line managers awarding or re-awarding contracts for supply and delivery to 'the company which has always done it' or to a company they have knowledge of through business or family connections. Qualifying effective suppliers under these circumstances is not only difficult but is a major risk to the client in terms of corruption, fraud and poor value for money. A professional purchasing department staffed by qualified personnel and with the right support and backing at board level will go some way towards mitigating this key risk.

Armed with an agreed product or service specification, the purchasing department can commence an invitation to tender process as a means for soliciting interest. This might start with a pre-qualification questionnaire (PQQ). Public sector buyers letting large contracts under the EU Directives would have to start with this when using the 'restricted procedure'. The benefit of using a PQQ is that it allows the buyer to carry out a wider 'trawl' of the market and eliminate all but the most suitable suppliers before moving to the full tendering process. Alternatively, there may be a list of 'preferred suppliers' maintained. In the public sector many organisations now use what are known as 'framework contracts'. These are in effect lists of 'approved suppliers' who have already been selected through formal competition for a place on the 'framework'.

In both cases, tendering creates the opportunity for competition between suppliers to benefit the client through access to price selection and quality or service differentiation. Placing new contracts or renewing contracts without tendering raises a significant risk of not obtaining the best solution which the market can offer. Single-source supply, for whatever reason, brings with it all the significant risks of being locked in to one supplier. In some cases single sourcing may be the only option. In those cases we need to be particularly vigilant about the risks that we are running. Careful drafting of contract terms so as to redress difficulties may help to some extent. However, we should not delude ourselves about the degree of dependence that exists and we should certainly be looking at longer-term strategies to reduce dependence. This might include 'reverse marketing' which aims to draw other suppliers into the market. Another option might be to reduce or eliminate our need for that product, commodity or service over the medium to long term.

The time, effort and cost of continually tendering has led to the practice of maintaining a preferred tenderer list which is made up of companies for whom we have already spent the time and energy on appraising using our standard procedures. By asking a few of these to tender for specific contracts we can obtain a double benefit by (a) mitigating the financial and other risks associated with a new supplier by using one we are familiar with, and (b) getting the best value for money from our own procurement resources.

There are times when tendering is not possible, usually because of single-source supply – utilities and some commodities used to be examples of this but, more and more, even these are being opened up to competition. The risks which have to be managed when there is only one credible supply source include the key risk of having no alternative supply. Mitigating the risk is difficult. Financial redress may be available but even tight contract terms cannot substitute for no supply. If there is a physical supply, a commodity for example, then strategic stockholding may be a possible means for risk mitigation but at the additional costs of financing these stocks. The fact that coal stocks at power stations were high when British miners started their strike in 1984 was a key factor in enabling the government to hold out and ultimately break the strike.

Tendering provides one of the best opportunities for avoiding poor value-for-money risks and for comparing quality and delivery. However, we must also ensure that monitoring post-contract is part of our standard procedures, not only to ensure that contract expectations are fully realised, but to make sure that anticipated risks are covered and no new risks have materialised. Line managers as well as buyers should carry out checks and audits from time to time on all aspects of the supplier's performance, and contract terms should include clauses which relate to redress in the event of non-compliance or poor performance.

Self-assessment question 11.2

Give details of the various techniques that you could use to avoid a supplier becoming complacent, after the contract has been awarded.

Feedback on page 178

11

11.3 Assessing financial health

Learning activity 11.3

Ask your finance manager for some advice on which are the most important financial ratios.

Feedback on page 178

In study session 10 some basic and common financial ratios were considered. Earlier in this study session, finance in relation to supplier appraisal was discussed. These should now be reviewed. This section looks at financial health as it applies to any organisation, client or supplier, and then considers the use and limitations of financial ratios in the assessment of suppliers.

When we identify and evaluate risk we are ultimately looking at a financial outcome and our mitigation strategies seek to reduce that possible outcome to as low a residual value as possible. Businesses are 'healthy' when they can continue in business for a foreseeable period of time – the 'going concern' principle. For our own company, we want to be sure that it will carry on in business and, for our suppliers, we want to be sure that they will be around long enough to fully meet whatever commitment they have made to us.

The general principles which apply to maintaining financial health begin with the ability of the business to at least achieve its projected margins and, at best, to exceed them. This allows the business to build up reserves and to invest. This principle of building reserves is essential if the company is to survive periods of downturn and remain in business. Also, without using reserves to invest in new equipment, new buildings and so on, the business will stagnate and be unable to take advantage of new opportunities. A healthy business will have assets which will either retain their value or appreciate in value with time so that they can be sold in times of hardship if really necessary.

Entrepreneurial flair keeps business alive but the skill of the entrepreneur is to spot good opportunities while avoiding putting every egg into one basket. Investment and/or takeover decisions should not involve putting the whole business at risk and, similarly, the healthy company will not rely on just one or a few main customers or suppliers for its survival.

Financial ratios are useful indicators of a firm's performance and health and can assist us in making decisions concerning a potential supplier's financial viability. Understanding what the ratios can tell us is an important first step. To ensure continuity of supply we need assurance in four main areas:

- profitability
- liquidity
- solvency
- operations.

In terms of profitability, we want to ensure that the supplier is making sufficient profits to make it worthwhile to remain in the particular business for which we want a supply. The profit earned allows the supplier to invest and stay in business, as we have already described. Remember that there is a gross profit margin, which is simply the margin after the cost of goods sold but not other costs, and a net margin, which is achieved after deduction of operating and fixed expenses, taxes and interest.

Liquidity describes the company's ability to meet its short-term obligations; staff wages and supplier payments are examples of these. In other words, is there sufficient ready cash to hand to meet these immediate requirements? For this purpose the business needs positive cash flow, short-term bank agreements like overdraft limits and stock which is readily converted to cash by sale to customers in the normal way of business or by quick sale of assets to other sources.

Solvency, unlike liquidity, measures the long-term stability of the company – its ability to meet debts when they become due like debenture repayment, shareholder debt and bank or other loans.

The cost of operations takes into account those costs beyond the cost of goods sold which you or your supplier has to spend to actually deliver the product or service to your customers. These will therefore include inventory cost, administrative overhead and any sales and marketing costs not directly attributable to the cost of goods sold.

Most ratios can be calculated by reference to the data in the public domain such as interim or final company reports, operational and financial reviews and stock market data. They can be used to analyse trends in addition to being compared with similar companies in the same sector or industry and, of course, the ratio results will provide you with sufficient data on a prospective supplier for good buying decisions to be made.

There are limitations in using ratios alone to indicate a company's financial performance. In the main, they should be used as indicators, although the more that are available, the better the overall picture will be. Extracting figures from year-end accounts only may be unrepresentative since there may be significant fluctuations in values over a complete year. Finally, most ratios by themselves are not highly meaningful. Ratios should be compared from one period to another historically to gain a good view of a picture which is stable or deteriorating. It is worth remembering that this is true of any system for monitoring the performance of your suppliers, be it quality, on-time deliveries, financial strength or any other metric. What you really want to know is: are they consistently hitting the agreed standard, are they getting better or are they getting worse?

The composition of various financial ratios is quickly and easily available on the internet and you should research those available. Several websites also offer calculators which can set up the ratios you select and work out the results for you to use from the data which you provide. The financial planning Toolkit is one such facility (at http://www.finance.cch.com/sohoApplets/Ratios.asp).

Self-assessment question 11.3

Discuss the limitations of financial ratios as a method of assessing supplier risk. Address at least five commonly used ratios.

Feedback on page 179

11.4 Early warning of supplier difficulties

Learning activity 11.4

Select a key supplier and try to list some events which could adversely affect their ability to supply the right quantity, quality or cost of products.

Feedback on page 179

Continuity of service delivery or supply is an important part of staying in business. To a greater or lesser extent all our businesses are reliant on the efficiency and effectiveness of supply chain management. Most organisations are not self-contained and depend upon incoming supplies in order to satisfy their own objectives, outputs and customers. Good procurement management recognises this and ensures a professional approach which includes identifying and evaluating the risks in the supply chain. Perhaps the greatest risk is that, having placed reliance on a particular supplier, that supplier fails, for whatever reason, to deliver as required.

Can supplier failure be anticipated?

Business continuity planning and disaster recovery contingency planning (which is dealt with in detail in study session 20) point us in the direction of the whole organisation being prepared to carry on in spite of what may appear to be catastrophic occurrences. It is no different for procurement – and part of this is being prepared for supplier failures which could put us out of business or, at the very least, prove to be a significant and costly inconvenience.

From a financial point of view we can seek early warning signs from a variety of sources. The ratios that we may have used while appraising suppliers can alert us to possible problems in the future – liquidity and solvency, for example. These ratios should be maintained and regularly updated for all of our major suppliers as a matter of standard procedure.

Financial market sources can often provide pointers and these include briefings from market analysts, share price fluctuations and changes in credit ratings from organisations such as Standard & Poor's or Dun & Bradstreet. Trade and professional organisations can be sources of market intelligence. These same sources may bring the first indications of mergers and takeovers which, although not apparently posing immediate risks, can quickly turn into a threat if the newly formed organisation decides to drop a particular line of business – which could be your main supply source – or becomes a virtual monopoly as a result of reducing the numbers of suppliers available. The same thing could apply to an overseas supplier which could easily be a single source of supply. Changes in political power or environmental issues could hasten the end of a well-established supply chain relationship.

The first step in getting an early warning system in place is to use our IT facilities to create a comprehensive database of all of our suppliers, categorised by type of supply and cross-referenced to the part which each supply plays in our own internal processes. This will allow the identification of significant supply streams without which we could not operate, cascading down through 'desirable' to 'not essential'. From all the other data that has been gathered through supplier appraisal, indicators can be built which will be activated as circumstances change. These changing circumstances will depend on the regular inputs to the system which can be made as supplier data is updated from all the sources already mentioned.

An example would be a change in a liquidity ratio affecting the supplier. This could result in the supplier having difficulty in paying short-term creditors with the result that deliveries to your company are delayed or cease altogether. If this change in the ratio had been input to the warning system at an early stage, it could have triggered an indicator which would have caused defensive action to be taken – seeking new supply avenues – much earlier than would otherwise have been the case. However, as we have said before, do not just rely on the ratios. There are likely to be other indicators that not all is well. Some delivery dates may already have slipped, the supplier may have been in touch pushing for prompt payment or offering very good discounts for early settlement. Equally, some of the supplier's key staff may be becoming uneasy and may already be moving on for fear that a round of redundancies is on the way.

Many other events could affect suppliers which would have an effect on the client and should form part of the early warning contingency plan. These could include labour disputes and overseas wars. Direct supplier contact is vitally important in the midst of IT and other solutions. Meetings and discussions with relevant supplier staff, particularly through relatively informal channels, may often be as good a means as any to glean early warning information. Financial data is important but good early warning systems will take account of many other matters as well.

Self-assessment question 11.4

There are currently only three suppliers in the world for your most important purchase. You have heard a rumour that two of them are merging. Describe the plan of action that you will now need to take.

Feedback on page 179

11

Revision question

Now try the revision question for this session on page 356.

Summary

Funding and finance are key factors in every organisation. Understanding how the financial stability of potential suppliers can affect client organisations' risk assessment is a critical part of the procurement process. Getting access to a potential supplier's financial data and then manipulating that data to provide useful information which will inform buying decisions can assist in selecting the right suppliers in the first place and, subsequently, ensure that there is continuity of supply. Putting contingency plans in place to attempt to avoid being caught out by the problems of our suppliers should be one of the standard procedures in every purchasing department.

Suggested further reading

Office of Government Commerce: http://www.ogc.gov.uk.

You could also read the relevant sections of Sadgrove(2005).

Feedback on learning activities and self-assessment questions

Feedback on learning activity 11.1

You should find that your company has a standard approach to appraising new suppliers. Key factors in the appraisal should be financial soundness, product quality, delivery and fitness for purpose, history of supply satisfaction with existing customers. The appraisal system should also include authority levels for approving new suppliers and the skills for carrying out the supplier appraisals. (Note that it is not just the purchasing function that needs to be involved. Other departments with an interest are quality assurance, finance, and so on.)

Feedback on self-assessment question 11.1

The plan should commence with the means to be used to assess the supplier's ability to meet your requirements:

- right product available
- your specification matched
- sample testing arranged
- company financial reports obtained
- financial appraisal carried out
- banker's reference obtained
- purchase questionnaire sent to supplier
- relevant personnel meetings.

Feedback on learning activity 11.2

You should have seen the schematic under the 'successful delivery toolkit' which covers the process from business case to contract management. You should also have reviewed the section on performance. Give some thought to the way in which contracts are awarded in your organisation; is there flexibility in the methods which are used? Are there standard procedures in your purchasing department which give details on the way contract performance should be monitored?

Feedback on self-assessment question 11.2

Methods should include frequent supplier contact; more formal agreements – contract terms – for periodic audits and checks. Standard procedures for checks on product quality and timeliness of delivery with reporting to the purchasing department so that action can be taken with suppliers. Contracted agreements for product return and re-supply when agreements are breached.

Feedback on learning activity 11.3

The importance of particular ratios depends very much on the use to which they may be put. Short-term creditors, for example, prefer a high current ratio (working capital ratio) because it reduces the risk of them not being paid quickly. Shareholders might prefer that ratio to be lower so that more of the assets are working to grow the business rather than being paid out quickly. The ratios which may be used by those interested in investing in your company, solvency ratios or dividend ratios for instance, may not be the ones you will want to consider in detail when appraising a potential supplier.

Feedback on self-assessment question 11.3

The ratios would have included examples from solvency, liquidity, profitability, asset turnover and operations. The limitations were referred to in the latter part of section 11.3 and should be revised in the light of your answer.

Feedback on learning activity 11.4

These events could include financial constraints, political or labour problems and failure of downstream suppliers. All of these could contribute to fluctuating delivery volumes and increased cost by suppliers attempting to pass on their own increases experienced when alternatives have to be sought. Poor substitutes in supply or labour may affect quality of product or service. Withdrawal of a single-source supplier might bring significant problems of cost and quality – if an alternative can be found – and business closure if an alternative is not available.

Feedback on self-assessment question 11.4

11

You should have started by expressing the hope that a contingency plan was in place. If there is no plan then you should be seeking the market and other intelligence which was described in section 11.4. You should then have considered the actions needed to clarify your position as client by contacting each of the companies to seek assurances as to continuity of supply.

11

Ethics, corporate social responsibility (CSR), health and safety

Introduction

Being ethical in business need not mean being uncompetitive. In fact, by making a virtue of such a policy, several companies have gained a competitive edge in their particular economic sector of activity. Procurement is often an area which is seen as being most vulnerable to unethical behaviour and the reasons are not hard to find: they include the imperative to get the best deals, ability to agree contracts and authority to disburse funds. Ethical and social responsibility can go hand in hand with effective and efficient operations, however, and this study session explores the relevant issues together with discussion of health and safety issues. Health and safety are often the areas which suffer most from poor ethical and social responsibility because it is easier and less costly to ignore these issues although, in the long run, such a policy inevitably incurs higher risks and potentially more costly outcomes.

'A combination of an ethical code, training on proper business conduct and a designated Ethics Officer or Ombudsman point the way to a comprehensive ethical programme.'
Ethics Resource Centre, Washington, USA

Session learning objectives

After completing this session you should be able to:

12.1 Demonstrate an awareness of the changing nature of global ethics.
12.2 Define the impact on the management of the supply chain of a corporate social responsibility policy.
12.3 Formulate a plan of action to deal with safety issues and understand the application of hazard operability analysis (HAZOP).
12.4 Predict some health and safety issues that may arise within the supply chain.
12.5 Assess the impact of corrupt practices and the effects of fraud, particularly as they apply to the supply chain.
12.6 Develop a policy of personal ethical conduct for all purchasing and supply management staff.

12

Unit content coverage

This study session covers the following topics from the official CIPS unit content document:

Learning objectives

3.1 Develop appropriate solutions to mitigate the inherent risks in the following supply chain issues:
 • Supplier appraisal, selection and management
 • Project failure (eg capital procurement – investment appraisal)
 • International sourcing
 • Implementation of new technologies

- Corporate social responsibility (CSR) including ethical, environmental and health and safety issues
- Public sector procurement

3.4 Analyse specific key risks and exposures in purchasing and supply and identify appropriate mitigating actions.
- Contractual failure, consequential loss and provision for remedies
- Supplier insolvency, monitoring and guarantees
- Quality failure, non-conformity and corrective action
- Project failure, project planning principles and corrective action
- Security of supply, contingency planning, stock holding and alternative sources of supply
- Technology failure, impact on supply, use of back-up systems and disaster recovery
- Security, theft and damage
- Fraud, accounting and payment exposures, conflicts of interest, purchasing ethics and codes of conduct
- Product liability, reputational damage, consumer confidence

---

Prior knowledge

Study sessions 1 to 11.

Resources

Internet access.

Timing

You should set aside about 6 hours to read and complete this session, including learning activities, self-assessment questions, the suggested further reading (if any) and the revision question.

12.1 The changing nature of ethics

The importance of ethics has always been a factor in business relationships. 'My word is my bond' has survived since antiquity as an indication of trustworthy transactions and is based on the character and morals of the individuals concerned. Integrity is the keynote of this type of approach. Each party to a transaction trusts the other to deliver their side of the bargain. It is the *absence* of trust and the gradual withering away of morality and principle which causes stakeholders to question the actions and behaviour of corporate leaders. Not just the loss of trust in face-to-face situations but also the contributing factor of lengthy chains of command in today's corporate bodies which may increase the scope for inappropriate behaviour at various decision-making levels.

Much of the fallout from corporate disasters such as Barings, WorldCom, Enron, Parmalat and All First has been laid at the door of poor corporate governance, in particular, poor ethical behaviour. The reason for this is not hard to find: ethics is about the way people behave and, when the pursuit of greed for personal or corporate gain is the main motivator, disaster is often not too far behind.

Ethical conduct is really as simple as putting into place the mindset of *do unto others as you would have done unto you.* It relies on a behavioural code which the majority of people will accept and behave accordingly because it accurately reflects their own outlook on business and personal life.

Codes of ethical conduct are becoming relatively commonplace in both public and private sectors in many of the world's economies. Such a code – which could otherwise be termed an ethical policy, statement of business practices or set of business principles – is simply a convenient way for boards and senior management to establish and communicate corporate values, responsibilities and obligations. The code provides guidance for employees in situations where a dilemma may arise between alternative courses of action, none of which may be obviously 'right' or 'wrong'.

No two codes will be exactly the same. Codes need to reflect the different business environments which organisations find themselves in and the parts of the world which are being dealt with. Unofficial payments may spell bribery and corruption in the UK but in other parts of the world they may be common business practice. Codes must also take into account the needs and concerns of the people most intimately concerned, both within the organisation and those with whom there are common interfaces outside the company. Otherwise, practical and realistic outcomes may be difficult to achieve. Like many other areas of corporate life, codes of ethical conduct will only work if they are effectively communicated, there is commitment from the top, there is organisation-wide application and the effectiveness in practice of the code is constantly monitored.

Religions have usually been the first to codify moral conduct. These codes have invariably been based on custom and practice for the time in which they were established. Practice, indeed, which the moral leaders of the time would have considered to be *good* in the sense of satisfactory outcomes for the majority of people concerned. Thus, the Christian Commandments provide a moral code which is as applicable nowadays, in the main, as in the times when they were first written. Similarly, much of the Koran provides moral guidance while the pacifist approach of Buddhists and their belief in the sanctity of all life provides an enduring example of ethical and moral behaviour.

So, an ethical approach to business should not be too hard to achieve; it is about a reasonable standard of behaviour both individually and corporately. Note the word *reasonable.* Perfection is not expected or required. But reasonable behaviour would seem to be a *reasonable* aspiration for the world's corporate leaders in all sectors of economic activity.

Learning activity 12.1

Investigate ethics websites such as http://www.ethicaltrade.org to identify some of the global principles.

Feedback on page 198

Various codes of practice now exist in this field although few are required by law. Ethical codes generally complement other codes – codes of business conduct, for example, such as the Combined Code in the UK for listed companies. In the USA, the knee-jerk reaction to all the poor corporate behaviour of the late 20th and early 21st centuries – culminating in WorldCom, Enron and others – was the Sarbanes-Oxley Act of 2002. While we shall not go into the details of that act, much of which is about financial control and public reporting, it is interesting to note that new rules introduced under the act require companies to disclose whether or not there is a code of ethics which applies at least to its chief executive and chief finance officers.

Many professional bodies, including the Chartered Institute of Purchasing and Supply, have their own codes of ethical conduct which members must sign up to on being admitted. Members usually have to commit to observing the ethical code in their day-to-day work and there are often sanctions included in the code for use against members who are found to have breached the code and, perhaps, brought the profession into disrepute.

The majority of ethical codes stress that there should be no *impropriety* – offending against moral law or legal requirement – and that there should be avoidance of doing any *needless harm* – to the environment, perhaps, or to individuals by an abuse of human rights. Applying these principles to business decision-making should not really be too difficult and the simple tests advocated by the Institute of Business Ethics (http://www.ibe.org.uk) are these:

- transparency – do I mind others knowing what I had in mind?
- effect – who does my decision affect or hurt?
- fairness – would my decision be considered fair in objective terms?

Many examples of ethical codes exist around the world. This is a very subjective area, however, and often difficult to codify; what works for one country or industry may not work for another. A good first step for developing a code or reviewing an existing one is for consideration to be given to those parts of the company's business or business relationships which might be particularly vulnerable to malpractice or similar risks. The following areas should feature in any ethical code or, indeed, a straightforward code of good business practice:

- honesty, objectivity and diligence in carrying out responsibilities
- loyalty to the company
- avoid conflicts of interest
- avoid acts which could discredit the company and its reputation
- accept no inducements to act in a particular manner
- avoid use of confidential information for personal gain
- ensure that all activities undertaken are within the law
- maintain high standards of integrity, morality and competence.

Integrity Works, a UK company specialising in providing customised ethical programmes for its clients, considers that each company needs its own type of code because this will reflect the national culture, the sector culture and the exact nature of its own structure. Importing a 'standard' code may lead to a poor match with the particular company and result in the code falling into disrepute and becoming counter-productive.

Although it is stressed that no two organisations in this regard are likely to be the same, all who are global stakeholders in virtually every type of organisation would certainly appreciate the high aspirations of those who are interested in improving business ethics. In risk management terms, the existence of a code of ethics, widely disseminated in an organisation and signed up to by all staff, can begin to mitigate some of the personal and relationship risks that can materialise in virtually every part of the supply chain.

Self-assessment question 12.1

Explain what has changed in recent years to make it necessary for most large organisations to adopt an ethical approach to the way they do business.

Feedback on page 198

12.2 Corporate social responsibility in relation to the supply chain

Learning activity 12.2

Identify some CSR issues in which your organisation has an interest which could influence the way you manage your supply chain.

Feedback on page 198

Modern organisations need to take account of many things which their predecessors of relatively few years ago would never have had to consider. Concerns, in particular about damage to the environment, have resulted in significant new legislation, much of it emanating from the European Union in the form of new directives. It is also worth remembering the role played by the environmental pressure groups which have had a very significant impact in raising awareness of environmental issues. Many environmental issues now have 'popular' overtones that nobody can afford to ignore. Nor is it just illegal activity which causes headlines. In 1995 plans by Shell to dispose of an obsolete oil rig, the Brent Spar, by sinking it in the North Sea resulted in a major popular outcry. This was despite the fact that, compared to the other disposal options open to Shell, sinking the rig was one of the better environmental options. Ethical and environmental issues are, therefore, not only a 'hot' topic; they are a potential minefield for the unwary.

Corporate bodies have a particularly significant role to play in the way in which they interact with society and the environment as a whole; gone are the days when their immediate workforce, markets and political influences were their only concern. Employees will be influenced by international working conditions, standards and pay norms; markets and customers may be found in any part of the world and, increasingly, it is regional and global politics which affect national policies and aspirations.

Corporate social responsibility (CSR) is difficult to define but a good attempt is evident in the UK Department of Trade and Industry definition which states that CSR:

'has a wide-ranging agenda and involves businesses looking at how to improve their social, environmental and local economic impact, their

12

influence on society, social cohesion and human rights, fair trade and the ways in which that fairness can be corrupted. CSR is an issue for both large multinationals and for small locally based businesses.'

CSR is generally not required by statute although some of its constituent parts may be; employment law, for example. Nonetheless, there are more pressures on organisations to take account of the requirements for CSR than not. 'Practice in time' is also important. What may be relevant in one moment in time may not be in another as the world and people's behaviour moves on. And, of course, ethical and social norms in one country may not be those which apply in another.

While it is difficult to identify a specific business case for CSR, there could be a high cost involved in ignoring CSR and in not managing the risks which it engenders. Corporate scandals ultimately reveal the high costs of socially irresponsible behaviour which could include:

- bankruptcy
- loss of shareholder value
- criminal and/or civil prosecutions
- loss of credit rating
- loss of reputation.

These and other CSR risks are often not generally well understood by line managers because many of the risks are external to our own organisation. For procurement managers, however, this is less the case since a large part of supply chain work is outside the client company and well within the normal operating environment for the purchasing department.

The quest for low-cost sources of supply has always been a feature of the capitalist economy. While this was seen as a benefit to the captive colonial countries of the past in terms of employment for the local population, education and the beginnings of local government, nowadays it is viewed as exploitation. Nonetheless, the lowest possible supply cost is still important to achieving profits for today's companies. Unfortunately, this can result in the exploitation of low-cost labour in poor countries where labour laws may be weak or (perhaps more likely) where basically sound labour laws are simply not enforced.

Continued exploitation of this nature has fuelled the new emphasis on CSR, not least because of reputational issues brought about by the 'naming and shaming' by activists of companies thought to be guilty of knowingly using child labour or cheap bonded labour sources of production. In recent times this has been just what has happened to international brand names such as Nike and Gap.

A company's ability to monitor and influence the working conditions and ethical practices of its suppliers tends to diminish as the geographical distance from the supplier increases. Despite this, the impact of poor practice (or simply practice which is seen as unacceptable in our own culture) in these suppliers can have a massive effect on the client company's brands, reputation and revenues when these practices are revealed.

Risks to revenue and reputation can be significant when supply chain impacts and outcomes are considered. CSR in procurement is exemplified by socially responsible sourcing and, while this may still be a relatively new concept, *not* to take account of it could have disastrous results. Consider, for example, the effects of a prolonged activist-driven campaign against your company: your supply source could be affected, your customer base diminished and reputation severely damaged. Additionally, the morale of your workforce will be affected and many will question why your senior management did not address these risks and act in a much more socially responsible fashion.

In fact, the drivers for more effective CSR can come from within: a desire from the company's own workforce, for example, to demonstrate a more acceptable ethical stance; pressure from shareholders and other stakeholders; a widespread and deepening public desire for governments and society in general to be more socially aware and to be more ethical in business dealings. All of these things drive the need for supply chain management to take more account of CSR in its sourcing decisions.

Appraising potential suppliers to take CSR into account needs to be widened when we consider the appraisal techniques which we discussed in study session 11. Now we should consider the social responsibility of the governments of overseas countries with which we may wish to do business. The labour policies of these countries need to be taken into account and the business norms need to be more closely scrutinised. The means for doing this can be difficult and time consuming. Ethical audits may be necessary before contracts are signed and more attention paid to undertaking due diligence – often more applicable to mergers or takeovers but necessary here for different reasons. Due diligence is the activity of attempting to make as sure as possible that what you are going to get in a takeover is exactly what was expected and entails close scrutiny of the other company's figures, operations and markets. The parallel to validating a potential supplier in terms of CSR is clear.

All this may add to the cost of supply but the ultimate value added is first, the risk of potential damage to the bottom line by taking account of CSR in the supply chain is diminished and, second, we improve our reputation.

Self-assessment question 12.2

What steps would you take to ensure that a supplier complies with your corporate social responsibility policy?

Feedback on page 198

12.3 Safety issues and hazard operability analysis

Management is responsible for the health and safety of all employees in an enterprise. Every individual has a personal responsibility also for avoiding potential dangers when they are apparent and for being aware of the need for personal safety. A good example would be an employer providing hard hats in a dangerous area with instructions on how, when and where to wear them and an employee disregarding this by not wearing the hard hat in appropriate circumstances.

The Health and Safety Executive (HSE) in the UK is empowered to oversee effective practice and compliance through legislation and the EC has, through its directives, required assessments to be undertaken in these areas. It is worth remembering that the HSE has very significant powers and that, in extreme cases, it can shut down an operation which it considers to be dangerous. Health and safety risks are present in every organisation and should be an integral part of the risk management approach. That means that relevant issues should form part of the enterprise-wide approach to identifying and evaluating risks and be subject to the same data collection methodologies together with timely monitoring and review.

Potential risk outcomes in this area can be extreme: death or serious injury, for example; and the loss of output following a possible closedown while an incident is investigated could be catastrophic. A death is a tragedy under any circumstances but the further implications could include the company being sued by the surviving relatives. While this is an insurable event, there could also be loss of reputation together with sanctions from the HSE. These could include prosecution for non-compliance with relevant legislation or regulation and could lead to curtailment of production or some other operational constraint.

Some risks may appear to be small in immediate impact but can accumulate in volume or severity as time goes on. Repetitive stress injury (RSI), for instance, may occur in only a few individuals initially but if work practices are poor, the number and value of the injuries can swiftly escalate.

Assessing risks depends on identifying potential dangers and hazards. Procurement managers should be particularly assiduous in identifying constituent parts of products being supplied which may have subsequent unwanted effects on our workforce. Are checks made on:

- production processes used by suppliers – any dangerous substances in use?
- any residual toxicity in products being delivered?
- toxicity build-ups while products are in storage?
- customer feedback on any strange outcomes which could be traced back to the product?

Some of these checks may be part of the standard procedures applied in the purchasing department as a matter of course. Buyers should ensure, also, that the supplier's instructions regarding the storage and handling of products are not being ignored and thereby causing unnecessary risks to arise.

Many companies have their own internal departments charged with training all employees in health and safety and also carrying out audits and reviews of the safety systems. Learning from experience is important and highlights the need to ensure that all accidents are reported and that there is a system in place, such as an accident log, which is available, known about and used by all staff. The key part of this activity is to ensure that all staff are aware of potential hazards and are properly trained to minimise both the effect of these risks and the risk of them arising in the first place.

It is essential that the audit and checking work carried out by health and safety officers is taken seriously by senior management and any recommendations implemented speedily. Proper training, audit and record keeping will assist in mitigating risks in these important areas and also

12

help in the event that a serious accident occurs. The fact that the company has done all in its power to minimise risks arising illustrates good faith and acceptance of the need for effectiveness in this area. This stands well with social awareness and is a good endorsement of the culture of the organisation in the event of subsequent litigation.

Hazard and operability analysis (HAZOP) was introduced as a methodology in an earlier study session. Now it is appropriate to look in more detail at this technique and consider how it can be applied to identify safety hazards.

HAZOP as a technique was originally developed by ICI but only started to be used more widely after the Flixborough disaster in 1974 where there were many fatalities and injuries following an explosion at a chemical plant. Through general exchanges in ideas the system was then used in the petroleum industry, followed by the food and water industries where similar potential for disaster was thought to exist, although more in the areas of contamination rather than explosion. The HAZOP methodology is perhaps the most widely used aid to loss prevention because it is easy to learn, can be easily adapted to almost all the operations that are carried out within process industries and no special academic qualifications are required.

The procedure basically involves taking a full description of a process and systematically questioning every part of it to establish how deviations from the design intent can arise. Once identified, an assessment is made as to whether such deviations and their consequences can have a negative effect on the safe and efficient running of a plant.

Typically used by a multi-functional team, 'brainstorming' is used to help identify both obvious and less obvious threats and hazards. An essential part of the questioning approach and critical analysis is the use of keywords, as follows:

- **primary keywords** which focus attention upon a particular aspect of the design intent or on an associated process or condition
- **secondary keywords** which, when combined with a primary keyword, suggest possible deviations.

The primary keywords reflect process design and operation and could include *flow, pressure, temperature, mix* and *absorb*. Secondary keywords suggest deviations or problems and are descriptive in nature, for example 'no' as in 'no flow' or 'less' as in 'less pressure'.

The methodology involves drawing up a table which shows the application of keyword combinations linked to the reason for a problem and the subsequent action needed to rectify it. An example is given in table 12.1 where a fluid flows from a tank via a strainer, is mixed with another fluid and ends up in a holding tank.

Table 12.1 HAZOP register

Deviation	Cause	Consequence	Safeguard	Action
Flow/no	Strainer block	No mixture	Pressure gauge	Pressure checks

This simple example shows that, if there is no fluid mixture then the consequence is that the second tank will not contain the expected product. The deviation in this case is 'no flow' because the strainer is not working and a pressure gauge in the system can record pressures which, if set at a pressure for the flow of the mixed products, will set an alarm for pressure deviation.

Figure 12.1 illustrates the iterative process.

Figure 12.1: Flow chart

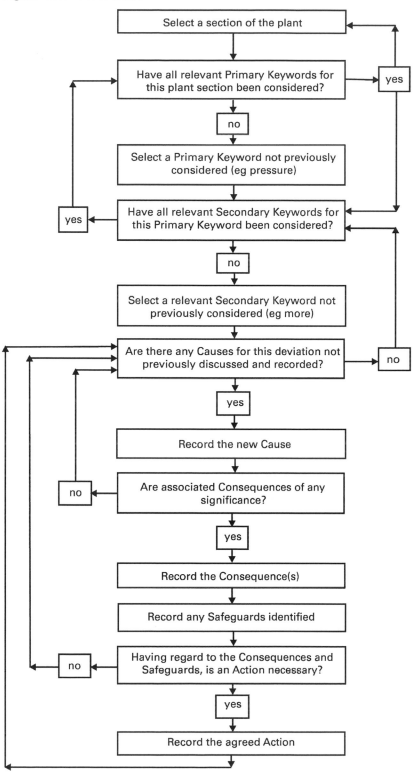

There are limitations to the HAZOP technique. It requires a well-defined system of activity and effective development of the keywords. It can be time consuming – brainstorming sessions take time – and, additionally, it needs considerable personnel resource since multi-function teams work best in reviewing the system or process and identifying potential deviations.

Learning activity 12.3

Look around your workplace, try and identify some hazards that may exist for visitors and then research your organisation's application of HAZOP principles. If your organisation does not use HAZOP, then consider what you have learned in this section and apply it to changing a plug on an electrical appliance.

Feedback on page 199

Now attempt the self-assessment question by applying all you have learned in this study session.

Self-assessment question 12.3

You are planning to purchase a new chemical that is highly flammable. Develop a plan of action to prepare for the arrival of the first consignment.

Feedback on page 199

12.4 Health and safety issues in the supply chain

12

Learning activity 12.4

Have a look at your organisation's safety record and accident log. Discover what your safety policy says and compare this to what happens in real life. If you discover a discrepancy, ask your manager what action should be taken.

Feedback on page 199

The corporate attitude to health and safety will be reflected in the way every part of the organisation implements internal rules and regulations designed to reduce and eliminate dangers. If the corporate culture is seen to be one of cutting corners in this area, perhaps to save cost, then this attitude is bound to be reflected in the way that all staff carry out their duties in the workplace. The risk appetite and the risk strategies of the enterprise should be sufficiently robust and apply in matters of health and safety just as they do in all other operations.

Risk management in the supply chain in terms of health and safety should be an integral part of the approach taken to securing the right product at the right price and at the right time. Thus, supplier appraisal should include assessment of products for their potential impact on the health and safety of our own workforce. Included in this should be evidence of compliance with relevant UK and EC directives or regulations which might apply to particular unique products or services. Similarly, there could be specific regulations applicable to the industry in which we operate and procurement managers need to ensure that suppliers and our own processes comply with these requirements.

Particular points on which assurance might be sought include:

- toxicity – dangerous fumes or leakages
- supplier instructions on storage and distribution methods
- training of the supplier's workforce on product dangers and hazards
- compliance with laws and regulations in supplier's production
- implementation of international standards.

Further checks should be carried out to achieve an independent view of the supplier's assurances by means of supplier audits, trade checks etc. Government lists on dangerous substances should also be reviewed since these can also indicate the laws and/or regulations which need to be complied with. The successor organisation to HMSO, The Stationery Office (http://www.tso.co.uk), provides lists of available data and there are links to the office of Public Sector Information and HSE Books (http://www.hse.books.com) where regulations of all types are available – the *Guide to Compliance with the Explosives Regulations* being just one example.

The health and safety of purchasing officers who may be involved in carrying out supplier checks and reviews is of particular importance. Confirmation in writing should be obtained prior to any visits taking place on matters such as recording of visitors' arrival and departure from sites, safety briefings for visitors, issue of protective clothing where appropriate and escorting of visitors at all times while on site. All of these should also apply to our own company and purchasing officers should verify our own approach to handling visitors to ensure that supplier representatives, for example, are treated in an appropriate risk-aware fashion.

The systems and procedures which have been discussed as applying to risk management in general apply equally to supply chain awareness of health and safety issues. It is important that all sourcing is treated in a way in which risks are identified and assessed before any purchasing agreement is entered into. The health and safety of our workforce is a paramount consideration for all managers for humanitarian reasons as well as for business continuity. Good practice in this area will pay off for our organisation's wellbeing as well as for our end-user, the customer paying good money for our product or service.

Self-assessment question 12.4

Imagine that the hazards that you identified in learning activity 12.3 above and the records that you saw in the activity above were actually those of a major supplier. What actions would you take?

Feedback on page 199

12.5 The potential for fraud and corruption in the supply chain

Fraud and corruption can exist in any organisation. Rather than define each term (it is difficult to find a simple legal definition for fraud), we should consider how they can occur and what some of the effects might be.

Fraud is an act of deception. Whatever act is carried out, the perpetrator does it with forethought and generally makes some attempt to ensure that the act is not discovered or else that it is blamed on someone else. Often, fraud occurs because a loophole is seen in a system or procedure and the fraudster exploits that weakness. It is generally seen as a 'white collar crime' in that it tends to be finance-oriented and the perpetrators tend to be administrators rather than shopfloor workers. This is, perhaps, becoming less the case as delayering takes place together with the implementation of relational database systems which involve direct computer input from base-level operations.

Corruption is generally seen as the use (more accurately, misuse) of a post or position of power in order to achieve personal or corporate gain. It is an immoral as well as dishonest act – immoral because an insidious attempt may be made to compromise an individual's core values and beliefs, and dishonest because the truth of any situation will be twisted to suit the eventual outcome. Corruption may not always involve the passing of money, it could be intangible favours; but the use of any kind of incentive, cash or kind, is termed a bribe.

Using gifts or allowing payments outside of contract conditions can be part of the normal way of doing business in certain parts of the world. Acceptance of this still does not make it appropriate but does make it much more difficult for the ethical values of one country to match those of, perhaps, an emerging nation. The payments, even if seen as absolutely necessary to gain the business, still corrupt the body making the gift as well as the receiver of the gift and remain illegal. What is really needed is for each party to work towards a global acceptance of an improvement in business ethics and much has been done to achieve this in recent years, such as the UK government initiatives, for example on making poverty history, and the Export Credit Guarantee Department's regulations on export sales, some of which are designed to prevent bribery.

Bribery and corruption have existed for centuries. Attempts have been made to legislate against them in modern times. In the 1970s and 1980s, events like the Lockheed Aircraft Company's attempts to bribe the Japanese government and the Watergate scandal all contributed to the Foreign and Corrupt Practices Act of the 1970s in the USA. In the UK the early Prevention of Corruption Act of 1916 and more recent Anti-terrorism, Crime and Security Act of 2002, together with legislation in the area of money laundering, have served to heighten the profile of fraud and corrupt acts. Despite this, we do not have to look far for crimes in this area: Barings, AllFirst and Parmalat, for example.

Fraud, bribery and corruption run parallel to the morals of society itself. Greed, self-interest and jealousy all fuel poor ethical behaviour in individuals and corporations alike and drive the potential for more and more dishonest acts to occur. There are several keys to eliminating this kind of behaviour,

12

not least of which is establishing a better corporate governance framework for companies and other bodies and, as far as possible, removing temptation from areas where fraud and corruption could be seen to thrive.

Supply chain professionals need to be particularly aware of the potential for fraud and corruption because of their unique position in the corporate body. Purchasing departments lie on the boundary between the internal organisation of their own company and the external mechanisms of those companies which may have the ability to satisfy the client company's sourcing needs. Buyers have corporate funds to spend and individuals in the purchasing department have authority limits commensurate with their responsibilities. It is not too difficult to see why procurement has been traditionally seen as an area where bribery and corruption could be a temptation.

Buyers have their employer's money to spend and every buyer is exposed to the possibility that suppliers will attempt to be the supplier of choice by offering the buyer incentives, some of which may well be inappropriate. Avoiding temptation is the carapace under which the purchasing professional must operate. The organisation takes the first step in employing professionals with the right qualifications and experience and with attitudes which match the organisation's own cultural outlook. Organisations should then also provide the ethical framework within which the purchasing department operates: codes of conduct, standard operating procedures and so on.

It is particularly important that conflicts of interest are avoided in the purchasing department. Avoiding these conflicts could include ensuring that buyers have no interests in any specific supplier – or at the very least that any interest is declared. This might include a close relative working for or even owning a supplier. It might also include the holding of shares in a supplier.

There are several indicators which can be used to spot procurement areas where fraud, bribery and corruption risks may be 'flagged' to raise awareness:

- Too close a relationship between procurement managers and suppliers – kickbacks can be in cash, foreign holidays, free use of car, and so on
- Inconsistent use or abuse of tendering procedures – one firm being constantly favoured over another
- Lack of delegation in the procurement function – senior buyers keep everything to themselves to avoid bribery detection or even just poor margins
- Favourable contract terms – some suppliers forced to bid with more stringent conditions than others
- Supplier demands for payment in cash – 'long firm' suspicion (false companies set up to invoice for goods but with no intention to deliver), avoidance of money laundering legislation, open to bribery.

Avoiding some of these risks by switching buyers between supplier categories from time to time, warning suppliers that anti-corruption forms part of the business norm and breaches will be reported and using only competitive tendering are all means for risk mitigation.

12

For purchases of any significance there should be a division of responsibilities between ordering of goods and services and paying for them. Thus, the purchasing department might raise and approve the order on receipt of an authorised requisition from the user department. Invoices should go directly to Accounts Payable who pay them automatically if all details match those on the order. If not, they log the invoice on the system and return it to the end-user for sign-off. Finance should monitor and analyse returned invoices in order to spot any suspicious patterns. Similarly, setting up supplier account information, although initiated from the purchasing department, must be independently entered into the information system, usually by the finance department.

Note that the recent adoption by many organisations of purchasing cards as a means of streamlining procedures for making low-value purchases effectively removes any separation of duties with these purchases. The cardholder effectively authorises the purchase, authorises payment and receives the goods. However, what purchasing cards may lack in pre-emptive control they more than make up for in retrospective control. Management receives comprehensive reports from the card issuer which make it very easy to see if suspicious transactions are taking place.

All of these, and more, are the checks and balances necessary to ensure that the offering of bribes or the establishment of corrupt behaviour is, if not impossible, at least very difficult. The integrity of the individual buyer is an essential ingredient in an anti-corruption strategy and we shall see later how a code of ethics can assist in this regard and forms part of an effective risk mitigation strategy.

Learning activity 12.5

Identify some possible sources of corruption within your organisation and consider how they could be avoided.

Feedback on page 199

Self-assessment question 12.5

As a purchasing manager, what steps would you take to protect your staff from false accusations of corruption and/or fraud?

Feedback on page 200

12.6 Developing an ethical code for supply chain managers

Learning activity 12.6

Read the CIPS ethical code on the http://www.cips.org website and compare this to what happens within your organisation. Make some notes on the

(continued on next page)

12

Learning activity 12.6 *(continued)*
reasons for any discrepancies that you may have discovered, taking particular note of any policy omissions in the area of possible conflicts of interest.

Feedback on page 200

We have seen earlier in this study session how ethical standards and corporate social responsibility have become significant drivers in trying to achieve better corporate governance. Corporate governance (the way companies are directed and controlled) is the generic term coined in recent years to describe the aspiration towards more accountability – an accountability that has appeared to be sadly lacking in the behaviour of some of the companies and their boards of directors in recent times.

Codes of conduct, be they ethical codes or any other kind of code, are usually voluntary in nature and define a level of behaviour which is deemed to be 'acceptable'. What is considered acceptable may vary from one individual to another but, in the case of a company, a code embodies the manner in which the company expects all employees to behave while conducting its business and being part of its corporate body. In this way companies can impose their own codes of conduct. However, the code will only work in practice if the vast majority of employees are prepared to accept the code as a reasonable way of working.

A company code of conduct may already be in place but it will have evolved from experience, consultation and fitness for purpose. In the case of procurement there are some clear ethical issues which need to be addressed in addition to more common areas of business practice. These issues include

- conflicts of interest
- integrity
- professionalism
- giving and receiving of gifts
- transparency of action.

Of course, these areas may well feature in a general code of ethics but are particularly relevant in the purchasing environment. It could be necessary for purchasing officers to accept the general code but, additionally, have additional or more clear-cut addenda to the code as it applies to them.

As we have seen earlier, the purchasing department is uniquely placed in terms of pressure being brought to bear on its staff from external sources. Negotiations mean dealing with people who are potential suppliers and who are keen for their products or services to be one of your key sources. They may be tempted to bring personal incentives into the discussion and the client may be equally tempted to accept that incentive. After all, who will ever know?

It is that very question – *who will ever know?* – which highlights the need for personal integrity in supply chain managers and an acceptance of good ethical conduct. It may appear clear that nobody *will* ever know, although in the fullness of time these things have a habit of being revealed. Once involved in any corrupt practice the individual is on a treadmill that is almost impossible to get off. Any future refusal to 'cooperate' by sanctioning or participating in fraud or corruption is likely to result in threats of blackmail – revealing, for example, that a bribe was offered or accepted in a previous transaction.

Getting the right people in the first place is important. Well-qualified, professional and with the right experience, staff also need to be involved in continuing professional development. They also need to be trustworthy and this may only be demonstrated by the way they work in their current jobs as well as their actions in previous positions.

Ensuring that there is a corporate code of ethics which is seen to be operating is important. Equally important are the additions which may be necessary for the purchasing department and include the main points listed above. A general company policy on giving and receiving gifts – and hospitality – should be in place and this may need to be a rigid 'don't do it' policy as far as the purchasing department is concerned. Purchasing officers should be required to make written acceptance of the ethical code as it applies to their department.

Senior managers should ensure, by monitor and review, that the code is working in practice. Any code is only as good as the extent to which it is accepted and put into effect. Having a code which is misused or falls into disrepute is the same as having no code at all.

Self-assessment question 12.6

Make notes for a presentation to new starters in which you will explain and justify the corporate policy relating to personal ethical behaviour.

Feedback on page 200

12

Revision question

Now try the revision question for this session on page 357.

Summary

An ethical approach to business is extremely important. Global communication and global trading have highlighted the different approaches there may be to doing business in various parts of the world. A code of ethics can help to avoid the pitfalls of bribery and corruption which may be endemic in certain economies.

An ethical approach helps to maintain the integrity of the individual and the organisation and promotes a better way of doing business. In the supply chain, particular temptations exist and a code is a clear means for assisting both clients and suppliers to be transparent and open while still getting the best deal for their respective stakeholders.

Suggested further reading

You could read the relevant sections of Manifest (2006).

Feedback on learning activities and self-assessment questions

Feedback on learning activity 12.1

You should have discovered that the main points cover areas such as honesty, loyalty, integrity and avoidance of conflicts of interest. For interest and comparison with your own company's ethical approach, you should log on to Standard Chartered Bank's website and review its Code of Conduct (http://www.standardchartered.com/csr/ethics).

Feedback on self-assessment question 12.1

All organisations have had to react to public opinion, which has generally condemned the conduct of corporate bodies and the conduct of their senior managers in the wake of corporate scandals. Much of this has come from well-publicised company failures and the perception that directors and managers were driven by greed and paid scant regard to their employees' or the public's good. The emphasis on better corporate governance which has become apparent in recent years implies a sound ethical approach and many organisations now have ethical codes which all employees should adhere to. In the USA, an ethical code has become mandatory for certain board members.

Feedback on learning activity 12.2

Depending on the sector in which your company operates, some of the issues will include fair trade issues and international labour law. This could include liaison with organisations such as the International Chamber of Commerce and international labour associations because of their focused view of financial stability generally in overseas countries – poor CSR thrives where fraud and corruption proliferate. Your company will also be interested in the manner in which potential suppliers approach corporate governance and ethical issues are handled, in addition to the way in which the environment features – care and attention to areas in the immediate area of the supplier's business, for example, or philanthropic interest in clean water supply.

Feedback on self-assessment question 12.2

Supplier appraisal methods should reflect the company's approach to CSR. This could include background research on countries of operation in terms of political approach; global or local credit rating agencies to ascertain financial health which may, at the same time, give us a view on corruption issues; and checks with labour associations. Our company's standard approaches, which will no doubt include some form of questionnaire, should include supplier visits and audits as a means for verifying the responses to questionnaires. A focused form of due diligence – investigating financial and operational 'health' – may also be appropriate since this will

12

inform our overall view of the way the organisation works and fits with its community.

Feedback on learning activity 12.3

HAZOP principles can be applied to less complex situations than those found in full-blown continuous processes. Using the principles, a questioning approach should highlight some of the more obvious safety hazards which, although familiar to you, may be less obvious and therefore more dangerous to a visitor.

Changing a plug could beg the questions: skilled to do it? Proper tools available? Supply switched off? Apply the consequences and actions to these areas as a simple exercise for your own interest.

Feedback on self-assessment question 12.3

Your plan should have included:

- Obtaining the supplier's detailed brief on the nature of the chemical.
- Recommended methods of transport and storage.
- Brainstorming with your own production staff using HAZOP or other technique designed to identify and evaluate risks.
- Develop and communicate an action plan.
- Ensure monitoring and review processes are in place to assess effectiveness of your action plan.

Feedback on learning activity 12.4

The safety record should form part of a regular report to senior management and the board. You should be able to find these reports and review their contents. Check back to accident logs and review whether safety reports really do reflect the situation as you have discovered it. Check the safety policy for current application: does it refer to current requirements of legislation or regulation? Are all staff aware of the policy? Ask some of your colleagues and consider their response.

Feedback on self-assessment question 12.4

Your actions depend on how appropriate your own and your organisation's approaches have been. Use this opportunity to be critical since you do want a potential supplier to reach the highest standards in this area in order to protect your own staff and, ultimately, your customers.

Feedback on learning activity 12.5

Reviewing the description of corruption should have helped you identify some areas which could have included some of the 'red flag' issues. In addition, you may have considered:

- Inappropriate authority limits (eg a manager having a very high limit when they have no need for it).

12

- Poor division of duties in authorising the purchase, receiving it and authorising payment to the supplier.
- Favouritism of a supplier even though they are recognised to be expensive and/or provide poor service.

Feedback on self-assessment question 12.5

Your answer should have included reference to a procedures manual, purchasing standards, a code of ethics and an adequate scheme of delegation. Management check of activity periodically should also have been mentioned or an internal audit to provide assurance of compliance.

Feedback on learning activity 12.6

You will have found that the CIPS code consists of principles and guidance. The principles cover things like the avoidance of improper business relationships, professional competency and compliance with legal requirements. Guidance tells you how to deal with declarations of interest, issues of confidentiality and other matters of that nature. Your own organisation should have some kind of ethical policy which is applied from the board down. There should be a procedure for all staff to have copies of the policy and to acknowledge that they have seen it and understand it.

Feedback on self-assessment question 12.6

Your notes should cover the general ethical points of honesty, diligence and avoidance of conflict. The need for trust to be in place should be explained and the way in which loyalty and confidentiality is central to the way in which the organisation does business should be highlighted. Policy on hospitality and gifts should be clearly explained.

Project management including project appraisals

Introduction

This session seeks to introduce concepts of investment appraisal in respect of projects which require capital funding. An understanding of the principles behind the various methods which can be used is essential, although there is plenty of help available in the form of software which removes the need to undertake complicated mathematics. Unfortunately, projects often fail to deliver up to expectations either of time or cost and some of the reasons for this are explored. The need for risks in projects to be recognised together with the role for supply chain managers are both made explicit.

The future can only be influenced by the plans we make today. Tomorrow's projects will succeed with the right mix of funding and physical assets, effective management and recognition of the risks to project success.

Session learning objectives

After completing this session you should be able to:

13.1 Explain the problems of investment appraisal.
13.2 Recognise the specific issues related to capital projects.
13.3 Deal with project failure in such a way as to minimise losses.

Unit content coverage

This study session covers the following topics from the official CIPS unit content document:

Learning objectives

3.1 Develop appropriate solutions to mitigate the inherent risks in the following supply chain issues:
  • Supplier appraisal, selection and management
  • Project failure (eg capital procurement – investment appraisal)
  • International sourcing
  • Implementation of new technologies
  • Corporate social responsibility (CSR) including ethical, environmental and health and safety issues
  • Public sector procurement

Prior knowledge

Study sessions 1 to 12.

Resources

Internet access.

Timing

You should set aside about 5 hours to read and complete this session, including learning activities, self-assessment questions, the suggested further reading (if any) and the revision question.

13.1 Approaches to investment appraisal

Learning activity 13.1

Identify the major methods of investment appraisal techniques. Search the DTI website and http://www.moneymatters.com, also http://www.investopedia.com. Follow the links on these sites to research terminology together with the availability and utility of software packages in this area.

Feedback on page 211

Capital investment decisions involve current outlays, perhaps at the expense of other immediate requirements, in return for future benefits of profit, asset improvement or service delivery. The investments may reflect the corporate strategy going many years into the future and require considerable funding inputs over a long period of time. Capital investment and strategy are inseparable, each being a factor of the other.

There may be a need for several projects to be considered at one time and capital investment appraisal is designed to provide comparative data which can show which of the projects may provide the best return on the capital which will be employed. In fact, the earlier that an organisation can realise the benefits from an investment the better since it will then be able to enjoy the gains which come from having made that investment. The mechanism which is used to measure cash flows at the current date rather than when they may occur at some time in the future is known as discounting. This technique, **discounted cash flow** (DCF), is used to recognise the value of money *now* instead of at some projected future date when an income stream may actually materialise.

Separate projects will inevitably have different finishing dates. DCF provides a means for comparing all these different projects in terms of their value at the present time. Thus, each project can be considered equally at a time which is common to all – the present.

The concept of compound interest is readily understood and means adding interest over a period of time, then adding interest to the sum which has had the interest added originally, and so on. For example:

£1,000 at 10% compound interest over three years is:

$1{,}000 \times 1.10 = 1{,}100$

$1{,}100 \times 1.10 = 1{,}210$

1,210 × 1.10 = 1,331

So the value of £1,000 is £1,331 in three years' time. DCF is really the converse of compound interest in that we say that the value of £1,331 in three years' time is actually £1,000 at present.

Investment describes how we lay out cash now in order to generate future income or benefits. This could be either better services in the case of a public sector organisation or profit-generating activities in the case of a plc. The investment decision seeks to be made based on all projects judged on an equal footing, that is, each compared on the same footing as the other. The way to achieve that is to calculate each project's present value (PV) by using the principles of discounting.

The best way of showing the calculations for the various approaches is to use very basic examples without complex mathematics or concerning ourselves with variables which may alter the final results. Whatever complexities are introduced, the basic method remains the same.

Net present value (NPV)

The formula for calculating **present value** is:

Future value = present value × $(1 + r)^n$

Where r is the relevant rate of interest and n is the number of years into the future. From this we can transpose the equation to get:

Future value × $1/(1 + r)^n$ = present value.

We can illustrate this concept by using the example of a company making an investment of £10,000 in a new machine. It is expected that there will be a net inflow in year 1 of £6,000 and in year 2 also £6,000. Is it worth investing in this machine?

For simplicity we can use an interest rate of 10% and to understand the discounting from these values to get to a net present value, we need to calculate the PV factors as follows (/ represents the division line):

Year 1 $1/(1+0.1)^1$ = 0.9091 that is, 90.91 pence is the value now of £1 in a year's time

Year 2 $1/(1 + 0.1)^2$ = 0.8264 that is, 82.64 pence is the value of £1 in two years' time.

Using these PV factors we can put the cash flows on to a consistent footing, expressing all in their present values (table 13.1):

Table 13.1

Year	Net cash flow	PV factor	Present value
0	−£10,000	1.0000	−£10,000
1	+£6,000	0.9091	+£5,455
2	+£6,000	0.8264	+£4,958
NPV			+£413

The above figure shows the value of the income *now,* bearing in mind that making the investment at the start of year 1 (shown in table 13.1 as year 0) means a cash outflow. The result is positive, indicating that the project to buy a new machine should go ahead. Had the result been negative, then the project should be stopped – the general rule being that a positive NPV means project acceptance while a negative NPV means, basically, think again.

The underlying principle in discounting to arrive at the net present value of a project is that money received in future is worth less than money received today, for the simple reason that we are obliged to forego the interest (at whatever the prevailing rate) on money that we are not going to receive for another one, two, three or four years.

Payback method

The **payback method** considers the length of time that a project will take before the investment is matched by the generation of cumulative positive inflows. In other words, when does the company recoup its initial investment? We can illustrate the concept by using again the figures we used in the NPV example but, this time, we assume that the £6,000 in each year flows in equal amounts of £500 from one month to another between month 1 and month 24.

The payback period is: initial investment/inflow per month.

Thus, £10,000/£500 per month = 20 months.

When comparing projects, the general rule in considering the payback is that a shorter payback period is generally preferable to a longer one. Net gains are achieved more speedily and financial exposure risk is reduced.

Note that payback is usually an easier and quicker method of calculating the likely viability of a project. It is also a very simple concept to grasp. However, it takes no account of the 'time value' of money. The £500 that we receive each month in the example above is given the same value as if we had received it today.

Accounting rate of return (ARR)

The previous two methods were based on cash flows. **Accounting rate of return** is expressed in percentage terms and aims to relate potential profit to the capital investment that has to be made, thereby giving a measure similar to the return on capital employed which was discussed when we looked at financial ratios. ARR, however, looks at a single project in terms of return rather than the whole organisation. The method is a simple calculation based on the average annual profit of the project and the average net book value of the investment at the start of the period and the end of the period, assuming that depreciation (the amount the asset loses in value each year) is done on a straight reducing basis, that is, equal amounts each year. **Net book value** is the value of the investment recorded in the company's accounts.

We can illustrate ARR by continuing to use the figures from the previous examples. The machine cost us £10,000 and was to be written down to nil over two years. The annual depreciation on a straight-line basis would be:

£10,000/2 = £5,000 per annum.

The average investment is calculated by adding the initial net book value (£10,000) and the final net book value (in this case 0) and dividing by the number of years of asset life:

£10,000 + 0/2 = £5,000.

We now need to know what additional sales income is forecast from having the machine, let's say £30,000, and any additional operating costs, let's say £24,000. Additional profit is calculated by subtracting operating costs and depreciation from the forecast income. Thus:

£30,000 – (£24,000 + £5,000) = £1,000.

The ARR of the project based on these figures would be:

£1,000/£5,000 × 100 = 20%.

As with the previous appraisal methods, ARR can be used against several projects and the percentage returns compared. In the above example the return was 20% so that, if the company is currently experiencing less than 20% as its return on capital, then this would be a good project.

There are limitations to this method, notably the assumption of straight-line depreciation, and also because of the way that accounting conventions may be applied in the company. Different accounting approaches could change the way these figures are extracted and used – which costs may be taken in as operating costs, for example, or cost of sales. Nonetheless, this is a good and relatively simple method for measuring profits and therefore value added. The complexities can be made simple by the use of software and this can also be valuable for assistance when there are multiple projects to choose from.

Investment appraisal techniques are designed to assist in making choices between several competing projects. The techniques provide comparative data and can also point to the financial risks which may be involved, for example, negative cash flows, small or nil profit, good or bad asset use. Bear in mind, however, that management judgement also comes into the equation and how well (or badly) potential projects fit with the overall company strategy.

Self-assessment question 13.1

Carry out an investment appraisal on XYZ Company which has the following data for a project:

Initial investment £30,000 for a new widget machine. Forecasted additional sales income £50,000 and operating costs of £40,000. The company uses

(continued on next page)

Self-assessment question 13.1 *(continued)*

the straight-line depreciation method and the machine is to be written down over four years with a residual value of £5,000.

Calculate the ARR for the widget machine and consider the risks which the project may incur.

Feedback on page 211

13.2 Issues in capital projects

Learning activity 13.2

There have been many high-profile projects which have gone wrong in recent years. Do some research into the Millennium Dome, in particular consider reputational issues in the project and any ongoing issues resulting from poor project conception and management.

Feedback on page 211

The defining characteristics of capital projects are the time periods involved and the amounts of finance required. In terms of time, then, a capital project will typically cover several years and certainly more than one. In terms of funding, the amounts involved are usually large and, because of this, the means for obtaining the funds and the treatment in accounting for these funds are markedly different from the short-term, day-to-day operations of any organisation.

A capital project is a major project, therefore, which requires a mix of skill, knowledge and experience to ensure acceptable outcomes. Common to all major projects is the large investment of money, developing and maintaining a competent project team, procuring the necessary equipment and/or assets to carry out the project and – despite deploying investment and project appraisal techniques – the final common factor is a reasonably uncertain outcome.

Large, capital-intensive projects are notorious for not delivering to expectations. The main issues revolve around time – usually missing completion targets, cost – usually over estimate, and finished product – not as initially expected.

Each of these areas tends to overlap into the others. If plans have to be amended as work goes on – a building project, for example, where ground conditions may be different to the original surveys – then design changes may be entailed. This change can mean additional time in solving the new problem, unscheduled costs in building work and, ultimately, a change to the finished building because of the design changes needed to cope with the unforeseen ground works.

All of these are high-risk areas:

- *Additional funding*. Funding required over a longer period than anticipated will affect original payback estimates and affect cash flow over a longer time. Depending on funding method there could also be immediate cash flow problems as a result of increased loan repayments and interest payments.

- *Manpower*. Different skills may be required from those initially forecast if new problems result in new methods of problem solving being required. Additional labour may be required as a result of new workings or to cut time overruns.
- *Reputation*. Client and contractor suffer when projects overrun. Bad publicity is inevitable and, in the case of a listed company, could affect share price and market confidence.
- *Social standing*. The finished construction may not meet public expectations. This has ramifications, not just for reputation but also for corporate social responsibility.

In addition to all of these, the way in which procurement of funds takes place may have impacts on the organisation which could be far reaching. If the project is financed using offshore funds or tax havens then there could be issues of ethical investment to be contended with – obtaining money which could have been raised through money laundering or other doubtful practices. If the investment is to be made into overseas countries then issues of bribery and corruption may have to be defended against in addition to issues such as fair trading and human rights. Projects involving extraction of minerals, changing of landscapes and other more esoteric areas such as animal testing can all bring external issues to bear on project planning and control which increase risk and contribute to the uncertainty of outcomes.

Procurement of money has many of the common problems of the supply chain: sourcing the funds at least cost; getting delivery of funds as and when required and minimising 'overstocking', in this case too much cash lying idle and not working to the benefit of the organisation. Poor cash flow management is a key risk since the correct timing of drawing down funds from a lender to finance ongoing project work can be critical to maintaining positive cash flow and minimising liquidity risks to the client. Source of funds is significant in terms of reputation and CSR.

The choice of projects may have to be made not just on financial grounds but with other drivers in mind. Political and social imperatives may drive public sector organisations regardless of the financial implications, and these operational concerns bring other problems to the management of projects. These could include external interference, frequent changes to specification and attempts to influence project direction.

The already difficult job of effective project management can only be made much worse by these difficult-to-manage interventions.

13

Self-assessment question 13.2

List at least five potential causes of capital project failure and identify a potential solution for each.

Feedback on page 211

13.3 Managing project failures

Learning activity 13.3

Consider what might be meant by the word 'failure'. What mitigating circumstances might there be?

Feedback on page 212

Failure may be construed in different ways. If every objective of a project is not met then, overall, it has failed. Projects such as the Scottish Parliament building may have failed in that completion dates were not met and costs appeared to spiral out of control. Nonetheless, there is a building in place and it is being used for the purpose for which it was constructed. Failures are, therefore, relative.

Projects generally fail because of over-optimism in terms of the time to be taken and the overall cost. They can also fail because there are constraints imposed by external factors such as a public undertaking to be complete by a date announced in the public domain. Often, the budgeted cost figure for a project will be announced ahead of project commencement. Again, this becomes the 'real' figure in people's minds so that any future cost implication is measured against this, perhaps hypothetical, figure. This is frequently the case in the public sector where projects are in competition for public funding and there could be a bidding process for getting funds in a particular financial year.

Projects can fail, also, as a result of management override of project planning. Despite the meticulous planning which may have taken place and the amounts of system-produced data, it can be difficult to resist the dictates of a senior manager who has the authority to make decisions based, perhaps, only on that individual's judgement. Without clear procedures for documenting variations from plan, accountability for this kind of interference may be difficult and constitutes a significant risk.

Project planning software is often based on earlier manual planning methods such as critical path analysis (CPA), network analysis and programme evaluation review technique (PERT). The laborious work and masses of paperwork have been taken out of the process by IT but the principles remain.

A project manager is essential for all projects and a good manager helps to avoid failure. This individual should be nominated and be given the authority to manage the project, reporting at agreed intervals to the board and/or senior management. Management-by-committee usually spells disaster for a project; there needs to be clear and decisive leadership with speedy decision-making processes. The project team may meet as a 'committee' but, in reality, the team should be a group of specialists, chosen for their expertise in a particular field as well as for their personal qualities which can contribute to the group dynamic. A weak project manager or a

13

committee approach to running the project constitute large risks which can only be compounded as the project moves on and any difficulties occur.

A lack of effective monitoring and controlling often contributes to project failure. Progress of project deliverables must be constantly under review. Key points and dates produced by the project planning system should be under frequent surveillance by the project manager. Whereas the whole team may only meet weekly, or even monthly, day-to-day progress must be monitored by the project manager so that any slippage can be quickly addressed. Modules of the package used to plan the project should also be in place to produce analyses and variances. The variances could include cost and cash flow variances, programme work variances and authorised variations to the original project specification and plan. Any problems highlighted by the reports should be addressed and rectified as quickly as possible.

Probably the biggest single cause of delay and extra expense in any project is change, particularly to the scope of work or to the original design or specification. Many small changes may seem insubstantial but, cumulatively, a large number of small changes may have a greater effect than one single large change. Changes will inevitably occur as projects run their course. The secret is to make sure that all changes or variations to specification are authorised, approved by the whole team and fed into the system so that time and cost implications can be seen by the project manager and, where necessary, remedial action taken to keep the project on track

All these areas, although mundane, are significant in avoiding failure. Cost overruns, for instance, are far too important to suddenly find out about when the initial funding has been used up.

Failures also often occur because the procurement function is not involved in the project at an early enough stage. If the company standard approach to procurement includes invitation to tender, tendering, selection, additional negotiation and final contract signing, then this process needs to be put in train at an early stage in a project to ensure that goods and services are delivered as and when required. Even where the process is curtailed, perhaps by pulling from an approved supplier list, sufficient lead time must be built into the project plan. Clearly, procurement professionals need to be closely involved in any project, both proposed and ongoing.

Failures in projects are not hard to find, be they construction projects, IT projects or simply introducing new products.

We have referred already to the Millennium Dome and the Scottish Parliament. The London Stock Exchange spent five years and £300 million on developing a paper-free settlement system. The system did not work effectively and was eventually abandoned.

The Child Support Agency has become notorious for its failures to meet any stakeholder expectations. Much of this was put down to its attempts to introduce a new £450 million computer system. More than half the cases entered into the system were delayed although this was reduced subsequently to about 10%. By 2006, the cost of running the Agency came to more than it had paid out to claimants.

13

Honda attempted to enter the motorcycle market in the USA as far back as the 1960s. The project centred around the bigger cc bikes rather than the small run-abouts. The project failed initially because of lack of market understanding and lack of adequate investment appraisal. Complete failure was only avoided by changing the project plan to include sales of the run-abouts. The dominance of the Honda brand is now history.

Self-assessment question 13.3

You have just taken over control of a capital project that is already late and overspent. What steps will you take to minimise further losses and embarrassment to your organisation?

Feedback on page 212

Revision question

Now try the revision question for this session on page 357.

Summary

This study session has attempted to show why projects can fail and has considered various methods of mitigating risks in projects by using a variety of techniques and methods. We have not over-complicated the issue by relying on a lot of complex calculations and formulae, but the principles have been laid out in as understandable a manner as possible. Where possible, learning by the use of examples has been used to clarify some difficult concepts such as discounted cash flow and other appraisal methods. The availability of software to make project management easier has been discussed but it has been emphasised that it is the management of the project which is important, not the complexity of the IT which is available.

Projects do often fail or, at least, do not reach the potential that had been envisaged at the outset. Some of the reasons for this have been reviewed with common causes such as overoptimism highlighted. Project risks have been discussed and means for mitigation proposed, not least of which is the involvement of the procurement function at an early stage in any project.

Suggested further reading

Association of Project Managers website http://www.apm.org.uk (see their 'body of knowledge').

Department for Work and Pensions. *Change Lifecycle Methodology.* Link from the OGC website http://www.ogc.gov.uk Contract Case Studies.

You could also read the relevant sections of Dyson (2004).

Feedback on learning activities and self-assessment questions

Feedback on learning activity 13.1

You will have found that discounted cash flow underpins the three main appraisal techniques:

- net present value
- payback
- accounting rate of return.

Investopedia shows some excellent definitions together with worked examples of the methodologies, which you will find of great interest. The links on the sites should have pointed you to some of the software packages on offer.

Feedback on self-assessment question 13.1

You should have used the formula in the example to arrive at an answer of

Additional profit divided by average investment = 12.5%

The risks could include that this figure may be less than current returns; external factors may change sales forecasts; residual value of the machine may be incorrect.

Feedback on learning activity 13.2

You will have found that the original plans set visitor targets at 12 million. This target was high and depended on early visitor satisfaction raising awareness and publicising the attraction. In fact, many exhibits were incomplete and others experienced queuing problems. Opening night difficulties with transport affected visitor perception. You should have found many reputational problems and project management difficulties together with doubts as to recouping financial outlays.

Feedback on self-assessment question 13.2

Problems could include:

- Poor planning – project planning and control software, eg Prince, could help this from the outset.
- Cash flows and profit margins not achieved – review sales and expenditure forecasting methods and improve; widen participation in project team to get more in-depth advice on project potential.
- Lack of contingency – anticipate contingencies of time and money and methods of resourcing to ensure 'quick fixes' can be made where appropriate.
- Inadequate financial appraisal – best project not pursued; improve project appraisal techniques and procedures for the future.
- Marketing plan not integrated with project plan – make marketing an integral part of main project plan to ensure realistic forecasts and promotional methods.

13

Feedback on learning activity 13.3

Failure is a relative term. There may be a final outcome from the project but at increased cost and overrun of time. Mitigation could include design changes which result in a better building or a better delivery of service, although at a later date. Changes in funding could result in lower interest charges, albeit incurred over a longer time. Increases in labour numbers or time (overtime) to meet deadlines and save reputation may avoid failure but, again, increase cost.

Feedback on self-assessment question 13.3

The steps you can take could include:

- Immediate termination resulting in curtailment of losses.
- Review of project outcomes and revision of objectives to comply with a lower overall spend.
- Review of contract obligations with contractors – evoke liquidated damages and appoint a new contractor.
- Renegotiate funding arrangements to achieve lower commitment.
- Put PR and media plan in place, if appropriate, to manage release of information and limit possible reputational damage.

Contractual issues and negotiations

Introduction

This session deals with complex matters of contract law but attempts to avoid legal jargon and terminology. Wherever possible, examples of each concept are given. Most contracts are drawn up on the basis that each party wants what the other has to offer and is happy to exchange a consideration, usually of money, to secure this. Contracts are entered into in good faith with the general expectation of a good outcome for all the parties involved. Unfortunately, contracts do sometimes fail to deliver and we try to assess the means by which this can be anticipated and reasonable remedies for non-performance arrived at. Since much of contracting is about negotiation, we also consider the ways in which disputes require negotiation and how this can be done without always resorting to the law.

A written contract with the backing of national and international law is the best way to seal an agreement which provides for both delivery and recompense if delivery fails.

Session learning objectives

After completing this session you should be able to:

14.1 Identify how contracts can fail to deal with specific scenarios.
14.2 Recognise ways to mitigate consequential losses.
14.3 Deal with project failure in a professional manner and obtain appropriate compensation.
14.4 Apply the most appropriate corrective action following failure of the contract.
14.5 Identify alternatives to resorting to the law to resolve disputes.
14.6 Formulate sound and appropriate negotiation strategies.
14.7 Apply strategic approach and negotiation techniques.
14.8 Identify keys steps in negotiation planning for success.

Unit content coverage

This study session covers the following topics from the official CIPS unit content document:

Learning objectives

3.4 Analyse specific key risks and exposures in purchasing and supply and identify appropriate mitigating actions.
   • Contractual failure, consequential loss and provision for remedies
   • Supplier insolvency, monitoring and guarantees
   • Quality failure, non-conformity and corrective action
   • Project failure, project planning principles and corrective action
   • Security of supply, contingency planning, stock holding and alternative sources of supply

14

- Technology failure, impact on supply, use of back-up systems and disaster recovery
- Security, theft and damage
- Fraud, accounting and payment exposures, conflicts of interest, purchasing ethics and codes of conduct
- Product liability, reputational damage, consumer confidence

3.5 Formulate sound and appropriate negotiation strategies to reduce future contract risk and supply chain vulnerability to enhance long-term business value.
- Key steps in negotiation planning for success
- Strategic approach and negotiation techniques
- Good practice methodology
- Tactics and standpoints
- Behaviours of successful negotiators
- Contractual issues and remedies
- Dispute resolution alternatives

Prior knowledge

Study sessions 1 to 13.

Resources

Internet access.

Timing

You should set aside about 7 hours to read and complete this session, including learning activities, self-assessment questions, the suggested further reading (if any) and the revision question.

14.1 Contract failure and remedy

Learning activity 14.1

Read one of your supplier's standard terms and conditions and try to identify areas of risk which you, as customer, are being forced to bear rather than the supplier.

Feedback on page 234

Contracts are generally entered into in good faith and can be evidenced in three main ways:

- in writing using a written agreement between the parties
- orally – on the basis of what was said by the parties
- through behaviour – if the behaviour of the parties indicates that they intended to enter into a contract.

It is very important to understand that, although it is advisable to have a written contract, should anything go wrong there does not have to be a written contract in place or even an oral agreement for a contract to be valid and enforceable in law. If for example you go to an auction and make a bid and yours is the winning bid, you have established a collateral contract with the auctioneer to buy and pay for the lot for which you have bid. There may be nothing that you have signed and you may have said nothing, but you still have a collateral contract with the auction house under which they could sue you for non-payment of the price and you could sue them if they did not have the authority to sell the goods. Similarly if you enter the London Underground and board a train without a valid ticket you are in breach of contract. Your actions demonstrate that you intended to board the train and your failure to pay for a valid ticket puts you in breach of contract with the supplier, London Underground Limited – regardless of the fact that nothing has been signed or said between the parties. As we shall see later, many procurement contracts are in practice established on the basis of behaviour. This in turn creates issues (and risks) about when the contract actually comes into being.

The whole purpose of a contract, whether written or oral, is to formalise an agreement reached by two or more parties with the terms of the agreement being recognised by the contract clauses. The assumption at the outset is that the contract will be honoured, since the contract itself merely articulates the wishes and desires of the parties in whatever endeavour is being embarked upon.

Procurement contracts formalise agreements between suppliers and users and, again, the assumption is that the contracts will be honoured. The client needs the supply in order to continue in business; the supplier wants to deliver since that is how income is achieved. The contract is an agreement or a promise, therefore, that can be enforced or recognised by the law. It creates an obligation on the parties to the contract to deliver the service or product which forms the basis of the contract.

The vast majority of contracts are undertaken without any problems arising. Unfortunately, some contracts will be disputed, some will not be honoured and these possible failures constitute a risk. Thus, there is a risk in all contracts that failure may occur and, like risk management in all areas, we need to assess the probability of failure of a contract and the potential impact this may have on our business.

Basic contract law addresses four main issues:

- When and how is a contract formed?
- When may a party escape the obligations of a contract?
- What is the meaning and effect of contract terms?
- What is the remedy in a case of breach of contract?

Without going deeply into law and legal practice, these main points can be summarised as follows.

There needs to be a contractual offer made and there needs to be acceptance of that offer. Parties to the contract must be competent to understand and enter into the contract and, in this context, a corporation is a legal 'person'

14

and fit to enter into a contract in the same sense as any other competent adult. There must be a consideration, that is, the conferring of money or other benefit, and the contract must have a lawful purpose. There is a presumption that commercial contracts (as opposed to domestic and social) are intended to create a legal relationship between the parties, that is, that procurement contracts will be legally binding, for example. There must be a mutual right to remedy in the event of a contract breach.

We have stated that contracts arise because the initial intention is that all of the contract terms will be fulfilled. That is the intention when an agreement for service or product delivery is made, for example – both parties want a successful outcome. There is little point in going through all the stages of tendering, appraising suppliers and reaching an agreement if there is no real intention for a deal to be made which will benefit all parties.

The use of IT and the impact of the global economy has made the concept of **non-repudiation** important. Using the internet may mean there is no ability to sign or seal a contract and even face-to-face meetings are becoming rarer. Non-repudiation means that a contract, once made, cannot be denied by one of the parties involved. This is particularly important when everything may be done on the web or by email, but remember that behaviour and intention of the parties can be the basis for a valid contract.

Sometimes things go wrong. Unforeseen circumstances may arise which may range from complete catastrophe (for example, bankruptcy of one or other of the parties) to late or below-quality deliveries. The manner in which the contract is written has to cover for as many eventualities as possible.

Contracts may fail for a number of reasons. If it never comes into existence it is considered to be void and will not be recognised at law. A contract based on an illegal purpose, for example, is judged never to have been in existence. If the terms of the contract are incomplete or uncertain, the contract may fail because it is clear that the parties did not, in fact, reach an agreement – a primary purpose for bringing a contract into existence. Despite this, the actions of the parties may create a contract: for example, accepting goods into your warehouse, unpacking them and putting them on the shelves means you will almost certainly have a contract with the supplier and be obliged to pay for them, regardless of the quality of the product or anything else. Again, your behaviour indicates that you intended to enter into a contract with the supplier. There may be an issue over whose terms and conditions apply but the court can decide this for you, where necessary. More commonly, there will be a contract, agreed in good faith, but which then fails because of unique circumstances in one of the parties. A supplier fails to deliver the quantity or quality of the product the client has ordered or a service fails to reach the standard stated in the contract. On the other hand, the client may fail to make payment at the time and in the amount contracted after the supply has been successfully delivered. In these cases we seek redress in the form of forcing the contract terms to be met where this is appropriate, or by the remedy of seeking monetary compensation for breach of contract.

The best remedy is to revert to the contractual terms and somehow get the supply which was promised. That's what the client really wants in order to

14

carry on the business, rather than go through the whole process of getting a new supplier with all the time and cost that will involve. This is termed **specific performance** but, in real terms, it will only work if the supplier is still in business. Also, while specific performance may be desirable from the client's perspective, in practice the courts are reluctant to order specific performance unless the contract is in some way unique, their preferred remedy usually being an award of damages. Similarly, an **injunction** may be sought from the court, which specifically causes a party to refrain from doing something that would breach the contract. There will, of course, be difficulty in seeking either of these remedies when the reason for non-performance is that the party has gone out of business.

Typically, the remedy for breach of contract is an award of money damages. This is assessed by considering what is necessary to put the injured party back to the position enjoyed before the breach occurred. Thus, the additional expense involved in obtaining the service or supply elsewhere (although not necessarily any additional cost in suffering a new, higher supply price), together with recompense for the inconvenience caused and cost of legal action, will typically represent the award made. Consequential damages may also be awarded. These recognise loss of product and consequent loss of profit or revenue.

Despite the monetary compensation of damages, supply chain failures are an additional burden to bear. Interruption of operations, additional administration and the cost of renegotiating supply all contribute to an extra overhead which all organisations want to avoid. If supplier appraisal methods (as laid out in an earlier study session) are applied robustly then this will minimise the risk of the supplier defaulting on the contract. If our appraisals are sufficiently effective, we will have reviewed the financial soundness of a potential supplier and have a higher confidence level of avoiding the possibility of contract failure.

Assessment of probability of contract default and the impact this may have is an essential link in the management of risk in the supply chain. Contract terms must reflect the importance of agreed deliverables and, in addition, provide for a reasonable remedy when things do not go as originally planned.

14

Self-assessment question 14.1

Give details and examples of four situations where contract clauses can fail to protect the buyer.

Feedback on page 234

14.2 Mitigating consequential losses

All risk management activity is geared towards identifying and evaluating the unwanted or unexpected events which may stop us achieving our objectives. The impact of potential risks is what we measure when, having identified the risk, we consider the probability of it ever arising and the consequences which may follow if the risk comes to pass.

Consequential loss or damage is the *indirect* loss or damage which has occurred from an event. For example, if a severe gale causes damage to our premises, then our insurance cover will provide recompense for the property damage directly caused by the gale. However, a tree may have been blown over and smashed our roof. If the damage caused by the tree also included a break in electricity supply – internal or external supply cable damage, perhaps – which resulted in loss of the contents of a freezer, then the consequential loss is represented by the value of the freezer contents.

Learning activity 14.2

Select one business hazard for your organisation. Try to identify what would be the consequential losses that would result from that hazard occurring.

Feedback on page 234

Strategies for dealing with risks formed part of our early study into risk management and adopting the right strategy for a particular risk area is a critical part of our mitigation, that is, minimising the effect of any risk event should it actually happen.

Some risks may have the potential to put us out of business, others scale down to those which are merely a nuisance – a brief period of lost production, for example. The risks which have the highest probability and may have the highest impact are going to be the ones which we want to put a lot of management effort into. Earlier study sessions have looked exhaustively at strategic approaches and some of the means to minimise the effects when a risk does actually arise. One of those mitigation strategies was to share or transfer risks to another party. In the case of consequential loss, we may have exhausted all our risk management approaches and still be left with a significant residual risk. One of the only ways to handle this risk could be to consider insuring against the potential loss.

The word **liability** implies legal responsibility and liability insurance may be the last line of defence against devastating claims for things over which you have little or no control. If a hazard is knowingly permitted to exist then there is a potential for negligence – you knew it was there but you did nothing (or not enough) about it. However, you may still be held liable for something about which you were not aware and where you have not been negligent or where a genuine accident has occurred. Nonetheless, some hazards can be identified in the workplace and its environs and action taken to remove the hazard or, at least, minimise potential impacts. Again we should revert to earlier study sessions to review the texts on CRSA and HAZOP, for example, and on other mitigating and managing methods and actions. Many techniques can assist in identifying hazards and reducing the potential for consequential losses. However, there is likely to be little option but to use insurance to deal with the residual risk of possible negligence claims.

General or public liability insurance will cover or help to cover payments required to be made under third-party claims for personal injury or property damage. The cover will usually extend to legal expenses incurred in defending against claims and for medical expenses accruing to the underlying incident. The cover comes normally with exclusions and limitations, the monetary value of which can still be a considerable risk to the organisation – hence the need for robust risk management to minimise residual risk.

For manufacturing businesses and those engaged in selling services, product liability insurance can mitigate potential losses for claims relating to poor service delivery, quality of product or breach of relevant regulations. For doctors, accountants and other professionals, this is often termed malpractice insurance or professional indemnity. Business interruption insurance extends consequential loss or damage coverage for such items as extra expenses, additional rentals, reduction of profit and similar items associated with an unexpected break in business activity. All of the foregoing insurances can be used in mitigation of consequential loss and other risks.

Compensation for workers who may be injured at work now or become ill at some time in the future, as a result of the work they did, is covered in the UK under law. The Employers' Liability (Compulsory Insurance) Act of 1969 is the original legislation and requires employers to have at least a minimum level of insurance cover to meet potential claims of this nature. Employers' liability insurance enables organisations to meet the cost of claims for compensation from employees. Current claims in this category could be large and future claims indeterminate, so that sharing this risk is the only mitigating action that can reasonably be taken. However, because of the numbers of this type of claim and the size of their settlement, cover is becoming increasingly expensive and more difficult to find.

We have looked at human resources risks in earlier study sessions but, because of the consequences which claims under employer's liability may have, it is wise to be sure that the review of risks in this area is robust and is up to date. Minimising the potential for some of the risks to occur means taking avoiding action now and this could include:

- environment issues such as air quality and pollution
- ergonomic issues such as effective training to avoid RSI and other similar occupational health issues
- policy on bullying and stress management
- research on the reasons for absenteeism and addressing some of the underlying causes
- firm application of health and safety regulations and industry-specific safety rules.

Consideration of consequential losses has led us into the risk management strategy of *sharing*. While we can still take many actions to mitigate the possibility of consequential loss, in the main we seek to cover our residual risks by using insurance of different classes, although it may be possible to use 'umbrella insurance', an all-inclusive liability cover that can cover liabilities exceeding the basic policy limits at a reasonable cost. Insurance premiums are a major expense item, however, and we need to be certain that all other risk management tasks are implemented with rigour as a contribution to reducing this cost as much as possible.

14

Self-assessment question 14.2

Give details of some clauses covering consequential losses that might be acceptable in an English court of law.

Feedback on page 235

14.3 Compensation for project failure

Contracts are drawn up, agreed and signed in good faith and in the expectation that the main purpose of the contract will be fulfilled. Experience, however, tells us that there can be difficulties in performing the contract, perhaps in meeting time targets, correct quality of product or in price variation. One of the ways in which we can anticipate possible problems and build in compensation to the contract is to have a **liquidated damages** clause.

Liquidated damages is a term used in the law of contracts to describe a contractual term which establishes damages to be paid to one party if the other party should breach the contract. In order for a liquidated damages clause to be upheld, two conditions need to be met. First, the amount of damages identified must be approximate to the damages likely to fall upon the party seeking the benefit of the clause and, second, the damages must be sufficiently uncertain at the time the contract is made that such a clause will likely save both parties the future difficulty of estimating damages.

A liquidated damages clause may seem to anticipate failure before the contract even comes into force. In fact, liquidated damages are merely a means for ensuring compensation without the need necessarily to argue a specific breach – it is a confidence-building mechanism which can establish a 'comfort level' for the contracting party in terms of minimising potential loss. The clause is not designed to be a punitive sanction or penalty. Indeed, the clause will not be enforced at law if the purpose of the clause is solely to punish a breach of contract (this would make it a **penalty** clause).

Payment for non-performance, where this type of clause is in the contract and specified by value, will be awarded to the aggrieved party irrespective of the actual loss incurred and, in this respect, is similar to liquidated damages. However, the specified amount may be reduced by a court on petition where it is deemed to be grossly excessive in relation to the loss resulting from the non-performance.

Liquidated damages are a common clause in many contracts and provide a hedge against failure to perform as well as building in monetary compensation should that failure actually occur. As we have seen earlier, breach of contract will bring the ability to sue for damages, although the general provision is that the sum eventually paid out should only put the aggrieved party back to the position he would have been in if the contract had been duly performed. The damages will cover the loss which he has suffered and the gain of which he has been deprived.

14

Learning activity 14.3

Review the subject of liquidated damages and penalties in any commercial law book, but preferably on the internet, and make notes on when they may be able to be used and what the impact would be on supplier relationships.

Feedback on page 235

The project may fail if the contract is terminated. If this were to occur then the customer may recover money paid for goods or services which he did not receive or which he properly rejected. While this brings possible monetary compensation, it still leaves the problem of seeking alternative arrangements with all the frustrations of delay and additional cost that this may bring.

Terminations may occur for a number of reasons, several of which may be contained in the contract clauses and have to be given by notice to the other party. It could be, however, that non-performance is fundamental to the project covered by the contract so that if, for example, the non-performance is a delay of a significant amount which prejudices the completion of the contract, then termination would be appropriate. A termination may also occur if an impediment arises which is beyond the control of the performing party and is not just a temporary situation. The impediment must be notified in writing with clear and concise reasons given. The excuse of an impediment may have to be tested in law if the two parties do not agree that it forms a reasonable reason for terminating the contract. Again, the aggrieved party can seek compensatory damages to the extent that costs have been incurred or profits foregone.

Contract law is generally for the protection of all the parties involved although it is a broad framework which leaves the parties concerned free to agree whatever they want, subject, of course, to overriding statutory requirements such as the Sale of Goods Act and the Unfair Contract Terms Act. The law will not provide protection, for example, against what may essentially be a poorly drawn-up contract. Contract clauses in procurement may often follow a standard format – standard terms and conditions being the terms normally applied to most of your contracts – although for specific purchases, specific terms and conditions may be required. The intention is for the parties to agree a supply and be satisfied, on the one hand with the delivery and quality of that supply and, on the other, with the monetary value gained. Generally speaking, all goes well. The binding nature of a contract is such, however, that it is designed to cope when things do not go well. Under these circumstances, it is essential that compensation for failure can be obtained and that, as far as possible, the compensation places the parties back on an even footing.

Some contracts are signed under what is called **heads of agreement**. This allows the details of the contract to be negotiated and agreed as matters progress under the general headings which form the contract. Care must be taken in these cases to avoid failures as a result of the original headings being either no longer appropriate or too vague in the first place.

14

Projects not subject to full contractual agreement may still have implied terms which can be tested in law. Letters of agreement, for example, can form the basis of a binding arrangement just as an oral contract can have the same effect as a written contract. Implied terms (as opposed to *express* terms – terms actually explicit in the contract) are important in relation to whether a statement made is a promise. Only if a promise is made can a party sue for breach of contract in the event the promise is not fulfilled. The nature of promises made is critical, therefore, whether the contract is oral, in the form of a letter or in a proper contract document.

If a contract is entered into in the right spirit by all the parties – for the purposes of a project, supply arrangement or any other legitimate purpose – failure should not be the first consideration. It makes sense, however, to anticipate the causes and effects of potential failures in good risk management terms. Appropriate contract clauses help to mitigate the consequences of failure and avoid the worst effects of a contractual dispute.

Self-assessment question 14.3

Frank has set up in business as a developer of games software. He has shown an aptitude for computers since he was 8 years old and has just begun selling his games from home at age 15. Frank needs a supply of IT equipment to help with his design and production and contracts with ABC Computers using email and web facilities only to make the supply. His father advises him that, in his view, all IT companies are liable to go out of business overnight and advises Frank to write a liquidated damages clause into the contract.

What is your opinion of the contract and its damages clause?

Feedback on page 235

14.4 Corrective action following contract failure

Learning activity 14.4

Assess the benefits and disadvantages of having a written contract.

Feedback on page 235

The reason for making a written contract between parties is to give a basis for agreement and as a reference point for any subsequent disagreement as the agreed terms have been expressly recorded. Although remedies for failure are part and parcel of the contract, the expectation at the outset is that the contract will succeed. Nonetheless, there are many reasons why the contract may not be fulfilled, despite initial optimism.

Circumstances may change beyond all recognition. Companies do not expect to go out of business or be bankrupted but this could occur between

14

signing a contract and the first delivery of product or service becoming due. The supplier may run into difficulty further along the supply chain with his own deliveries which may make manufacture or onward supply difficult or impossible. Strikes or other labour relations failures may cause delivery delays and, of course, catastrophic physical events such as an earthquake may interrupt utilities. War or political instability may affect commodity price and delivery.

We dealt in section 14.3 with contractual remedies for compensation in the event of a contract failure. Now we need to consider the actions that need to be taken when a contract fails, both in terms of seeking compensation, but more importantly, perhaps, ensuring continuity of the business.

Our own business may depend upon the delivery of the service or supply which will not now be delivered as expected. First, we need to be sure that we have conformed with our side of the contract terms up to that point, for instance, making payments on time, if appropriate. Second, we need to simultaneously take action to:

- secure a new supply
- start the compensation procedure.

Initially, we can seek to force the remedy of *specific performance* referred to earlier, but this may be impossible if the supplier has ceased operating. If the client wishes to consider the contract void or terminated, then written notice must be given. This should be attempted by using registered mail or equivalent (even although it is obvious that the supplier is defunct) in order to make any subsequent court action clear of any doubt that a reasonable attempt had been made to contact the supplier. It must be quite clear that the original supplier is unable, or cannot, or will not complete the contract before the client begins to take the actions necessary to keep his business going. Not to do so raises the risk of counterclaim by the supplier when further actions by him are refused.

The main concern for the client is to secure a new supply. Preparedness for this eventuality is part of the fundamental approach to risk management: is there a probability of a supplier ceasing to function? Mitigation of this risk will include having a portfolio of alternative suppliers drawn up ready to contact. This could also include a preferred supplier list which contains suppliers already 'qualified' by your own procedures. From this list a selection of a new supplier can be made who, although not the original successful supplier, is ready – at least to be approached – for a speedy alternative supply. Alternatively, an entirely new process must be commenced and, since the whole process is time-consuming, it should be started upon as soon as possible.

Supplier failure means you are in difficulties in terms of meeting your own customers' needs. Since speed is of the essence you should consider temporary or short-term contracts as a means for securing supply quickly while retaining the ability to think again once the temporary problem has been solved. In this respect, bear in mind the *heads of agreement* contract mentioned earlier which allows speedy exchange of contracts with the ability to negotiate detail later.

14

Continuity in your business by securing quick replacement suppliers may be your first priority. Equally important is getting procedures under way to seek compensation for non-performance of the original contract. In this respect, the essential priority is getting legal advice and then pursuing the various remedies which are available to you. Legal proceedings take time to initiate and can be a lengthy process when started. If the opportunity arises, any offer to negotiate financial settlement from the defaulter should be given consideration. Given the time and uncertainty of any damages claim outcome, it is often a better option to take a potentially smaller figure which is capable of earning interest for us rather than waiting it out for a doubtful future benefit.

Self-assessment question 14.4

Your organisation has lost a lot of money as a result of a supplier invoking a force majeure clause. Detail what actions you will take to avoid a recurrence.

Feedback on page 236

14.5 Alternative approaches to settling disputes

Disputes may be settled by going to law and many of the problems and remedies which we have considered up to now in terms of projects and contracts have concentrated on this legal approach. Going to law has drawbacks. Litigation can be lengthy, key personnel may be tied up over long periods of time and outcomes are not guaranteed. Also it is *public*. Anyone can go and sit in court and report on proceedings – as journalists do. So if you want your business troubles aired in the mass-audience tabloid press, having your day in court will be money well spent. Most people, however, don't want this. Inevitably also, by going to law, there will be a breakdown in relationships between buyers and sellers. There are other methods available, however, for settling disputes which might have occurred in supply chain contracts and we refer to these as alternative dispute resolution techniques (ADR).

Arbitration is a dispute resolution process where the opposing parties select or appoint an individual called an arbitrator. The arbitrator will arrange to hear and consider evidence and review arguments and will bring the two parties to a point where the arbitrator proposes an award. When the award is decided and agreed upon, the parties will honour this position. Arbitration clauses may already be in contracts, but often the agreement to go to arbitration will be voluntary on the part of both parties and outwith any contractual clauses.

The key to arbitration is the agreement of the parties concerned to use the process (it cannot be used if only one party agrees but the other refuses to cooperate) and the appointment of an acceptable, independent arbitrator. There may well be a relatively lengthy process involved but it is more than likely that setting up the arbitration, undertaking the process and agreeing the awards will be of far less duration than going to court. The very fact that arbitration is outside legal proceedings has the added benefit of making it possible that relationships between the parties can be maintained or, perhaps, repaired where breakdowns have occurred. A further benefit is likely to be a saving in legal costs, although there will be a cost for the services of the arbitrator.

Another ADR process in which the parties freely choose to participate is **mediation**. Mediation is done solely by the parties concerned, without any outside interference. A mediator is selected by mutual agreement and will be responsible for making sure the process runs smoothly. The mediator makes no decisions but, instead, acts as a facilitator in making the parties understand the dispute and the issues, oversees constructive discussion and helps the parties reach an agreement. The costs of mediation are generally agreed in advance, as are the contributions which each party will make to those costs. If the parties involved in a mediation process fail to reach agreement, they are free to follow other options but, again, mediation gives the opportunity for relationships to be preserved, given some goodwill from all sides.

The last ADR to be considered in this section is **conciliation**. Similar to mediation, conciliation involves the appointment of a conciliator whose principal role is again as a facilitator, but in this case the conciliator acts only as a guide for the parties to achieve a settlement, based only on his recommendations. Usually the parties will agree in advance whether they will be bound by the conciliator's recommendations and the initial agreement will also be firm on the sharing of costs.

Learning activity 14.5

Research the internet for any bodies or organisations which provide out-of-court advice using a model such as the Arbitration, Conciliation and Advisory Service (ACAS) for employment disputes. Consider how some issues such as product quality could be resolved without resort to law.

Feedback on page 236

14

There is much to be gained from settling disputes using ADR, including the fact that they are all *private* – unlike litigation. Indeed, ACAS was born from disputes between employers, employees and unions when strike action was almost endemic in the UK and opinions seemed to be polarised. Significant recent advances in this area include the Employment Act 2002 (Dispute Resolution) Regulations which came into force in the UK in 2004.

ACAS states that it hopes to reach an acceptable solution to any dispute or disagreement at work without having to go to court or to an employment tribunal. This aspiration neatly encapsulates ADR: avoid going to law, keep relationships intact and work to achieve an agreed settlement.

Other avenues for ADR do exist: regulating bodies for particular industries such as water and electricity, for example, and ombudsmen, whose role is to look at complaints about public and private organisations. Usually, ombudsmen provide a route for a final appeal to be made after all other complaint avenues have been exhausted. They are free to use, do not take sides and make decisions which are not binding so that recourse to a court of law is still possible after the ombudsman ruling. Ombudsmen look at decisions which have been made and consider whether or not there has been maladministration. They do not consider whether the decision itself was right.

Self-assessment question 14.5

Draft a short report to your purchasing manager detailing some areas which you consider should be standard purchasing department procedures as a result of your research into alternative dispute resolution.

Feedback on page 236

14.6 Appropriate negotiation strategies

Negotiating is a part of normal supply chain activity. Negotiation is also a tried and tested ADR. Negotiation becomes *mediation* when a facilitator becomes involved and the facilitator's role is to keep the parties talking and bargaining. The facilitator keeps a record of each party's position and prepares a memorandum of agreement containing all the points which, after discussion, have been agreed by all parties. Negotiation and, indeed using facilitators, can result in settlements which avoid resorting to law. This has the benefits of (1) avoiding the risk of a costly and lengthy court action, and (2) avoiding the risk of irretrievable breakdown in relationships between buyers and sellers. Risks remain, however. Negotiation may fail so that nothing has been gained by attempting ADR rather than going directly to law. Poor outcomes from negotiation may affect reputation – both the personal reputations of the key negotiators and the reputation of the companies concerned – and mitigating these risks can be difficult once the outcome is in the public domain.

14.7 Strategic approach and negotiation techniques

Learning activity 14.6

Review the project life cycle and consider with whom we may need to negotiate at each stage to get the best final outcome.

Feedback on page 236

Negotiation depends on the approach which is taken and the two common standpoints are:

- win–lose
- win–win.

There may also be some integration of both extremes.

With the win–lose approach, one party to the negotiation wins at the expense of the loser. In essence, there are fixed resources to be divided up so that, of these resources, the more one party gets, the less is available for the other. Often, in this kind of bargaining, one party's interest opposes the other and the dominant concern is to maximise one's own interest. Strategies employed by the dominant party will include manipulation, force and withholding of important information.

In the win–win situation there is a variable amount of resources to be divided up and both sides can win equal amounts, should they so wish, or at least gain enough to be satisfied. The dominant concern is to maximise joint outcomes by using cooperative strategies, information sharing and mutual problem solving. The perception of each should be that they are happy with the outcome.

Successful negotiations seek to lean towards the win–win situation as otherwise losers will be disgruntled and dissatisfied. Whatever the agreement made, it will rankle with the loser and he will wish to return another day – sooner rather than later. There is doubt, therefore, over the efficacy of this strategy as a long- or even medium-term solution.

In procurement we often see elements of both approaches. In negotiating prices, for example, your supplier wants as high a price as possible whereas, as the buyer, you want as low a price as possible, taking account, of course, of all the other factors involved in the deal. To some degree, however, the interests of buyer and seller coincide; each wants a successful deal where both go away satisfied. Integrative bargaining (an alternative term for win–win) has the following characteristics:

- positive attitude on entering negotiations
- plan ahead – establish your own key points
- have options to hand which can lead to mutual gain
- separate the people concerned from the problem – forget the personalities
- focus on mutual interest rather than on positions
- be prepared to allow the negotiation to flow – allow participation
- be an active listener
- communicate effectively.

There are constant trade-offs in negotiations. We can start by identifying best and worst possible outcomes and gradually move our position towards the middle ground by making a series of incremental changes. We can also identify those areas which are of lesser importance to us but are greater to the other party. These can be used as 'concessions', although, in fact, we are conceding little, since these are of small value to us. In monetary terms, it is good practice to try and establish early on in the negotiation what the 'spread' might be, that is, your own lowest (or highest) figure and the same for the other party. With this knowledge you can begin the incremental changes previously referred to – appearing to make concessions but, in fact, moving closer to the figure you had in mind at the outset.

Win–lose begins from the position that you care little for the other party's needs or interests and the negotiations are based on you winning regardless of all else. Openness is not the character of this type of negotiation. Typically, information is jealously guarded, misinformation is common and manipulation is used at every step. The other party may still leave the negotiation with something rather than nothing, usually because you have

14

ensured that their expectations are so low that any upward improvement on that is seen as a bonus.

A previous study session dealt with ethics. In this context, is it ethical to negotiate using concealment, lies and misinformation? This is a personal question which affects everyone who takes part in negotiations. Our personal values, determined by the culture we live in and the way we conduct business, influence our ethical approach. A sound ethical approach is fundamental to the advances which are being made to achieve better corporate governance. It follows, therefore, that negotiators should be guided by a code, based on the company's ethical code but formatted to cover the behaviour which the company expects from those it entrusts with negotiating on its behalf.

Negotiations between companies and individuals from different countries and cultures pose particular problems. It may be necessary to use a 'go-between' or facilitator familiar with the situation on the ground and it may be necessary, also, to use a mix of approaches which combine your cultural approach and theirs.

Using negotiation and mediation as ADR techniques in contract disputes can lead to establishing better relationships through good communication and face-to-face meetings; a human face is put on things. By contrast, court proceedings are stiff and formal and do not allow for interaction between parties. There is little scope for retrieving relationships which have been soured by protracted legal action which, inevitably, will result in one winner and one loser.

Self-assessment question 14.6

Most negotiators have a preferred style of negotiation. Some are collaborative; some are adversarial. What are the risks in each style of negotiation? What can be done to manage or minimise these risks?

Feedback on page 237

14

14.8 Key steps in negotiation planning for success (good practice methodology including tactics and standpoints)

An effective team should always identify its objectives, expectations and alternatives while preparing the negotiation. In all cases, objectives, expectations and alternatives should be identified beforehand. The following eight steps represent good practice in terms of planning for a successful contract negotiation:

Step 1

Identify your client organisation objectives, expectations and alternatives to help manage risk:

- develop objectives, etc for all aspects of the contract
- focus on the least acceptable alternative and the most desirable outcome for each aspect

- identify potential negotiation positions that will facilitate achieving the most desirable outcome.

Step 2

Identify each contractor(s)/supplier(s) key business drivers, least acceptable alternative and most desirable outcome and benefits that will result from addressing them. This will help reduce vulnerability. Examples might include:

- contractor/supplier needs this contract to absorb excess capacity = more aggressive pricing
- demand for contractor/supplier services is growing (profit potential increasing) = secure resources to meet our needs while offering supplier competitive margins
- contractor/supplier may be seeking multi-year contracts = better pricing and supply assurance
- contractor/ supplier market is increasingly competitive = lower cost, better service, etc.

Step 3

Identify each of the contractors(s)/supplier(s) representatives involved in the negotiations to help manage risk:

- who are they?
- what prior dealings have you had with them ?
- what are their experiences?
- what role are they playing in the negotiation?
- what is their personal stake in the negotiation?
- how will the outcome of the negotiation impact them?
- what are their authority levels?

Step 4

Identify your strengths (and weaknesses) and plan on how to take advantage of (compensate for) them during the negotiation. This will better position you in terms of reducing vulnerability. Examples might include:

- this is first of many similar projects in your business plan = promise of long-term contract or relationship
- competitors are anxious to break into this market = threat to take business elsewhere
- market is very tight and supply constrained (contractor(s)/supplier(s) market) = your willingness to commit to a long-term agreement.

Step 5

Identify lists of issues that you might expect the contractor/supplier to raise during the negotiation and prepare to deal with them. This will better position you in terms of leverage and reducing vulnerability. Examples might include:

- use of incentives
- escalation terms

14

- performance metrics
- terms and conditions.

Step 6

Identify the key messages(s) that we want to deliver based on analysis of information from previous steps. This will better position you in terms of leverage and reducing vulnerability. Examples might include:

- the competition is very aggressive in seeking this contract
- we are looking for a long-term relationship that looks beyond current short-term market conditions
- we are not satisfied with the technical (or commercial) quality of your proposal.

Step 7

Establish and organise your negotiating team (plus roles and responsibilities) to help manage risk:

- considering the information developed, identify the experts needed to support the negotiations
- determine roles and responsibilities in preparing for and conducting the negotiations
- identify spokesperson for each aspect of the planned negotiation
- establish procedures and protocols for calling conference breaks, seeking clarification, etc among team members
- practice by role playing using different tactics for each side to better anticipate issues and outcomes.

Step 8

Develop a detailed strategy that properly considers all of the information developed and takes advantage of the strengths of the negotiating team. Recognise that this strategy may vary with each of the contractor(s)/ supplier(s) involved but ultimately will add value in terms of the risk management process and reducing overall vulnerability in a negotiation.

Learning activity 14.7

Review the structure of a typical negotiation and identify the steps that should be followed to ensure a satisfactory outcome for you in terms of reducing contract risk and vulnerability for your organisation should you conclude a contract with the party you are negotiating with.

Feedback on page 237

Gaining control through negotiating techniques to reduce risk and vulnerability is important. Consider table 14.1:

Table 14.1 Negotiating tactics, techniques and behavioural characteristics

Tactic	Techniques
Keep discussions unemotional	Provide only necessary information when required Show little emotion as points are made Avoid surprises
Make orderly concessions	Create 'hierarchy' of concessions, from wants to needs Make concessions slowly Match concessions to those of other party
Legitimise your position	Establish credibility with the other party through: • Size of company/order • Historical precedent • Desire for long-term relationship Show less confidence in legitimacy of other party
Stress unmet needs	Stress areas of unmet needs in supplier offer: • Product's deficiencies • High price • Delivery problems Create impression of unsatisfactory supplier response
Use competitive leverage	Enter negotiations with alternatives: • Other suppliers • Make internally • Alternative product Create demand through perception of enhanced value
Encourage supplier investment of time	Allow supplier to invest significant time in the process: • Preparation of information • Multiple bargaining cycles • Discussions before session • Ensure supplier vulnerability to loss • Encourage long-term relationship
Ensure commitment of team	Ensure understanding of and commitment to goals by all team members. • Project unified position to supplier
Achieve mutual identification	Determine real needs of other party rather than wants • Show understanding of and empathy with needs • Incorporate other party's ideas into discussion • Transform two separate goals into one mutual goal • Form basis for long-term relationship
Show expertise	Present image of confident, self-assured team through understanding of: • Information • Issues • Products and applications

The behaviours of successful negotiators

Research has consistently shown that certain behavioural characteristics are
exhibited by successful negotiators in the field of supply chain management

across all sectors of industry. Salient characteristics of successful negotiators are that they:

1   Consider a wide range of outcomes or options for action, especially options that might be raised by the other party.
2   Give significant attention to areas of common ground.
3   Pay attention to the long-term implications of issues.
4   Plan their objectives in terms of upper and lower limits.
5   Identify major issues and plan for each one separately.
6   Learn all they can about the other party: their needs, current business results, expectations, style, past practices, trustworthiness, deadlines, constituencies they must please, and decision-making authorities.
7   Try to clear up or diffuse any rumours or misinformation, or resentment left over from the past.
8   Are careful to avoid provoking, and being provoked by, the other party and getting caught up in a 'defend/attack' spiral.
9   Avoid using words and phrases that have negligible negotiation value but cause irritation with the other side (ie generous, fair or reasonable offer).
10 Are able to articulate a vision or image of an ideal outcome to the negotiation in a way that attracts or 'pulls' the other party in his or her direction.
11 Recognise that negotiators who expect more, and who ask for more, settle at higher levels than those who have lower aspiration levels and make more modest opening demands.
12 Are not afraid to say they are unprepared to discuss a certain issue or reach a conclusion.
13 Are less apt to make a unilateral concession early in a negotiation.
14 Do not respond immediately to another party's proposal with a counter-proposal. Immediate counter-proposals are perceived as blocking or disagreeing by the other party, rather than as proposals.
15 State their position clearly, directly, and succinctly, and are willing to repeat it until they sense that the other party has heard and takes it seriously.
16 Avoid 'argument dilution'; that is, they stick to their two or three strongest points.
17 First give the reasons or explanation for their disagreement, and then state that they disagree.
18 'Test understanding' and 'summarise' more frequently than average negotiators.
19 Reflect back on what the other person has said to obtain a further response.
20 Ask significantly more questions than average negotiators.
21 More frequently disclose both proprietary data and information about their underlying needs. This is apparently done to increase the trust level so that the other party will disclose similar information.
22 Avoid large or unilateral concessions near the end of a negotiation to meet a deadline or avoid a deadlock.
23 Check out any ambiguities, possible misunderstandings, or reluctance to close before the end of the negotiation rather than leaving them as potential hazards during implementation.
24 Take frequent breaks and caucuses to confer with associates, review the other party's proposals, and/or to formulate their own position.

14

25 Ask for something in return when they make concessions.
26 Take steps to avoid being placed under deadline pressure.
27 Set aside review time after the negotiation to capture lessons learned and identify best practices.
28 Avoid emotional or value-loaded behaviour.
29 Attack hard and without warning. Attacks that build up gradually allow the other party to build up their defences, leading to an 'attack/defend spiral'.
30 Are more likely to give information about their feelings or motives than average negotiators.

Self-assessment question 14.7

Consider a negotiating theme of 'We must stop our relationship unless you can be more competitive'.

What messages would you deliver in terms of situation, method, qualifications and benefits?

Feedback on page 238

Revision question

Now try the revision question for this session on page 357.

Summary

The topics covered in this study session have been wide ranging. We have looked at the use of contracts in procurement and considered where contractual arrangements can fail. The various losses which may result from failure require to be handled in particular ways and we have reviewed the means by which redress can be obtained. The importance of contract clauses as a basis for carrying out the contract and of protection when things go wrong has been stressed. When things do go wrong, there has to be a way of trying to regain as much as possible of the position we were in before the problem occurred. In this respect, we have considered the protection and redress given by the courts and alternative means of resolving disputes. The importance of understanding how relationships may be maintained has been illustrated by discussing the use of negotiating techniques.

Suggested further reading

Department of Trade and Industry. *Resolving Disputes – a new approach in the workplace.* Department of Trade and Industry: http://www.dti.gov.uk.

Department of Trade and Industry. *Standard Terms of Contract* Department of Trade and Industry: http://www.dti.gov.uk/about/procurement/.

14

Feedback on learning activities and self-assessment questions

Feedback on learning activity 14.1

You should compare your supplier organisation's approach with an industry benchmark or the standard terms which can be found for the Department of Trade and Industry at http://www.dti.gov.uk/about/procurement. Standard terms cover some of these points:

- definitions and interpretations
- service of notice and communication
- waiver
- severability
- confidentiality
- invoices and payments
- provision of service/supply
- indemnities and insurance
- law and jurisdiction.

Key issues might include payment terms, transfer of ownership and liability, termination rights, issues surrounding warranty, and so on. You will find that the supplier's terms and conditions are written so as to favour the supplier if anything goes wrong.

Feedback on self-assessment question 14.1

Your answer could have included:

- The other party is unfit to make a contract – either they are not legally competent, eg an ultra vires act by a company, or they do not have the appropriate authority, eg an agent seeking to enter a contract for which he was not authorised by his principal.
- The contract is voidable – one of the parties has the option to terminate the contract and has done so legally.
- An unenforceable term in the contract – eg if a term of the contract conflicts with a statutory provision then the statute will take priority and the term of the contract will be unenforceable.
- One of the parties is bankrupt – criminal proceedings may be brought but remedies under the contract cannot be enforced fully and will be subject to the bankruptcy.
- The contract is void – if it is deemed to be concerning an illegal purpose it is considered not to have existed at all and hence no enforceable rights have been created.

Feedback on learning activity 14.2

Your answer will depend on your organisation and the economic sector in which you operate. For an example, we can use a chemical processing plant. Explosion could be a specific hazard and consequential losses might include:

- total loss of power affecting all production and operations
- damage to buildings off-site owned by third parties
- injury to third parties off-site

- pollution and other environmental damage beyond the plant boundaries
- litigation arising from any breaches of industry regulations or wider legislation.

Feedback on self-assessment question 14.2

A force majeure or act of God clause protects the contracting party against events such as wars, earthquakes and so on which may make a contract impossible to deliver.

A clause could also be included requiring the other party to put their own insurance in place to cover possible consequential losses on the client's part.

Also acceptable would be a liquidated damages clause by which the contracting parties agree a sum of damages that will accurately reflect the loss that they will suffer in the event of specified breaches of the contract. It is important that the agreed sum is a genuine pre-estimate of loss and does not constitute a penalty clause, which would be illegal.

Feedback on learning activity 14.3

You could have found Principles of European Contract Law at http://www.lexmercatoria.org and other contract data at Contracts Case Summaries http://www.4lawschool.com/contracts.htm. Parties to contracts may choose to have their contract governed by the 1998 Principles of European Contract Law but, nonetheless, should allow for the effect of national, international and supra-national laws. Agreement by the parties as to which country's law is to apply to the contract is essential.

You would have found that liquidated damages are designed to compensate but not be an express sanction and that other remedies for non-performance and contract failure include terminating the contract and seeking damages.

Invoking any of these processes means that any relationship with a supplier is going to be subject to change. Previous good relations are bound to sour when penalties are sought and actions at law commence. Future negotiations may be too difficult to contemplate and there may be complete termination of any existing relationship.

Feedback on self-assessment question 14.3

Your answer should have pointed out that the contract would be void because Frank is below legal age – using electronic procurement facilities means that neither party may be aware of age as a constraint. The nature of the business might have suggested a non-performance clause rather than liquidated damages – the contract being void, however, this clause could not be invoked.

Feedback on learning activity 14.4

Contracts, both written and oral, make any agreement binding on the parties involved. The major benefit of a written contract is that the terms are laid out and explicit and each party knows what is expected of them.

14

The expectation at the outset is that the contract will be honoured on both sides. A further benefit is that remedies for non-performance form part of the contract at the outset.

Disadvantages include the need for legal knowledge to be available to ensure that the contract terms are appropriate. Getting the contract right takes time (even allowing for standard contract terms) and a further disadvantage is the probable lack of flexibility allowed by the contract terms – although, of course, the parties are free to have in the contract exactly what they want and can amend the terms as long as both parties agree to the amendment. Price and delivery may be non-negotiable unless otherwise stated.

Feedback on self-assessment question 14.4

Acts of God (events outside of human control) include sudden floods or other natural disasters for which no one can be held responsible. Force majeure (French for 'greater force') is a common clause in contracts which essentially frees one or both parties from liabilities when acts of God or other extraordinary events occur. This is a 'catch all' phrase although it refers to out-of-the-ordinary events. Nonetheless, some natural events can be anticipated and managed such as non-catastrophic flooding, fire and wind damage. Detailed analysis of the avoidance by the supplier needs to be undertaken so that the grounds for invoking force majeure can be understood and, where possible, written into future contracts.

Feedback on learning activity 14.5

Disputes over the quality of products should be avoided initially by tight specification, including reference to international standards, where appropriate. Standard-setting bodies may also provide arbitration in matters where product quality is an issue. There are several bodies which provide out-of-court advice on disputes. Apart from ACAS there is the mediation service of the Office of Government Commerce (OGC) and the Centre for Effective Dispute Resolution (http://www.cedrsolve.com).

Feedback on self-assessment question 14.5

You should have considered having a clause in your standard contract terms which details the means to be used for settling disputes, other than resorting immediately to civil action. Training needs assessments in the purchasing department should consider whether there ought to be awareness training for all personnel in ADR techniques such as mediation and conciliation.

Feedback on learning activity 14.6

A project life cycle covers the initial objective setting and end user requirement, establishing any design needs, procurement involvement including stockholding and control, budgeting, timescales for funding and procurement, implementing delivery, monitoring and reviewing. Internal and external negotiations will be required for at least:

- Release of manpower to project – negotiating with relevant line managers

14

- Obtaining funding – internally with finance managers; externally, finance managers with fund providers such as banks and capital markets
- Dealing with suppliers – negotiating variable deliveries, for example, dependent on project progress
- Downstream arrangements – internal and external customers; the need to maintain customer loyalty in the face of problems.

Feedback on self-assessment question 14.6

The collaborative style lends itself to win–win. There is openness and a fair exchange of information. One of the goals is to maintain a relationship in addition to achieving a settlement. Conversely, an adversarial approach alienates one of the parties and is associated with win–lose – it is difficult to re-establish relationships from a poor outcome for one of the parties. Some risks are common to all negotiations and include:

- dissatisfaction with the settlement
- negotiation breakdown
- loss of relationship
- reputational loss.

Your mitigation of these risks should have referred to the ADR techniques which have been covered in this study session, including the possibility of using a facilitator. You might also have pointed out that failure of ADR can lead to action in the courts, incurring the risks of even more expense and, of course, an unknown outcome.

Feedback on learning activity 14.7

Step 1

Identify your client organisation objectives, expectations and alternatives.

Step 2

Identify each contractor(s)/supplier(s) key business drivers, least acceptable alternative and most desirable outcome and benefits that will result from addressing them.

Step 3

Identify each of the contractors(s)/supplier(s) representatives involved in the negotiations.

Step 4

Identify your strengths (and weaknesses) and plan on how to take advantage of (compensate for) them during the negotiation.

Step 5

Identify lists of issues that you might expect the contractor/supplier to raise during the negotiation and prepare to deal with them.

14

Step 6

Identify the key messages(s) that we want to deliver based on analysis of information from previous steps.

Step 7

Establish and organise your negotiating team (plus roles and responsibilities).

Step 8

Develop a detailed strategy that properly considers all of the information developed and takes advantage of the strengths of the negotiating team.

Feedback on self-assessment question 14.7

Situation	Method	Qualifications	Benefits
We want you to be our supplier due to our past relationship, but you need to be in this price range _____ in order to continue	We are in a strategic sourcing process, and we must choose contractors/suppliers that provide max value	In other areas, we have disqualified suppliers with 20-year relationships	Maintain a profitable account Derive benefit from association with us

Public sector issues

Introduction

The public sector is a unique economic sector. As a result it has a distinct role to fulfil which is different from the private sector and has very different objectives. The public sector provides a framework within which strategic services of national importance can be delivered and which is funded, in the main, from tax revenues collected from citizens. This study session considers the unique nature of funding and service in the public sector which brings some different approaches to running organisations, differences in governance and accountability and differences in relationships between stakeholders. In addition, the nature of government in the UK brings other dimensions into play in the way that national, regional and local government operates. Additionally, there are challenges to be considered in the relationship between the UK and the EU, together with the way in which EU laws and regulations are subsumed into the UK economy and legal system.

'There is no overarching definition for public private partnerships. PPP is an umbrella notion covering a wide range of economic activity and is in a constant evolution.'

Frits Bolkestein (EU Commissioner for Internal Markets)

Session learning objectives

After completing this session you should be able to:

15.1 Define what is meant by the public sector.
15.2 Recognise some of the risks that are inherent in public sector projects.
15.3 Describe the workings of EU public procurement directives and the remedies available for infringement by public sector organisations.
15.4 Explain the role of audit bodies in the public sector.
15.5 Summarise the work of the Office of Government Commerce in assisting public sector organisations to manage and mitigate risk.
15.6 Identify the risks, including reputational risks, that can derive from access issues in the public sector which relate to the free availability of information.

15

Unit content coverage

This study session covers the following topics from the official CIPS unit content document:

Learning objective

3.1 Develop appropriate solutions to mitigate the inherent risks in the following supply chain issues:
  • Supplier appraisal, selection and management
  • Project failure (eg capital procurement – investment appraisal)
  • International sourcing

- Implementation of new technologies
- Corporate social responsibility (CSR) including ethical, environmental and health and safety issues
- Public sector procurement

Prior knowledge

Study sessions 1 to 14.

Resources

Internet access.

Timing

You should set aside about 7 hours to read and complete this session, including learning activities, self-assessment questions, the suggested further reading (if any) and the revision question.

15.1 The public sector in context

Learning activity 15.1

Identify some public sector bodies and show how the management structure differs from the private sector.

Feedback on page 254

Private sector businesses exist to make profit. Profit is the reward for entrepreneurial enterprise and investing capital in a venture which has no guarantee of return. The public sector is formed from organisations created by successive governments to provide services which are in the public interest. Allocation of funds to these bodies is on the basis of government priority which is, itself, reacting to public desire and election promise.

Many of the services are strategic in nature and many are there because the government is the 'provider of last resort' – in other words, no one else is either willing or capable of providing these services. Achieving profit is not generally a goal although achieving value from all the money spent is a consistent objective of the public sector. Originally seen as aiming for effectiveness, economy and efficiency, the term *value for money* remains important but has been extended to encapsulate *adding value*. This approach seeks to benchmark various activities in the public sector against alternative delivery methods in order to ensure that the best possible use is made of the resources used in any activity.

Funding of the services (the phrase 'state funded' is often used) comes from publicly generated funds, which could be by taxation, some sales of services or goods, and loans. Loans may be raised in the financial markets, by the selling of gilts (government bonds) or by publicly subscribed savings schemes. Where loans are used to generate income, the interest payments must, of course also come from publicly generated revenue streams. At various times, diverse governments have attempted to introduce alternative funding schemes and some have been more successful than others. The Public Finance Initiative (PFI) is an example of one such scheme which encourages partnership approaches to public projects by seeking private sector investment.

The manner in which the public sector is governed is markedly different from that in the private sector. Policy is set at the level of elected representatives, based on perceptions of public need and election manifesto. Administration of government business is done by departments managed by civil servants. Although these departments may have quasi-management boards, the powers of the board and its individual members differ from the legal responsibilities of company directors. The board of a company is executive in nature and collectively responsible for its actions and the actions of its employees. Civil servants may act only within the authority handed down from government and are not responsible to the public at large.

Local government is administered by officers who are implementing decisions taken by elected representatives. These elected representatives are accountable to their constituencies, as are Members of Parliament (MPs) and Members of the European Parliament (MEPs), also, of course, Welsh and Scottish parliament members. Like civil servants, local authority officers can act only within the authority handed down from the elected council.

Accountability and governance are key differences between economic sectors. The private sector answers to its shareholders for business success. Companies are self-governing. They must operate within the law, but they are subject to market forces and follow their own strategies – their policies are not directed by government. In the public sector, accountability is ultimately to every citizen, although there may be layers of officers and elected members between the highest elected representative and the ordinary citizen.

The defining factor of the public sector is that it is in place to deliver services which every citizen needs but which it is inappropriate for a commercial organisation to provide if it is in a position to remove or curtail a service purely on the grounds of lack of profit. A public service should exist without a profit motive and purely for the public good. Of course, this high ideal is subject to the vagaries of public opinion and the need to share limited funds between many competing bodies – hence the establishment of new initiatives like the PFI together with a variety of innovative methods of service delivery, some of which may be undertaken by private sector organisations.

Bureaucratic bodies, such as are found in the public sector, are sometimes less responsive to change than private sector bodies because the day-to-day fight for profit and commercial survival is less evident. Nonetheless,

15

entrenched ideas about public sector provision are constantly being challenged. This is exemplified by the privatisation of former nationalised industries such as the electricity supply industry, the water industry and the railways. All of these would have been considered essential strategic industries not long ago and, because of that, secure in the public sector and subject to public directions represented by a government minister or department.

Some public sector services may be difficult to provide in any way other than by public funding – social work and education, perhaps. Even here, however, innovative schemes for part-privatisation or outsource provision to the private sector have been tested and are changing perceptions as well as introducing new ideas about public sector activities. Hospital trusts, for example, have been helping to clear their waiting lists by paying for patients to be operated on in private sector hospitals.

The ultimate model – in local government first, perhaps – is for the public body to become a contracting body only. There would still be the need to elect public representatives, but after that, a handful of officials would negotiate with private sector contractors for all the services required and be responsible to the elected representatives for the efficient and effective spend of public funds on the contracted-out services. This kind of change would mirror the private sector model where change is seen as a constant and organisations which do not act quickly enough are lost forever. (This is an example of how provision of service may change in the not too distant future – it's already happening in the USA – and reflects how change may happen in the UK beyond the Best Value-type agenda.)

Self-assessment question 15.1

Identify the main differences between the public sector and the private sector.

Feedback on page 254

15.2 Risks in public sector projects

Learning activity 15.2

Do some research into the successes and failures of public private partnerships (PPP) and identify some of the factors which contributed to these successes or failures.

Feedback on page 254

The only way to avoid risk is to do nothing at all – which ensures that nothing is achieved. As we have seen, the role of the public sector is different to that of the private; nonetheless, each public sector service has a purpose and objectives to achieve. We defined risk much earlier in our studies as being any event which might affect the achievement of objectives and, by this yardstick, the public sector is as vulnerable as any other to the threats and hazards with which we are all surrounded.

Public sector risks are different only in that the funding, operation and management of public sector services differs from that in the private sector. There is a common approach to risk management. Exposure to risk is the combination of impact and probability of the events which might prevent objectives being achieved, and the strategic approach to the risk cycle is common with other sectors and approaches, as illustrated in figure 15.1.

Figure 15.1: Strategic approach to risk

Identify risks
↓
Evaluate the risks
↓
Assess risk appetite
↓
Identify risk response
↓
Assure the process
↓
Embed and review

The major differences in the risk management approach in the public sector compared with the private sector flow not just from unique operations but from variances in the risk appetite and the accountability of service provision.

The manner of funding public sector bodies means that all citizens have a stake in the way organisations are run and how well they perform since it is public money, in the main, which is being used to finance activities. As we have seen, there are limitations on the way in which public money can be raised and the use of that money is under public scrutiny – taxpayers do not expect speculation with their funds to the same extent that shareholders may accept higher risk in return for higher profit. This can easily affect the attitude which managers in the public sector have towards taking risks and, in general, this tends towards the risk-averse end of the scale. Accountability concerns also affect this attitude. Accountability is to the public at large and not to a relatively small group of shareholders as in the private sector. The strategic approach to risk management and its operation in each service area is akin to the position in the private sector. Despite there being some significant differences between the sectors in inputs, management and outcomes, the process of making risk management effective is very similar. Thus, relating risks to objectives at each level of a public sector operation follows much the same path as in the private sector. There needs to be a good understanding of objectives at each level and there needs to be a process which can identify and manage the risks which could arise.

Resources of all kinds in the public sector are available from the public purse. Despite innovative schemes for sharing investment and reward with the private sector, public services must still compete for funds from a limited

15

pot. Going out of business may not be a real possibility for most public sector organisations but, nonetheless, poor performance in delivery or in spending can affect the future funding and viability of these organisations. Thus, lack of performance could mean loss of future funding and loss of public credibility – just as in the private sector missed profit targets and loss of reputation inevitably lead to loss of investment and shareholder departure.

Many new projects arise in the public sector as a result of manifesto aspirations or changes in public need. Managing these projects and forecasting their risks can be difficult because they may be in new areas of provision or taking radical approaches to existing areas of service. Despite tending towards the risk averse, many of these projects can be much more risky than more normal departmental operations. This high-risk factor may lead to higher-than-average project failure but does provide an opportunity for learning from mistakes. Again, because of the public accountability requirement, it is essential that all the techniques of project appraisal which we have covered in earlier study sessions should be applied. Unique to the public sector may be the high level of authority for project spend which is needed before projects can commence. High government levels may be involved which, in itself, is no bad thing for managing the accountability risk. The higher the authority level, the greater the need to manage project resources and risks to ensure ultimate success and the maintaining of reputations.

Projects delivered under a public private partnership (PPP) aim to provide an alternative to the traditional ways in which the state funds, procures and provides services and assets. PPPs can be seen as a means both for accessing new sources of funding, particularly for major capital projects, and for obtaining the input of private sector expertise into public sector projects. There is the added benefit of spreading the risk by sharing the provision and/or investment with one or more partners.

The UK is one of the foremost EU countries involved in rolling out PPPs and the Private Finance Initiative (PFI) provides a good example. PFI projects are designed to allow the public sector to retain a substantial role in projects, either as the main purchaser of services or as an essential enabler of the project. It differs from straightforward contracting-out in that the private sector provides the capital asset and finances it. Under the PFI, the public sector does not own the asset but pays the PFI contractor a stream of committed revenue payments for the use of the facility over an agreed contract period. Good examples would be hospitals or schools – large, capital-intensive projects which, under PFI, avoid the need for a large public investment of funds.

Government has been actively involved in promoting effective risk management for some time. The National Health Service (NHS) has embraced the risk standard AS/NZS 4360 virtually in its entirety and applies its principles to the NHS risk management framework. The Association of Local Authority Risk Managers promotes risk management in local government and, in central government itself, there is the 'orange book' (*Management of Risk – Principles and Concepts*), in addition to the Treasury's *Strategic Risk Management Overview*.

15

Accountability at whatever level of the public services means that not achieving objectives is often a matter of public debate. A disgruntled electorate, at local or national level, makes its voice heard by changing government. That is the ultimate political risk. However, the opportunity for wielding that particular weapon comes perhaps only every four or five years. In the meantime, it is in all governments' interest to ensure that the risks which may stop their objectives being achieved are understood and managed.

Self-assessment question 15.2

What are the benefits to public sector organisations of PPPs?

Feedback on page 255

15.3 EU public procurement directives

The purpose of European Directives is not to harmonise all national rules on public procurement but to align the procedures to be followed in each member state whenever a contract is to be awarded which is over a certain threshold (in 2005 this value was £99,695.00). The directives fall into two groups: those governing the traditional areas of public procurement and those dealing with water, energy, transport and telecommunication. Both groups are based on the principle of freedom from discrimination and transparency of awarding procedure.

There is a choice of three procedures – open, restricted or negotiated. *Open* allows any supplier to bid whereas the *restricted* procedure comprises a two-stage procedure whereby suppliers need to pre-qualify before being allowed to put their bid forward. The restricted procedure is designed to allow for the customer to be sure that potential contractors are actually capable of providing specialist supply items, thus avoiding time wasting on both sides. In both these procedures, the potential bidders can request clarification of the contract with replies being circulated to all contracting entities which have expressed an interest.

The *negotiated* procedure can only be used in limited circumstances such as those where there is only one suitable source of supply, where no suitable bids have been received in response to a previous open or restricted procedure, or in the case of an emergency. Another suitable case for the negotiated procedure would be the partial replacement of goods where integration with the current equipment is necessary – IT equipment might be an example. There are minimum time limits set down for stages of the particular procedures chosen. For more information see the 'EU Procurement Thresholds' section of the OGC website http://www.ogc.gov.uk/ – it will be found in the main 'Policy & Standards Framework' section.

The directives specify two award criteria: lowest price or MEAT (most economically advantageous tender). If the first option is chosen and the

15

tender figure is abnormally low it cannot be rejected for this reason alone without the tenderer being given the chance of justifying it. If MEAT is chosen then the heads of advantage should be expressed in order of importance. Typical parameters will include price, delivery, date, quality and aftersales service.

Public procurement also requires a prior indicative notice (PIN). This is used to provide advance notice of those contracts which a public body may be contemplating during the course of the forthcoming financial year. This is not a call for competition, only a means for advising potential contractors of contracts which may be of interest to them.

Learning activity 15.3

Read the CIPS document reference files on the EU directives, and identify the penalties that can be applied for non-compliance.

Feedback on page 255

The public procurement regime in the EU is in line with the basic principle of ensuring a free flow of goods and services between member states. The directives enter into UK law by means of statutory instruments (SIs). The Services Directive, for example, appears on the UK statute books as The Public Services Contracts Regulations, SI 1993/3228. Whereas the directives made little impact in the early years (the first was in 1971), they now have to be taken seriously by all who are involved in purchasing in the public sector, not least because of the existence of the Remedies Directives which provide a channel of appeal for suppliers who feel that they have not received fair treatment. The directives are as follows:

- the Services Directive
- the Supplies Directive
- the Works Directive
- the Utilities Directive
- the Remedies Directive
- the Utilities Remedies Directive.

Each of the directives above appears in the UK as an SI and each SI specifies the rules and obligations applicable to relevant categories. The Public Services Contracts Regulations, for example, embodies the Services Directive which divides services into priority services and residual services and specifies the rules for the regulation of service contracts (refer again to the TRFs for more detail).

Some of the risks in contracting can be alleviated by the directives concerning remedies which provide contracting parties with a means for redress if things go wrong. The Remedies Directive sets out to provide equitable remedies at both national and EU level which would be capable of suspending a contract award procedure for sufficient time to prevent irreparable damage that might result if the contract were awarded unlawfully. It also provides that member states have a system by which aggrieved parties can ask for damages and interest from the parties at fault. The Utilities Remedies Directive provides similar alleviation in the utilities sector of activity.

Self-assessment question 15.3

A unitary local authority in the UK wishes to seek tenders for a contract to supply specialist equipment worth £1.5 million at 2006 prices. Outline the steps which would need to be taken to be in compliance with EC procurement requirements.

Feedback on page 255

15.4 The role of audit bodies in the public sector

Auditing in the public sector may be *internal* or *external*, as is the case with other sectors and bodies. Internal auditing is defined as:

> 'an independent, objective assurance and consulting activity designed to add value and improve an organisation's operations. It helps an organisation accomplish its objectives by bringing a systematic, disciplined approach to evaluate and improve the effectiveness of risk management, control and governance processes.' Institute of Internal Auditors (2004)

Internal auditing, as the title implies, is carried out by an internal team at the behest of the board and management in order to provide them with the assurances they need that risks and internal controls are being managed effectively. The Combined Code already referred to several times in your studies has as one of its provisions 'that companies which do not have an internal audit function should from time to time review the need for one'. Thus, companies listed on the London Stock Exchange are required to comply with this requirement and, in practice, a large majority of listed companies do, in fact, have an internal audit function.

Internal auditing is, in the main, a non-statutory requirement. There are a few exceptions to this – the Local Government Act, for example, has an implied requirement in the Accounts and Audit Regulations which flow from the Act – but in the public sector in general, internal auditing is seen as an essential aid to management in assuring an effective approach to risk management and internal control. The vast majority of public sector bodies, therefore, have an internal audit provision which may be in the form of an in-house service or a contracted-out service provider.

External audit is a legal requirement in the public sector just as it is in the private sector and for the same reason: it is designed to provide an independent review of an organisation's financial position – the 'true and fair view' given by the financial statements – and to report findings in an open and transparent manner. In the private sector the external auditors report to the shareholders and are appointed by them at an annual general meeting as it is the interests of the shareholders that the external auditors are primarily seeking to protect. In the public sector, parliament appoints specific bodies to undertake the audits and to report via the Comptroller and Auditor General (C&AG). The historical role of the C&AG dates from the Exchequer and Audit Act of 1866. Nowadays the C&AG heads the National Audit Office (NAO) and reports to the House of Commons, in particular, the Public Accounts Committee. There are similar Auditors General offices for Wales, Northern Ireland and Scotland. The remit of the NAO is to audit central government departments and bodies including many non-departmental government bodies and agencies. The work they do may be directly provided or may be contracted out in part to suitably qualified audit firms.

Learning activity 15.4

Read the websites of the Audit Commission (http://www.audit-commission.gov.uk) and the National Audit Office (http://www.nao.org.uk) and identify how they deal with non-compliance in the bodies which they audit in terms of statutory or other duties.

Feedback on page 255

While predominantly a financial audit, the NAO developed its initiative 'Audit 21' early in the new millennium to take account of the need for the achievement of value for money in the audited bodies, the shift in these bodies to a risk management approach and the need to recognise the business-oriented focus of the bodies being audited. Auditors will, thus, take time to understand the business, assess the approach to risk being taken in the audited body and review internal controls analytically in operational as well as financial areas where these are relevant to the body's financial statement.

The Audit Commission (and equivalent bodies in Northern Ireland and Scotland) is the other large independent government external auditor and is responsible for the audit of local government, NHS bodies such as hospital trusts and strategic health authorities and some other bodies. Its remit includes assurance over value for money and provides the necessary independent assurance for local communities that the elected members of their local authorities are achieving objectives with financial probity. Much of the audit work is actually carried out by the District Audit Service on behalf of the Audit Commission and some work may be undertaken by contracted firms also. The Audit Commission has developed an approach called the 'managed audit' which involves internal and external audit teams working closely together so that there is both full cooperation and coordination of effort.

Given the proliferation of public sector auditors – central and local government, NHS and other agencies, audit bodies separate from England

15

for Scotland, Wales and Northern Ireland – there is plenty of ground for different approaches and different ideas. In an attempt to gain a single unified focus, the Public Audit Forum stated three firm principles as far back as 1998:

- independence of public sector auditors
- wide scope – financial statements, value for money and 'best value'
- results of audits available in the public domain.

The concept of an audit committee, mandatory as part of the Combined Code for listed companies in the private sector, is present also in the public sector. The non-executive directors which are required to form the private sector audit committee do not exist in exactly the same way in the public sector. Nonetheless, audit committees have been formed in virtually every government department and agency and in the NHS. To gain the independence required of those who serve on public sector audit committees, appointments are made to governing bodies from outside of their number by means of secondments or by appointments specifically for that purpose.

Self-assessment question 15.4

What is the role of the National Audit Office (NAO) and how does it carry out this role?

Feedback on page 256

15.5 The role of the Office of Government Commerce in promoting risk management

Learning activity 15.5

Do some research into the current initiatives of the Office of Government Commerce (OGC) and make notes on those areas of risk that would be reduced through following OGC initiatives.

Feedback on page 256

15

The mission of the Office of Government Commerce (OGC) is:

'To work with the public sector as a catalyst to achieve efficiency, value for money in commercial activities and improved success in the delivery of programmes and projects'. (http://www.ogc.gov.uk)

The OGC delivers this mission by supporting public sector organisations in the role of 'trusted adviser' in areas such as meeting efficiency targets, achieving more savings in central government civil procurement and improving the success rate of critical programmes and projects. The manner in which OGC attempts to achieve these high ideals is through initiatives such as the OGC 'buying solutions' service which aims to provide the public sector with better value for money from procurement, the provision of a procurement excellence model and the OGC Gateway process. All of these initiatives assist in ensuring that good risk management processes have been used by the OGC clients and, in themselves, provide an overview of good procurement and risk management for senior managers in client organisations.

The OGC Gateway process examines a programme or project at the critical stages in its life cycle to provide assurance that it can progress safely to the next stage. The process is designed to be applied to operational programmes and procurement projects and is based on proven techniques that can lead to achieving predicted benefits together with more predictable costs and outcomes.

Areas which will be reviewed using the Gateway process include:

- use of skills and staff experience
- stakeholder understanding of project
- time and cost targets are realistic
- in-house project review teams encouraged
- programme stages are achievable
- stage completion and advancement.

In undertaking the reviews, OGC will consider the risk process as it has been applied by the organisation's management to the project or programme and give additional assurance as to the effectiveness of risk identification and evaluation. By using the five points above as a guide, the project stages and targets can be compared to the risk register and/or risk map for the project and a view taken as to the reasonableness of the impact and probabilities of the threats foreseen by the project owners.

A Gateway Review can assist in capital investment projects by providing a check on the assumptions and timings involved in funding decisions and those decisions involved in providing asset utilisation forecasts. The work done by the client organisation in these areas will have included an analysis of the risks involved and their possible cost and impact. The OGC review will provide a quasi-independent view of the issues involved and will be able to advise the client's management of the effectiveness of their on-going risk processes and of the appraisal techniques employed in the original decision.

Self-assessment question 15.5

Explain how a public sector organisation can benefit by using the Gateway process for managing capital projects.

Feedback on page 256

15

15.6 Risks associated with free access to information in the public sector

Learning activity 15.6

Recognise the complexity of the British central government and local government structure and identify the chain of command and communication from ministers to local officials.

Feedback on page 257

The main role of government departments and agencies is to implement government policy and to advise government ministers. Departments are staffed by civil servants who are impartial and have no political bias. Funding is provided through parliamentary agreements and most departments are headed by a government minister. Some departments cover the entire UK, while devolved government to Wales, Scotland and Northern Ireland means that the work of some departments covers those areas only.

A non-departmental public body (NDPB) is a national or regional public body which works independently of ministers but to whom they are accountable. NDPBs may be executive bodies or advisory bodies. Executive bodies carry out set functions within the framework of government but have a degree of operational independence which varies between bodies. Advisory NDPBs are set up by ministers expressly to give advice on particular matters but not to take any executive action.

Some ministers do not have specific departmental responsibilities and are available for the prime minister to allocate special work or special tasks as necessary. Ministers in charge of departments are usually Cabinet members and, once the government has decided its policy, each minister is expected to support the government or otherwise resign.

Cabinet members are the most senior government members. Below them are junior ministers who may have specific responsibility for departmental functions. Below them come the under-secretaries of state who report to the junior ministers but who may also have specific responsibilities assigned to them by the junior minister. At each level, ministers are expected to support government policy once it has been settled. This principle of collective responsibility means that there is unanimity among ministers and junior ministers once policy has been decided and, if there is any dissent, a resignation should follow.

Ministers are accountable for the work of their departments and have a duty to Parliament to answer for their policies, decisions and actions. On taking office all ministers must resign directorships in private or public companies and must ensure that there are no conflicts between their private and public interests.

Local government in the UK operates under statutory powers laid down by various acts. Authorities look after many functions, some of which are mandatory under law and some of which are discretionary. The main link between central and local government is the Department of Communities and Local Government (DCLG), although other government departments which may have a direct interest in a local authority service – education is a good example – are also concerned. In Scotland, Wales and Northern Ireland, local authorities usually deal directly with the devolved parliament or assemblies.

Local government is both a major employer and a big spender, accounting for about 25% of all public spending and employing around 2 million people. Funding for this enterprise comes from the raising of local revenue through council tax and some charges for services, redistribution of non-domestic rates and grants from central government.

All of this can result in a complicated hierarchy, complex administrative and financial arrangements and difficulties for citizens in understanding 'who does what'. This raises particular risks for politicians and for administrators.

A major risk is the dichotomy of management between elected representatives and officials. Perception can often be that the line is blurred and, without clarity, there is difficulty in assessing accountability. Although it is the elected representatives who have the final responsibility, many of the actions taken to put policy into action are taken by non-elected officials. Mitigation can only come with clear, published schemes of administration together with clarity of schemes of delegation.

Financial arrangements are another risk issue. Local and central government has moved to a system of accounting more akin to that in the private sector (so-called 'resource accounting') but, even so, there are many rigid rules surrounding issues like obtaining loans, under- and overspending and building up and using reserves. There is competition for limited resources of funds and this leads to additional risks arising when new or innovative sources of finance are sought. Central government often wields a heavy hand when it comes to controlling local government finances and the heaviest tool is the use of 'capping' – putting a ceiling on the amount that a particular local authority can actually spend. The risks to elected members who disregard this action include personal surcharge and removal from office.

Significant reputational risks also exist in government. Policy failure can mean resignation for ministers and, in extreme situations, can result in a 'vote of no confidence' in the House of Commons. If carried, this will force the resignation of the government and the calling of a general election. Financial irregularity risks the reputation of individuals and organisations if fraud or corruption are discovered. Failure to deliver on election promises also raises a significant political risk at central and local government level. A disaffected electorate can be its own self-regulating risk mitigation strategy.

Openness and the increase in transparency of operations sought by all levels of government in recent years has led to new risks in public access to information. The Freedom of Information Act, operative from 2005, gives the right to see a wide range of information held by the public sector. The act covers nearly all public sector organisations, including:

- parliament
- local assemblies

- government departments
- local authorities
- health trusts
- GP surgeries
- many other public bodies such as publicly funded museums.

The act gives a right of wide access to information although there are defined exemptions and conditions, and the 'public interest' may be considered even where an exemption applies. There are powers of enforcement contained in the act and an independent Information Commissioner exists, with a tribunal, to hear complaints brought in terms of the act.

Open public access to matters such as notes of meetings, minutes, the background to formal decisions and, most importantly perhaps, personal information brings significant new risks to the apparatus of government. The intention of the act is primarily to promote openness and accountability on the part of public authorities and the way in which they make decisions. This means not only that the reasons for decisions must be rational and well founded but that everything must also be recorded. In the field of procurement, for example, anyone can now ask why a particular supplier was awarded a particular contract or why a contract was not tendered or why only certain suppliers were invited to bid. Provided that the reasons can be justified, the authority will have no problems. However, if there is little or no justification or if all the evidence has been lost or was never recorded, further challenges could follow.

The impact of realising some of these risks can be significant since remedies can include awards of damages, out-of-court settlements and reinstatement of employees who have been wrongfully or unfairly dismissed. All of these can have unwanted knock-on effects. All of them spell the need for anticipating future risks and managing them in an effective manner.

Self-assessment question 15.6

What action under the Freedom of Information (FOI) Act can be taken by a member of the public in the UK, who is dissatisfied with the service or actions of a public sector organisation? What are the implications of FOI for the reputation of a public sector organisation?

Feedback on page 257

15

Revision question

Now try the revision question for this session on page 357.

Summary

This study session has covered the manner in which the public sector is governed and operates, and some significant differences between public and private sectors have been highlighted. We have considered the relationship with some European laws and how these can affect life in the UK. We have also looked at the complex issues of separation between central and local government, together with the manner in which elected representatives interact with government departments and officials. The arrangements for auditing in the public sector have been discussed as well as the role of the Office of Government Commerce. Both these areas are important in achieving an understanding of how public sector operational activities can be improved and made more accessible to all interested parties. The need to always be future-oriented in risk management has been highlighted in this study session by our discussion concerning accountability and freedom of information, both of which are expectations of all stakeholders who have dealings with the public sector.

Suggested further reading

Visit the Audit Commission and National Audit Office websites: http://www.audit-commission.gov.uk and http://www.nao.org.uk.

Further information on the workings of government can be obtained at http://www.direct.gov.uk.

Feedback on learning activities and self-assessment questions

Feedback on learning activity 15.1

Many public sector organisations have significant monies to manage and large workforces. A large local government unitary authority, for example, will turn over £600 million annually and have anywhere between 8,000 and 10,000 staff. There is no board of directors, however, and management is divided between elected members who take the significant decisions and staff who implement the decisions. Accountability is to the citizens in the local area, not to shareholders.

Feedback on self-assessment question 15.1

You should have identified differences in these areas:

- governance
- accountability
- funding
- administration
- policy.

Using these main points you can compare each sector for the differences in approach. The role of a board of directors, for example, as compared with an elected council; the raising of funds from tax as opposed to the need to generate revenue by selling services to customers in a competitive market.

Feedback on learning activity 15.2

PPPs include several different approaches to public/private sector initiatives including joint ventures and the Private Finance Initiative. Partnerships

UK is the body, set up in 2000, which assists both sectors in preparing, planning and implementing PPPs. The OGC also has a role to play and its Gateway process includes the 4Ps local government initiative for securing funding and accelerating development, procurement and implementation of PPPs. Research these websites (http://www.ogc.gov.uk and http://www.partnershipsuk.org.uk) for examples of projects which will provide answers to this learning activity.

Feedback on self-assessment question 15.2

The main benefits are:

- share of funding requirement for investment
- release of funds for other projects
- access to management expertise
- maintaining public sector involvement
- spreading and sharing risk.

You could expand on this list by describing the various ways in which funding can be obtained, the risk appetite of the public sector and the differences in management in public and private sectors, all of which impact on PPPs.

Feedback on learning activity 15.3

Go to http://www.cips.org and find 'topic reference files' (TRFs). Remedies are available regarding supplies, services and works (Remedies Directive 89/665/EC) and include in summary (a) suspending a contract award, and (b) a system for damages and interest. Directive 92/13/EC provides remedies in the utilities sector including (a) a non-litigious procedure (b) a corrective mechanism, and (c) an attestation procedure which could include an independent report.

Feedback on self-assessment question 15.3

This is a public sector procurement and you should have pointed out that notice is required for all contracts in excess of the 2005 threshold of £99,695.00 by advertising in the OJEC. Then, to comply with EC Directives and UK Regulations, there is a choice of open, restricted or negotiated procedures in respect of tendering. In this case, it seems likely that the restricted procedure would be appropriate because there is specialist equipment involved and there may be a need to pre-qualify potential bidders. This appears to be neither an emergency nor a single-source supply, therefore negotiated procedures would not apply.

Feedback on learning activity 15.4

The Audit Commission is the independent public body responsible for ensuring that public money is spent economically, efficiently and effectively in the areas of local government, housing, health, criminal justice and fire and rescue services. It is required to provide assurance over the

15

financial accounts and reports of the bodies it audits and to report on the achievement of value for money. The NAO is the external auditor for central government departments and agencies and has similar tasks and reporting requirements to those of the Audit Commission. Non-compliance on the behalf of bodies which they audit can have serious consequences which can include surcharging for serious breaches of acts in the case of councillors, funding restrictions, dismissal of employees and, for government departments, can mean reports to Parliament and the Public Accounts Committee.

Feedback on self-assessment question 15.4

The NAO is the external audit body for central government departments, agencies and non-departmental public bodies. Its role is to provide assurance to government and the Public Accounts Committee that public funds are accounted for accurately, that the business focus of the body is appropriate and that value for money of taxpayers' funds is being achieved.

Feedback on learning activity 15.5

You should have visited the OGC website (http://www.ogc.gov.uk) and reviewed the projects, programmes and reviews which are on offer. In particular, the Gateway process offers reviews at four different stages and you should have taken note of the differences at each stage. The reviews provide assurance at defined stages of projects and assist in verifying the project risk analyses which the organisation will have already established.

On the OGC website an OGC Gateway Review is defined in simple terms as a review of an acquisition programme or procurement project carried out at key decision points by a team of experienced people, independent of the project team.

There are five OGC Gateway Reviews during the lifecycle of a project, three before contract award and two looking at service implementation and confirmation of the operational benefits. A project is reviewed at the OGC Gateway Review appropriate to the point reached in its life cycle. Retrospective or combined OGC Gateway Reviews are not supported. There may be additional OGC Gateway Reviews if required, such as the decision points between OGC Gateway Reviews 3 and 4 for construction projects. The process emphasises early review for maximum added value.

Feedback on self-assessment question 15.5

A Gateway Review can be undertaken by OGC on any relevant programme or project. On a capital project, it would be expected that the review would consider the appraisal methods used and verify the conclusions reached. The stages of the project as it proceeds would be reviewed with, again, the project planning strategy and control technique being scrutinised. Decisions taken at each key point of the project would also be considered and the initial risk analysis would be subject to review in the light of actual project progression.

15

Feedback on learning activity 15.6

You should have reviewed the information available at http://www.direct.gov.uk which gives comprehensive details of the structure of central and local government, the powers available and the division between government and the civil service and local government and its staff. You may also wish to visit the website for your own local council to see the services offered and the extent to which there is local accountability.

Feedback on self-assessment question 15.6

The first redress is to the offending body itself with a request for appropriate action to be taken. Thereafter, recourse is to the Information Commissioner's Office (http://www.ico.gov.uk). This office provides guidance to organisations and individuals and rules on eligible complaints. Action can be taken when the law is broken and can include ordering compliance and, ultimately, prosecution.

Several risks were reviewed in this section and you should look at these again. They include:

- accountability
- transparency of operations
- open access to information
- recording sufficient information on decisions.

15

15

Technological and environmental issues

'To provide the information that the enterprise requires to achieve its objectives, the enterprise needs to manage and control IT resources, using a structured set of processes to deliver the required information services.'
The IT Governance Institute

Introduction

Using IT to make procurement more efficient has come a long way since early attempts to use electronic funds transfer represented the cutting edge in supplier payment methods. The use of electronic systems for all administrative steps in the purchasing process – from raising the requisition through to authorising the order – is commonplace in many organisations. However, new processes bring new risks and we need to understand what these risks are and how we can mitigate them. IT has become all-pervasive and has often provided opportunities to introduce better ways of working. Failing to grasp IT and environmental challenges bring threats to survivability which most organisations cannot afford to ignore.

Session learning objectives

After completing this session you should be able to:

16.1 Understand how IT can make procurement more efficient.
16.2 Assess the impact of new developments on people and processes which can be seen in product design, manufacturing, and so on, as well as in IT applications.
16.3 Give examples of situations where failure to manage changing technology has led to financial or operational damage.
16.4 Identify the impact of legislation on procurement.
16.5 Compare a number of techniques for assessing environmental risk.

Unit content coverage

This study session covers the following topics from the official CIPS unit content document:

Learning objective

3.1 Develop appropriate solutions to mitigate the inherent risks in the following supply chain issues:
  • Supplier appraisal, selection and management
  • Project failure (eg capital procurement – investment appraisal)
  • International sourcing
  • Implementation of new technologies
  • Corporate social responsibility (CSR) including ethical, environmental and health and safety issues
  • Public sector procurement

16

Prior knowledge

Study sessions 1 to 15.

Resources

Internet access.

Timing

You should set aside about 7 hours to read and complete this session, including learning activities, self-assessment questions, the suggested further reading (if any) and the revision question.

16.1 Procurement efficiency gains from information technology

Learning activity 16.1

Research and evaluate the extent to which your organisation uses web-based applications for purchasing and makes use of the intranet for access to procedures and management directives.

Feedback on page 274

Speed, storage capacity and ease of use characterise the significant benefits that can be obtained from IT. Calculations can be undertaken quickly and with accuracy. Despite this, some of the cost savings anticipated from the early days of introducing computer systems to replace labour-intensive manual processes have never been realised. This has been the result of the costs of hardware and software development alongside employing and training the skilled staff necessary to operate computers. Efficiency gains can and have been realised in other areas, nonetheless, and will continue to be available from the continual extension of networked systems and desktop user-friendly applications.

The introduction of enterprise-wide computing systems has hastened the move towards an integrated approach to all systems and procedures. The computing power now available in network applications means that there is huge potential for real-time data entry for transactions which can, in turn, maintain the management information system (MIS) completely up to date. Efficiency gains from an integrated data system are significant. When transactions occur they can immediately update disparate data files. For example, input of a purchase order updates purchase ledger and supplier files with a commitment (an accounting term which indicates that the organisation is committed to a future payment) which, in turn, allows the MIS to reflect the actual financial position at any given time.

The introduction of a good IT management and security system can assist in promoting efficient and effective operations and a comprehensive

16

way of doing this is the application of the international standard BS EN ISO 17799.

The standard enables the organisation to identify risks facing its IT processes and introduce controls to mitigate these risks. Undertaking this activity helps to identify the assets that will be included, together with defining the scope of a security policy. This exercise can also define the strategy for the use and holding of personal information – critical in terms of both the UK Freedom of Information Act and the EC Data Directive 95/46/EC. Additionally, other organisations with whom we may wish to deal can gain confidence in our systems and approach – reassurance, in other words, that we are protecting our own data and that of our business partners.

Another standard which can assist in reducing IT risk and in increasing IT value delivery is COBIT (acronym for control objectives for information and related technology). Version 4 of this standard was released in December 2005 and provides an IT governance framework based around defined processes and control objectives used by managers, auditors and others with an interest in IT regulatory and compliance requirements. Using this standard as a framework will assist in addressing compliance and regulatory risk issues while, again, assisting in improving our credibility in the eyes of business partners.

Most organisations are highly dependent on IT systems. Consequently, when systems are down, it is almost impossible for organisations to continue to operate effectively. Efficient organisations have a contingency plan in place to minimise the risk of IT failures, which can come from a number of sources. These could include unavailability of the system through virus attack as well as power failure or physical damage to buildings and equipment.

Use of the internet for many things from procurement to product promotion encourages effective access to a huge global market. This kind of access improves prospects for product penetration in addition to allowing innovative approaches to sourcing and potential suppliers. Similarly, development and use of the intranet provides an efficient and effective means for internal communication, speeding up dissemination of important information in addition to making bulletin boards easily available to appropriate levels of staff. Internal email is also an aid to speedy communication, although there are dangers of overload just because the system is so easy to use.

16

The term e-procurement includes the use of online auctions (e-auctions), supplier identification (e-sourcing), e-payment and electronic catalogues. The early generations of e-procurement projects have not been fully analysed yet although most have been benchmarked against expected outcomes. The financial benefits are, therefore, difficult to establish. Nonetheless, from an administrative point of view, the process is delivering efficiency gains and use of diagnostic tools such as the Oracle I-SAVE (developed with CIPS) will help to evaluate cost benefits for the future.

Electronic procure-to-pay systems now enable the automation of each stage of the procurement process from identifying requirements through to payment of the supplier. Abolishing laborious paper routines brings change in the way people work and encourages a more efficient approach. Doing away with bureaucratic delays can also create better relationships between buyers and sellers. The initial learning curve may be steep but the initial cost of training and introducing new systems will be recouped as the use of the system improves and delivery of benefits can be seen.

Opening up the opportunities for supply and tendering by use of the internet can mean better sourcing, while the use of electronic reverse auctions can introduce more aggressive competition to the bidding process. The openness of the process, together with its potential for speedy resolutions when used appropriately, means that e-auctions can be a significant contributor to more efficient and effective buying practice.

Paying suppliers can benefit from IT solutions and can take the form of electronic fund transfers, direct debits and the use of electronic payment cards. All of these provide speed and accuracy but can also introduce new risks of fraud. The traditional approach of division of duties – between, for example, raising an order and authorising payment – can sometimes be difficult to achieve. Payment cards will often be used by the same person who orders and authorises payment, although the cards do tend to be used for low-value purchasing and other controls can be applied. Nonetheless, access to payment methods needs to be carefully monitored and the controls over payments going to the correct recipients need to be particularly tight. The impact of these risks can be considerable and this is an area where operational efficiencies need to be offset carefully against the potential for loss and irregularity.

The Office of Government Commerce (OGC) is the central government department dedicated to best procurement practice in the public sector. Its work is focused on assisting government at national and local level (and all associated bodies) to achieve real benefits from bringing buyers and sellers together in an electronic marketplace. In addition to providing generic advice, OGC provides several tools which can assist in the procurement process and has developed a 'procurement excellence model' which can be used for benchmarking purposes. CIPS provides professional guidance and advice on best practice also and is instrumental in providing position papers on topics of interest to procurement professionals.

Seeking value for money from the use of scarce resources compels all organisations from all economic sectors to continually find better and better ways of utilising assets. IT is no exception. Mainframe computers still have a part to play, particularly in specialised environments, but more and more it is distributed computing which fuels the drive for speed, data access, data integration and value for money from the investment in, and use of, IT resources.

16

Self-assessment question 16.1

List some of the risks you think exist in using the internet for purchasing. Are there any mitigating strategies which you think could be applied?

Feedback on page 275

16.2 The impact of new developments

Learning activity 16.2

Ask a senior manager in your organisation how fundamental business changes are planned for. If possible, read a post-implementation review or audit of a major system or process change and assess the impact of any recommendations made.

Feedback on page 275

Many organisations claim that change is a constant in today's fast-moving business environment. Managers and others often claim that moving to a company with a reputation for embracing change meets one of their requirements for staying motivated. Conversely, many organisations seem moribund and almost have a resistance to change. It is the prevailing culture in a business which primarily influences an individual's view of change – the shared values, ideals and beliefs. Much of this is shaped by the attitude at the very top of the organisation.

Change usually becomes necessary as a result of a disparity becoming evident between actual and desired performance. A performance gap emerges and requires attention, the gap itself being seen as a threat or an opportunity. A product, for example, could be at the end of its useful life although the organisation selling it still considers it to be fit for purpose. The market gives its verdict through falling sales and, as a result, revenues fail to achieve targets. A performance gap emerges which is both a threat to profitability and an opportunity to research and produce a new product which meets customers' needs.

People's behaviour as a factor of change can be illustrated by the same example. Those who relish a challenge will see the short-term downturn in sales as regrettable but use it as a challenge to find the right product to get sales back on target. Those who resist change will see the downturn as the beginning of the end for the business – nothing can save it – and take the attitude that it was not their fault anyway.

Examples of both extremes are easy to find. At the peak of its performance, British Airways saw its competition as the other major world airlines and aspired to be the best in that class. It largely succeeded in that aim but failed to see the emerging low-cost competition as the threat which it very quickly became. Although other factors at the time also played a significant part (9/11), British Airways suffered large drops in profits and staff layoffs, exacerbated by resistance to changes in working practices by its air staff, all of which impacted also on its reputation as a world-class airline. Its response eventually showed results but to achieve this it had to rebrand and reprice many of its short- and medium-haul routes and alter working practices in order to compete with its low-cost rivals.

On the other hand, Sun Microsystems introduced procurement changes which involved key suppliers in developing close working relations with Sun buyers. Key personnel from both organisations worked closely to resolve problems and achieve an understanding of each other's business requirements. For both organisations this involved changes in technology, processes and roles. It also resulted in a harmonisation of expectations and greater success for both companies.

The essence of both these examples can be seen in greater detail in Chapter 11 of *Management: An Introduction* by David Boddy. At Sun, change is constant and flexibility, adaptability and enthusiasm are encouraged because the attitude to change is positive. At British Airways, change did come but only because of force of circumstances, not because of enthusiasm for new products or new markets.

Information technology has been implemented like any other change in society: embraced wholeheartedly by some and, by others, accepted grudgingly and in the smallest possible increments.

Any change, but in particular the massive changes brought about by IT, requires to be managed as effectively as possible. The approaches used include following the project life cycle methods discussed earlier in our studies; taking a participative approach; an emergent change approach and a political approach.

The life cycle perspective follows successive stages in an orderly and predictable way. A project manager plans and guides the process and monitors progress, making changes as necessary to ensure the project objectives can be met. The participative approach encourages personal involvement and, because of this 'hands-on' participation, individuals are motivated by their ability to make a difference and live with the results of their efforts. The emergent perspective relies less on the planning phase although having a fixed idea of the strategy to be achieved. As the project advances, new behaviours or innovative approaches emerge which had not been anticipated at the outset. This allows flexibility in implementation while still achieving a satisfactory final outcome. A political model of the change process brings power as a factor into the equation. Personal or corporate ambition may drive change and the achievement of power may be the most decisive element in the process rather than the benefit a potential change can bring in itself.

All of these issues affect the success or otherwise of a change programme. Implementing e-procurement into supply change management gives us a good opportunity to consider how this fundamental business change has affected all our organisations. How well did your organisation do in bringing in this change? Was there an overview in place before the change to full implementation was planned and commenced? Check your own experience against this checklist:

- Objectives – was there a good set of reasons for change and a business case?
- Personnel – are our culture and staff attitude right to accept change; will there be resistance, even sabotage?
- Relationships – can we cope with internal and external relationship changes?
- Technology – do we have in-house development skills; do we have the knowledge to buy in the right solution where necessary?

- Finance – has the project been properly appraised and are the end results worthwhile?
- Power – will the new system shift power from one department or set of managers to another and, if so, what might the effects be?

All too often projects, like new management ideas, are 'the flavour of the month' and are brought in only for the reason that it seems that everyone else is doing it so it must be good. In fact, without a clear need or reason to change and a strategy for attaining an end objective, there will be little chance of any progress. The project will become just another in a long line of failed management innovations.

In IT the approach to projects usually follows the systems development life cycle. This follows the project from user requirement and system analysis through specification and testing to implementation. This process allows integration of risk assessment and control strategies to be taken into account as the system is developed rather than at a more costly later stage when the system is live. Rapid application and development techniques can supplant the more traditional life cycle approach but speed of development should not allow the sacrifice of attention to control. Mistakes in recognising risks and mitigating them can be as costly in IT developments as elsewhere.

Self-assessment question 16.2

Assess the HR and other risks which might arise if senior management proposed giving line managers authority to make all purchases, thereby disbanding the purchasing department.

Feedback on page 275

16.3 Limiting the damage from failures in change

Learning activity 16.3

Try to identify some projects, either in your own organisation or in the public domain, where designers or project engineers have attempted to implement new technology without success. Evaluate the main factors which contributed to failure.

Feedback on page 276

Computer projects have left a long trail of damaged organisations and unhappy individuals. Implementing new technology is notoriously difficult so this is not surprising. What is surprising and, indeed, disappointing, is that there seems to have been so little learning from the mistakes of the past.

The overarching problem seems to be over-optimism. Given the complexity of most projects, there always seems to be insufficient time allowed and insufficient finance. The Child Support Agency has become notorious for its many failures: delays in payment, wrong payments and an IT system which has never achieved its objectives. The agency, by the end of 2005, was costing more to run than the value of the payments it was making to its clients. The difficulties of attempting a large number of changes in systems, client relationships and new IT developments all seem to have conspired to make sure that the Child Support Agency failed to deliver up to expectations.

Other examples abound. One of the most notorious is the failure of the London Ambulance Service (LAS) which aimed, in 1992, to automate the labour-intensive manual dispatch system. Changes were going to be significant, therefore, to the manner in which personnel carried out their work and the introduction of new technology to streamline the whole process from dispatching of ambulances to speeding up the arrival of patients at hospital. There were several risks evident in the process at the outset: in personnel terms, changes to the working procedures of dispatching staff, changes to communications to ambulance drivers; to the system, from manual to computer; and to the hardware, setting up and implementing a local area network. LAS managers set a tight timetable which was said to be non-negotiable, despite many prospective suppliers raising concerns over the time allowed. Advice on procurement was delegated to the systems manager – who was aware that on implementation of the system he would be made redundant – and the contract analyst. There was no input from the professional procurement manager, who was believed to have no expertise in IT. The tenders were evaluated by only these two individuals.

The system was built by a small software house which was the lowest tenderer although it was known that the company had no previous experience in developing this kind of system. The systems requirement specification (SRS) was detailed but took little account of other interfacing systems such as communications. The system was to run on a series of networked PCs and file servers supplied by Apricot Computers using the software developed by the software house. There was little input from ambulance crews at the SRS stage because of disputes and most of the SRS was written by the systems manager and the contract analyst. Thus, those who would be primarily affected had little effect on the specification of the system.

The prime objective of the new system – to deliver a better service to patients while achieving better utilisation of staff and vehicles – was not realised. Despite being lightly loaded at the start, the system soon built up backlogs caused by crew faults, radio blackspots and incorrect system allocations based on incomplete or inaccurate vehicle information. The backlogs scrolled offscreen and became increasingly difficult for staff to attend to and the size of the information queues slowed down the system. The effect on patients was late arrival of ambulances, multiple attendance of vehicles to single incidents, and delays in accepting initial calls. Crews (as well as patients) became increasingly frustrated, which increased radio traffic and contributed to even more communications bottlenecks.

Project management failed in virtually all respects in this example. Poor procurement, poor communications, lack of consultation and training, lack

16

of system testing – all of these contributed to a failure which should never have occurred. Customer satisfaction was never achieved and the reputation of LAS reached rock bottom.

There is often only one way of dealing with this kind of significant failure and that is to start again. Use this bad experience as a learning opportunity. Carry out a post-implementation review and use the mistakes to inform a new approach to project planning and control. The LAS experience shows that calling for a system without the ability to deal with peaks and troughs of capacity results in a system which cannot deal with exceptional loadings. More time and flexibility in implementing the main system would have resulted in a more controlled test phase before live running, and a better backup system would have helped deal with the initial crisis. Critically, involvement of users in system design and training in new methods and practices is essential to the success of a live system.

In the meantime, damage limitation must address the means by which some kind of credibility can be rebuilt both internally and outside the organisation to the important people in the process – the service user. The experience of the LAS points us in the direction that can be taken. In the first place, those with key responsibility must be seen to act. In the case of LAS, the chief executive resigned. Thereafter, a workable, temporary manual system was reintroduced with some limited IT involvement and an entirely new computerised system was devised. Alongside all of this, significant public relations efforts were used to rebuild public confidence while staff involvement and training was increased to a much higher degree.

Other examples of unwanted outcomes from the handling of change are not hard to come by. HM Revenue & Customs was criticised for having poor systems and management approach following the introduction of the tax credits system. Overpayments in 2003/04 amounted to £2.2 billion, much of which had come about through the system being unable to cope with the volume of changes in recipients' circumstances. Interestingly, one of the most fundamental errors was a failure by those responsible for planning the changes to the tax credit system to understand that an organisation like HMRC, which had traditionally only ever collected money for the government, might struggle with the complexities of giving money out without losing control. In yet another case, the Department for Work and Pensions was criticised by the Public Accounts Committee as a result of an estimated £3 billion loss through fraud and error, much of which was caused by staff making errors in benefit payments.

The loss of reputation to HM Revenue & Customs and to the Department for Work and Pensions again shows the effect of failing to manage effectively. Regaining credibility after these events with a constituency which is a generally unwilling contributor to tax anyway provides a real challenge. Mitigating the risks in the first place is a far better strategy than persuading reluctant taxpayers that repayments will be sought and system changes made.

The results of failure to manage change can be significant and risk management has a strong role to play in any project planning and implementation process. Recognising the risks to service delivery and

16

reputation at the earliest of stages gives the opportunity for projects to be better managed. In the case of LAS, the risks of time inflexibility, using a supplier with untested expertise and the lack of involvement of critical parts of the staffing structure could all have been identified by risk management procedures and mitigated accordingly.

Self-assessment question 16.3

List some project management software and tools available which can assist in effective control and the mitigation of risks.

Feedback on page 276

16.4 Legislation and procurement

Learning activity 16.4

List some steps that a purchasing manager can take to reduce the production of waste material in the supply chain.

Feedback on page 276

This section is not designed to give a full review of legislative requirements in the field of procurement. Legal aspects of procurement form a separate part of your course and, in addition, section 15.3 deals with the EC procurement directives. The main areas required for legal knowledge in procurement are:

* UK law – English, Scottish or Northern Ireland as appropriate
* EC law relevant to purchasing – directives
* international law relevant to purchasing – mercantile law, competition law, e-commerce law.

Of further relevance is a knowledge of TUPE (Transfer of Undertakings (Protection of Employment) Regulations), environmental legislation, health and safety legislation and sector-relevant legislation or regulations such as best value. A detailed knowledge of law is difficult to obtain and maintain up to date for anyone other than specialists in law or those concerned with drafting legislation. Nonetheless, purchasing professionals generally have a good knowledge of contracts and are able to access sources of information on other legislative areas such as EC directives or national regulations. For environmental matters, for instance, a good source is the Environment Agency's *NetRegs*, an online resource available at http://www.environment-agency.gov.uk.

Many UK regulations flow from a European Union directive which is the result of a collective decision made by member states acting through national government ministers in the Council and in the Parliament. Both Council and Parliament must approve a text in identical terms in order for a proposal to become law. The overriding principle of law throughout the EU is that national law should prevail over European law where appropriate. Thus a directive requires national implementing legislation in each member state before it comes into effect in that state. By contrast, an EU regulation relies on existing legislation and is self-executing; it does not require any corresponding national legislation to come into force. If a member state fails to pass the necessary national legislation or that legislation does not adequately cover the requirements of the directive, the Commission can initiate action against that state in the European Court of Justice.

A directive is generally justified by a need for harmonisation to reduce market barriers and help create a single market within the EU. Implementing a directive leaves a degree of choice to member states in that, although the directive is binding, national authorities may choose the form and method of implementation. In the UK, most directives are brought into being via Statutory Instruments.

There are several directives which are now regulations in the UK. The Directive on Integrated Pollution and Prevention and Control, designed to prevent or reduce emissions of pollutants to land, air and water, is the UK Pollution Prevention and Control Regulations 2000, and there are the Air Quality (England) Regulations 2000 which protect human health and the environment. The Environment Act of 1995 transferred many environmental issues to the Environment Agency and these include responsibility for flooding information and control, water quality, air quality and control of waste.

The Health and Safety Executive (HSE) is responsible for implementing and controlling areas such as the Health and Safety at Work Regulations and, with the Environment Agency, matters like major accidents and hazards and control of substances hazardous to health. The latter two regulations are usually referred to by the acronyms COMAH (Control of Major Accidents and Hazard Regulations) and COSHH (Control of Substances Hazardous to Health Regulations).

Virtually all products sold in the EU have to be compliant with directives and the 'CE' mark denotes this compliance. Categories covered include:

- pressure equipment machines
- electrical or electronic equipment
- medical devices and equipment
- personal protective equipment
- equipment for use in a potentially explosive environment.

The EU specifies a date for a directive to come into effect in the member states and if the deadline is missed the Commission can commence proceedings in the European Court of Justice against the country concerned. EU citizens can sue the state for damages because of tardy transposition of directives into national legislation and, when national laws may have multiple interpretations, a judge must choose the interpretation that conforms to EU law.

16

Breaches of directives are, in essence, breaches of national law as a result of the process explained above. Appropriate remedies at law or by contractual agreement for non-compliance can therefore apply. These may include breaches under relevant UK laws to which appropriate directives apply and could include breaches under the environmental legislation, health and safety legislation and human rights legislation, to name just a few. Other legislation within which any directives may have been subsumed may also form the basis for seeking a remedy such as damages where it is the breach of the regulation flowing from the directive that has caused a breach of an agreement.

The risks to organisations of non-compliance with laws, regulations or directives include substantial fines, imprisonment and loss of reputation. All of these can impact on survivability and constitute significant risks for any organisation. They should be recognised in the identification and evaluation of risk and appropriate action taken to both lessen the likelihood of their occurrence and mitigate their possible effects. An understanding of the issues in the first instance together with compliance with the requirements of the appropriate legislation is the best strategy. Mitigating actions such as safety audits and seeking assurance from suppliers of their compliance with law should be taken as a matter of course. Environmental audits using the ISO 14000 framework could also be undertaken.

Redress may be sought in a court of law in common with any other matter in which justice is sought. In the public sector, for example, the EU emphasises this right by reference to its Remedies Directives on public procurement in the mainstream sector (89/665/EEC) and public procurement in the utilities sector (92/13/EEC), which allow for damages where breaches occur and also allow judicial review or review by a proper court or tribunal.

Self-assessment question 16.4

Draw up a checklist of UK and European laws and regulations which could affect your organisation's relationship with environmental issues.

Feedback on page 276

16

16.5 Assessing environmental risk

Learning activity 16.5

Read the Defra/Environment Agency guide to environmental risk assessment.

Feedback on page 277

Environmental risks cover the threats caused by various waste materials, toxic materials and pollution of air and water. There may be inherent risks in these threats as well as reputational risks for those involved in perpetrating their causes. Environmental issues are core to the increasing awareness of corporate social responsibility (CSR) because of increasing public awareness of the harmful effects of emissions and pollutants. For most organisations, the penalties for not complying with environmental laws and regulations are increasingly outweighing any benefit from ignoring them.

The Complete Guide to Business Risk Management (Sadgrove 2005) lists eight ways to pollute:

- emissions to air
- discharges to water
- solid waste
- owning (or acquiring) environmentally damaging assets
- producing or using toxic or hazardous materials
- consuming fossil fuels or energy derived from them
- consuming scarce or non-renewable resources
- damage to nature through destruction of natural habitats or amenity space.

It is the attitudes of society which have changed the way in which enterprises have had to organise themselves in order to be more environmentally friendly. Whereas pollutants and emissions used to be seen as part and parcel of industrial activity and therefore unremarkable, increasing knowledge has highlighted the dangers which these wastes can bring and society as a whole has reacted accordingly. Because of the pervasive nature of environmental hazards, organisations have to consider not just the internal risks to their own personnel and assets but also the wider external risks caused by pollutants perhaps being carried long distances from their point of origin and thus affecting potentially large areas and populations. This is the reason that environmental issues are such an important component of CSR.

Pressure groups have had a significant part to play both in raising awareness of environmental hazards and in taking direct action to prevent environmental damage. The tactics of these groups vary from 'tree sitting' in an attempt to prevent building on ground seen as being a natural asset, to sophisticated public relations and media exercises such as preventing the sinking in the Atlantic of the redundant *Brent Spar* oil rig undertaken by Greenpeace. Risks from pressure group activity are likely to increase and become more sophisticated as time goes on. IT systems are certain targets when, by immobilising technology, it can be seen that unprepared corporations can grind to a halt. Just as effective, if not more so, than blockading a factory.

There is much about environmental risk assessment which should be familiar to us as a result of our earlier studies. The assessment process is similar to risk identification and evaluation in any other area of operation, while there is also similarity with HAZOP. Environmental risk assessment tends to consider potential *hazards* and defines these as 'a property or situation that in particular circumstances could lead to harm' and this in broad terms could include impacts of road transport on the environment or the adverse impacts of induced climate change due to fossil fuel emissions. This is not too different from our earlier broad definition of a risk: any unexpected event which may prevent the achievement of objectives.

In common with a good management system and a good quality system, the approach to sound environmental management should focus on a specific method for doing things in order to make expected outcomes more certain. The management system most clearly tailored to environmental requirements is that provided by the ISO 14 000 framework.

ISO 14 000 requires the production of a register, not unlike the risk register with which we are already familiar. This register is termed an 'aspects register' (an 'aspect' is ISO 14 000 terminology for an activity, product or service which may interact with the environment) and serves to illustrate the organisation's environmental impacts in a simple way. Like the risk register, the aspects register can help us recognise the areas where we need to take more action for mitigation purposes or where we are satisfied with the current situation. Table 16.1 illustrates a simple aspects register with a few examples of some possible activities.

Table 16.1 A simple aspects register

Aspect	Normal conditions	Abnormal conditions	Incidents, accidents	Future activities	Past activities
Air emissions Solid waste Toxic material Noise					

It can be seen from table 16.1 that even a simple aspects register may be used to feed into the corporate risk assessment process including the risk register and risk map. Thinking back to the risk map idea, it is easy to imagine that a chemical manufacturing company would have environmental issues 'HH' and coloured red in the top right-hand corner of its board's 10 or 15 biggest risks.

Undertaking an environmental risk assessment follows the steps of understanding our objectives at all corporate levels of activity, considering what events may prevent or hinder achievement of the objectives and then planning reasonable mitigating actions. Environmental risk mitigation starts with the high-level board or governing body consideration of the equivalent of risk appetite: *environmentally friendly*, conforming with best environmental practice; *environmentally neutral*, doing just enough to conform; or *environmentally unfriendly*, doing nothing to conform, even making matters worse by continuing with poor or banned practices.

Environmentally friendly organisations not only conform but make a positive attribute of their approach to the environment and, using this as a marketing tool, turn risk into opportunity. Environmentally unfriendly organisations risk much: there may be financial consequences in the shape of

16

fines and there could even be jail sentences for officials. Various insurances may become increasingly expensive to obtain and even impossible in some cases as a result of taking insufficient or no action to control such things as pollution and waste. Because the environment is so important an area for most consumers, at least in the West, there are huge reputational risks in not conforming. Demand is bound to suffer and market share diminish. Further, the medium- and long-term future is likely to bring even more control and sanction over defaulting companies – future survival could be in doubt. Finally, the neutral organisations will survive but will win no new friends – they may even see themselves as having no interface with environmental issues. Few organisations can afford to be in this position given the way people and processes react and, for future success and customer satisfaction, these organisations also will have to improve their response to environmental risks and realities.

In procurement, clients want to be sure that their suppliers are being as environmentally friendly as possible as well as doing all they can to avoid becoming an environmentalist's target. Supplier appraisals should take account of these needs and, where appropriate, evidence of environmental compliance should be requested in tender documents. Above all, there should be organisational policy which clarifies the organisation's position on environmental issues and follows through to an annual plan which sets targets in particular areas for improvement. These targets could include lower carbon emissions, less water use and a greater use of energy from sustainable sources.

Environmental auditing is an accepted means for providing assurance to management that the environmental management system is working effectively. This is not a statutory audit and may be carried out by the organisation's own internal auditing function or by specialist environmental auditors brought in from outside. The need is to make the audit independent from operational management so that a good, objective view of the situation can be taken. Typically, the audit will review the performance of the environmental management system against the organisation's own stated objectives and against those of ISO 14 000 (there is also a similar EU eco-management and audit standard). The audit report should guide the organisation's management to a more effective compliance with the standard or provide satisfaction that the standard is, in fact, currently being achieved.

Environmental risks have always existed. Now, however, the importance of leaving the planet in a suitable condition for our successors, as well as improving current conditions, means that managing the issues effectively is of ever greater importance. Being a socially responsible neighbour in the environmental context is a good thing in itself. Managing environmental risks effectively brings the added bonus of customer satisfaction, safe reputation and avoidance of detrimental financial consequences.

16

Self-assessment question 16.5

You are the purchasing manager for a large manufacturer of cardboard cartons. Your managing director has asked what the implications would

(continued on next page)

Self-assessment question 16.5 *(continued)*

be of insisting that your major suppliers have ISO 14 000 or 14 000.1 accreditation. What would your suppliers have to do to become accredited? How realistic would it be to insist on this?

Feedback on page 277

Revision question

Now try the revision question for this session on page 357.

Summary

This study session has discussed the gains which can be achieved through the effective use of IT. Innovative ways of using IT, in particular, use of the internet, can bring benefits to the procurement process in terms of speed of transaction and wider access to sourcing. Internal communications can also be more effective by utilising IT. New developments in IT inevitably bring the need for changes in operations, activities and relationships. We have considered how change can impact on organisations and how change in any circumstances needs to be properly managed if the expected outcomes are to be achieved. Finally, we have considered environmental issues in terms of risk assessment and management and how the environment can be used as a source of opportunity or as an area where reputation and financial loss may signal the demise of established enterprises.

Suggested further reading

DEFRA (2000)

International Organisation for Standardisation. *ISO 14 000* http://www.iso.org.

Sadgrove (2005), chapter 7.

Feedback on learning activities and self-assessment questions

Feedback on learning activity 16.1

Your organisation may make use of a wide range of e-procurement methods which could include reverse auctions, supplier partnerships for stock provision (eg JIT agreements), cataloguing and electronic fund transfers for swift and easy payment of suppliers. Web-based applications could also include seeking out new suppliers and researching travel arrangements, while the intranet is an internal network resource which can be accessed at different levels of security for particular applications. The intranet is an ideal medium for bulletin boards, internal correspondence and for posting document drafts which need the input of a variety of people throughout the organisation. Standard procedure manuals and standard documents can be held on the intranet and easily accessed when necessary.

16

Feedback on self-assessment question 16.1

Your list of risks could include:

- Limiting access to sensitive data
- Maintaining confidentiality
- Payment fraud.

Mitigation of these risks can be achieved by (among other things) systems access controls including login and password, system reports of unauthorised access attempts, restricted access for external users, supplier identification systems and the setting of authority levels for all access and payment levels. Payment cards can be used for avoiding the administrative burden and achieve some efficiencies but are usually only for low-value purchases because of the risks they can bring through poorly controlled use, for example risk of personal purchases, misuse of spend limits and poor supervision.

Feedback on learning activity 16.2

Your research should find that often changes are linked to gaps becoming evident between objectives, targets and goals, and actual achievement. Systems, methods, procedures – all may be inappropriate through passage of time or poor application. Small changes may also have occurred gradually to the extent that the original intention is no longer clear. Fundamental change may also occur through merger and takeover, also as a result of moves into new or different markets. Planning methods for change could include scenario planning, brainstorming and using mind-mapping or decision tree analysis as an aid to getting the best answer. Review of previous projects can be a good guide to avoiding past mistakes – in particular, recommendations from post-implementation reviews – were they relevant and can they help current and future projects?

Feedback on self-assessment question 16.2

This classic example of making a change is not uncommon and runs the risk of alienating all staff unless they can be convinced that this change is for *their* benefit as well as the benefit of the organisation. Reputational risks also exist in terms of impact on markets and society if lay-offs are not well handled.

The objectives of the change need to be communicated along with the expected outcomes in terms of future employment as well as future profit. Line managers need to be convinced of their having access to additional training in order to be effective in purchasing. It might also be advisable to implement an electronic procure-to-pay system to enforce compliance in the use of preferred suppliers – although this raises the question as to who, with no purchasing department in place, is going to maintain the preferred supplier list. Demotivation of all managers is a risk if the IT system is not ready for the change and if line managers see that they are regarded in the same light as their purchasing counterparts, that is, dispensable at any time.

16

Feedback on learning activity 16.3

In 2003 it was reported that more than £1.5 billion in taxpayers' money had been wasted on delayed or cancelled UK government projects over the previous 6 years. These included an estimated £698 million spent on a cancelled project to develop smartcards for benefits payments and £134 million overspent on the LIBRA project to overhaul the IT systems for magistrates' courts.

The major contributing factors to failure include:

*   poor specification
*   lack of the right technical expertise
*   poor project control
*   underestimates of both cost and time.

Feedback on self-assessment question 16.3

Accessing the internet should have given you a vast list of software. As examples you could have found MS Project at http://www.microsoft.com, the P2netPRINCE 2 toolbox at http://www.concertosupport.co.uk (and elsewhere), time and project tracking software at DOVICO, the Tract IT suite at http://www.timetrackingsoftware.com and Easy Projects NET, particularly relevant for IT projects, at http://www.easyprojects.net.

Feedback on learning activity 16.4

There are various EC directives covering waste which are subsumed into UK legislation by Statutory Instrument. An example is the EC Directive on Waste Incineration which, in the UK, becomes the Waste Incineration Regulations 2000. Regulations concerning waste and its disposal must be complied with so it is incumbent on all management to minimise waste – besides, waste means additional cost. Procurement should ensure that the steps taken include some or all of the following: correct products are specified and deliveries exactly meet specification in terms of price, quality and time of delivery. Contact should be maintained with operations management to review the supply and to obtain feedback on performance. This will assist in refining product specification and informing suppliers of any deficiencies which need to be remedied – time wasted and product rejected will be minimised.

Feedback on self-assessment question 16.4

Your answer could have included:

*   EU Directive on Waste (also on hazardous waste, waste incineration, landfill waste)
*   Clean Neighbourhood and Environment Act 2005
*   EU Directive on Integrated Pollution Prevention and Control (UK Pollution Prevention and Control Regulations 2000)
*   Environment Act 1995
*   Health and Safety at Work Regulations etc 1974 – augmented by the Management of the Health and Safety at Work Regulations 1999

16

and, in terms of the environment, Control of Noise at Work
Regulations 2006
* EU Directive on Waste Electrical and Electronic Equipment.

Feedback on learning activity 16.5

Defra on its website (http://www.defra.gov.uk/environment/risk/eramguide)
provides guidelines which you should have found cover the framework for
environmental risk assessment and other matters including the social aspects
of environmental risk.

At the Environment Agency site (http://www.environment-agency.gov.uk)
you will have found, among other things, the Agency's management
guidelines which give information about compliance with various
environmental edicts – see *NetRegs* on this website.

Feedback on self-assessment question 16.5

The ISO 14 000 'family' is concerned with environmental management.
ISO 14 000 is concerned with the way in which organisations achieve
efficiency and effectiveness in terms of their environmental management
system (EMS) while meeting customer quality requirements, complying
with regulations and meeting environmental objectives. Organisations
seeking accreditation aim to minimise the harmful effects on the
environment caused by their activities and to achieve continual
improvement of their environmental performance. ISO 14 000.1 specifies
the requirements for an EMS that may be objectively audited for self-
declaration or for second- or third-party audit. Thus, your suppliers would
have to seek certification of their EMS by an accredited body that has
audited the system and declared that it conforms. This will entail both time
and cost for your supplier and may not be of sufficient benefit to win your
business – although, of course, the certification can be used for general
publicity and marketing and may be seen as an overall benefit. You can
specify what you wish in your tendering provided it is lawful, so seeking
ISO 14 000 can be specified provided it is not anti-competitive or in breach
of any other contracting requirement.

16

16

International issues

Introduction

Communications, IT and the growth of multinational corporations have all contributed to the 'global village' effect which ease of travel and increased world trading has brought about. International trading brings with it particular risks, however, as well as significant opportunities. This study session explores several issues that may impact on the supply chain, all of which can affect the way buyers may approach the initial setting up of international deals or of maintaining existing arrangements. Various bodies and agencies are available to provide assistance in this area, both national and international. The manner in which interactions may occur between international bodies and enterprises trading globally is considered in addition to the way in which geophysical issues impact on travel, trade and competitive advantage.

Session learning objectives

After completing this session you should be able to:

17.1 Demonstrate how the effective management of some key operational areas such as tariffs, quotas and alternative supply sources, eg in commodities, can make a major contribution to an organisation.
17.2 Analyse the impact of culture, language and economic development on international business relationships.
17.3 Prepare a plan of action for improving relationships when dealing with foreign suppliers.
17.4 Summarise the possible geographical causes of delays and damage in your supply chain.
17.5 Distinguish between the payment methods commonly used for international sourcing.
17.6 Assess the implications of different standards by foreign suppliers and service providers and the effect this may have on goods or services sourced for the UK market.

Unit content coverage

17

This study session covers the following topics from the official CIPS unit content document:

Learning objective

3.1 Develop appropriate solutions to mitigate the inherent risks in the following supply chain issues:
* Supplier appraisal, selection and management
* Project failure (eg capital procurement – investment appraisal)
* International sourcing

- Implementation of new technologies
- Corporate social responsibility (CSR) including ethical, environmental and health and safety issues
- Public sector procurement

Prior knowledge

Study sessions 1 to 16.

Resources

Internet access.

Timing

You should set aside about 6 hours to read and complete this session, including learning activities, self-assessment questions, the suggested further reading (if any) and the revision question.

17.1 Global and international purchasing

Understand the role of overseas agents

Learning activity 17.1

Select one of the UK's trading destinations, eg Nigeria, and use the PESTLE analysis to list the key risks in trading with this country.

Feedback on page 295

Global sourcing and international purchasing are two different but similar terms applied to obtaining goods from foreign suppliers. Global sourcing has been defined as the integration and coordination of procurement requirements across worldwide business units, looking at common items, process, technology and suppliers. It is practised by large corporations as they have the need and leverage to gain competitiveness from global sourcing and the facilities around the globe to enable them to apply the process. It is characterised by contractual arrangements with other large corporations who have the ability to supply products to the globally located sites of the multinational purchaser.

International purchasing is the purchasing from another country of the products or services required by the purchasing organisation. In other words, it involves importing. All organisations can practise international purchasing although it does require knowledge and skill to ensure that the expected benefits are attained. It does not require the global integration and coordination of the purchaser's demand with the supplier's global ability to supply, which characterises global sourcing.

For many organisations, particularly initially, entry into new and unknown international markets can be facilitated by using the local knowledge of

17

agents already established in-country. Agents know the local situation, are conversant with law and culture, understand tariffs and customs procedures and can ease the introduction of buyers to sellers. They will charge a fee for their expertise which will need to be built in to the costing profile but, in the fullness of time, the buying organisation's own expertise may supersede the need for agency involvement.

The reasons for sourcing overseas are many. In some cases there may be no local supply available – commodities such as coffee and tea, for example – although there may be more than one commodity-supplying country. In other cases the buyer is looking for other advantages which could include:

- price – lower supply price through labour cost advantage, exchange rates or economies of scale
- delivery scheduling – continuity of supply may be better overseas through larger capacities
- satisfaction – home market demand stimulation by combination of price, quality and product availability factors.

Offsetting these potential benefits will be other factors which may complicate the process of sourcing from overseas and eradicate the advantages considered above:

- Lead time – shipping from an overseas location will take longer than home supply.
- Stockholding – shipping methods will have an impact on cost but also on needs for additional 'buffer' stocks; if quotas exist, stockholding may have to compensate for peaks and troughs of supply.
- Funding – credit terms may vary, thus affecting cash flows; additional insurances may be necessary; special packaging may add to base cost; exchange rate fluctuations may affect earlier pricing strategies.
- Customs – tariffs or duties may be imposed on commodity and other supplies; customs may also be poor facilitators of speedy exports.
- Quality – rejects may be difficult to return or obtain credit for (increasing acceptance of ISO 9000 should offset this substantially).

The impact of any of these and the probability of them affecting your overseas trade need to be evaluated as with any other organisational risks. The competitive advantage which you see from sourcing overseas may be wiped out by some or all of these risks occurring. In fact, it may be worse than just that if, by sourcing overseas, you have then effectively cut off home-grown supply by ceasing relations with local suppliers or by reducing the production volume of the home industry.

Commodities are undifferentiated products whose market value arises from the owner's right to sell rather than the right to use, that is, raw materials sourced in a country which, with little or no processing, are available for sale on world markets; examples are wheat, coffee and oil. They have several vulnerabilities on both the supply side and the demand side. For the producing country, it may be the only source of wealth and can be subject to political vagaries because of this. Abnormal weather may be another factor affecting production and, therefore, income and, of course, world demand variations will also affect national income, causing price fluctuations over which the producing country has little control, although, of course, many

17

other factors can affect price also. Price and availability affect the demand side, causing possible production peaks and troughs in addition to pressure on consumers. Mitigating these risks by finding substitute products or sources is often impossible, given the basic nature of commodities.

The General Agreement on Tariffs and Trade (GATT) began as the means for liberalisation of world trade following the damaging effects of protectionism in the global trade depression of the 1930s. Protectionism leads to tariffs being imposed to discourage overseas supply, usually in an attempt to protect local industry. The side effect of this is often to encourage poor efficiency and limit customer choice. Various rounds of GATT have sought to reduce or eliminate tariffs by multilateral trade liberalisation and GATT itself was superseded by the World Trade Organization (WTO) in 1995. The current round of negotiations, the Doha Development Agenda, includes negotiations on agriculture, non-agricultural market access, trade facilitation and the environment.

The trading risks referred to above could be compounded by political changes in any potential trading partner or trading bloc. The UK, as part of the EU, promotes the so-called Helsinki Principles (agreed in Helsinki, Finland, in October 1999) which aim to promote greater efficiency and private sector participation in international commodity bodies. The principles include the encouragement of liberalisation of commodity markets and reducing the negative social, political and economic impacts of commodity dependence in the poorest of countries. Unfortunately, this kind of agreement, or any WTO diktat, may not impress a totalitarian regime in a country with heavy dependence on a few, or only one, commodities. Political considerations of that regime may override any other consideration and cause significant problems for buyers who do not have alternative sources of supply.

Protectionism is costly. Trade barriers and tariffs distort domestic markets, protect inefficient sectors from competition and push up consumer prices. Foreign producers are penalised and there are inefficient allocations of resources both domestically and globally. The UK is committed to the lowering and eventual elimination of all tariff and non-tariff barriers to trade. International trade can, however, assist buyers in gaining access to a wider choice of supply and is a major focus of help for developing nations in establishing products and markets and in reducing poverty.

Self-assessment question 17.1

What are the advantages and disadvantages of using agents in foreign countries to act on behalf of your organisation?

Feedback on page 295

17.2 Cultural and language impacts on overseas relationships

The United Kingdom is made up of a variety of countries, cultures, dialects and even languages. There are legal variations between some of the constituent countries and the well-publicised 'north/south divide' epitomises the perceived differences between those in the south of the country and those in the north. So, even in our own country, many cultural and other differences contribute to our national identity. Despite this, the UK has a more or less common understanding of trade, business relationships and the way things are done.

Culture is an amalgam of attitudes, practices, behaviours and laws, formed by history and tradition and, to a certain extent, current affairs and characterised by the phrase 'the way things are done round here'. Elsewhere in the world, the way things are done may vary considerably from our traditions in the UK. Nonetheless, if we wish to trade with other parts of the world then we need to gain an understanding of the differences which can apply so that we can source and subsequently contract effectively for the supply which we need.

Many of the raw materials necessary for production in the UK are only available overseas. Therefore, if we want to commence or continue production using these materials, we need to work with producers in these countries to ensure, as far as possible, a secure supply. Gone are the days when the British Empire provided the largest trading bloc and exploitation of commodities from the Empire formed the basis of British industry.

However, buyers still seek to obtain the best deal. Global trading and the fact that the old Empire's 'captive' market has long since ceased to exist mean that the UK is in competition for the world's scarce resources just like any other trading country. Part of gaining competitive edge is to have a good understanding of the way things are done in the country of potential supply.

There are huge differences between markets. The emerging markets of Eastern Europe pose different challenges to those in Africa and the Middle East, not to mention China. History shapes nations in a variety of ways and the way in which trade is carried out depends on the ways in which cultures have developed and the length of time that has been involved. There can be significant differences in the way companies are directed and controlled; responsibility and authority levels may be different – decision makers may not be at the same level in some countries as we are familiar with in the UK; monetary payments to encourage preference may not be seen as bribes but as the normal way of doing business; attempting to influence officials in order to get government approval may, in fact, be the way business is expected to be done rather than 'corruption' in our terms.

English is widely accepted as the international language of business. This is both a benefit to British business people and a potential disadvantage. The benefit is that many people in other countries speak our language and speak it well. The disadvantage is that we tend to be bad at learning foreign languages. Failure to speak the local language in a foreign country can be a major barrier to understanding the local culture. This can be a problem for us in Europe, never mind the more exotic areas such as Africa, South America, the Middle and Far East. Not understanding the national language of a potential supplier means relying on translators. This can create problems with negotiations and sometimes in agreeing contracts. Knowledge of language also can help greatly in understanding the legal framework in different countries and this may be particularly relevant when trying to

17

reconcile practices and attitudes with the laws and regulations which apply in the UK and Europe.

Culture defines a nation. Procurement success in other countries is enhanced when there is real understanding of different ways of doing things and where the objectives of both buyer and seller can be complemented. The greatest risk is not understanding these things and failing because of that to secure the supply you want at the quality and price which makes it worthwhile for you.

Learning activity 17.2

Look at Transparency International's 'corrupt perceptions index' and discuss with colleagues or with your tutor why the top three and bottom three are in those positions. Identify the main reasons why you think these countries find themselves in the positions they are in.

Feedback on page 296

Economic differences also impact on culture, relationships and understanding. Free market conditions such as we are familiar with in the West may not exist in countries where new supply opportunities are being sought. Centralised economies behave in different ways and require very different approaches to government officials who deal with trade. Even the recently freed command-and-control economies of the communist bloc in Eastern Europe are very different to those in the West despite their attempts to emulate Western market conditions. Attitudes are still shaped by history, even to the extent that some of the markets in Eastern Europe have swung to the opposite extreme and seem to be free of all control, not just central control.

Some of the cultural differences may seem to act as barriers. The ethical approaches of UK countries tend towards the moral high ground because this can, in fact, contribute to competitive advantage in winning and keeping customers. The policies of the Cooperative Bank, for example, are instrumental in maintaining its reputation and include a policy of not investing in weapons manufacturing companies or in countries where human rights are less respected or where environmental impact has not been taken seriously. These barriers can, however, also be used to advantage. By not trading with these companies or countries, changes in behaviour can be encouraged so that, as things change, the chances for trade increase and the benefits for those countries can be seen by its population.

The real problem in understanding the differences in culture is in finding the right balance between forcing change and allowing it to happen at its own pace. Bribery and corruption cannot be stamped out overnight but, by encouraging gradual changes in attitude and practice, they may become less and less endemic. Encouragement of social policies, for example, and funding some of these policies by donations is an excellent way of diverting funds from individual incentive to incentive for the whole community. Directly funding the provision of doctors, nurses and healthcare supplies in

17

an area where there may be basic buildings but not professional staff would be an example of this.

Many countries encourage and, indeed, rely upon foreign direct investment. These investments may be the only way that emerging economies can fund large projects such as dams and power plants. A survey carried out in 2000 jointly by the World Bank and the Brookings Institute of Washington, USA, concluded that corruption acts as a strong deterrent to foreign direct investment. Changes in attitude to corrupt behaviour could be seen to bring benefits, therefore, since companies will be more willing to invest in countries when bribery and corruption cease to be normal practice there.

Changes in practice by companies and by countries can be tracked relatively easily and risk perception changed accordingly. The World Bank produces a periodic 'blacklist' of companies and individuals known to have infringed its procurement guidelines. We have already mentioned the anti-corruption body, Transparency International (TI), which publishes an annual list of the countries it considers to be the most or least likely to be corrupt. The TI list, known as the 'corrupt perceptions index', is compiled by using expert assessment and surveys and should be part of the research done by any purchasing department considering sourcing overseas. TI also gathers and provides data on the supply side of corruption, companies known to be involved in seeking to give bribes, and, again research on this index helps to establish as much data as possible on countries where investment or operations are being contemplated.

The World Bank has also introduced (2005) a World Governance Index. This has been done to reflect the upsurge in interest in effective corporate governance around the world. Ethical behaviour which includes anti-corruption and fair trading features strongly in good governance and is yet another area in which to seek indicators for the way commerce is approached in any country of interest.

Language difficulties can be overcome simply by taking the time and trouble to learn the language of the countries with which we trade now or hope to trade in future. Beyond that, translation is usually available although with the ever-present risk of interpretation nuances. Culture, on the other hand, may take a long time to understand while the need to start trading is urgent. Risk management in this area requires much research and strong management from the purchasing organisation. Strong management includes adhering to the ethical standards which reflect the attitude and culture of reasonable people. This in turn encourages behavioural changes which will help to avoid exploitation and benefit the supplier as well as the buyer.

17

Self-assessment question 17.2

Draw up a list of the main points for a training course which your organisation has decided to establish for purchasing officers dealing with overseas countries.

Feedback on page 296

17.3 Improving relations with foreign suppliers

Learning activity 17.3

Consult the DTI website and investigate the statements regarding doing business in a country of your choice. How would these statements affect a decision to trade with that country? Review, also, Foreign and Commonwealth Office advice on its website.

Feedback on page 296

Global and international sourcing are similar but slightly different concepts as we saw in section 17.1. Relationship issues apply to both forms of sourcing but there may be more of an arm's-length relationship position when dealing with international purchasing; the buying client may not have global locations and deals with the supplier as a straightforward import source.

The first step is to allocate specific international responsibilities to appropriate buyers. This may require development of several new skills including an understanding of the culture of the country to be dealt with, its language and currency differences; an international perspective; and an understanding of the new risks which dealing with a foreign supplier may pose. Many of these have been dealt with in section 17.2, eg lack of language and cultural understanding is a significant risk in making deals and closing contracts and currency fluctuations in foreign exchange dealings pose a key financial risk – and these risks have to feature in supplier appraisal and other buying decisions.

The PESTLE analysis can be particularly helpful in assessing the development levels of prospective suppliers in foreign countries. Political awareness is a key factor in successful overseas trade – not just understanding the vagaries of local politics but being able to influence decision making by fostering contacts with both political leaders and civil servants.

There may be barriers to change in moving from local or domestic suppliers to an international supply source. These barriers could be either personal or nationalistic: (i) personal in that local employment threats may be perceived by switching to overseas supply or there may be a lack of confidence in the ability to deal with a different buying approach, at least in the early stages – if quality and delivery does not work well, there could be an immediate downturn in sales and, therefore, job threats, and (ii) nationalistic in the encouragement of overseas jobs at the expense of both domestic supply and production employment. Recognising these fears and clearly identifying the reasons for the change (eg cost benefit or quality benefit) help to ensure that motivation is maintained.

Part of starting or maintaining and developing a supplier relationship with foreign suppliers is to gain or keep trust, although, of course, this is true of any supplier in any country. Achieving this depends upon the seller perception of making a good deal without exploitation, while the buyer must be genuine in the desire both to get the best deal for his company and to help the seller gain or keep a market for his goods. Helping the supplier to develop the best production and quality systems not only assists the supplier's ability to achieve the buyer's required standard but is helpful in boosting the supplier's motivation and willingness to work with the buying company.

Many of the methods which buyers would apply in the home market to improve relationships apply also when developing foreign suppliers. These include sharing of business strategies, where appropriate, cross-transfer (seconding) of staff for temporary periods – particularly from the supplier to the buyer – and on-site training of the supplier's staff. All of these help with the task of mutual understanding of each other's culture, business and way of life.

The solutions to domestic interrelationships may be similar to those overseas but there can be significant problems which need to be overcome. Foreign suppliers may not be at either the educational or technical level of home suppliers and this can make communication and training difficult. Knowledge of import/export issues may be at different levels and issues of cultural difference can be significant. Political systems may be very different to those in the home country and the way business is done may also be significantly different. Successful foreign relationships are nonetheless essential if anything other than a one-off single supply is to be obtained.

The FTSE4Good London Stock Exchange listing index is a means for responsible investors to identify companies which meet globally recognised corporate responsibility standards. The index provides socially responsible investors with a benchmarking tool to both make investments and develop investment products. Companies in the index must first be listed in the FTSE All Share Index (UK) or the FTSE Developed Share Index (global) and there are five criteria for inclusion:

- working towards environmental sustainability
- developing positive relationships with stakeholders
- upholding and supporting universal human rights
- ensuring good supply chain labour standards
- countering bribery.

The criteria can be used as a framework, also, for maintaining or developing relationships with your suppliers and agents in foreign countries. The way in which a buyer or a buying company is perceived is a critical factor in building trust and the five factors above can give us the means to win the seller's confidence by showing our acceptance of these aspirations. Conversely, we can apply the criteria as a 'scorecard' against the way in which the seller is currently doing business and aim to help in improving the standard in each of these areas should this be necessary. Assisting in development of a supplier's business and products is a critical part of building a successful relationship and work in the appropriate areas will build trust in a future mutually beneficial relationship.

17

Finance may be a problem which needs to be overcome. Developing countries may not have either the capital markets or the understanding of strategic investment which is common in the home country. There may be currency barriers as well as trade tariffs to overcome and all of these add to the cultural barriers which affect our relationships with suppliers. Often the buyer needs to be the catalyst in solving these problems and, for UK buyers, there is plenty of help to hand. The Export Credit Guarantee Department is a resource available to offset some risks by providing insurance against political risk in equity or loan investment overseas (as its name implies, it is a large player also in export insurances) and the Foreign and Commonwealth Office (FCO) maintains many overseas embassies, high commissions, consulates and missions, a significant part of whose duties is to assist trade and help build trading relationships. The local knowledge provided by these offices is invaluable and can also give an insight into the availability and competence of agents appropriate to a buyer's business. Contact with these offices and getting as much up-to-date information as possible on a continuous basis from other sources such as the Department for International Development and UK Trade and Investment all helps to get the right 'feel' for a particular country and is essential for maintaining relationships in the countries.

Trade missions sponsored by government and chambers of commerce among others also provide an excellent medium for obtaining first-hand information about a country by being part of the mission or getting information from it on its return. These missions are a two-way process, allowing the members of the mission to visit in-country and see for themselves what conditions are like, but also encouraging meetings with agents and suppliers which will be the foundation of future business relationships. Contact will also be made with the country's government departments and officials. Political lobbying, that is, making attempts to influence decision making at government level, is an essential part of relationship building and assuring good future treatment by appropriate local government departments.

In summary, a plan for building and maintaining foreign relationships will have the following features:

- nominated responsible individuals
- education and training in appropriate country culture and language
- contact with appropriate UK and overseas government departments
- confidence building with agents or directly with suppliers
- help with developing standards and quality
- sharing the financial burden, eg possible payment default.

Self-assessment question 17.3

Explain how you would deal with an outbreak of political instability in a country from which you obtain strategic supplies.

Feedback on page 297

17

17.4 Geographical effects in the supply chain

Learning activity 17.4

When taking a business trip or holiday abroad, what are the geographical issues against which you might take out insurance?

Feedback on page 297

The economics of a geographical area can be influenced by climate, geology and socio-political factors. These factors also affect the interaction between geographic areas – which could be single countries or regions – and are often influenced by historical associations as well as relative distances.

Geological factors can have a major influence on natural resources – agriculture and forestry products, for example – and affect the way in which land is utilised. Natural geographic features such as mountain barriers and oceans affect transportation methods and cost and can also dictate working methods, the extent of mechanisation, for example in hilly terrain, and, therefore, productivity levels.

Infrastructure can also play a large part in economic development. The extent to which raw materials can be accessed and transported to a point of shipment, for example, can have a significant effect on the volume of a country's exports and therefore the value of its foreign trade. Natural barriers and climate can have a major impact on the extent to which commodities can be extracted or grown and on the way roads or railways can be established and maintained. Constant rainfall and flooding can make road maintenance both difficult and costly while silting in rivers may lead to port blockages and shipping delays.

Early economic geography models like that of Huntington (Ellsworth Huntington, Yale University, in the early 20th century) postulated that climate had a significant effect on economic development. He arrived at this conclusion by comparing the well-developed economies of northern temperate and colder countries like those in Europe, North America and Japan with those in hot, tropical countries which were far less developed and, additionally, appeared to have less stable political regimes. This rather simplistic model has been superseded by theories which take into account other factors, notably distance, travel time and size of the economy. These models tend to be referred to as spatial or locational rather than economic geographic models because of their use of a wider variety of factors.

One such model is the gravity model of trade which predicts bilateral trade flows. Geography in this model accounts only for distance, while the other variables consider economic size, usually GDP measurements and can also include tariffs, language and any colonial history. Another model is the Porter's cluster (Michael Porter, Harvard University). This model postulates a competitive geographic cluster where:

* resources and competences amass and reach a critical threshold

17

- a key position is held in a given branch of economic activity
- there is a sustainable competitive advantage.

Two types of competitive cluster are recognised based on (a) a high-technology orientation, and (b) historic knowhow. Porter claimed that clusters have the potential to affect competition by increasing productivity of companies within the cluster, driving innovation in the field and stimulating new business in the field. An alternative to clusters which recognises a more global approach are the geographic locations of so-called hubs and nodes. Examples of these geographic clusters, hubs or nodes include:

- 'Silicon valley', California: computer technology
- Toulouse, France: aerospace industry (and Seattle, USA)
- Rotterdam, Holland: main European container port
- Bangalore, India: software outsourcing.

Risks linked to economic geography include the factors of time, distance and methods of transportation and, of course, the nature of the good concerned. Product volatility affects some raw material (eg oil, coal) and may dictate particular vessel types for shipment which, in turn, may affect travel time and cost. Achieving an economic volume of product also affects method of shipment, time and cost. A good example of this is chilled and frozen products from Australia and New Zealand which require refrigerated transport to survive the long journey times from these countries to a destination in Northern Europe. Some risk share or transfer can be achieved by using commodity markets to buy and sell rather than dealing directly with source suppliers, and marine insurance can also be used to offset loss or damage to cargo in transit.

Geography may well be the prime factor in single-source goods or commodities. Distance from the market combined with natural geophysical barriers and lack of alternative supply or the ability to substitute brings risks which are difficult to mitigate. These risks can include increased costs in the form of holding buffer stocks in order to have some influence on supply, and in increases in product base cost through real or engineered scarcity. Again, adroit use of futures markets can help to mitigate some of these risks.

The availability of relatively cheap air travel has had the effect of shrinking the world for tourism and business. There are few exotic locations which are not now accessible within a reasonably short time frame. This has tended to lower barriers of cultural understanding while making it easier for business to access far-flung markets. IT has had the same effect. Global communications, instantly available 24/7, and universal air travel tend to make us forget that it still takes a ship a long time to traverse an ocean carrying the goods which were ordered instantly by email.

Most tourists are not interested in economic geography. Geography for them means the opportunity to visit lands and peoples with different lifestyles, culture and language to our own. Geography for some tourists means, in fact, going further and further afield to find the ideal, golden deserted beach. This tourist geography brings with it different risks. Travellers need to be aware of new medical risks which they would not be exposed to in their home country. Air travel now also means hijack and terrorism risks and the need to be aware of the differences in political systems and the instability of some regimes in particular global regions. There is an awareness now, also, of geophysical risks such as the tsunami of 2004 and recent earthquakes in Turkey and Pakistan.

- Traveller awareness is the key to risk mitigation in these areas. Use of the FCO website, for example, which gives useful information on climate, current weather, medical problems and political stability, can help to inform the decisions we make about the countries we visit. Good and comprehensive travel insurance is also mandatory for the experienced traveller.

Self-assessment question 17.4

List some of the geographical problems that may be faced when sourcing from Central America (eg Nicaragua, Panama).

Feedback on page 297

17.5 Payment methods for international settlements

Learning activity 17.5

Compare the payment methods that you use with your local suppliers with those methods used for international suppliers.

Feedback on page 298

Methods of paying for transactions stem from early systems of barter and move on to commodity-based payments. Commodity money comes from the underlying value of the commodity from which the money is made – gold, for example. Although more convenient than barter, it is inconvenient to use as a medium of exchange or standard deferred payment due to the logistical difficulties of storage and transport. The value of commodity money stems from there being a guarantee of the value being represented by an amount being held in store somewhere secure 'on account'.

Paper money begins to solve the storage and transport problems but has limitations and other payment methods evolved to overcome some of these. Payments by cheque or bill can represent large sums but take up little space themselves, although other problems clearly exist when there is no 'cash in hand', only a promise to pay. Means for providing assurances that due payments will actually take place are at the heart of the credit system of payment and form the foundation of the system for international payments.

International trading involves international bodies at various levels. At the macro level, the International Monetary Fund (IMF) is the lender of last resort for its member countries who find themselves in financial

17

distress because of imminent default on debt payments, for example, or when a currency crisis occurs. The IMF has other roles to play in macro-economics but, where transactions between organisations in different countries are concerned, it has little effect. Other global organisations, such as the Bank for International Settlements which fosters cooperation between central banks, pursue goals of monetary and financial stability. It is banks and institutions at the micro level, however, to whom we must look for mundane settlement of international transactions.

The main risks for supply chain managers lie in (a) guaranteeing payment to suppliers for products or services ordered, and (b) receiving the good for which deposits or advance payments have been made. Subsidiary risks of foreign exchange rate fluctuation, below-quality standard and return of rejects also exist since each of these may have involved payment in one direction or the other.

Payment methods aim to remove risk by being as secure as possible while meeting contracted dates agreed by the parties concerned. This can be achieved by a bank guarantee, whereby a bank guarantees to a supplier that the recipient of goods is able to meet the agreed commitment and will, itself, pay out on default.

Letters of credit provide a similar guarantee up to the value stated and, again, are aimed at the avoidance of hard cash or cheque transactions which are unfavourable methods of undertaking international trade. Deferred payments achieve a similar result by ensuring that payments are only made at specific points of time or volume of delivery. Risks of default on payment or failing to deliver all the goods are mitigated to a certain extent by this method.

Bank transfers (formerly wire transfers), referred to as electronic funds transfer (EFT), are secure and require only that each party in the supply chain has a bank account. Bank account holders must have been identified and the transfer is made between each bank. The risk of payment not reaching the correct recipient is therefore transferred to the bank.

In the UK the Export Credit Guarantee Department (ECGD) is the body which can provide much in the way of risk mitigation for UK international traders. The bulk of ECGD business involves buyer credits individually tailored for exporters who seek to cover the risk of non-payment or late payment from overseas customers. ECGD can also provide insurance for political risks in overseas countries where investments may have been made or where loans have been made to finance local projects to facilitate future supply contracts.

17

Self-assessment question 17.5

What risks are involved for government departments in using loans and grants to support the development of international supply chains?

Feedback on page 298

17.6 The effects of international standards

Learning activity 17.6

Research the background, rationale and current work of the International Organization for Standardization (ISO) and the International Labour Organization (ILO) and make notes of the impact of those bodies on supplier appraisal, selection and monitoring.

Feedback on page 298

The British Standards Institution has a long history of setting standards for many processes and functions. Many of the British standards have formed the basis for subsequent international standards – BS 7799, the IT management system standard, being a good example, having become ISO 17799. The benefit of international standards, however, is that they can form a common basis across all companies and organisations in whichever process or service is being undertaken. Thus, sourcing from a supplier who holds the relevant standard assists in mitigating some of the risks we might have in terms of quality or reputation of a prospective supplier.

ISO is the international standard-setting body and is a network of the national standards bodies of 156 countries. It is unique in bridging between both private and public sectors and providing standards which meet the needs of society, varied stakeholders, consumers and users. When the large majority of products or services in a particular sector conform to international standards, a state of standardisation can be said to exist. This standardisation is achieved by the agreement of those involved in ISO – governments, regulators, suppliers and users alike – on matters of specification, testing and analysis, terminology and provision of service. In this way international standards provide a common technological language between suppliers and customers which facilitates both trade and the transfer of knowledge and technology.

The application of international standards allows businesses to compete more effectively on the world stage through:

- confidence in product development based on the standards
- acceptance of the standards as a mark of quality
- reputation in the supply chain and with end users of products or services.

Customers benefit from the global compatibility of products and services based on the standards, thus widening choice through competition between suppliers. Governments benefit from the technical and scientific bases underpinning international standards concerning health, safety and environmental issues. International trade benefits since the standards provide a level playing field for competition, avoiding possible barriers being erected by insistence on application of a national standards approach only. International standards provide the defining characteristics that products and services need to meet on the open market, thus assisting developing

17

countries in achieving production and supply standards which will help them compete in exporting. Finally, in general terms, the international standards assist sustainability and corporate social responsibility by encouraging emission control, air quality and water quality, all of which will benefit our own and future generations.

ISO standards are voluntary although some of the standards are referred to in some legislations, notably in matters of health and safety. The market drives the standards, however, as with ISO 9000, the 'quality' management system standard, which is a good example of how some of the standards have become market requirements. Similarly, the World Trade Organization in its Agreement on Technical Barriers to Trade recognises the important contribution which ISO standards and conformity assessments can make to improving efficiency of production and facilitating international trade.

Some countries have their own standards, much like the British standards referred to above, but the benefit of accepting ISO standards is the common benchmark it provides between different organisations in different countries. Product specification in tendering matters becomes much easier to handle than would be the case if a variety of different country standards had to be taken into account. Customer understanding benefits since the ISO accreditation is meaningful in consumer terms. There are cost benefits also, since products do not require to be assessed to many differing standards at various points in the supply chain.

Applying any standard to achieve better quality or more effective management is a benefit to consumers and producers alike. Compliance with the standard is important in order to give confidence and enhance reputation. The effect of international standards is to give buyers and sellers alike the confidence that they need to bring products to market from a variety of competing sources.

Self-assessment question 17.6

How would you respond to a challenge from a major shareholder who is concerned that attractive supply prices are being achieved overseas only because international agreements on fair labour rates are being flouted?

Feedback on page 298

17

Revision question

Now try the revision question for this session on page 357.

Summary

International trading is a means for widening the choice for sources of supply. The benefits may include better cost than in the home market, but may bring other problems which raise new risks. Dealing with these risks needs an understanding of different languages and culture and a good understanding of different ways of doing business. A variety of relationships may need to be nurtured from the use of agents to dealing with foreign civil servants. Payment processes which may seem simple in the home market may be markedly more complex overseas and also need a different approach. All of these matters add up to a need to understand international issues to the full before embarking on a process of overseas sourcing.

Suggested further reading

International Chamber of Commerce. http://www.iccwbo.org.

You could dip into Smith (1776).

Feedback on learning activities and self-assessment questions

Feedback on learning activity 17.1

P – many African countries have totalitarian regimes, the presence of which often brings political unrest, revolutions or rebellions. Regimes such as these may impose protectionist policies which increase prices through tariffs, or control supply through volume quotas.

E – economic factors include control of supply, countertrade agreements or imposition of unfair tendering arrangements.

S – poverty may be endemic as a result of commodity trading price variations and the failure of regimes to pass the benefits of export deals into the infrastructure.

T – technological advances may be slow, in manufacturing processes and in IT, as a result of inability to encourage inward investment or through lack of internal investment in infrastructure.

L – legal processes may vary widely from those expected in the West or the UK. Standards of evidence may be lower and the system of justice may have legacy issues from earlier ethnic forms of justice.

E – environmental standards may not be those which are accepted and encouraged in the West. Environmental practices may still avoid issues of sustainability, pollution and best practice.

Feedback on self-assessment question 17.1

Agents can smooth the path for a new incursion into a supplying country through:

- local knowledge
- political awareness
- range of contacts
- language and culture.

Actions and responsibilities need to be clearly understood by both agent and principal so that both parties benefit from the arrangement. Agents can continue to make a contribution by becoming familiar with the

17

client's business and industry needs but are an additional cost to the client. Depending on the volume of business being placed by the buyer, the cost of using an agent can be much lower than the buying organisation trying to do the work itself. Even if it can avoid having someone 'on the ground' in the country concerned, someone will have to research the local market, identify suppliers and set up any deals. It is also likely that someone will have to visit the supplier from time to time. This can involve significant cost in terms of travel and time. In time, the volume of business placed by the buyer and his knowledge of country culture and business practice may alleviate the need for an agent in favour of the buyer's own representation in-country.

Feedback on learning activity 17.2

You would have found Transparency International at http://www.transparency.org and accessing their corruption perceptions index would show that, of 158 countries listed, Iceland is top, Finland and New Zealand are second equal and Denmark third. At the very bottom is Bangladesh, then Chad, Haiti, Myanmar and Turkmenistan equal second bottom and Cote d'Ivoire, Equatorial Guinea and Nigeria are third bottom. The reasons for these placings include (at the top) open and accountable way of doing business; strong environmental, ethical and social policies; adherence to international standards and commitment to open elections and universal franchise. The opposite tends to be true of the bottom countries with, additionally, graft and corruption featuring in antisocial policies.

Feedback on self-assessment question 17.2

Selection for attendance on the course should include the need to show a positive attitude and a propensity for quick learning so that an understanding of the way things are done in the foreign country can easily be assimilated. The course should include:

- differing attitudes to negotiation
- attitudes to gifts
- ethical stance in different countries
- key aspects of commercial legislation, including contract law
- social conventions (how to meet and how to greet, what to wear or not wear, what to say or not say, and so on)
- national and regional values – differences and how they are shaped or influenced by culture and tradition.

Feedback on learning activity 17.3

You should have found the relevant DTI site (http://www.dti.gov.uk/ewt) which contains a wealth of material on the UK's trading policies both worldwide and within the EU. You could have accessed the section on 'trade by region' to find out about a particular policy and you could have reviewed the information on the Doha Agreements to consider any restrictions or special arrangements which might apply to the country of your choice.

The FCO website (http://www.fco.gov.uk) would have given you information about the role of embassies and consulates operated on behalf of the government and the countries in which they may be found. The FCO also gives information on terrorist alerts and other travel information which may assist in considering trade with a particular country.

Feedback on self-assessment question 17.3

You should have undertaken a PESTLE analysis at the outset of your relationship with the country concerned. This would have highlighted significant risks for which you should have mitigating strategies in place. Since this is a strategic supply, you will already have alternative sources ready if necessary. At this stage, you should be able to implement your fallback strategy but, if that was not already in place and this is an unexpected event, you could start with a SWOT analysis which will indicate to you whether you can consider this a short-term situation or indicate the need for a speedy change of supplier, perhaps by country as well as producing organisation. Scenario planning can also help, that is, planning for several different future threats or outcomes by posing the question 'what if'. You can base the scenario on known trends and forecasts but then ask the 'what if' question or pose entirely new scenarios. In this case, you may have considered price increases or the effect of world trade but did you consider the possibility of political instability? The basis of scenario planning is to attempt to anticipate even the most bizarre future event so that plans can be made to meet those eventualities should they ever occur.

Feedback on learning activity 17.4

Climate is affected by natural features such as mountains, oceans and rivers. These geographical features have known effects on weather and, by ascertaining the weather expected for the time of your visit, you can prepare for that weather or postpone your trip to a more favourable period. Geography also dictates the prevalence of some medical risks against which you should seek inoculation, if appropriate. The possibility of socio-economic factors such as political unrest or labour disputes may be anticipated (in some areas more than others) but access to various websites can give current information on these issues. You should also consider insuring against the possible effects of any of these actions.

Feedback on self-assessment question 17.4

Nicaragua, with capital city Managua, has unique geographical features such as Lake Nicaragua, one of the largest freshwater lakes in the world, the world's second largest rainforest and many volcanoes. The main east coast (Caribbean) port is Bluefields. Coffee is one of the main commodity crops and has to be transported from its growing area in the central highlands to the main port. This entails transport through humid, wet, sparsely populated areas to the relatively small port of Bluefields which lies below a natural barrier of volcanic mountains. Geography therefore contributes to slow, low-volume transport and low-volume shipping because of port size restrictions.

Panama's economy depends on services and tourism and has little or no indigenous crop or natural resource. It has great strategic importance

17

because of its geographical location in the middle of the Central American isthmus through which runs the Panama Canal. There is little raw material sourcing to be done in Panama but it has huge importance as a saver of distance between the Pacific and Atlantic Oceans and, therefore, is a contributor to cost reduction.

Feedback on learning activity 17.5

Electronic funds transfer is a common payment method for domestic creditors and is both secure and fast. The same method can be applied to foreign payments. In each case, both parties require bank accounts for the method to operate. Cheque payments are still used for domestic payments but are generally inappropriate for overseas payments through time factors and lack of payment guarantee for the supplier. Procurement cards are common for payment of low value, one-off transactions.

Feedback on self-assessment question 17.5

The key risk in giving loans is in the possibility of default on repayment. Political changes may change policy in the country to which the loan has been made or corrupt practices in the organisation receiving the loan may result in the money not being used for the agreed reason. Risks also exist in the currency agreed for repayment since exchange fluctuations could affect the final amount repaid. Straightforward grants run the risk of misappropriation or being misapplied which could ultimately affect your reputation.

Feedback on learning activity 17.6

ISO is the world's main developer of standards. Its principal activity is with technical matters but it also considers the social and other issues on which its standards may have an impact. The standards help to avoid a proliferation of national standards standing in the way of international trade. Access the ISO website for more information at http://www.iso.org.

The ILO is a UN body and is headquartered in Geneva. While labour relations is its main interest and area of influence it is also concerned with general employment issues and social issues as they impact on labour. The ILO is concerned with international health and safety of workers issues and is interested in both the supply and demand side of the supply chain and its impact on labour and workers' rights, for example, exploitation. It is concerned also about the use of child labour, available employment opportunities and labour rates in relation to poverty. Find out more at http://www.ilo.org.

Feedback on self-assessment question 17.6

Law, regulation and custom and practice are very different things. The first step would be to ensure that your company's policies comply with and are being enforced in terms of international law. Any evidence of labour rates being flouted would be sought and the reasons for this investigated. If your company can show that it is complying with international agreements in terms of process and procedure rather than specific rates of pay, then you can claim competitive advantage from good buying skills. If you can also show that your company's buying practice has enhanced cash flow in the country concerned and that this is enhancing living conditions, this would put you in a strong position. Similarly if your investment through buying is helping to reduce poverty, again you can show good social responsibility from your actions.

Quality issues

Introduction

Quality control and quality assurance are the terms we immediately associate with striving towards a continuous improvement in the quality of our products and services. In fact, quality relates to the needs and wants of consumers and in satisfying these factors with products and services which are fit for purpose and will achieve customer satisfaction. The level of quality which achieves customer satisfaction is the one to be aimed for and all our procedures and processes should lead to that end. Designing in quality aids prevention of quality loss, and ensuring that quality is the responsibility of every employee helps make sure that systems work effectively. This study session looks at a range of issues associated with achieving the right quality of input and output and considers how standards and methodologies can assist in this task.

There is a strong relationship between price and quality: 'Speeding out into space I reflected that every component in the craft beneath me had been selected from the lowest bidder.'

John Glenn, astronaut

Session learning objectives

After completing this session you should be able to:

18.1 Summarise what needs to be included in effective specifications.
18.2 Evaluate the relative impact of the costs of quality.
18.3 Show how product liability needs to be addressed by supply chain managers.
18.4 Summarise some quality management systems that are used in modern business.
18.5 Learn how to use tools and techniques for measuring quality.

Unit content coverage

This study session covers the following topics from the official CIPS unit content document:

Learning objective

3.4 Analyse specific key risks and exposures in purchasing and supply and identify appropriate mitigating actions.
   • Contractual failure, consequential loss and provision for remedies
   • Supplier insolvency, monitoring and guarantees
   • Quality failure, non-conformity and corrective action
   • Project failure, project planning principles and corrective action
   • Security of supply, contingency planning, stock holding and alternative sources of supply
   • Technology failure, impact on supply, use of back-up systems and disaster recovery
   • Security, theft and damage

18

- Fraud, accounting and payment exposures, conflicts of interest, purchasing ethics and codes of conduct
- Product liability, reputational damage, consumer confidence

Prior knowledge

Foundational understanding of quality assurance and total quality management.

Resources

Internet access.

Timing

You should set aside about 6 hours to read and complete this session, including learning activities, self-assessment questions, the suggested further reading (if any) and the revision question.

18.1 Quality issues in specification

Learning activity 18.1

Identify three situations at your place of work where the product or service was over-specified and three where it was under-specified.

Feedback on page 315

Specification is the means by which we communicate our requirements to the suppliers of the products or services which we need as input to our own operations. A specification is a set of requirements agreed to by the user prior to forming the basis of a procurement process. In procurement terms, the specification is an official document which clearly and accurately describes the essential technical requirements for items, materials or services which we seek to source on behalf of the user function, department or business unit for whom we are acting.

The needs and wants of our own customers will already have been identified by various means including research, and translated into the products or services which are at the heart of our business. Now, as customers ourselves in the supply chain, we want the right product delivered at the right time in order that our own operations can run efficiently and without waste. The task of procurement is to take the specification which has been agreed by the user and then source the product or service in the most efficient, effective and economical way.

In IT, a formal specification can mean a technical description of software or hardware that is then used to develop an expected output. It describes what the system should do, not necessarily how the system should do it. Given this formality and technique of specification, it is possible to verify each competing supplier's proposals against the accuracy of the specification. Failure to meet the verification criteria leaves little room for doubt: specification not met.

Aside from partnership sourcing, the common approach to specification has been to specify in great technical detail and then seek tenders for competitive supply. Deviations from the specification are not encouraged and the emphasis is on price at the point of evaluation. Performance specification moves on from this prescriptive approach to one in which buyers explain their broad needs to suppliers in terms of the performance expected from the product and then allow selected suppliers to propose their best solution. In partnership sourcing one supplier is selected, usually by running a competitive tendering exercise, and the emphasis is on a long-term relationship, working together to meet specifications while reducing cost and improving quality.

Specification is the means we use, therefore, to make the best attempt possible to get the product or service that we want. Accurately stating what is expected is the first step. A clear, concise, complete and accurate description of the product or service required is the essential component of a satisfactory specification. The description may be framed in technical terms or output terms or, most likely, a combination of both. Communications between the users and the purchasing department should be strong so that buyers can put their experience at the disposal of operations staff in matters of similarity of products, product substitution and varying levels of quality to achieve a desired result. This avoids over-specifying (seeking a higher than necessary level of quality or performance) before the tendering process even begins. Conversely, under-specifying – substitution on grounds of lower price only, perhaps – runs the risk of performance not being achieved and a failure of customer satisfaction.

Price and quality may not be issues at the point of user specification since operations managers will have identified a need in their process or function and will then go on to specify what they believe to be necessary to fill that gap. It is the expertise of the procurement function which can help to get the best supply at the best price for the desired quality level. So how can the buyer influence the specification?

- The specification may state that components must be tested to a recognised level, eg ISO 105–F01:2001 tests for colour fastness for wool garments.
- The specification may state the need to conform to environmental standards, eg ISO Guide 64 'The inclusion of environmental aspects in product standards'.
- The buyer can specify 'guide prices', eg a range from published catalogues and so on.
- The buyer can specify target delivery points and times.

Buyers may seek bids from suppliers holding particular accreditations such as ISO 9000 and 14 000 and immediately set a standard which imparts credibility to the product to be supplied. The standards bring greater

18

303

confidence in accepting the supply with minimal need for checking of quantity and quality of deliveries, thus providing the opportunity for savings in the overall process since rejects and returns will be fewer. The accreditation can also obviate the need for separate quality standards for individual parts of a supply and, thus, give the opportunity for additional cost saving. By stipulating a specific delivery schedule, potential suppliers who cannot meet this – but might meet cost – may still be excluded because delays will add cost to the process.

Specifications going out as part of tenders must have sufficient detail to allow informed buying evaluations to be made when bids are submitted. Over-specifying brings the risk of imposing too high a quality standard – unnecessarily high – which will result in tenders being overpriced to meet that standard. Under-specifying brings the reverse risk: a poor quality of product which causes rejects and, ultimately, customer dissatisfaction. The procurement function can mitigate these risks by ensuring that specifications are only as detailed as is absolutely necessary to achieve a standard that is neither too high nor too low in relation to the true needs of the user. Buyers can also influence specification methods by using innovative supply methods such as partnership sourcing.

Partnership sourcing helps to avoid the risk of over-specifying since the partner is being relied upon to give advice when a different approach, product or service will still provide a solution but at a lesser price. Acceptable quality standards, such as ISO accreditations, should be part of the selection of the partner. The relationship with the supplier is long-term and the emphasis is on both parties working together to reduce cost and improve quality. It is normally a single-source supply solution. The partner may have been selected from an initial competitive tender but continuing value for money, including quality of supply, will depend upon benchmarking performance and regular re-tendering to ensure market advantage.

Self-assessment question 18.1

Detail up to ten most important elements that may need to be specified when outsourcing the catering service for a manufacturing business.

Feedback on page 316

18.2 Evaluating the relative costs of quality

Learning activity 18.2

Select a process that you are regularly involved in such as raising a purchase order or signing off invoices, for example. Consider the impact on the process of spending more resource on quality assurance aspects of the tasks.

Feedback on page 316

There is a cost to achieving the desired quality level. Most people concerned with quality tend to look at things the other way round: *poor* quality costs money. Nonetheless, the sources of quality cost include:

- prevention – getting the systems right
- appraisal – measuring how the systems are performing
- external failure – faults found by customers
- internal failure – faults found during checks inside the operation.

In craft production the quality of output is critical. A good quality product attracts a customer who is willing to pay. Additionally, the craftworker takes pride in their work, always striving for improvement and this reflects on the end product. Without this pride and interest in quality there would be a poor output and customers would not be persuaded to return. This ideal was lost when the factory system evolved and managers began to subdivide the work; by having only a small part in the production of an object, there was no pride taken in the end product. Quality was separated from production with 'quality control' being seen as an add-on rather than an integral part of the same process.

Rediscovering the fundamental truth about craft production – pride in product – was the impetus for the re-emergence of quality as a main plank of management improvement schemes following the Second World War. This is now at the centre of the drive for quality: quality is everyone's responsibility, support staff as well as production staff. Quality is directly related to customer satisfaction and each customer throughout the chain must receive top quality performance for the business to survive.

Quality control and quality assurance are two separate aspects of additional costs in the production process. Quality control is a means of preventing below-standard quality by inspection and by test. It is an add-on rather than an integral part of a process and depends upon finding rejects either individually or by the statistical sampling of batches at various points of production to indicate the level of possible rejects in a batch. Quality assurance aims to be an integral part of systems, processes and behaviour so that quality is built in rather than added on.

Controlling the costs of quality depends very much also on the standard of product or service which is set. The question is: what is the quality expected of the service or product to be delivered? Customer requirements should dictate this and ultimate customer satisfaction will be the proof that the quality level achieved is the right one. Aiming for a level of perfection which may be difficult or impossible to achieve and which customers do not require simply adds unnecessary cost to the process. The level of quality desired is therefore the first determinant of cost and affects both inputs from other parts of the supply chain as well as every part of our own production or service delivery system.

The cost of introducing the concept of quality being the responsibility of all will include the need for training; changes in product design may be necessary and changes to systems and processes may also be required. Consultants may also have to be employed at the outset to begin the process of change. All of this will bring additional cost but will also be a step-change for the organisation. Once the change has been made the continuing costs

18

will fall dramatically and, if the change has been embraced enthusiastically, the volume of waste will reduce and rejected product will diminish.

The evaluation of cost in changing from quality control to quality assurance may have to wait until the effects have had time to filter through to a measurable period of customer satisfaction. Nonetheless, the abolition of add-on quality control procedures and staff can immediately be counted as a saving.

There is a direct cost to be considered in attaining a quality accreditation. There is a fee involved in initial acquisition of the certification and in recertifying at particular points in time. Additionally, there will be indirect costs involved in developing the internal procedures to the level required by the certification body which will require both time and expertise. Actual costs can be determined by contact with relevant certification bodies, Lloyds Register Quality Assurance in the UK for example.

Self-assessment question 18.2

Detail four examples of internal failure and four examples of external failure and explain how these failures can be reduced or eliminated.

Feedback on page 316

18.3 Product liability

Learning activity 18.3

Discuss with a senior manager your organisation's product liability insurance. Does the insurance cover you against negligence or bad practices? If you cannot discover this, do some research on the internet.

Feedback on page 317

Product liability encompasses a number of legal claims that allow an injured party to recover financial compensation from the manufacturer or seller of a product. The claims most commonly associated with product liability tend to be negligence, strict liability, breach of warranty and consumer protection claims. Each type of product liability claim requires different elements to be proven to present a successful claim.

Product liability is the area of law in which manufacturers, distributors, suppliers, retailers and others who make products available to the public are held responsible for the injuries those products cause.

Product liability claims usually fall into one of three possible types:

- those claiming a design defect
- those claiming a manufacturing defect, or
- those claiming a failure to warn.

18

Dangerous or defective product claims may succeed even when products were used incorrectly by the consumer, as long as the incorrect use was foreseeable by the manufacturer (or other party in the supply chain).

A basic negligence claim consists of proof of:

1   a duty owed
2   a breach of that duty
3   that the breach caused the plaintiff's injury, and
4   an injury.

Product liability claims are generally not based on negligence, but rather on a liability theory called 'strict liability'. The difficulties of an injured customer to prove what a manufacturer did or did not do during the design or manufacture of product has led to the development of newer product liability claims such as strict liability. However, some legal experts consider claims of 'failure to warn' to be negligence-based claims.

Rather than focus on the behaviour of the manufacturer (as in negligence), strict liability claims focus on the product itself. Under strict liability, the manufacturer is liable if the product is defective, even if the manufacturer was not negligent in making that product defective. Because strict liability is a harsh regime for a manufacturer, who is forced to pay for all injuries caused by his products, even if he is not at fault, strict liability is applied only to manufacturing defects (when a product varies from its intended design) and almost never applied to design and warning defects.

There is some confusion in judicial opinions as to whether strict liability is being applied in cases of design and warning defects. The courts may even state that they are applying strict liability. However, when the court proclaims to apply strict liability while determining a product's defectiveness through the use of a consumer expectations test or risk-utility test, it is applying negligence principles and not strict liability. Although the tests are not based on the conduct of the manufacturer, rather focusing on the product itself, they attempt to determine if the product's design or warning is reasonable. It is widely known that reasonableness is the staple of negligence, not strict liability.

Proponents of strict liability for defective products argue that strict liability is necessary because between two parties who are not negligent (manufacturer and consumer), one will still have to suffer the economic cost of the injury. The proponents argue that it is preferable to place the economic costs on the manufacturer because it can better absorb them and pass them on to other consumers by the way of higher prices. As such, the manufacturer becomes the insurer of consumers who are injured by its defective products, with premiums paid by other consumers.

A related argument arises from the fact that the manufacturer of any given product is in a better position than the consumer to know of its particular dangers. Therefore, in order to fulfil the public policy of minimising injury, it is more reasonable to impose the burden of finding and correcting such dangers upon the manufacturer as opposed to imposing the burden of

18

finding and avoiding unsafe products upon the consumer. These arguments are often mentioned in cases of design and warning defects and less so in the case of manufacturing defects, since the latter are thought to be less preventable by the manufacturer because he is already acting with due care.

The risk of a product liability claim occurring can be built into the cost or the price as insurance. However, there is a risk that, as a result of strict liability for their products, manufacturers may not produce the socially optimal level of goods, that is, by quality and/or price. Where consumers are very price-sensitive, the manufacturer by definition cannot pass on the economic costs to the consumers as a form of insurance without pricing many of those consumers out of the market for that good or service.

Critics also argue that applying strict liability to products results in substantially higher transaction costs. One example of these transaction costs is the creation of maintenance of legal disclaimers on products that would be unnecessary to the reasonable person. This results in a waste of time and resources for the producers who have to create these warnings. This also lowers the consumer 'surplus' from these transactions, as all reasonably diligent consumers will read the unnecessary instructions, whereas the consumers likely to misuse the product are unlikely to be sufficiently diligent to read the instructions.

The EC Product Liability Directive was issued initially in July 1985. It establishes the concept of strict liability and there is no need to prove negligence by the producer. From this point on, only a damage and a causal relationship are required to win the case.

Warranties are statements by a manufacturer or seller concerning a product during a commercial transaction. Unlike negligence claims, which focus on the manufacturer's conduct, or strict liability claims, which focus on the condition of the product, warranty claims focus on how these issues relate to a commercial transaction. Breach of warranty-based product liability claims usually focus on one of three types:

1   breach of an express warranty
2   breach of an implied warranty of merchantability, and
3   breach of an implied warranty of fitness for a particular purpose.

Express warranty claims focus on express statements by the manufacturer or the seller concerning the product (for example, 'This chainsaw is useful to cut turkeys'). The various implied warranties cover those expectations common to all products (for example, that a tool is not unreasonably dangerous when used for its proper purpose), unless specifically disclaimed by the manufacturer or the seller.

Procurement managers need to be aware of the risk of a product liability claim arising and must be aware, therefore, of the multi-tier effects of the supply chain. Poor quality can leapfrog along the supply chain and cause unforeseen repercussions. Warranties given as part of branding or marketing exercises can be equally dangerous. Mitigation of these vulnerabilities begins with a commitment to high levels of product quality, sharing of risk with insurers and the embracing of total quality management concepts.

18

Self-assessment question 18.3

What processes should you have in place to facilitate a prompt and effective product recall?

Feedback on page 317

18.4 Quality management systems summarised

Learning activity 18.4

Investigate the quality management systems that operate within your organisation to ensure that accurate payments are made only for goods and services actually received in good condition. Make notes on which elements add value and which simply add cost.

Feedback on page 317

Quality control and quality assurance are two different concepts. Quality control focuses on inspection and check to ensure that the end product is right; in other words, checks are made on the end product to see if it has achieved designed specification. At various points in a production process, for example, random or statistical checks may be made to ratify specification and, therefore, the desired level of quality. Quality assurance, however, seeks to ensure that poor quality is prevented at the outset rather than remedied after the event. Quality assurance concentrates more on systems and people on an ongoing basis as being the best way to eliminate waste, reduce costs and meet customer requirements.

Total quality management (TQM) is the aspiration of many organisations such that *quality* is not a separate issue or function but an integral part of every system and every action. The underpinning philosophy of TQM is that not having consistently appropriate quality wastes resources. Some waste is more obvious than others. Scrapped material in manufacture as a result of equipment failure is one example but waste resulting from bad systems or poor communications may be less obvious and more difficult to both find and measure. TQM advocates continuous effort to improve and is an holistic process, that is, it covers everything and everyone in the organisation. The principles of TQM (after Boddy: *Management: an Introduction*) are as follows:

- Philosophy – waste reduction through continuous improvement
- Leadership – committed and visible from top to bottom of the organisation
- Measurement – the cost of quality failures
- Scope – everyone, everywhere across the whole supply chain
- Methods – simple control and improvement techniques, implemented by teams.

18

Progressive small improvements pay disproportionate high returns. Small shifts also reduce costs progressively since the system experiences less and less waste and resources are used more effectively. Leadership is necessary to keep the effort going. Better quality comes from better attitude and visible leadership, committed to TQM. This can change the culture of the organisation to one of constant quality consciousness.

Each and every link in the supply chain from raw material to final consumer is formed between an individual or group acting as customer to a supplier. The customer is in turn supplier to another. Thus, the next customer in the chain immediately feels any failure in quality. TQM should therefore strive for the effect of the philosophy to extend throughout the supply chain, each taking responsibility for quality in the relevant part of the chain so that the entire supply chain becomes a total quality system.

TQM is a philosophy and approach which embraces the whole organisation and can extend outside the organisation to enhance relationships in each part of the supply chain. Quality accreditations and quality marks, on the other hand, can be associated with individual systems or a series of systems. Investors in People, for example, is an award relating primarily to the systems for HR relationships, excellence in developing skills and abilities, formal approaches to training needs and recognising people as a major organisational asset. Winning the award motivates people within an organisation and, by publicising gaining the award, also adds to customer satisfaction. ISO 9000 and ISO 14 000 are generic management systems standards by which is meant that the standards can apply to any organisation, large or small, whether it is a producer or a service organisation and whether it is in the public or private sector. The management system of these standards refers to what the organisation does to manage its processes or activities.

ISO 9000 is concerned with quality management, meaning everything the organisation does to enhance customer satisfaction by meeting any relevant regulatory requirements and continually improving performance to meet this objective. The procedures and processes which we put in place to achieve our objectives are the basis of our own 'quality system'. Design, specification and process are in place to provide the outcome which we desire, that is, the satisfaction of our internal and external customers with the product or service which is at the heart of our business. We start from the premise that we are not in business to produce something that nobody wants; thus, the quality of our product depends on the systems we have put in place to meet that quality criterion. A good example is the National Health Service (NHS) in the UK which has a series of National Service Frameworks (NSF) based on:

- setting clear quality requirements for care based on the best available evidence of what treatments and services work most effectively for patients
- offering strategies and support to help achieve these.

The NSFs have been developed in partnership with healthcare professionals, patients, carers, health service managers, voluntary agencies and others. They indicate clearly the requirements for a 'quality system': understanding customer (patients in this case) requirements; designing systems to meet objectives; getting everyone involved; providing help to achieve an effective system and maintaining its efficacy.

Gaining the ISO 9000 recognition indicates that our own systems have been independently verified to contain a number of essential features which are spelled out in the standard. Retaining the standard means, again, independent verification – this time, that the requirements of the standard are still being complied with. In fact the standard contains a number of principles:

- customer focus
- leadership
- involvement of people
- process approach
- systems approach to management
- continual improvement
- factual approach to decision making
- mutually beneficial supplier relationships.

Other avenues exist for obtaining quality awards. There is, for example, the Business Excellence Model, developed in the UK by the British Quality Foundation as a framework for an overall quality approach to doing business (see figure 18.1). The model, which has now been adopted by the European Quality Foundation, is based on self-assessment. The EFQM describes the model as 'a non-prescriptive framework based on 9 criteria'. Five of these are 'enablers' and four are 'results'. The 'enabler' criteria cover what an organisation does. The 'results' criteria cover what an organisation achieves. 'Results' are caused by 'enablers' and 'enablers' are improved using feedback from 'results'. Organisations that want to can enter the annual EFQM awards contest. This requires independent, external verification of the progress that the organisation has made in improving its approach to quality. Further details of the EFQM model can be found at http://www.efqm.org.

The EFQM model can also provide a basis for benchmarking for best practice. The whole idea of the model is that you keep on reassessing yourself year after year in a quest for continuous improvement. This allows organisations to 'benchmark' their own progress over time without having, necessarily, to involve any other organisation in the process.

Figure 18.1: Business excellence model

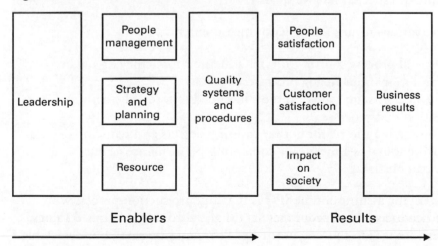

The significant risk inherent in attaining a recognised standard is that it will be seen as a 'one-off' exercise. Having obtained the accreditation, quality is guaranteed for all time. Of course it is not, and the principle of continuous improvement is significant in the application of ISO 9000: nothing stands still, people must continually review their actions, and systems should be monitored to ensure that redundancy is eliminated and quality improvement pursued at all times.

Another risk is in not recognising that the ISO quality standard is accrediting a documented system and process – it is not guaranteeing the product or service. A supplier can have ISO 9000 accreditation but produce a poor-quality product or service. All that ISO 9000 will confirm is that the product or service consistently meets the specification set by the supplier and that the supplier has monitoring systems in place to alert him should quality fall below the standard that he has set. He is also supposed to have systems in place which ensure that corrective action is taken – but only to bring quality back up to the set standard. It is really a case of 'caveat emptor'. ISO 9000 is not a guarantee of supply quality for the lazy buyer. You still need to monitor and manage your suppliers. In the case of your key suppliers you should make sure that you visit them and assess or reassess them on a regular basis.

Self-assessment question 18.4

What quality management systems do you think may be operated in the Emergency Room (also known as Casualty or Accident & Emergency) of a general hospital?

Feedback on page 318

18.5 Measuring quality

Measuring quality may be subjective, eg 'it's good quality' or 'it's poor quality' – but what do these terms mean? Each may be different depending on the beholder. Objective measures, on the other hand, attempt to put values on a particular level of quality or, more often, measure the variance away from an expected level of quality.

There are various means available for measurement:

- Statistical process control (SPC) is a method for achieving quality control in manufacturing processes.
- Control charts are statistical tools intended to assess the nature of variation in a process.
- Six Sigma is a metric for both measuring defects and reducing defects.
- Benchmarking is a means for comparing performance against comparable data.

The underlying assumption in SPC is that any production process will produce products whose properties vary slightly from the designed values, even when things are running normally. There may be small but detectable

18

differences in each product and there may also be changes in the machinery – through wear and tear or through slight power fluctuations. If these variances were allowed to continue unchecked then the product could fall outside the manufacturing tolerances and also fail to meet customer requirements. These variances can be analysed statistically to control the process and be used to correct problems, thus reducing or eliminating rejects and waste.

A control chart is a run chart of a sequence of quantitative data with three horizontal lines drawn on the chart: a centre line drawn as the process mean, an upper control limit drawn three standard deviations above the centre line, and a lower control limit drawn three standard deviations below the centre line. The chart is a tool for distinguishing between common and special cause variation; common cause being those in the system itself and special cause something outside of that. Without going deeply into statistics and interpretation of deviations, suffice to say that the chart plots irregular patterns usually within the deviation limits when common cause variations are observed. Anything outside of these limits signals a special cause.

Six Sigma is a methodology to identify process variations that cause defects which are unacceptable deviations from the mean or target and then to work towards managing variation in order to eliminate those defects. Six Sigma has two key approaches – to improve an existing business process (DMAIC) and to create new product design in such a way as to result in a more predictable and defect-free performance (DMADV). These terms are explained below. Tools which can be deployed in the Six Sigma approach include the control charts already referred to above, Ishikawa diagrams, histograms and process maps – many of these have been described in earlier parts of our studies. In summary, the Six Sigma approaches are:

DMAIC – *Define* the process; *measure* to define baseline; *analyse* to verify factors and relationships; *improve* to optimise the process base on analysis; *control* by establishing pilot runs, transition to production and subsequent production runs.

DMADV – *Define* the design goals; *measure* capabilities, risks and so on; *analyse* design alternatives and capabilities; *design* the process and simulate if appropriate; *verify* the design from pilot runs through to production.

Software is available to make measurement easier and examples are DataLyzer (http://www.datalyzer.com) and Infinity QS (http://www.infinityqs.com).

Statistical sampling is often used in quality control since it can avoid the use of costly and time-consuming 100% checking. Statistical methods provide a means for achieving an understanding of large volumes of data by selecting samples of that data which will be truly representative of that entire data set or population. Rather than taking a random sample of the population which could be either biased or simply unrepresentative, statistical methods can be used to improve the confidence of the user that the sample taken is as representative as possible. The higher the confidence level and probability that the sample is, indeed, representative of the whole population, then the better the conclusions which can be drawn from it.

18

Statistical sampling is based on various mathematical processes which can mostly now be done using appropriate software – either developed specifically for the systems to be tested or as a standard package. There may be times, however, when a total check of a process or procedure cannot be avoided, such as when there is a strong probability of contamination, perhaps, or when there is doubt in the ability of a supplier to deliver expected quantities – a prior history of short deliveries, for example.

Learning activity 18.5

Under what circumstances would you decide to operate 100% inspection of a product or process?

Feedback on page 318

Benchmarking provides a means for comparison rather than straightforward measurement. The Cabinet Office gives a good description of benchmarking as follows:

'In practice, benchmarking usually encompasses:

- regularly comparing aspects of performance (functions or processes) with best practitioners;
- identifying gaps in performance;
- seeking fresh approaches to bring about improvements in performance;
- following through with implementing improvements; and
- following up by monitoring progress and reviewing the benefits.

'Although benchmarking involves making comparisons of performance, it is not:

- merely competitor analysis – benchmarking is best undertaken in a collaborative way
- comparison of league tables – the aim is to learn about the circumstances and processes that underpin superior performance.'

There are a number of groups or organisations which can help businesses that want to do benchmarking. For example, the EFQM, referred to above, has what it calls a Community of Practice (basically a group of similar organisations in similar sectors of activity), and by paying a joining fee your company can participate in the relevant benchmarking group.

Cost–benefit analysis provides another simple method for measuring the cost of any quality initiative. The costs, direct and indirect, are collected in relation to all the activities connected with the quality initiative and then compared with the benefits attained (or expected), quantified in the same terms. The difficulty here is in being able to measure benefits in sufficient detail to make a direct comparison with costs possible or meaningful.

There are some areas where measuring quality in terms of monetary or production values is either inappropriate or cannot be done. Quality of life,

18

for example, is important in economics and political science but many of the constituent parts – freedom, happiness, environment, health, art and innovation – are very difficult to measure.

Self-assessment question 18.5

Under what circumstances would you decide when to operate a zero inspection of a product or process? Give details of some upstream quality tools that would need to be in place to enable this situation to occur.

Feedback on page 318

Revision question

Now try the revision question for this session on page 357.

Summary

Various aspects of managing towards quality have been covered in this study session with the aim of considering how systems and procedures can help us to achieve 'fit for purpose' in all our activities. The dangers and costs of not achieving the desired quality level have been reviewed, while we have also considered that over-specifying the necessary quality level can be costly too. There are risks to reputation as well as to revenue when we consider quality in the entire supply chain. Mitigating the risks depends on many factors, however, from staff motivation to external accreditation by gaining a recognised standard.

Suggested further reading

You could read the relevant sections of Boddy (2005) and Womack and Jones (2003).

British Standards Institution website: http://www.bsi-global.com.

International Organization for Standardization website: http://www.iso.org.

Feedback on learning activities and self-assessment questions

Feedback on learning activity 18.1

Depending on your type of organisation, these could include specifying a level of product testing or inspection not necessarily required, insisting on an ISO or other accreditation when not strictly necessary (this could also be anti-competitive) and seeking that a product or service is delivered to almost impossible conditions of delivery time. Conversely, under-specification may have given the supplier too wide a range of delivery times, low standard of quality and no clear idea of where deliveries were expected.

18

Feedback on self-assessment question 18.1

The elements could include (in no particular order):

- product description and variety, eg sample menus
- ingredients identified, eg free from allergy contents; religious or cultural requirements, if appropriate
- initial source, eg fair trading
- production methods, eg amount of subcontracting; hygiene certification
- quality accreditations of supplier
- hygiene etc qualifications of staff
- staff continuous training scheme
- volume of each product, eg expected quantities
- delivery points, eg number of canteens, vending machines
- delivery times, ie service availability times.

Feedback on learning activity 18.2

Some processes are particularly important and can have significant adverse effects if not carried out correctly. Raising a purchase order creates a commitment which we are bound to fulfil and therefore involves us in both trust and payment: the supplier's trust in us that we will pay and depletion of our cash when we pay. Both of these factors make it essential that we get it right:

- Are we using an approved supplier with whom we already have a contract? If not, why not?

Invoice payment involves us in the same way and is a similar imperative to get it right: the right payment at the right time to the right supplier:

- Is there a matching purchase order? If not, why not? Is there a goods received note or formal acceptance that the goods or services have been received? If not, how do we know that we have received what we are being invoiced for?

Financial controls over all these processes should already be comprehensive so that additional quality assurance need only provide evidence that the expected controls were in place and did work; this can be achieved by management review. These additional assurances should be built in to the designed control system:

- How often did an invoice arrive for which there was no order? How often did the order and invoice fail to match? Who were the culprits – which suppliers and which user departments? Why is non-compliance happening? What are we going to do about it? What targets for improvement are we going to set? How will we measure progress?

Feedback on self-assessment question 18.2

Internal failure might include failing to detect short deliveries, below-standard deliveries or entirely wrong product delivery; information

(IT) systems may not provide the right or sufficient information for good decision making; and the quality of product moving from one part of a production process to another may be substandard. TQM and application of quality standards can alleviate all of these occurrences. External failure includes failing to achieve customer satisfaction by late delivery or substandard products causing rejects, out-of-date products and overpriced products through over-engineering to meet an unnecessary quality level. Market research, application of quality standards and internal quality assurance processes can all help to eliminate these failures.

Feedback on learning activity 18.3

You could have researched http://www.wikepedia.org for a thumbnail sketch of product liability. Insurance is a mitigating strategy which can be effective in providing risk transfer; however, the cost of insurance may be affected by your organisation's approach to quality of product or service as shown by your internal procedures, history of claims and holding of any recognised quality awards.

Feedback on self-assessment question 18.3

Process control and other quality control and assurance methods should alert you to the possibility of deviation from expected standard. The extent of this deviation will determine the point at which production should not flow through to customers before corrective action is taken. In the event that procedures have failed and there is doubt as to whether products have actually been delivered and may not be at the required quality level, a fallback procedure should include:

- identification of possible faulty batches and destinations if sent
- removal from stock if not yet delivered
- customer identification and contact; return of goods at our cost
- financial systems alerted to stop invoicing of faulty goods
- public relations plan implemented to minimise reputational damage
- communication with customers to build future confidence – discounts, and so on.

Feedback on learning activity 18.4

You may have a TQM system already in place which is backed by board endorsement, with policies and procedures available to all staff and geared towards goal achievement at the desired quality of output. You may have ISO 9000 and/or ISO 14 000 in addition to other standards which assist in assuring quality of input and output. Goods inwards procedures should be documented and flow from the raising of a purchase order based on tendered procurement procedures at the correct authority levels. Internal controls over goods inward should reflect the laid-down procedures and be subject to management review periodically; this should include short delivery procedure. The systems may be part of an accredited ISO or other process. Services should follow a similar path although without a physical good being received. The actual service received should be verified against that originally contracted before payment is made. Any 'double checking'

18

in the systems adds cost whereas a system of commitment accounting adds value.

Feedback on self-assessment question 18.4

Hospitals have their own plans, strategies and procedures. Many will be based on advice and recommendation from the Department of Health and other bodies which provide advice to the various levels of Health Authority (National Institute for Clinical Excellence, NICE, for example). Hospitals are subject to the Health Commission's performance ratings (star ratings) based on performance indicators and performance against these targets. A&E have indicators set and performance in this area is fed into the hospital's overall results. The approach to achieving targets and seeking overall improvement fits well with establishing a quality approach to patient care in A&E.

A reasonable expectation for any hospital would be for it to base its systems around a quality standard – either those provided by the National Service Frameworks (NSFs) or ISO 9000. NSFs set quality requirements into patient treatments and services; they have the following objectives:

- Set national standards and identify key interventions for a defined service or care group
- Put in place strategies to support implementation
- Establish ways to ensure projects are completed within agreed timescales.

NSFs are just one of a range of measures to raise quality and decrease variations in service across all areas of patient care, and a system of TQM embracing the performance measurement approach will assist in achieving this.

Feedback on learning activity 18.5

The criteria for a 100% check include:

- Life threatening – nothing less than a complete check will do.
- Security – national or local security depends on every item being checked.
- Perfection – medical product or process must be perfect otherwise purpose cannot be achieved.
- Doubt – reason not to be confident in quality or delivery.

Seeking perfection in any circumstance will require a 100% check and a 100% success rate from the checks. This is rarely achievable through cost, manpower and time available. Some of the above circumstances could, however, justify such an approach.

Feedback on self-assessment question 18.5

Confidence from past experience can help to justify a no-inspection regime. Other tools in place, however, would be a better justification such as statistical methods being continuously applied and variations investigated. These tools could also include SPCs and control charts with benchmarking being used as a continuous validation process. Software application of these tools can provide quick and easy solutions.

18

Controlling the risks

Introduction

How can organisations be controlled? There is a close relationship between organisational objectives, understanding the risks which may prevent these objectives from being achieved and the role of control in mitigating risk occurrence. Managing those risks effectively means using internal control as one of the mechanisms which can help to avoid some of the risks from actually materialising.

Internal controls are not a haphazard collection of activities or events designed to hamper the operation of particular systems. If they are to be effective then they need to be carefully thought out, discriminately applied and constantly monitored. If controls are no longer appropriate because of system change or system decay then they must be amended or removed entirely. In other words, internal control should not hinder systems in achieving their goals but actively support them while contributing to the attainment of desired results and minimising the opportunities for operational surprises.

Effective control provides reasonable assurance – not guarantees – that the desired objectives will be achieved, and it does so at reasonable cost while relating to the structures and processes which are current within the organisation. But internal control has to be seen as an integral part of the *objectives, risks and control* continuum. If objectives are not clearly stated, understood and communicated then the risks which may prevent the achievement of those objectives cannot be identified and assessed. Similarly, without knowledge of the risks, controls appropriate to the level and magnitude of those risks cannot be devised.

'The cause of all business failures can be traced to failures of internal control.'
Sir Adrian Cadbury, chairman, Committee on Corporate Governance (1991)

Session learning objectives

After completing this session you should be able to:

19.1 Design a programme of risk-based internal audits which could be carried out in the purchasing department or suggested to the chief audit executive.
19.2 Explain the value that can be derived from effective external audits and external specialist consultants.
19.3 Demonstrate the value of control models, feedback and appraisals as monitoring and control techniques.
19.4 Propose some software solutions that can be used to test risk on an ongoing basis.

19

Unit content coverage

This study session covers the following topics from the official CIPS unit content document:

Learning objectives

3.2 Evaluate and apply monitoring and control techniques for testing risk on an ongoing basis.
- Internal audits
- Interdepartmental exchanges
- External experts: advisers, mystery shoppers, research companies and the police
- Use of benchmarking to assess and mitigate external risk
- Use of competitive intelligence
- Quality systems, total quality management (TQM), quality inspection and quality control

Prior knowledge

Especially study session 18.

Resources

Internet access.

Timing

You should set aside about 6 hours to read and complete this session, including learning activities, self-assessment questions, the suggested further reading (if any) and the revision question.

19.1 Internal auditing in relation to procurement

Gain an understanding of your organisation's internal audit function.

Internal auditing operates *within* an organisation to undertake objective reviews of all operational activities and provide management with opinions on the effectiveness of controls in the operations so reviewed. Internal auditing differs from inspection. It seeks to go beyond merely reporting on compliance (or non-compliance) with policies and procedures and seeks to make recommendations for achieving better use of inputs and outputs, thus contributing to downstream business outcomes and the achievement of added value – for company and shareholder benefit.

Internal auditing, by its very nature, can never be absolutely independent but it can achieve quasi-independence by being disassociated from routine operational matters, its level of reporting and the independent state of mind which it brings to its work.

Modern internal auditing dates from the establishment of the Institute of Internal Auditors (IIA) in 1941. A *Statement of Responsibilities of Internal*

19

Auditing was first published by IIA in 1947 and has featured in regular updates right up to the present time. The IIA *Standards for the Professional Practice of Internal Auditing* were first published in 1978, have been subject to frequent review and updated regularly. As a result of these reviews, IIA published its updated *International Standards for the Professional Practice of Internal Auditing* (the Standards) for implementation in January 2004.

The Standards are designed to provide a framework for all internal auditors to undertake their work in a professional and responsible way, integrated with the risk assessment of the organisation as a whole. Their purpose is to:

- lay down basic principles that represent the practice of internal auditing
- give a framework for performing a wide range of internal audit activities
- establish a basis for measuring internal audit performance
- seek to improve organisational processes and operations.

The internal audit function has become an increasingly important management tool in providing assurance over risk management activities and the effectiveness of internal control. The UK Combined Code of October 2003 which incorporated various earlier and recent review work – The Turnbull Report, internal control; the Higgs Report, non-executive directors; the Smith Report, audit committees – in its Code Provision C.3.5 states, amongst other things, that 'the audit committee should monitor and review the effectiveness of the internal audit activities'. It goes on to say that companies which do not have an internal audit function should annually review the need for one and, significantly, the code requires the absence of an internal audit function to be explained in the annual report.

The current emphasis on the role of the internal auditor in matters of corporate governance seems to have come about because of the increased importance of the role of the audit committee and the general need for boards and managers to become more accountable. Quite clearly, internal auditing – when properly mandated and resourced – is an invaluable tool to the audit committee when that committee is endeavouring to carry out its delegated responsibilities. A strong relationship between the chair of the audit committee and the head of internal audit can provide any organisation with a formidable bastion against adversity.

The quality and value of the work done by internal auditing is enhanced by the manner in which it reports within the organisation. As stated earlier, internal auditing can never be seen to be totally independent because it is provided by the organisation for the organisation. The reporting lines for internal audit are important, however, if it is to make a contribution worthy of its cost and professionalism and to be accepted as a real catalyst for change. The most effective reporting relationship is for the head of internal audit to report directly to the chief executive officer (CEO) and to the chair of the audit committee.

Reality for most organisations is that the head of internal audit reports, in terms of line management, to the CEO and is, thus, reaching the highest levels of the organisation. The purpose of this high-level reporting is to ensure, as much as possible, that the work of the auditor is not being 'censored' by lower levels of management. In addition, the internal auditor should be reporting to the audit committee – in the sense that written and oral reports are given to the committee to assist it in reaching a view on the effectiveness of risk management and internal control. The head of internal audit will, in addition, be charged with maintaining a close relationship with the audit committee chairman.

Learning activity 19.1

Identify some of the errors that might have been avoided or detected if an effective internal audit were regularly carried out.

Feedback on page 336

In relation to the procurement process, the head of internal audit (also known as the chief audit executive) will hold periodic discussions with senior managers in the purchasing department in order to get a view on the risk management activities being undertaken within the department. Audit will also have taken a view on procurement at the level at which it features in the risk profile of the whole organisation; this will assist in prioritising internal audit work areas. Following the discussions, the head of internal audit will programme work in the procurement department into the internal audit plan for the organisation.

The work of the internal auditor is based on the risks which have been identified and the actions taken to mitigate these risks. The actual risk management work is the preserve of line management so that internal auditing will carry out its work by reviewing the risk assessment process in the purchasing department and then concentrate on testing the controls which have been put in place to mitigate the risks. This testing will consider all the procurement processes, including contractor appraisal and e-commerce interfaces.

The results of internal auditing work will be in the form of a report to the most senior line manager, containing recommendations for improvement in control actions where appropriate. The report also goes to the CEO and the audit committee will be kept up to date on the issues raised by the head of internal audit. These internal audit reports are designed to bring about improvement in systems and processes, not just to criticise any failures which may be found, and it is the added value provide by the audit work which benefits the whole organisation.

Internal audits or checks can be carried out by the purchasing department's own staff – indeed, monitoring of systems and controls is part of the line management task. Standards such as the ISO 9000 series require quality audits to be carried out as part of compliance with the standard, and this will typically be done by the standard holder's own staff. Similarly, health and safety checks should be part and parcel of normal management review.

Effective internal auditing can assist procurement managers in achieving their objectives by reviewing systems and controls in place for assessing and

19

managing risks. The process provides assurance to the board and the audit committee as well as management of the procurement activity.

Self-assessment question 19.1

Identify the team members that you would select for an internal safety audit team and justify your choice.

Feedback on page 336

19.2 The contribution from external audit and external consultants

Learning activity 19.2

Review the work you did earlier in study session 15 researching the work of the Audit Commission and the National Audit Office and make notes on how their work can facilitate the control of risks.

Feedback on page 336

Consultants are often called upon to advise organisations in areas where specific expertise is lacking in-house or where the existing workload is such that augmentation is needed from outside to assist in driving projects forward. There are several benefits available including:

* specialist knowledge and skill
* independent view
* limited timeframe
* skill exchange or skills transfer.

There are disadvantages also in that there will be additional expenditure involved over and above own staff costs and existing staff can be demotivated by the presence of outside people. Indeed, the most common reaction from internal staff to a consultant's report is 'we could have told them that anyway and saved the money'. Despite this, the use of consultants is continually growing and there is no doubt that, used effectively, they can make a large contribution to an organisation's success.

The key to getting good results from the involvement of external consultants is to be sure of the objectives for the project, to be clear about the expected outcomes and be robust about containing work done within the remit and contracted cost. Contractual arrangements should stipulate the skills expected to be brought to bear and the experience level expected of consultants. Working relationships should be laid down and the timing and type of reports should be agreed. Variations to time and cost should be the subject of strict agreement. Above all, the outcomes from the consultants' work should actually be used. The considerable expense involved can only

19

be justified if the work done actually informs change within the organisation and contributes to better performance.

Consultants can also be used in roles such as price checking or service delivery checks where anonymous individuals test the way a service is performed. Testing of call centre service is a good example where the consultant poses as a normal customer, assesses the service against given criteria and reports to the client. Similar tests may be carried out in the retail sector where shopfloor prices can be checked against daily price lists and reported upon anonymously.

The use of consultants is a choice which is usually made by the board or senior managers in an organisation. The driving force is to improve performance by using specialist advice. External auditors, on the other hand, are required by law. The only choice an organisation has in the matter is in the appointment of one firm from among many.

External, or statutory, auditors report to shareholders (ultimately to citizens in the case of the public sector). The company pays the audit fee incurred in the work done to provide a report to the members of the company – shareholders – which states the extent to which the company's financial statements and reports show a 'true and fair view' of the company's operations at a point in time. The statutory auditor is independent by virtue of being external to the company and the audit fee is the only financial reward the auditor should expect.

In terms of corporate governance, the external auditor is a critical part of the board's *accountability* to shareholders. The independent nature of the external audit, undertaken by independent outsiders looking into the company's financial affairs, provides strong reassurance to those who wish to place reliance on company reports. Additionally, the external auditors will almost certainly review the board's approach to corporate governance when they consider the way in which the company deals with risk management, internal control and internal audit.

Virtually every company in the world is subject to an external audit. It is a long-established practice and its main reason for being is to protect shareholders from unscrupulous company directors and managers. It is a *financial* audit. It is designed to confirm that the financial results which the company reports from time to time are accurate, complete and reflect the actual state of the business referred to in the company's published data. External auditors are required to be qualified – and that generally means qualified as an accountant under the examination process of a recognised accounting professional body.

Because the statutory audit is reported upon in the public domain, users of accounts need to have confidence in the work of the accountant who has prepared the reports concerned. This confidence consists of several factors:

- the history of the external audit firm in working in similar industries and sizes of company
- the experience, skill and qualifications of the firm's partners and staff
- the amount of time spent on the audit

- the extent of audit testing to establish the completeness and accuracy of all the transactions which, together, have formed the input to the final accounts
- the manner in which any inconsistencies have been handled when reported to management
- the application of international standards for external auditing and reporting.

Additionally, and perhaps most importantly, there is the question of independence of the audit firm. Despite the safeguards of being appointed by shareholders and receiving only the fee for the audit, reality for most companies is that *management* selects the auditor and recommends the appointment at the annual general meeting. Reality, also, is that the audit firm will do other work for the client company not related to the audit. This practice can easily compromise the auditor's independence despite the artificial mechanisms which may be put in place by the audit firm to prevent it such as 'Chinese walls' which, in theory, ring-fence one part of the firm from another. Audit firms claim that they need the additional income which non-audit work brings and suggest, also, that from their knowledge of the company gathered during audit work, they can do other work at (a) a better price than competing consultants, and (b) with shorter learning times and more efficient output.

Large audit firms have, in the main, divested themselves of their consulting arms following the events surrounding Enron and Arthur Andersen in 2001. Indeed, the extent to which audit firms may take on additional work has been curtailed in many countries because of perceptions, if not actual, compromises of independence. In the USA, for example, an external audit firm may not provide more than 40% of a company's internal audit requirement.

External auditors consider risk in the work that they do but, in the main, they are not required to comment on the manner in which a company has identified and assessed the risks it faces. Nonetheless, the external auditor will want to ensure that management control extends to consideration of the appropriate risks against which the architecture of the internal control system has been designed to defend. The key external audit risk factor is, in fact, consideration of the risk which faces them if they have not carried out the audit effectively or in some other way have compromised the work that has been undertaken. The demise of the accounting and auditing firm Andersen in the wake of the Enron situation amply illustrates this issue.

The external auditor will be interested in the internal control system because, by undertaking a review of this system, the auditor will be able to formulate an opinion as to its effectiveness in contributing to good financial management. A good internal control system will improve the external auditor's confidence in the operation of financial control. A good internal control system will also allow the external auditor to calculate the extent to which testing of all the transactions may be reduced – for example, the use of sampling in conjunction with statistically valid confidence levels.

In carrying out their work, external auditors need to understand both the standards which are applied by companies in completing their accounts

19

and the internationally accepted standards which apply to the practice of external audit. Companies will follow either the Generally Accepted Accounting Practices applied in the USA and elsewhere or the International Accounting Standards which apply globally and have replaced or augmented many national accounting standards – the European Union countries, for example, follow International Accounting Standards as from 2005.

Communicating audit results has posed three main problems for external auditors:

- the paucity of information when all the stakeholder sees is a brief 'true and fair view' certificate
- the role of the external auditor in matters of fraud
- the loss of credibility attached to company collapses which follow an apparently 'clean' external audit.

Each of these contributes to the phenomenon known as 'the expectations gap'. This gap is created as a result of a misconception on the part of users of financial information who think that the auditor has carried a 100% check of all transactions that lead to the compilation of final accounts and financial statements. Users also hold – or at least *held* in the past – the mistaken belief that the auditor would also uncover fraud during the examination of the accounts. In fact, the auditor no longer scrutinises *all* transactions but sufficient only to provide the auditor with an opinion on the content and accuracy of the accounts, and sample sizes vary dependent upon the confidence level which the auditor is seeking. Similarly, the auditor is required only to be vigilant when reviewing transactions and financial data and maintain a healthy degree of scepticism in order to spot the indicators which may mean that a fraud is being or has been committed.

The external auditor's report is prepared in accordance with international and/or national standards and usually conforms to the legal framework for companies in that particular country. The report usually forms part of the company's annual report, a document available more often than not in the public domain. Getting more information about the audit beyond the auditor's report and certificate is difficult, however. The reasons for this are not hard to understand – confidentiality of client data, primarily – and usually mean that the only avenue for further information is questioning of the auditor at the annual general meeting. Again, because of confidentiality and the public nature of annual general meetings, auditors are not generally forthcoming in those forums.

There are no guarantees, then, from the external auditor but an **opinion** – an opinion that gives an assurance that, on the basis of the work done, there are no material discrepancies in the company's financial statements.

International Standards for Auditing – and those for accounting – seem to give the best avenue for the future. If accounting is done honestly, diligently and to a common benchmark then the audit which follows, also done to a common standard, should provide stakeholders with the kind of assurances they seek: honest financial statements which properly represent the past and point accurately to the future, certified in a manner which can maintain stakeholders' confidence.

Self-assessment question 19.2

What are the benefits of having a regular external audit?

Feedback on page 337

19.3 Control models, feedback and appraisal

Use of benchmarking to assess relative risk with suppliers

Learning activity 19.3

List some good and some bad techniques that you may have experienced in supplier appraisals. Research the availability of benchmarking or comparison data for your main suppliers.

Feedback on page 337

Control is an action taken to assist in achieving an objective – it is an action which helps to avoid failure. Internal control is the collective term used to describe all the management actions taken within an organisation to assist in achieving the objectives of the organisation. This contrasts with external control which is applied from outside the organisation; laws, regulations and external audits are all external control.

The environment within which control works is as important as the framework, or models, for control which follow later. The control environment sets the tone of an organisation and indicates the extent to which the board and senior managers embrace control concepts and are seen to be applying them. The attitude and actions of the board in this context are crucial to the success of the control systems and processes. Control environment factors include ethical values, individual integrity and managerial competence and this environment is the foundation upon which the rest of the control framework is built. If the board doesn't get it right and then send the correct message to the rest of the organisation, effective internal control is not likely to be achieved.

Monitoring and review are the classic techniques for 'closing the loop' in any system and these factors feature in all the well-known control models which are part of any management control and risk management system. Two models, or frameworks, are most commonly referred to: the COSO model (Committee of Sponsoring Organisations of the Treadway Commission, USA) and the CoCo model (Criteria of Control Board of the Canadian Institute of Chartered Accountants). While North American in origin, both models have achieved worldwide recognition and use.

The COSO model, developed in the early 1990s, relates control to the environment of the organisation – its culture, the attitudes of its people,

19

its approach to assessing risks – and the way in which the control processes are put into practice. It exemplifies internal control from a definition which places responsibility firmly on directors, managers and other personnel for a process which is designed to provide reasonable assurance that objectives will be achieved in the categories of:

* effective and efficient operations
* reliable financial reporting
* compliance with relevant laws and regulations.

In the context of organisational structures, COSO puts into context the *why* of control but not the *how* or the *where.* COSO illustrates the relationship between risks and controls and emphasises the responsibility of management in any organisation to be proactive in seeking ways in which objectives can be achieved – using control, in other words, as one of several risk mitigation strategies which may be available to managers.

COSO is generally seen as the 'hard control ' model because it is concerned with actions within operations, processes or systems; is dependent on management action and puts an expectation on managers to monitor and review their own success in achieving goals through the application of appropriate internal controls.

Figure 19.1 illustrates the COSO model, which – as will be seen later – had, by 2004, been extended from a foundation of internal control into a comprehensive enterprise-wide risk management model.

Figure 19.1: The COSO model

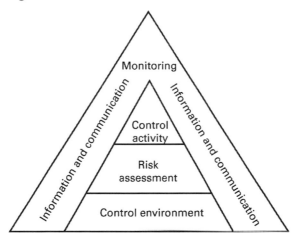

Another internal control model commonly referred to is the CoCo model. Developed in the mid-1990s by the Canadian Institute of Chartered Accountants, this model is usually seen as the 'soft control' approach because of its emphasis on areas of corporate activity which are usually thought of as being outside the scope of traditionalists. And yet, these are the areas which are closest to organisational success in terms of output and outcome, the very areas where risks may be at their highest in respect of preventing achievement of objectives and, therefore, perhaps, the areas in greatest need of effective control.

The three main areas of the CoCo model cover the purpose of the organisation, the commitment of assets to meet the purpose and the capability of all these assets to actually achieve strategy and objectives. Interestingly, closing the loop – the fourth area in the CoCo model – is not just monitoring the process and its outcomes but *learning*; learning from mistakes rather than using mistakes to impose sanctions or punishments.

The model is illustrated in figure 19.2.

Figure 19.2: The CoCo model

Monitoring and learning
- external and internal environment monitored
- performance against targets tracked
- challenge of assumptions behind objectives
- information needs regularly reassessed
- follow-up procedures in place
- periodic review of effectiveness of control

Purpose
- objectives set
- risks identified and assessed
- policies established and communicated
- plans established and communicated
- performance targets and indicators

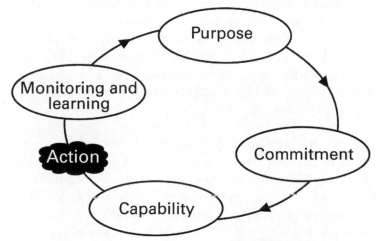

Capability
- knowledge, skills and tools
- communicate processes to support objectives
- timely and relevant information
- decisions and actions coordinated
- control an integral part of the company

Commitment
- shared ethical values
- consistent HR policies and practices
- clear authority, responsibility and accountability
- atmosphere of mutual trust

There are other specific control standards, for example, related to IT. These cover the following four main components, or domains:

- planning and organisation
- acquisition and implementation
- delivery and support
- monitoring.

This standard covers security and control for IT systems in support of business processes and is designed for management, users and auditors. Known as the *Control Objectives for Information and Related Technology*, the standard is usually referred to by the acronym CobiT.

The Basle (or Basel) Committee on Banking Supervision has spent some time in developing internal control principles which relate exclusively to the banking environment. The principles – thirteen in all – are broadly in line with those already discussed but with the additional proviso that national banking supervisory authorities should oversee the adequacy of internal control within all the banks, whether large or small, in their country's banking sector.

All these models provide a benchmark for control in an organisation which can be used to measure and improve the approach taken. They also amply illustrate that internal control is part and parcel of any organisation's approach to trying to ensure that its laid-down objectives are achieved as expected. Additionally, they illustrate emphatically that control cannot exist in a vacuum. Control is only necessary when a risk has been identified which may prevent – or at least make it harder for – objectives to be attained. It follows, therefore, that internal control should be seen as a positive contributor to corporate endeavour, although not a guarantor of success.

Internal control processes often combine the 'soft control' and 'hard control' approaches which have been referred to earlier, seeking to capitalise on the strengths of both. Hard control tends to flourish in what may be considered to be a, perhaps, traditional or scientific approach to managing organisations. This is epitomised by the view that people are inherently dishonest, lazy and eager to avoid significant effort. The organisation itself is seen as a machine and control is effective when it can be seen that people do exactly as they are told by managers, have no individual flexibility and can use no personal innovation.

Conversely, the humanistic or behavioural view believes that people are generally honest, hard-working and eager to do the best they can to assist in achieving organisational objectives. Often, the organisation's objectives coincide with individual objectives and the organisation is seen as a social organism. In an earlier study session we considered the use of appraisals in connection with 'qualifying' suppliers. The use of appraisals also fits well into this model since, other than appraising or reviewing operational plans, investment projects and similar proposals, appraisals tend to be most familiar in the HR setting where their use is predominantly as a control over personal performance.

In common with other control techniques, an appraisal can only work if an individual's personal objectives have been set out and agreed within the context of desired corporate achievement. The means to achieve that level of performance include a training needs assessment followed by any actual training necessary. Key points or dates need to be agreed so that performance can be monitored throughout, rather than at the end, of an agreed period. This is not unlike any other ongoing project appraisal where critical paths and progress are constantly monitored.

Feedback is the critical part of all approaches to control and monitoring; it is the link between planning and control. Whether achieving targets or missing them – in either case, without appropriate feedback, corrective action cannot be taken and the loop cannot be closed. Procedures need to be in place to ensure that appropriate managers get the feedback at the time and of the quality needed to either continue to achieve successful outcomes or take action to get back on track.

Internal control needs to help management achieve objectives. While directors and managers are responsible for an effective framework of control, it cannot be achieved without the motivation of the workforce – despite the advent of sophisticated technology. Thus, the best parts of all the control models should be extracted and moulded to the exact requirements of each company or organisation. As with benchmarking, control models provide a standard which can be aspired to as 'best practice' but, like most things in business, there is no *one size fits all* for internal control. It's what works best for individual organisations.

Self-assessment question 19.3

You are planning to visit a potential new supplier to carry out a formal supplier assessment. You are going to meet a number of his key staff in different functions. List five things that you need to find out from your visit.

Feedback on page 337

19.4 Using IT to assist in risk management

Learning activity 19.4

Consider how IT system controls could assist the purchasing department in planning purchases, managing suppliers and reporting management information.

Feedback on page 337

We discussed control models in section 19.3. The COSO model referred to has been developed into a complete enterprise-wide risk management tool and is reproduced in figure 19.3.

Figure 19.3: The COSO model, extended

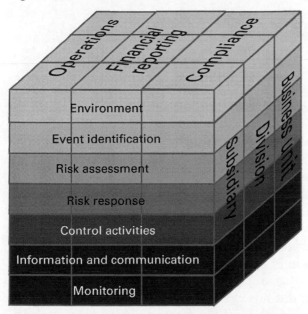

Again it is illustrated that control, specifically internal control, is not just financial control but is all-pervasive. Operations require management control just as much as finance does. Accepting that control is a response to a risk, it is clear that if objectives are known, then the interrelationships between every organisational function and unit can be expressed in terms of the risks which may prevent achievement of objectives and the controls put in place to mitigate these risks. This systematic approach to risk management fits well into the logical approach of computer technology.

The enterprise-wide approach to risk management lends itself to embedding the controls necessary to mitigate risk into every system and every procedure. Thus, all the procedures referred to in earlier study sessions covering identification, evaluation and action can transfer into operational systems. Controls need to be built in to systems at the development stage since amending systems after they become operational is costly and time-consuming. The way to achieve this is to ensure that the risk management system is accepted as part and parcel of the systems development process.

The systems development life cycle provides the basis for any new system and should follow the steps in figure 19.4.

Figure 19.4: Systems development life cycle

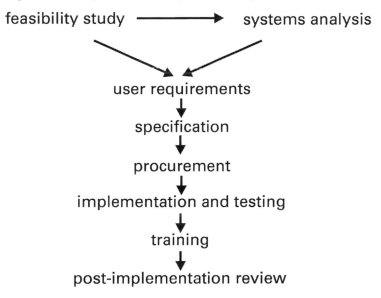

Following this development cycle allows risks to be addressed at the early stages and controls to be embedded as part of the system specification and implementation. The use of rapid application design techniques (RAD) and other proprietary development tools makes it even more important for control to be addressed as a normal part of any system design, development or amendment. It makes sense, also, to have risk and control specialists involved at the early stages of development so that there is the best chance of building in control rather than adding it on later.

While this addresses risk and control in the IT environment, we need to understand how IT can help in the risk management process itself. A technique referred to in an earlier study session was control and risk self-assessment. The role of IT in this process can be significant in that it can help to automate the process, thereby saving time and getting a quicker and easier-to-use set of output data. Data gathering and analysis software can be developed in-house using Excel and even Word but proprietary packages such as OptionFinder™ and TeamMate™ do the job well and at reasonable cost.

A good e-procurement system can be very effective in ensuring that end-user functions only use 'approved' suppliers. In fact, a good e-procurement system can allow much more day-to-day purchasing (calling off) to be delegated to end users without fear of loss of control. This frees the professional buyers to get on and do what they are meant to be doing: monitoring supply markets, setting up new deals and managing the key strategic suppliers so as to reduce risk in this area.

Embedding risk and control into systems is done from the point of view of addressing management need to have effective systems but should also include the ability to report on how well the system objectives are being achieved. In other words, are anomalies being reported? If there is an attempt to override a system control, is this immediately flagged for action? Even when embedded correction takes place automatically, there should be a report generated of a fault detection. Preventive and detective controls can be built into systems so that errors can be (a) automatically corrected (preventive controls) or (b) detected and the transaction or process stopped. In both cases, it is essential that management receive a report and act on the detail of the report, thus allowing the risk management of these events to be implemented.

In addition to embedding control, software can be developed or purchased which will report on particular criteria using analysis and data mining applications. Fraud detection and prevention software is a good example of this; packages are widely available and include IDEA and ACL.

The most important part of embedding risk and control initiatives is to follow through by introducing them into IT systems and implementing their use. Thereafter, it is essential to take action when things are going wrong. If the report data is not used to take corrective action, there is little point in having it in the first place.

Self-assessment question 19.4

Identify a software solution that can raise an alarm when a particular supplier's deliveries display a trend of increasing unpunctuality.

Feedback on page 338

Revision question

Now try the revision question for this session on page 358.

Summary

The relationship between objectives, risks and controls has again been emphasised in this study session. Control models have been introduced

19

as a means for implementing high standards of risk management and internal control and ideas about benchmarking risk approaches have been discussed. The role of internal auditing, external auditing and external consultants has been explored in relation to controlling risks and appraising risk management in general. Great benefits can be achieved from integrating risk management into systems and to making this an essential part of all systems development. In addition to embedding controls to mitigate risks, some software solutions were also discussed which can assist in taking action when anomalies or irregularities are discovered.

Suggested further reading

Committee of Sponsoring Organisations of the Treadway Committee (COSO) (2004) Criteria of Control Board (CoCo): Canadian Institute of Chartered Accountants (1998 to date) *Control and Governance*. http://www.cica.ca

You could also read the relevant sections of Pickett and Pickett (2002).

Feedback on learning activities and self-assessment questions

Feedback on learning activity 19.1

Internal auditing helps the organisation achieve objectives. It does so by providing assurance over the effectiveness of risk, control and governance processes. Thus, detecting errors is not the main objective of an internal audit although it may be a byproduct of audit work. What the audit will do is review systems and test the risk assumptions together with the controls activated to mitigate the risks. This audit testing may find system faults which could indicate errors. Specific testing may be undertaken purely to detect errors if controls were found to be less than adequate.

Feedback on self-assessment question 19.1

Any staff members who have been trained in line with quality audit requirements would be the first choice – these individuals should have the skill and experience to carry out an internal safety audit. Failing this, staff with good experience in the department and who have attended in-house briefings on safety issues would be a good choice. The objective of the team should be to monitor the application of the organisation's own rules and procedures (and any other external requirement) in the areas of health and safety of personnel and to make improvements where necessary.

Feedback on learning activity 19.2

The external audit of public bodies requires an approach which covers financial probity and achievement of value for money. In both these areas, an effective risk management process should feature strongly and the external auditors should review the risk process in place. The auditors will be trying to find assurance that the underlying risk and control systems are effective to the extent that final accounts and other operational information is accurate and reflects a 'true and fair' view of the organisation at a point in time.

Feedback on self-assessment question 19.2

The external audit provides an independent view of an organisation's financial position (in the public sector there will also be a view of value for money). The auditor's report goes to shareholders and allows all stakeholders to take a view on the organisation's performance independent from any view given by management. The work of the external auditor can assist also in reviewing the approach to financial risks and the control actions taken to mitigate these risks. The auditor's report will also be beneficial in circumstances where a takeover or merger is being contemplated since it provides an independent view of financial stability at the point when the work was done.

Feedback on learning activity 19.3

Good appraisals depend on a frank exchange of views based on as much background data as possible. In all cases it is helpful to agree objectives before the contract even begins. Without this there is little against which to measure or judge results. Data gathered over a longer rather than a shorter period of time benefits a good appraisal and there should be openness on both sides. Bad appraisal techniques are characterised by a one-sided approach, argument over what each party thought were the main objectives, withdrawal or lack of participation and vague, inadequate or unconstructive feedback.

Benchmarking uses comparative data on a number of similar organisations so that best practice can be attained by all, based on 'best in class'. This relies on data collection in some key indicator areas and willingness to impart as much information as possible into the public domain. Industry analyses, indices and benchmark groups are easily accessible on the internet and in trade or professional journals.

Feedback on self-assessment question 19.3

Your list could include:

* financial stability
* product quality
* product availability
* ability to deliver when and where agreed
* reputation
* knowledge of market
* application of industry and other standards.

Feedback on learning activity 19.4

Your answer could have included:

* price movement histories for the same product from different suppliers

- what is actually bought from any single supplier
- who in the organisation is buying or ordering from a supplier
- the number of suppliers used who are all supplying the same thing
- quality and delivery performance, standards of service, and so on
- savings achieved or price increases conceded to suppliers by specific buyers.

System controls allow constant monitoring of data flows, indicating alerts and generating reports when controls are breached or attempted breaches occur. Additionally, parameters can be set to generate all the information you require as a buyer and, also, you can use query functions to specify exactly the data you want to interrogate.

Feedback on self-assessment question 19.4

The solution must include the ability to input expected delivery dates at the commencement of the supply and use these dates to generate a report when there is no confirmatory input of a receipt. Aldata G.O.L.D. Events is one example of many such systems which provide alert messages and can be purchased as a completed procurement solution or in modular form. Other solutions can be found on the internet and a good index site is http://www.uk.logismarket.com.

Study session 20

Contingency planning

Introduction

Having a contingency in place means having a fallback position ready in case something goes wrong. In finance, we may have a reserve account available for unforeseen costs – an amount available for no particular purpose other than to deal with unexpected events; not allocated, in other words, for specific expenditure. The same applies to general **contingency planning**. The term means ensuring that we have plans in place to provide for business continuity, as much as is possible, should something unforeseen occur. The terms contingency planning and disaster planning are often used to mean the same thing and, in fact, the important issue is not the terminology but the fact that a need has been recognised and plans developed to meet emergencies should they ever arise. It means, at one extreme, being prepared for the worst possible disasters that can be thought of and then trying to plan beyond that to situations that we simply do not think will ever occur – just as we learned with scenario planning, our mindset needs to be: 'what if'. At the other extreme, crises may emerge which require more than the normal management response to contain them but are not a full-blown emergency. Disaster recovery and contingency planning covers these extremes and everything in between.

'If you can keep your head when all about you are losing theirs.'
Rudyard Kipling, *If*

Session learning objectives

After completing this session you should be able to:

20.1 Explain the need for key staff succession planning.
20.2 Give examples of how disasters can be avoided through good design.
20.3 Demonstrate a number of IT disaster recovery solutions.
20.4 Formulate a plan of action to deal with disaster recovery in the supply chain.

Unit content coverage

This study session covers the following topics from the official CIPS unit content document:

Learning objectives

3.3 Develop contingency plans designed to overcome risk situations.
  • What is meant by a contingency plan?
  • The key components of a business continuity plan (BCP) and disaster recovery plan and how such plans are put into practice
  • Key contingency measures used by a BCP: telephone cascades, emergency and fire wardens, use of IT systems to help co-

20

ordinate activities, use of alternative accommodation and back-up information technology systems

- The benefits of business continuity planning from an operational, financial and reputational perspective

Prior knowledge

Study sessions 1 to 19.

Resources

Internet access.

Timing

You should set aside about 4 hours to read and complete this session, including learning activities, self-assessment questions, the suggested further reading (if any) and the revision question.

20.1 Key staff succession planning

Learning activity 20.1

Consider your own job. Draw up a list of tasks for which you have specialist knowledge. If you were promoted, how would you ensure a seamless transition?

Feedback on page 351

Succession planning encapsulates the senior management task of ensuring that capable personnel are trained, prepared and ready to fill an appropriate vacancy when that need arises. Like many another management task, it is about anticipating future events and one of those future events will inevitably be the departure of key staff members whose going will affect the company's operations. How significant that effect may be will depend on the specialism and seniority of that individual.

Management succession planning aims to ensure that a sufficient supply of appropriately qualified staff are available to meet the contingency of operational failure through lack of a key staff member. Some staffing events are foreseeable, like promotion or retirement, but death or sudden resignation are the unwanted surprises which constitute one of the significant HR risks.

Key staff members are those without whom a function or operation would not carry on effectively or the delivery of which would be severely curtailed. Identifying what the really significant tasks are, the key, essential tasks

20

without which the operation cannot proceed, is the first but often the most difficult process. The more senior these key people are, the more vulnerable the organisation is likely to be to their sudden departure. It makes sense to begin mitigating this kind of risk by first of all minimising the threat by spreading the knowledge and capability required for a particular task beyond just one or two key personnel. Sometimes this will not be possible. There is usually only one managing director, for example, but good succession planning by the board's staffing committee should ensure that at least one replacement is immediately available should the need arise.

The key risks are:

• operational crisis
• loss of continuity (from one individual to another)
• vacancy with no immediate replacements
• diminution of product or service delivery.

The response to these risks begins with a commitment to staff training and development – both across the entire organisation and resident in each individual manager.

Training fits an individual for the tasks at hand and should be continuous in order to reflect changes in methods and technologies and to allow a certain amount of progression to take place. Development, on the other hand, should be aimed at preparing staff for new roles and new positions which may require both additional and different skills. Thus, a management development programme should be in place and have specific goals and expectations which may include:

• continuous improvement in managers' performance
• improved motivation by being part of a programme aimed at the future
• improved retention and a 'hook' for improving recruitment quality
• training for today's jobs and tomorrow's
• a wider 'pool' of prepared managers with deeper knowledge
• involvement of managers from differing disciplines; this will improve communication together with knowledge of different functions.

Management development programmes should go well beyond the technical knowledge required to undertake a particular job. Professional training for buyers, for example, can be designed very effectively to prepare people to get the best out of the supply chain for the benefit of their companies. Developing buyers to be ready for board positions, however, requires the acquisition of different skills and necessitates a different approach.

Recognition of the need for succession planning should begin with the board and cascade down to senior management. No succession planning means putting up with a substantial unmitigated risk and, for most organisations, this would be unacceptable. The only way to mitigate the risk effectively is to have either a nominated successor always available or a group of people, any one of whom could fill any senior position when it becomes vacant. The nominated successor is possible but often a wasteful use of resources: consider a 'deputy' to a post holder – if the biggest part of the job description is to understudy the principal officer, this is probably not the

20

best use of resources or the best solution available. Better to have a group, from which a choice can be made, trained and ready to step in immediately.

HR departments provide the necessary skills to assess the skills, knowledge and capability required for the types of jobs common in the company in which they operate. They have the specialist knowledge which can be applied to recruiting staff at various levels and can provide great assistance in the selection process. All of these tasks help to mitigate the day-to-day staffing risks experienced by every company at all but the most senior levels, such as skills analysis, labour relations and remuneration packages. They should also be the facilitators of a management development programme.

The role of HR as facilitator in a management development programme means that time can be allocated in an off-line function to assess the availability of various development programmes or, if necessary, develop an in-house scheme. HR can take a wide view of the management needs of the company and of the individuals who might be part of the programme. Thus, the programme should be designed to extend participants' capabilities by widening their exposure to ideas, principles and methods about which they might not otherwise be aware. The goal is to provide managers with a rounded knowledge base and heightened intellectual capability to help them in becoming the leaders of tomorrow.

HR departments cannot do this task alone. Commitment from the board and other senior managers is essential. Many parts of the programme, if it is to be successful, may well be off-site and require time to be made available which might be to the detriment of the immediate management task. Far-seeing managements will see this as a temporary setback only and look to the greater opportunities in the future rather than the inconvenience of a few days' absence. We should not forget, either, that every manager in post has a responsibility to look out for successors and actively encourage their development. This should be part and parcel of any manager's contingency planning process.

Knowledge management – understanding the key philosophy and principles of the corporate ethos as well as the organisation's operations – is an important senior management task in environments where technology drives change at increasing rates. Loss of a key staff member can threaten this resource and part of effective knowledge management is to ensure that there are the people and equipment available to capitalise on what may be an organisation's unique knowledge base. A contingency plan in place and ready to deal with management succession is an essential part of future-oriented organisations keen to maintain continuity and capitalise on staff resources.

Self-assessment question 20.1

List the steps that may be necessary to ensure that an effective succession plan is in place in a purchasing department.

Feedback on page 351

20

20.2 Avoiding disasters by implementing good design

Learning activity 20.2

Think about the construction of houses in areas vulnerable to natural forces such as flood or earthquake. What is normally done to minimise the dangers?

Feedback on page 352

In 1995 in Kobe, Japan, 5,500 people died as a result of an earthquake. Many parts of Japan are known to be vulnerable to this form of natural disaster and there had been much research into the improvement of construction methods which could aid survival from earthquakes. It is possible that the death toll would have been even higher had improvements in materials and methods not already taken place. Because of its geophysical location, Japan will continue to experience earthquakes. Nothing can stop this but research continues into better and different ways of constructing buildings to better withstand the effects of tremors of varying strengths. The fact is, however, that optimism prevails over experience and people will tend to want to stay in their home area and rebuild despite knowledge of a possible repeat disaster.

Natural flood plains exist in many parts of the UK. Several have not flooded in recent memory although historic flooding events are well known. Carlisle in 2005 suffered significant flooding despite there having been no major flooding event in the city for the previous 100 years. Boscastle in North Devon was devastated by catastrophic floods in 2004, having previously experienced severe flood damage in 1987.

Flooding often occurs as a result of rivers becoming unable to contain higher volumes of water within their normal banks. The overflow runs off into well-established flood plains and causes little damage to structures or people. Sometimes, however, particularly after spells of prolonged rainfall, ground becomes saturated and is unable to absorb any more water. The rain has to find somewhere to go and runs over the ground, following contours into valleys and causing so-called 'flash floods' – large volumes of water cascading into already swollen rivers – in areas not normally prone to flooding.

Areas which are vulnerable to natural disasters must rely on building defences against these events to mitigate the risks. Similarly, advances in design need to be encouraged as a means for reducing the vulnerability of all the people and assets which may be deployed in known risk areas. Unfortunately, the prioritisation of resources means that, often, it is only the known danger areas which get the funds to provide adequate protection.

At the macro level, defence against natural disasters is managed by strategic planning and decision making. Large investments have to be made in designing and building major projects such as flood defences. The London flood barrier is a good example of this. A less costly defence is to use planning law to prevent new building in known flood plain areas.

20

Unfortunately, pressure on available building land sometimes allows homes to be built in areas which are known to be vulnerable and the only defence becomes awareness of possible flooding through use of the Environment Agency's flood warning system. Nonetheless, UK rivers known to be prone to flooding are carefully managed and the design and construction of weirs, reservoirs and banked channels are measures taken to minimise the impact of flood damage. At the micro level, the design of homes in these areas should take into account their vulnerability and be built on high foundations with as much ground sloping away from the dwelling as possible. Additional or larger-volume drainage systems should also be part of the design brief for sites in these areas.

Japan is one part of the world where several oceanic plates meet and this is the cause of frequent earthquakes. The western coast of the USA is another earthquake-prone area and there are many others around the world. Japan has been at the forefront of building design through research into innovative methods of earthquake-proof foundation work. Various schemes have already been designed in to buildings such as floating foundation blocks and hydraulic springs beneath columns and walls. Much work has also been done on the ways in which different construction materials react under earthquake-type stresses and, in particular, the patterns which materials adopt when collapsing. All of this has been done to encourage builders to use design as the means for mitigating earthquake risks since avoiding earthquakes themselves is simply not possible. Interior design has also played a key part in this approach, following research which showed that many deaths and injuries in earthquake-affected buildings were found to be caused by falling objects within living or working spaces.

The USA has also taken prevention seriously in its approach to building design. The Building Seismic Safety Council has issued regulations which require compliance where construction sites lie within earthquake-prone areas. Specifications for material quality and building procedure are laid down and there is a series of inspections during the build period.

Fire is another hazard where prevention can be a powerful mitigation strategy. Using the design stage to ensure that fireproof materials arc used for products is not only sensible but essential where there needs to be compliance with particular safety standards and legislation. British Standards such as BS5839-1: 2002 cover detection and alarm systems for buildings and there is a code of practice for systems design and installation. Other issues can be built in at the design stage of any building such as the use of fire-resistant materials, isolating higher-risk areas such as heating plants and boiler rooms, and constructing safe escape routes.

Building processes, for large construction projects or for manufactured products large or small, benefit from a total quality management (TQM) approach. TQM is a management philosophy that requires all staff in all parts of the organisation to be responsible for quality. Underpinning the philosophy is the idea that not having as perfect quality as possible wastes resources. Thus, a quality control process provides a remedy for finding rejects or faults after the event and feeding back the lessons learned from these failures. Quality assurance, on the other hand, seeks to ensure that quality failure should be prevented rather than corrected.

Thinking about quality at the design stage brings important benefits. Information from as many sources as possible should be incorporated; customer feedback, design forums (including 'quality circles') and shopfloor ideas can all inform the design process and epitomise the idea of prevention of faults and 'getting it right first time'. The whole organisation can benefit from working towards the business excellence model, a means for linking leadership with quality systems and processes which will enhance business results. The model, promoted in the UK by the British Quality Foundation, provides a framework which makes quality an integral part of every action and outcome and constantly contributes to continuous improvement. Various other standards are often required of companies in order that they become approved providers of the goods or services which they design and produce: ISO 9001, for example. These standards give the framework for a quality process within the organisation and also provide a measure of credibility for consumers outside the organisation.

International, national and other standards provide a system which guides users in a particular way and gives confidence to stakeholders that an accepted quality system is in place. Compliance with internally set standards is the first step, however. A design can only be translated into a process and, ultimately a product or service by adhering to the manuals and procedures provided to achieve the desired outcome. The right design, made to accomplish an agreed objective and produced by complying with the agreed system, will provide the best insurance against future failure and disaster.

Self-assessment question 20.2

What steps would you take as a designer to ensure that the components on an aircraft cargo door that you are designing are correctly reassembled during routine maintenance?

Feedback on page 352

20.3 IT disaster recovery planning

Learning activity 20.3

Investigate IT disaster recovery solutions, through the internet or preferably with an IT manager, and list the alternatives that may be available for particular 'disasters'.

Feedback on page 352

IT is central to the efficient operation of all organisations. If IT fails, survivability can be in doubt for many enterprises and, for all but the smallest, reverting to a manual system is virtually impossible, certainly in the short time available when a disaster strikes. That means planning for recovery from an IT disaster must be a high priority.

20

The process is shown in figure 20.1.

Figure 20.1: Planning for IT recovery

Disaster plan

↓

Staffing: skills and contacts

↓

Equipment: facilities; contracts

↓

Premises: buildings, prefabs

↓

Operating procedures

↓

Software: copies, back-ups, etc

↓

Transport arrangements: to new site; staff collection

↓

Procurement: new software; call off contracts, etc

Minor service interruptions of a much lesser nature than a disaster will be handled by risk responses such as maintaining standby generators in case the main power supply fails. Similarly, equipment to smooth out unexpected power surges will feature as part of the standard installation. Mechanical or electrical breakdown in networked systems can be compensated for by use of other parts of a local area network or by arrangements with other users in a wider area network.

The failsafe way to ensure IT recovery in a mainframe environment is to maintain a complete duplicate of the IT asset, remote from the main site, and to ensure regular back-up of data. The majority of commercial organisations cannot sustain this level of investment or justify the resource input necessary. Even within large strategic organisations such as national defence or intelligence gathering, this level of duplication is rare. More appropriate is a standby arrangement of some sort which can be activated at short notice.

Traditional measures for a standby arrangement generally consisted of a back-up where a minimum level of hardware could either be held in a separate building owned by the organisation where back-up software was available, or a contracted arrangement where service was provided on-call by a specialist supplier using the hardware configuration agreed with the supplier. These arrangements are no longer fully adequate for distributed computing environments where continuous operation is a must in an e-business, web-speed world.

Disaster recovery in IT now means engineering security, availability and reliability into business processes from the outset rather than retrofitting a recovery plan. However, distributed computing means that business continuity is not just the responsibility of the IT department. Decentralised processes and applications mean that all managers in every discipline must participate in making the continuity plan a working solution. Too much can be lost in minutes in today's electronic environment if systems are down rather than, perhaps, the hours or days that were available to recover in times gone by.

Client/server computing means that the cost of duplicating data and holding redundant storage arrays is achievable at reasonable cost thereby creating near-online data mirroring in-house. This is not the only requirement for a continuity plan, however, and there still needs to be consideration of a separate location from the main production equipment together with power failure back-up. Sufficient capacity needs to be available to allow frequent testing without disrupting current operations and there should be procurement arrangements in place to allow for speedy re-equipment in the case of a major disaster.

There remains the alternative of using an outside contractor to provide back-up facilities and many large and small companies exist who will provide a continuity plan to your specifications, although there will be the additional cost of a contracted retainer fee. Every organisation will have to balance the cost of maintaining spare capacity in-house as against the annual cost of maintaining a contractor at instant readiness. The ability of the contractor to keep up to date with your changes, both in technology and personnel expertise, also needs to be considered. A further risk to consider is: to what extent can we be sure that the contractor is equipped to maintain our approach to data protection? This risk also requires to be addressed when our own disaster plan includes data back-up and copying in different locations and using a variety of media.

A checklist can help the review of your readiness to cope with IT disaster recovery:

- Have you identified all critical business activities?
- What is the essential information needed for these critical systems to perform?
- Is there a record of all IT downtime with reasons why?
- Is the downtime record used to identify frequently occurring problems?
- Are any legacy systems and all other IT resources virus and hacker protected?
- Has the recovery or continuity plan been tested recently?
- Is there a change control mechanism which informs the continuity plan as process, organisation and technology changes take place?
- Do you have confidence in the current recovery plan – will it keep you in business?

Self-assessment question 20.3

What steps can you take to protect your computer files?

Feedback on page 352

20.4 Planning for disaster recovery in the supply chain

Learning activity 20.4

Evaluate the extent to which existing disaster recovery plans for the purchasing department in your organisation have been tested.

Feedback on page 353

Natural disasters and catastrophic events will happen. The past informs the future in this respect: we know that floods, earthquakes and hurricanes will occur from time to time. Aircraft will crash and terrorist acts will take place. We also know that power and energy supplies will fluctuate and that any number of other events may test our preparedness – and that is the key to disaster recovery: being as prepared as possible for the surprises we know will occur. What we don't know is when, where or how bad these events may be.

Disaster recovery is about building in the capability of carrying on as near as possible as if nothing has happened – to cope with the adversity and carry on delivering a service or making a product with as little delay as can be achieved. The only way to make sure of this is to plan for as many eventualities as is reasonably possible.

For businesses, the aim of disaster planning is to maintain continuity. Business continuity management is a process which aims to identify the potential impacts that could threaten an organisation and provide a framework for effective responses which will safeguard the interests of key stakeholders.

Most organisations will approach disaster planning much as they would risk management – it is, after all, just another area in the corporate risk portfolio. Procurement should, therefore, be part of the process for identifying and evaluating risks which build from the bottom up to feed into the corporate risk management plan. The procedure for contingency planning follows the familiar pattern but needs to reflect the particular needs of responding to the potential impacts and consequences of catastrophic events:

- Identification and evaluation – brainstorming, analysis, scenario planning: what disruptions and disasters may affect us? Can we look at historic events to gain insight? Are there any time-critical processes or deliveries in the supply chain without which operations must cease? How long would downtime be before everything stops? Is there a time period after which recovery would be impossible?
- Internal and external control – controls can mitigate the risks: what reasonable controls can be put in place which would contribute to operational continuity? Is it possible to increase stockholding, for example, to cope with supply disruption or to establish an 'emergency' stock? Are strategic commodity stocks held in-country and would we have access to them?
- Response procedures – who does what, where and when? Are there published plans for disaster recovery in place corporately and in the

purchasing department? Are nominated staff aware of their duties? Have staff been trained in the recovery procedures?

- Communications and operational control – is there a stand-alone alternative communications mechanism? Are key personnel known and can they be contacted? Is procurement represented on the main crisis management team? Are responsibility and authority levels clear and understood?
- Testing the plans – an essential part of making sure that the scenarios which might arise can be handled is carrying out verification trials of the plans and procedures. Does the alternative communications system work? Are assets available to the extent expected in the plan? Can essential personnel turn up where and when expected? Can external partners perform up to the expectations of our plan?

Companies often wish to prioritise emergencies and disasters into categories requiring particular responses. A crisis may be contained at a lower level of response than a full-blown emergency or a catastrophic disaster. Planning should take this into account so that incremental steps are taken as each phase of the events unfolds. A labour crisis may begin with a core team of managers dealing with the event from a meeting room and escalate to activation of an emergency operations centre only when the business is on the point of being closed down and creditors are clamouring for payment.

The corporate response to disasters will need to take into account matters such as public relations and broader stakeholder communication. Although this may not need to be taken into account in the purchasing department as a separate issue, it will be necessary for senior purchasing managers to be trained in media relations so that they can both provide input to the corporate PR response and be part of the response team dealing with external stakeholders, should that be appropriate.

The procurement function has extensive external relationships by the very nature of its work. Understanding and nurturing these relationships is part of every purchasing manager's daily workload. It is particularly important that these relationships are documented wherever possible so that the supply chain contingency plan clearly indicates key points where, for example, alternative supply is available – or is contracted for availability in the case of a crisis – and the means for calling off that supply are documented and available. An example would be the contract for 'hot start' IT facilities from a specialist supplier, activated only when our own IT crashes. Another simple example is the annual contract made with farmers by some councils to have their tractors available for snow shifting when the authority's own equipment is overstretched.

Two key issues are apparent in supply chain continuity. First, the visibility of the chain – *reduced* visibility in reality – in that the visibility often ends at the first-tier supplier and, second, loss of control at second- or third-tier supplier level. Where there is multiple supply in the chain, then it is essential for the client to get to know where each intermediate supply is sourced, at least in general terms. This allows the contingency plan to address the possibility of direct contact with each part of the chain should this become necessary.

20

Procurement managers need to be adept also at understanding means and methods for payment of suppliers. Creditors quickly materialise when crisis looms. This is particularly important when overseas sourcing is used. Suppliers may require advance payments, yet a crisis in that country may arbitrarily terminate supply before the contract is complete. This may be a relatively normal commercial kind of risk (and money values may be recouped by insurance or export credit guarantee) but unavailability of the supply in a crisis could be significant and should be planned for. Nonetheless, difficulties of contingency planning are compounded when overseas supply is involved. The country of source may have its own local difficulties which may take time to become evident and may only reach the level of a crisis for the client long after alternatives could easily have been brought into play. Supply chain intelligence gathering is essential as a means for mitigating this type of risk. Knowledge is everything and advance knowledge can be worth its weight in gold.

Testing of plans is a must. Tests and exercises, although as close to the real thing as possible, will rarely come up with the unexpected events which characterise the real thing. If the same floods which threaten your factory have also affected large areas of the surrounding countryside, can staff get to the emergency centre? Will alternative communications such as cell phones operate when signal stations are inoperable because of wet equipment? In procurement, can you carry out the necessary work away from your own premises? Is there remote computer access and will that work in an emergency? Does your emergency procurement plan allow for immediate payment to new suppliers (granting credit may take time) with whom you have no credit or payment record? Is there access to procurement cards or even cash in an emergency?

Contingency planning is an essential part of managing risk. The process has its basis in identifying and evaluating risks but needs to provide assurance at the level of business resilience and continuity. Planning for disasters which may never happen is not wasteful of resources. On the contrary, it is a reasoned and cost-effective way of staying in business when the enormity of huge events may overwhelm those less prepared.

Self-assessment question 20.4

What questions would you need to ask one of your suppliers in order that you can develop an effective disaster recovery plan for the supply chain?

Feedback on page 353

Revision question

Now try the revision question for this session on page 358.

Now try the revision question for this session on page 358.

Summary

Human experience tells us that disasters will always happen. The effects of these disasters can be lessened if we are prepared for as many contingencies as can be foreseen. This study session has emphasised the dependence on IT which characterises most organisations today and the fact that this reliance means loss of customer service and revenue which may affect survivability very quickly. We have emphasised that there needs to be a measured response to disasters; nonetheless, it is critical that communications and equipment are available at the level and at the time they are needed. Disaster recovery plans depend on people as well as equipment and some of the HR issues have been considered in addition to the manifestation of natural and man-made disasters. Business continuity planning is an holistic process. Nonetheless, we have looked at supply chain management in terms of its functional response to disasters as well as its part in being a component of the corporate disaster response.

Suggested further reading

You could read the relevant sections of Boddy (2002) and Sadgrove (2005).

The Business Continuity Institute: http://www.thebci.org.

Feedback on learning activities and self-assessment questions

Feedback on learning activity 20.1

You should have started by reviewing your job description. Using that as a base and your knowledge of your own key tasks, you could then have considered some of the following:

- identified staff with the correct level of experience to take over
- reviewed the current level of training of staff with the experience needed
- identified individuals with relationship skills (to ease the transition)
- identified those with the right attitude to success (motivation to succeed)
- used the assistance of HR to help plan the succession.

Feedback on self-assessment question 20.1

Your answer should include:

- identification of key tasks and objectives
- annual appraisal system to review success in achieving objectives
- a training needs assessment procedure
- availability of personnel trained to the right level for succession
- access to management development schemes run in-house or externally
- a budget for training and development
- willingness to participate in development schemes.

You should ensure that senior purchasing managers have addressed the need for a succession plan and that there has been liaison with HR to ensure involvement with training schemes and management development programmes. Remember that succession planning is essentially recruitment from within – hopefully with an able individual ready to take over –

20

rather than waiting for a vacancy to occur and seeking a wider recruitment solution.

Feedback on learning activity 20.2

Review historical data to establish frequency and severity of past events. Having done that, construction should be limited to those areas where past effects have been minimal. In the UK, for example, the Environment Agency should be consulted for information on flood plains. Other countries maintain data relevant to other dangers. Techniques for limiting damage by using new construction techniques should be made mandatory for the vulnerable areas and any quality or regulatory standards imposed, where they exist, to ensure use of the recommended materials. Inspection regimes during construction should be rigorously applied.

Feedback on self-assessment question 20.2

There have been many fatal air accidents due to aircraft cargo doors opening when the aircraft is in the air. A number of these have been the result of incorrect assembly of door-lock components following routine maintenance. Accident investigation reports have suggested:

- Making it impossible for parts to be reassembled incorrectly (ie designing the door-lock components so that they simply will not fit together unless assembled correctly).
- Designing the lock so that it will not operate (or appear to operate) unless all parts are correctly assembled and installed.
- Making it impossible to dismantle and repair certain parts or assemblies. If they fail on test (eg due to excessive wear) then the whole assembly must be replaced with a new one.
- Designing the door-lock mechanism so that it can be subjected to a series of simple tests following reassembly which will show conclusively that it is working properly.

Feedback on learning activity 20.3

There are many suppliers of business continuity packages and many varieties of service level available. A good research report is available at http://www.continuitycentral.com, the research actually undertaken by the Michigan State University, and focuses on supply chain continuity planning.

You could have found outsource suppliers including SunGard (http://www.availability.sungard.com/united+kingdom) and IBM (http://www.ibm.com/services/continuity). Many others are available and level of service depends only on client need and cost of each solution.

Feedback on self-assessment question 20.3

Protection includes copying data by system back-up routines as part of normal procedures. Integrated data systems will update files constantly and automatically and there should be regular data dumps as part of the contingency plan. Additionally, you should be copying files locally on the network or to other software assets such as removable discs. Other protection required includes access controls and virus and hacker exclusion.

Feedback on learning activity 20.4

You should obtain copies of the recovery plan and check:

- current and updated
- system and operational changes are fed into the plan
- staff trained and aware of the plan contents
- records of plan testing
- programme in place in the purchasing department for regular testing
- reports made to senior managers of test results.

Feedback on self-assessment question 20.4

Questions should include:

- his ability to continue supply in an emergency
- level of supplier's stockholding
- number of tiers in his supply chain
- source of supply for each tier.

Additionally, an understanding of financial consequences for the supplier if your own payment methods are compromised by the emergency, for example, delays in payment or different methods of payment (cheque to electronic funds transfer (EFTR) perhaps or, even cash for small amounts) and prior agreement with him for flexibility in payment terms to be permitted under those circumstances. It would be helpful for you to know that your supplier also has a recovery plan and this could have been part of your supplier appraisal/assessment procedure.

Revision questions

Revision question for study session 1

You have been asked to train some new employees in the concepts of risk and the practice of risk management. Produce a set of notes that you will use for a presentation to those new employees.

Feedback on page 359

Revision question for study session 2

Compare and contrast the risks that stem from within the organisation (internal risks) and those that are created outside the organisation (external risks).

Feedback on page 359

Revision question for study session 3

Explain the differences between strategic, operational and project-based areas of risk.

Feedback on page 361

Revision question for study session 4

In attempting to avoid referring only to shareholders in terms of company ownership and influence, the phrase 'wider stakeholder community' is often used. List those who may be part of this community and give brief descriptions of the effects on all these groups if a company is poorly managed and governed.

Feedback on page 362

Revision question for study session 5

Discuss the following statement: 'The implementation of total quality management eliminates risk from the supply chain.'

Feedback on page 362

Revision question for study session 6

Design a risk management strategy for a firm that supplies and erects scaffolding for building works.

Feedback on page 363

Revision question for study session 7

In terms of risk management define the terms *impact* and *probability* and illustrate the following risks by means of a risk map (eg an aircraft crashing onto a building housing a mainframe computer would be *high impact, low probability*):

1 Loss of revenue to 'flag carrier' airlines caused by low cost entrants to the market.
2 The effect of several consecutive years of losses on shareholder confidence in any company.
3 Multi-million pound awards against an NHS primary care trust with a poor record of patient care.
4 The effect on a consultancy firm of poor advice being seen as the reason for a principal client being in difficulties.
5 Release into the atmosphere of a harmful substance by a chemical firm with a poor emissions record.
6 A product is advertised as 'being of the highest quality' and is subject to complaint by consumers because of perceived poor quality.
7 The effect on a rail company of a death of a rail worker despite adequate safety supervision at trackside works.
8 The discovery that a bank had unknowingly breached the law by accepting large cash deposits from a doubtful source.

Feedback on page 364

Revision question for study session 8

Develop a plan of action to increase the risk awareness of a group of finance staff.

Feedback on page 365

Revision question for study session 9

Develop five clauses that you might include in a contract with a new supplier to ensure that they take responsibility for supply chain risks.

Feedback on page 366

Revision question for study session 10

Select two qualitative and two quantitative risk management methods and describe how they can be effectively used by a modern business to gain competitive advantage.

Feedback on page 367

Revision question for study session 11

Select at least five key parameters that need to be considered in potential supplier appraisal. Explain how you will obtain sufficient information for each parameter and how you will validate the information.

Feedback on page 369

Revision question for study session 12

You have just moved from the public sector to take on the role of purchasing manager in a company in the entertainment industry. Explain how you will deal with the change of culture regarding gifts, hospitality and other issues that may impact on your personal and professional ethics.

Feedback on page 370

Revision question for study session 13

Project management requires many skills. Discuss the advantages and disadvantages of running a project by means of a multi-skill management team.

Feedback on page 371

Revision question for study session 14

List ten clauses that you would want to include in a contract for the supply of heating oil. Rank them in descending order of priority and justify your ranking.

Feedback on page 372

Revision question for study session 15

Write a report detailing the risks that are specific to or more prevalent in the public sector.

Feedback on page 373

Revision question for study session 16

Give details of five methods that you might use to reduce the risks posed by changes in environmental legislation.

Feedback on page 375

Revision question for study session 17

Give details of at least three advantages and disadvantages of each of the modes of transport used in international trade. Analyse the risks of using each mode of transport.

Feedback on page 376

Revision question for study session 18

Explain the tools and techniques you would use to ensure that a new training company is providing you with good-quality training. Justify your choice of tools and techniques.

Feedback on page 377

Revision question for study session 19

Explain the principles of statistical process control and show how it could form part of an enterprise-wide risk management system.

Feedback on page 378

Revision question for study session 20

The Bangladesh cyclone warning system established in the 1980s significantly reduced death from cyclone tidal surges. Following the Indian Ocean tsunami disaster, there has been much discussion about creating a similar simple warning system. In the aftermath of these world events your chief executive has been thinking about whether there are any risk reduction strategies that your organisation could introduce to minimise the risk of a disaster happening. This would complement your existing IT disaster recovery plans.

You have been asked to conduct a review to determine what preventive steps might be taken to reduce the risks of a disaster occurring and to make a speedy recovery possible. As a first stage, you are asked to prepare a report identifying the areas that you would include in your review and explaining why they have been selected.

Prepare a draft report as requested.

Feedback on page 379

Feedback on revision questions

Feedback on revision question for study session 1

Your notes should include the following:

- A definition of risk: an unexpected or random event, but one for which we can make an assessment of probability and which may affect the achievement of objectives. This can be developed into the idea that threats and hazards are risks and that organisational risks may be different to personal risks.
- Objectives flow from an organisation's strategy; objectives, risks and controls are inextricably linked.
- A risk can be as simple as the potential for an employee to be exposed to RSI or as complex as the risk to reputation of a company because of a failure of quality.
- Organisational risks occur in all sectors of activity but there may be differences in management and accountability between the private and public sectors.
- Risk management is the means by which risks are identified, assessed and evaluated. Management action to mitigate risk follows the cycle of identifying the risks which may prevent achievement of an objective, assessing their likelihood or probability of occurrence and evaluating the impact which the organisation may suffer.
- The risk culture of an organisation can be defined as risk averse – little appetite for taking risks; or risk enthusiastic – eager to embrace a controlled approach to risk management (these are the 'risk appetites'). Risk enthusiasts tend to find the upside of risk – opportunity.
- The board or governing body is responsible for risk management and should cascade the culture and process all the way down the organisation. This should include the setting of risk strategy – the '4T' approach: treat, transfer, tolerate, terminate.
- Every staff member should become his or her own 'risk manager' by identifying and assessing risks in his or her immediate work environment.

Feedback on revision question for study session 2

Internal risks are created by the people, resources and operations used inside the organisation – the causes are internal although the effects may extend beyond the organisational boundaries. In contrast, external risks are caused by events outside the organisation and often beyond the control of the organisation's management. Risks can be categorised in accordance with the Risk Standard AS/NZS 4360:

- commercial and legal relationships
- economic circumstances
- human behaviour
- natural events
- political circumstances
- technology and technical issues
- management activities and controls
- individual activities.

Thus, some risks may be created from either inside or outside the organisation. The important thing is to identify the possibility of a risk arising, along with the impact and probability, and to take appropriate action to manage the risk.

Internal risks can occur through a lack of understanding of organisational strategy and objectives – management can fail to cascade these sufficiently well or to a low enough level for all staff to become motivated to meet common targets. The behavioural aspects of managing teams may be poorly understood and cause a lack of cohesion giving rise to risks of fragmented effort, loss of corporate focus and overall poor performance. HR management may not be handling recruitment and retention policies adequately, giving rise to employee unrest and lack of striving for attainment of objectives. Technology, both in communication and operations, may be better understood below senior management level and create risks of gaps appearing between high-level expectation and operational application. Poor quality of service or product – which may occur for any number of reasons, eg poor machinery maintenance, employee disgruntlement, poor procurement specification – will affect not only immediate revenue but also reputation.

External risks can occur as a result of any number of events taking place in the world outside the organisation which may, at some point in time, have an effect on the way the organisation operates. A common response to identifying these risks is to use the PESTLE (or PESTEL) analysis which considers the risks which may occur from:

- Political impacts – the effects of a change of government on business activity or policy changes by existing governments which might nationalise industry sectors or, indeed, denationalise them.
- Economic – the effects of inward and outward investment policies; corporation tax changes, perhaps, or capital investment rule changes (these may be political as well as economic); foreign labour rates; commodity prices.
- Social – the effects of an increasing awareness of corporate social responsibility; changes in demography; buying habits, eg decline in tobacco consumption.
- Technological – lack of awareness of technology impact on competitiveness; high cost of outdated equipment and machinery.
- Legal – awareness (or lack of it) in relation to appropriate laws and regulation; noncompliance and the effects of an increasingly litigious society.

- Environmental – effects on business survival of ignoring 'green' issues; costs of noncompliance with anti-pollution and emission regulations; sustainability of energy sources.

A variety of tools and techniques are available to assist in identifying and evaluating risks arising from both internal and external sources. The Office of Government Commerce offers a 'toolkit' which can assist and other tools which can be used include Porter's five forces matrix, Kraljik's segmentation approach and the Boston grid.

Feedback on revision question for study session 3

Strategic risk management is based around alternative courses of action which an organisation may take in order to minimise the effects of potential risks which may detract, or even prevent, the strategy being achieved. These risks could affect the continuing survival of the organisation.

An organisation's strategy implements the vision and mission of the organisation's founders and/or its highest management level. Thus, the board and senior management may consider the strategic direction of the organisation and, by analysis, review the risks which might stop the strategy being achieved. They may then decide on different methods of achieving the same end or, even, consider ending a line of business or an activity altogether because it is just too risky to continue.

The strategic approach applies the four tests of:

- Can we treat the risk? *Treat* – identify, evaluate and manage risks as an integral part of doing business.
- Can we transfer or share the risk? *Transfer* – seek ways of sharing risks or of passing them completely to another organisation.
- Can we tolerate the risk? *Tolerate* – either (a) accept the risk and manage it as in 'Treat' or (b) the risk is minimal and will never be large enough to impact on the organisation.
- Do we have to terminate to avoid the risk? *Terminate* – the business is so risky that it cannot be managed down to acceptable levels and the only realistic consideration is to get out.

Strategy flows down into objectives which will be achieved by applying resources – money, manpower, machinery, together with appropriate skill and knowledge – to the processes and procedures which make up the organisation's operations. Thus, operational risk occurs in every facet of the business functions and activities which are pursued in order to achieve objectives. Often they will have been recognised and managed before a formal approach to risk management takes place, eg if an inappropriate action is likely to occur in a process, management will have taken steps to make sure this does not happen as a matter of course. Risk management formalises this approach and attempts to identify all the risks which might arise and manage them in a manner which takes into account their possible impact and probability of occurrence.

Although *operational risk* manifests itself at a lower level in the management of the organisation it can still threaten business survival. For example, failure to manage debtors and cash flow can quickly and easily lead to bankruptcy. Classically, it is the relatively small operational risks which, either unrecognised or badly controlled, build up to a pitch where business survival becomes impossible. Barings Bank provides a good example of where this has occurred.

Project risk embodies all the approaches to risk management which are common to other business activities albeit related to a single project which, in itself, may be relatively simple or extremely complex. Projects tend to be of a finite timescale and directed toward a specific system or business improvement or change, and are often managed as a separate entity from mainstream management activity. The significant risks in projects, therefore, tend toward time and resource overrun which will then have a knock-on effect on implementation timescales which may, in turn, affect anticipated changes to operations and the fulfilment of strategy. Manpower diverted to project management may also affect the risk profile of normal operations when overruns occur.

Cause-and-effect diagrams, mind maps and software such as Prince can assist in the analysis of risks in the strategic, operational and project areas.

Feedback on revision question for study session 4

- Shareholders: those who have purchased shares and expect improvement in share value coupled with reasonable returns on investment, ie dividends. Poor management means no or low dividends and a declining share value.
- Employees: if the company fails to perform employees could be out of a job – with or without redundancy payments and with effects on pensions.
- Suppliers and contractors: late or irregular payments as a result of cash flow difficulties – even no payment if the company goes out of business – affect the ability of suppliers to stay in business.
- Customers: users of the company's goods or services want quality and continuity of supply and the company wants to retain customer loyalty.
- Government – local and central: lack of profits will affect company taxation returns and business rates will suffer if the company goes out of business.
- Neighbours: local businesses which obtain a significant part of their income from the spending of company employees will feel the effect of lay-offs; local people generally may have future employment expectations dashed by the company running down or closing.

Feedback on revision question for study session 5

Effective risk management seeks to maximise the chances for an organisation to avoid an unexpected event which could affect the achievement of objectives. By following a process which identifies and evaluates potential risks, organisations can then put in place mitigation strategies which will assist in managing the risks to a tolerable level. The outcome from good risk management should therefore be an organisation which is better placed to meet its stakeholder expectations by achieving its strategies, objectives, targets and goals. Additionally, there should be an expectation from implementation of risk management processes that both the downside and upside of risk will be identified, ie opportunities will be identified as well as drawbacks.

Total quality management (TQM) is the term applied to the way in which the culture of the organisation embraces the need for all individuals to be aware of (and apply) the level of quality desired to achieve an output which will consistently achieve customer satisfaction. It requires commitment and leadership from the top and a philosophy which promotes waste reduction through continuous improvement. Simple control and improvement techniques are used and these can best be employed by teams, all of whose members are committed to the same ideal of quality output. TQM accepts that the real cost of quality is not in providing assurance but in the costs endured by quality failures: customer dissatisfaction, waste and unnecessary repeat processing.

TQM enhances the possibilities for consistently achieving the desired level of quality and, to that extent, it contributes to effective risk management. The philosophy of TQM which says that everyone becomes responsible for his or her proportion of the quality effort fits well with the risk management concept that every employee should become a risk manager – in other words, those nearest to the point of delivery are best placed to understand what might prevent that expectation of delivery. Similarly, the tone at the top of an organisation sets the culture and philosophy which will be mirrored by every employee – so that the way the board approaches TQM and risk management will be the way in which these issues will be approached by the entire organisation.

In fact, there is nothing that can totally eliminate risk from the operations of any organisation. Whatever actions are taken to manage risk, there will always remain a residual risk beyond which it becomes too difficult or too costly to continue mitigation. If that residual risk still remains unacceptably high, then the organisation must consider the possibilities for transferring the risk or terminating it altogether. Thus, TQM can be a significant contributor to effective risk management but neither eliminates it nor replaces it.

Feedback on revision question for study session 6

The risk appetite of the firm – risk averse or risk enthusiast – will determine the approach to designing a risk strategy for the scaffolding firm. Applying the 4T approach to strategy could result in fewer high risks being identified in the supply part of the business as compared with the erection side but, since the erection business is in place and contributing, it may be difficult to consider termination as a strategy. Treating the risks by effective risk management seems to provide the best way forward.

Competitive activity in this sector will have to be taken into account – the approach to health and safety, for example, may be a restriction for all participants in this sector just as the extent to which operatives are trained will be (the cost of training will have an effect on competitive labour rates). Supply of scaffolding may be generically a less overall risky business than the erection of scaffolding and this needs to be taken into account also although matters such as the right kind of scaffolding – length, strength, couplings and so on – and the quantity to be held as ready stock, all contribute to the financial risks of stockholding in order to cater for as many job types as possible.

A corporate framework for managing risk begins with a clearly stated and coherent risk policy, based on globally accepted standards and which includes the types of risks which are unacceptable to the organisation. There needs to be suitable forums set up where risks can be discussed in a meaningful manner and risk management should feature heavily in any management discussion of new initiatives or any new projects. Day-to-day experience of frontline staff, particularly in the erection side of the business, should be taken into account when responsiveness to customer demand is considered or any initiatives to manage costs more effectively – safety should not be sacrificed to speed or cost cutting.

There needs to be clear responsibility for accepting risk and the authority to manage risk should be defined and assigned to key staff – this embodies *risk ownership* and *risk championing*. An effective framework should also cover the implementation of suitable systems for documenting risks and for the reporting of any significant risk events or experiences, thus providing for learning from experience. Finally, but certainly as important as anything else, there must be suitable monitoring and reviewing of the risk management system to provide assurance that it is operating effectively.

The strategy needs to address how risks are identified, how information about probability and impact is obtained, how risks are quantified, how effective communication mechanisms are set up and supported and how actions are evaluated for their effectiveness.

For the scaffolding company the strategy should mean fewer surprises, more efficient use of resources, better service delivery and better management through improved decision making.

Feedback on revision question for study session 7

Impact and probability are the words used to define the effect that a particular risk might have on the operations of an organisation. Impact is the evaluated effect or result of a particular outcome actually happening in terms of cost, value or consequence. Probability is the evaluation of the event ever actually coming to pass – its likelihood of occurrence. Probability may include consideration of the frequency of the event occurring, eg annually, every ten years, almost never, and so on.

The risk map should look like figure 21.1.

Figure 21.1: Risk map

Impact	low	medium	high
high		4	2, 3, 5
medium		6	1
		8	7

Probability

1   high impact, medium probability (hm)
2   hh
3   hh
4   (reputation) hm
5   hh
6   mm
7   hl
8   ml

Feedback on revision question for study session 8

Two approaches are required for this group of staff:

- raising awareness of the organisation's overall approach to risk management, and
- raising awareness of specific financially-oriented risks.

The organisation's overall approach will depend on its risk appetite. Nonetheless, many organisations have recognised the need to raise risk awareness, and methods include:

- training from induction onwards
- self-assessment (CRSA) or 'healthchecks' (how well are we doing?)
- implementing recommendations from external and internal audit
- cross-functional review teams and quality circles
- initiating and updating risk registers
- rewarding and publicising successful risk identification
- changes in responsibilities to dispel complacency.

It is also generally recognised that embedding risk management into every business process provides the best added value to the organisation and represents one of the best ways of recognising risk as opportunity. In fact, the more that risk identification and evaluation becomes an integral part of the normal way of working, the more likely it will be that (a) every employee takes responsibility for managing risk, and (b) new opportunities will emerge for undertaking new or improved business activities.

A plan of action should therefore include moving to embedded risk management if it is not already in place and implementing the appropriate steps from the above list.

Making staff aware of risks can help identify new threats and take action to minimise them. Thus, finance staff should be exposed to the overall approach to managing risks in the organisation and, in addition, receive training in some of the areas specific to finance where difficulties may occur. Finance risks could include interest rate increases, foreign exchange rate fluctuations, debtor payment risks, cash flow and capital funding risks and the ever-present risks of fraud and theft. Budgetary control, automatic bank reconciliations, debtor and creditor updates all form part of the financial control regime.

The plan of action in finance should include a comprehensive approach to internal control, ie preventive controls, detective controls and directive controls which should operate in financial systems. The purpose of the controls is to mitigate risks by ensuring that there is compliance with laws, regulations and internal policies and procedures, that assets are safeguarded and that financial and operational information is reliable, timely and complete. Finance staff require training in internal control so that the appropriate control can be used in the right context. There also should be training in monitoring the results of control and the means used to report irregularity.

The traditional approaches to control – segregation of duties, authority levels, double signatories, for example – need to be seen in the context of electronic purchase-to-payment regimes. Traditional controls may not be appropriate but other controls still need to be in place. These will include embedded system controls including exception reports and supervisory checks. Management reports and the action taken when irregularities occur form an important part of this approach.

Feedback on revision question for study session 9

A variety of clauses could apply and might include:

- *Currency of contract* – provision of supply for a stated time period passes the onus to the supplier to obtain the good or have it ready in stock for the period of the contract ready for your call-off.
- *Price* – price reviews only at agreed intervals and at agreed levels, eg inflation plus passes the risk of short-term price rises to the supplier for his absorption.
- *Insurance* – requiring the supplier to provide product liability insurance passes some of the risk of quality failure and/or defect to the supplier.
- *Liquidated damages* – inclusion of an agreed sum in the contract provides you with redress from the supplier or contractor if the contract is breached.
- *Information* – a requirement to share information concerning the good or service being supplied can mitigate the risk of sudden shortages or

exceptional price variations or difficulties with the supplier's own supply arrangements.

Additionally, you could have just-in-time supply arrangements by contract with your supplier, thus passing the costs and risks of stockholding to your supplier. You could also have clauses requiring your supplier to hold particular accreditations, ISO 14 000.1, for example, which thus shares and minimises the risk of being seen as environmentally unfriendly.

Feedback on revision question for study session 10

Qualitative, or subjective, methods are often used first in risk analysis to obtain a general indication of the risk issues to be faced and their possible outcomes. The method is often used, also, where numerical data is insufficient, inadequate or simply too costly to collect. Qualitative analysis uses words as descriptors for impact and probability, generally in three bandings: high, medium and low. Once a risk has been identified, judgement is used to rate risks relative to each other. Thus a risk may be judged to have a high impact but a low probability. Combinations of high, low and medium descriptions can then be shown either in matrix form or listed by rank in a risk register.

A risk map is a common qualitative method and depends on judgements being made concerning the potential impact and probability of risks which have been identified within the organisation. By deciding for both factors whether there will be high, medium or low results, the risks can be illustrated on a matrix or map which instantly clarifies those areas where management attention should be concentrated. The risk map can be refined further by adding 'traffic light' colouring to emphasise high-risk areas in red and grading down through amber to green, where the residual risk is either negligible or tolerable.

Scenario planning is another qualitative technique which is used in situations in which we are obliged to make assumptions about a 'scenario' turning out as we expect. Scenario planning can be very useful in assessing strategic risk. For example, we are planning to launch a new hand-held computer. Possible scenarios that we might need to consider could include:

- a competitor comes to market just before us with an even better product
- our system is less reliable than predicted in service
- customers will not pay the slightly higher price at which we plan to sell our product
- the Bank of England suddenly increases interest rates and the economy goes into recession in six months' time.

Scenario analysis poses 'what if' questions based upon various possible – or even apparently impossible – situations arising. Scenario analysis allows managements to move away from total reliance on traditional forecasting methods and gives the benefit of at least some preparedness when unexpected or unusual circumstances arise.

Quantitative research begins with the collection of statistics, based on real data, observations or questionnaires. Quantitative research is the numerical representation and manipulation of observations for the purpose of describing and explaining the phenomena that those observations reflect. It is used in a wide variety of natural and social sciences, including physics, biology, psychology, sociology and geology.

Regression analysis. It is relatively easy to plot a probability distribution when the data involves a single variable – for example, the number of reject items that we can expect when we examine a batch of, say, microchips from a supplier. Frequently, however, situations occur where there are two or more associated variables to be considered. One particularly important group of these is concerned with trying to predict the unknown value of one variable from the known value of the other variable. For example, a farmer may have information on the springtime rainfall in his area over the last five years and information on his crop yields. But how good is the level of spring rainfall as a predictor of crop yield later in the year? While there is likely to be some connection, the farmer will want to know how closely the two variables are related. Using *linear regression* we can develop an equation which allows us to plot a straight line on a graph which provides the 'line of best fit' to the observed data. The two axes on the graph will be, in this case, crop yield and rainfall. We can then plot the actual observations onto the graph and, depending on how tightly the observations are grouped around the line, we can infer the strength of the link between rainfall and crop yield. A wide scatter around the line means a weak link between the two variables. A tight scatter around the line suggests a strong link.

In many cases there are more than just two variables. The farmer (or the supermarket buyer who needs to predict future price movements) might want to look at the link between crop yields on the one hand and spring rainfall, temperature and hours of sunshine on the other. The technique which enables us to do this is known as multiple regression and is an extension of the techniques used in linear regression.

Ratio analysis. Applying ratios to financial data can give information which will assist in assessing how a prospective supplier company – or potential customer – is placed to meet short- and medium-term commitments. This can assist us in assessing which suppliers can work with us in terms of the prices we can negotiate and their being in business long enough to ensure our required period of supply. Similarly, we can make judgements on the risk which potential and existing customers pose in terms of ability to pay. Ratios can tell us how a company has fared over recent times and provide a guide for future performance.

Part of competitive advantage is having as much information as possible about your own capabilities and those of your competitors. Identifying and evaluating risks within our own organisation provides us with the opportunity of managing resources more effectively to meet customer demands of delivery, quality and price. By using a mix of qualitative and quantitative risk management techniques we improve our chances of both becoming more competitive with our existing operations and discovering new opportunities which might not otherwise have become apparent. Some of the techniques, ratio analysis, for example, can assist us in analysing our competitors' financial position, thus giving us good information in relation to market penetration and future investment ability.

Feedback on revision question for study session 11

In summary:

- Design engineering capability (visit and check out)
- Manufacturing capability (visit and assess against checklist)
  (a) experience of making this or similar product
  (b) ability to meet future increases in demand
  (c) recent investment in new machinery
  (d) flexibility to meet changes in our need
  (e) housekeeping
  (f) recent health and safety record
- Quality control – QA/QC accreditations, ISO, EN standards used
- Management – organisation, lines of responsibility, dedicated account management? and so on (visit and ask questions)
- Financial; how strong, how big, how profitable (get published accounts + D&B report)
- Aftersales service (ask for names of other customers who you can talk to)

In detail:

The specification for the product or service which is required will be provided by our own line management together with an idea of the anticipated timeline; new product manufacture commencement, for example, or the date for introduction of a new or improved stock item. We may have a selection of potential suppliers from previous buying exercises or from electronic pre-tendering enquiries but now we need to 'qualify' suppliers for this particular supply. Generally this will be approached using a mixture of assessment and appraisal methods which will include questionnaires and both procurement and financial review.

Following an accurate specification, the source of supply is our first consideration when approaching potential risks: single source or multiple source and any other potential sourcing difficulty, eg overseas supply. The questionnaire should include appropriate questions to make the source clear.

Reputational effects. Reputational risk can also be a major consideration when we are appraising potential suppliers. The main ways in which our reputation might be damaged by our suppliers include:

- If suppliers fail to meet our standards of quality, timeliness and customer service this may affect our ability to meet our own customers' expectations.
- Poor consideration of ethical and environmental issues.

We can evaluate all these issues by referring to previous performance if the supplier has been used before, by seeking market intelligence if a new supplier and by asking questions on our questionnaire concerning quality and environmental accreditations.

The financial position of the supplier can be assessed by asking questions concerning key ratios such as liquidity, profitability and so on, and this may be sought direct from the supplier or by using published financial information such as company reports. Evaluating financial information is a key factor in selecting a supplier since this provides a guide to business continuity and ability to continue to fund our supply requirements. Enquiries could also be requested from your own bankers and the supplier company's bankers as to the creditworthiness of the supplier company. This would be done as a matter of course when undertaking due diligence – a term applied to undertaking audits of a prospective partner, takeover or merging company to ensure that expectations can actually be realised – and can be used in a limited application to potential suppliers.

Gaining an understanding of the potential supplier's approach to standard setting in its industry can also give valuable added information to the supplier selection decision. Industry awards and national awards can give a flavour of the supplier company's approach to quality, HR investment and customer satisfaction. Investment in People awards, Queen's Awards to Industry and so on are all indicators of an organisation's culture and approach. Again, the questionnaire can include these areas in order that the supplier can respond accordingly.

Assessment of performance in the case of existing or previous suppliers is a common method of gaining confidence in supplier ability to meet requirements. Questionnaires to potential and existing suppliers provide the basis for information gathering which is then evaluated to assess ability to supply. Other methods should not be forgotten such as face-to-face meetings with the supplier's staff and, in the case of existing suppliers, the use of customer audits, ie audits carried out by your staff within the supplier's business.

Feedback on revision question for study session 12

The majority of ethical codes stress that there should be no *impropriety* – offending against moral law or legal requirement – and that there should be avoidance of doing any *needless harm* – to the environment, perhaps, or to individuals by an abuse of human rights. Applying these principles to business decision making is not difficult and the simple tests that can be applied are:

- Transparency – do I mind others knowing what I had in mind?
- Effect – who does my decision affect or hurt?
- Fairness – would my decision be considered fair in objective terms?

Many examples of ethical codes exist around the world. This is a very subjective area, however, and often difficult to codify; what works for one country or industry may not work for another. In this case, the approach in the public sector, which concentrates on the need for public trust and accountability and frowns upon any action which could be construed as corruption, will not be the same as the approach in the entertainment industry. The main principles should still apply, however, although application may be different. The following steps should feature in any ethical code or, indeed, a straightforward code of good business practice:

- Honesty, objectivity and diligence in carrying out responsibilities.
- Loyalty to the company.
- Avoid conflicts of interest.

- Avoid acts which could discredit the company and its reputation.
- Accept no inducements to act in a particular manner.
- Avoid use of confidential information for personal gain.
- Ensure that all activities undertaken are within the law.
- Maintain high standards of integrity, morality and competence.

Many of these are reflected or implied in CIPS's own Code of Ethics to which all members are required to adhere. In particular, CIPS is clear about gifts and hospitality; gifts should have little or no intrinsic value and hospitality should not be on a scale which could not reasonably be reciprocated.

The culture of the entertainment industry is certainly different from that in the public sector. Hospitality and the giving and receiving of gifts may be more part of the way of doing business. This should not mean that the basic principles of an ethical approach need be broken – there can be no case for breaking the law of the land, for example, or for the abuse of human and other rights. The use of any inducement, for example, can very quickly escalate into a corrupt act since, by their very nature, inducements tend to increase if they become part of a 'normal' transaction – more incentive is needed as time goes on and greed becomes a part of the equation.

In fact, various inducements and incentives to use particular suppliers form part of everyday business practice. Price cuts as incentives to buy, bulk buying discounts and special promotions of one kind or another form the usual backdrop to buying and selling. Where this can go wrong is in passing some of these benefits as personal inducements to buyers to influence their buying decisions – or in other ways seeking to get buyers to act in ways which will benefit their companies but also personally benefit them.

Ethical approaches are often about personal actions and reactions; we should follow the idea of 'do unto others what you would have done unto you'. Tolerate nothing, in other words, which you would not like happening to you. None of us would like to be in the position of having lost business as a result of the corrupt practice of a competitor. It's unfair – but it's also unethical.

Feedback on revision question for study session 13

Management 'by committee' is usually a recipe – if not for disaster, at least for missing targets – in any situation. A project manager is essential for all projects and a good manager helps to avoid failure. This individual should be nominated and be given the authority to manage the project, reporting at agreed intervals to the board and/or senior management. Thus, any project will benefit from strong and clear management with authority residing in one individual.

The management-by-committee approach often spells disaster for a project because it lacks clear and decisive leadership along with speedy decision-making processes. The project team may meet as a 'committee' but, in reality, the team should be a group of specialists, chosen for their expertise in a particular field as well as for their personal qualities which can contribute to the group dynamic. In fact, almost all projects benefit from the contributions of a whole range of skills. All projects require sound financial input and control regardless of their fundamental nature. Similarly, IT input will help the project planning process in addition to any specialised input to the core of the project.

The nature of the project will determine the skill levels, experience and knowledge required of the main participants driving the core project requirement. A construction project will require architects, surveyors and building experts as key team members but will benefit, also, from the input of accountants and computer specialists. Clearly, there are advantages in having a mix of participants in a project team so that both the fundamentals and the peripherals of the project can be adequately covered. The advantages can be dissipated without a strong leader, however. Skilled professionals and managers, perhaps all at or near the same level within an organisation, will each feel that their view should prevail; it needs good leadership to harness this energy and knowledge to make it work for one common aim.

The main enemies of successful project completion are time overruns and overspending. A team without a leader will fall prey to these much more easily as a result of the time and energy wasted on issues such as political infighting which will not drive the project forward. Additionally, lack of knowledge of project management can be a significant drawback, since there are particular skills which can be applied to the running of a project, eg use of appropriate software, understanding of project management techniques and the experience of where things can go wrong.

A weak project manager or a committee approach to running the project constitute large risks which can only be compounded as the project moves on and any difficulties occur. On the other hand, strong leadership and a mix of the right skills provide the best chance of success in any proposed project.

Feedback on revision question for study session 14

Getting the supply you have specified at the times and place required and at the price agreed are the main contractual requirements that you would wish to see fulfilled. You would want to seek redress if this does not happen.

- Payment – you would agree to pay the agreed price within a set number of days after receipt of invoice. *Receipt of invoice allows you to check price and quantity against your delivery note/receipt note and allows you time to process payment.*
- Price escalation clause. *The price of crude oil has to rise by more than X% before the supplier can pass on any increase to you.*
- Price reduction clause. The supplier must share with you or pass back to you any reduction of more than Y% in the cost of crude oil.
- Rejection – if the quality and standard (eg octane level, burn rate) is found not to conform then you can reject this and subsequent deliveries if the same applies. *You can test for quality and any other agreed specification and reject substandard deliveries.*
- Breach of contract – where a fundamental part of the contract is not fulfilled, the contract can be voided and redress sought. *This allows you*

to terminate the contract if you are certain that a fundamental breach has occurred. No deliveries for a long period, for example.

- Indemnity – the contractor undertakes to indemnify you against any loss, damage, injury or liability resulting from a breach of contract. *This is usually accompanied by a stated insurance limit against this liability, often in excess of £1,000,000.*

- Liquidated damages – an amount agreed in the contract to allow for compensation should the contract fail to be completed. *This allows you to claim compensation in the event that the contractor can no longer supply and you have to seek new arrangements.*

- Force majeure – avoidance of the contract in the event of act of God. *You could use this to escape obligations under the contract if an extraordinary event such as a flood or earthquake prevents you from carrying on to take the full contracted deliveries.*

- Waiver – waiving of any right or remedy under the contract does not mean that all other rights and remedies are waived. *This gives you the flexibility, should you want it, to waive only one clause without affecting the rest of the contract.*

- Amendments and variations – should be stated as not valid unless agreed in writing. *This safeguards you against the contractor changing the terms of the contract without your express knowledge.*

- Law and jurisdiction – states the legal structure and framework within which the contract is to be undertaken. *This could be important if you contract with an overseas supplier: the contract should be stated to be under the laws of the United Kingdom.*

Feedback on revision question for study session 15

REPORT

A REVIEW OF RISKS UNIQUE TO PUBLIC SECTOR OPERATIONS

1 Background

Differences between public and private sectors lie mainly in the governance arrangements, accountability, the manner of funding, style of administration and policy.

Public sector risks are different only in that the funding, operation and management of public sector services differs from that in the private sector. Exposure to risk is the combination of impact and probability of the events which might prevent objectives being achieved and this defines risks in all sectors of activity. There is, therefore, a common approach to risk management. Where there are differences, they flow not just from unique operations but from variances in the risk appetite and the accountability of service provision.

2 Risk appetite and funding

The manner of funding public sector bodies means that all citizens have a stake in the way organisations are run and how well they perform since it is public money, in the main, which is being used to finance activities. There are limitations on the way in which public money can be raised and the use of that money is under public scrutiny – taxpayers do not expect speculation with their funds to the same extent that shareholders may accept higher risk in return for higher profit. This can easily affect the attitude which managers in the public sector have to taking risks and, in general, this tends towards the risk-averse end of the scale.

3   Accountability

Accountability concerns also affect risk attitude. In the public sector, accountability is to the public at large and not just a relatively small group of shareholders as in the private sector. Despite there being some significant differences between the sectors in inputs, management and outcomes, the process of making risk management effective is very similar. Thus, relating risks to objectives at each level of a public sector operation follows much the same path as in the private sector. There needs to be a good understanding of objectives at each level and there needs to be a process which can identify and manage the risks which could arise.

4   Governance and policy

Shareholders own companies, and boards of directors appointed at annual general meetings manage companies on behalf of shareholders. Although there is much debate as to the composition of stakeholders in the private sector, accountability of the directors is, in the first instance, to the shareholders. Governance, ie the way the organisation is directed and controlled, is also in the hands of the directors and they have sole responsibility for the level of success in growing the business, achieving shareholder satisfaction and meeting the strategic objectives of the company. The policy and procedures of the company are those laid down by the directors and are designed to achieve the strategy and objectives of the company only. In contrast, in the public sector it is often elected members or publicly appointed governors who have responsibility for direction and who have to answer for their actions to citizens, ie the public at large. The policies may be driven by government requirement and/or political ends, and success in achieving objectives is judged, not by a small group of shareholders and investors, but by general public opinion.

5   Key risks

The key risk for those who are elected to office is that they will fail to be re-elected as a result of public disillusionment. This may arise from lack of success in meeting the aims for which they were elected; loss of reputation through their own or their immediate associates' behaviour; overspending to a critical degree; and social or environmental pressures where public perspective is such that blame is laid at the politician's door. The next tier of this same risk is that officers who are responsible for policy implementation fail to achieve expected performance and responsibility is laid again – and quite properly – at the elected member's door.

The key risk in government departments and non-departmental public bodies (NDPBs) is failure to achieve their stated purpose, coupled with lack of value for money, at least in public perception. The consequent loss of reputation and credibility impacts not only on the particular organisation but also on the government or other sponsoring body.

The key risk in other public sector organisations, such as not-for-profit organisations, is the failure to achieve sufficient funds to adequately carry out the organisation's main objective. This may be through excessive administration costs, poor fund raising or misuse of funds. Regardless of cause, the outcome will be a perceived lack of success which will result in loss of public confidence and a continuing downward spiral of lack of support through loss of funding and volunteer activity.

6   Conclusion

Since the underlying cause of risks is common to all sectors of activity, the approach to risk management is generally similar between private and public sectors. Where differences do exist it is as a result of the structure and framework of management where governance, accountability and methods of funding can vary between sectors.

J.Bloggs

30 May

Feedback on revision question for study session 16

The board and senior management should be aware of the risks posed by noncompliance with laws and regulations in general. In terms of environmental legislation, in common with health and safety issues, the board should take steps to ensure that the organisation is prepared to identify and manage its vulnerable areas. The following steps would be appropriate:

- A comprehensive and holistic approach should be taken to risk management. Methods for identifying and evaluating risks (such as CRSA) should be in place and must include addressing legal and environmental issues by using risk analyses such as PESTLE.
- Risk management processes should be subject to constant review and update so that the board is aware of new risks from whatever cause, eg new legislation.
- Significant risks should be allocated ownership, ie the responsibility of a named individual who will be accountable for the success of managing the appropriate risk. Environmental legislation should be one such area.
- An environmental management system such as provided by ISO 14 000.1 may be adopted and will, in itself, provide a response to the risk of changes in environmental legislation by ensuring systems are subject to supervision and review.
- A programme of internal audits should be put in place which will provide assurance over the adequacy of control over environmental issues and give recommendations for any improvements which may be required.

Once the risks have been assessed, appropriate mitigation action should include consideration of the ability to reduce the risk by effective management action such as tighter internal control, changes to procedure, or more adequate training. There may be an opportunity to share the risk with another department or supplier or it may be that the new legislation involves so much added cost without added value that termination of the activity may be necessary.

Feedback on revision question for study session 17

Choice of mode of transport in international trade depends upon geography and the factors of time, distance and expediency, eg the speed with which the good must be obtained. The choice of transport comes from the three areas of surface, sea or air and the nature of the good concerned. Advantages, disadvantages and the risks associated with the mode of transport are linked to all these foregoing issues. We can consider the matter using table 21.1 as follows:

Table 21.1 Surface

Advantages	Disadvantages	Risks
Easy to arrange	Maximum load size limitation	Traffic delays
Wide choice of operators		Customs/border delays
	Unfamiliarity with road system	Impounding of goods
Variety of load parcel		
	Regulations may vary with country, eg driver's hours	Vehicle breakdown
Speed of delivery		Theft
Lower insurance and unit costs		Hijack

Table 21.2 Sea

Advantages	Disadvantages	Risks
Large volumes/low cost	Cost of shipping	Weather delays
	Cost of insurance	Cargo loss (shipwreck)
	Unitised load (containers)/specialised vessel	Theft
		Ship and crew standards (flag of convenience)
	Long delivery time	
	Tariff impositions	Docking and unloading delays
	Onward transport cost	Customs/impounding of goods

Table 21.3 Air

Advantages	Disadvantages	Risks
Speed	Cost	Air traffic delays
Perishables easily delivered	Small unit load	

(continued on next page)

Table 21.3 *(continued)*

Advantages	Disadvantages	Risks
	Small overall capacity	Sent to wrong destination
	Insurance cost	
		Theft
	Onward transport cost	
		Impoundment

Other risks linked to methods of transportation include the nature of the good concerned – product volatility, for example, which can affect some raw material (eg oil, coal) and may dictate particular vessel types for shipment which, in turn, may affect travel time and cost. Achieving an economic volume of product also affects method of shipment, time and cost. Some risk share or transfer can be achieved by using commodity markets to buy and sell rather than dealing directly with source suppliers – and maritime insurance can also be used to offset loss or damage to cargo in transit.

Geography may well be the prime factor in single-source goods or commodities. Distance from the market, combined with natural geophysical barriers and lack of alternative supply or the ability to substitute, brings risks which are difficult to mitigate and exacerbate the advantages and disadvantages of different forms of transport.

Feedback on revision question for study session 18

The term 'good-quality training' is subjective – the training we want should be delivered to the standard which we desire and specify. It follows, therefore, that our specifications should clarify for the training company exactly what we expect and the contract should state our expectations in terms of cost and outcome.

- At the pre-contract stage our first step should have been to ensure that the company is capable of delivering up to our expectations. This would have been done using appraisals and face-to-face meetings or audits in the prospective company. Among the matters to have been discussed would have been the training company's prior experience, specific experience in our field, qualified personnel, and financial standing. Any evidence of TQM quality standards such as ISO 9000 or other accreditations such as Investor in People would add to credibility. Gathering of this data is necessary for us to make an informed decision as to the capability of the training company.
- Specification is the means by which we communicate our requirements to the suppliers of the products or services which we need as input to our own operations. A specification is a statement of the user's requirements. In procurement terms, the specification is a document which clearly and accurately describes the essential technical or performance requirements for items, materials or services which we seek to source on behalf of the user function, department or business unit for whom we are acting. The specification must be absolutely clear since it will be the basis of service delivery by the training company and will also be used as the basis for performance measurement as the contract progresses.

- The outcomes expected as a result of the training should be stated in terms of measurable targets. These targets may be financial in terms of increased sales per head or total revenue increase but may also be subjective: improved staff morale and motivation, perhaps. Other targets may be non-financial but more easily measured – reduction in complaints, for example. Successful delivery of the contract should depend on achieving measurable improvements so our review of progress should include consideration of the extent to which the training is showing improvements.
- Benchmarking our own performance against industry or competitors' standards will give us the opportunity of measuring any improvements which can be put down to a better-trained workforce. This exercise depends on frequent comparisons being made – one of which must have been taken before the training contract commences. Other factors need to be taken into account with benchmarking such as market conditions and competitor activity but it does, nonetheless, provide another means for measuring progress.
- Evaluating the costs of the training against the benefits attained – such as increased sales, improved profitability or reduction in unit costs – is another means for measuring the changes which ought to have occurred as a result of the training. A cost/benefit analysis of this nature provides a guide to the success or otherwise of the money spent in training.
- A value-for-money audit could provide similar results to the cost/benefit analysis. The audit would consider the terms of the contract and its costs and evaluate against the specification the extent to which outcomes have been achieved together with the extent of any added value gained from the exercise. This evaluation provides a good indicator for future training and the outcomes which could be expected.

The key to this and any similar exercise is to ensure effective supplier appraisal, specify accurately and in detail and review performance at regular intervals. Outcomes and expectations should be clear and, despite difficulties being perceived in measuring deliverables in areas such as training, the penalties for non-performance should be clearly understood.

Feedback on revision question for study session 19

Statistical process control (SPC) is a method for achieving quality control in manufacturing processes. The underlying assumption in SPC is that any production process will produce products whose properties vary slightly from the designed values, even when things are running normally. There may be small but detectable differences in each product and there may also be changes in the machinery – through wear and tear or through slight power fluctuations. If these variances were allowed to continue unchecked then the product could fall outside the manufacturing tolerances and also fail to meet customer requirements. These variances can be analysed statistically to control the process and be used to correct problems thus reducing or eliminating rejects and waste.

The enterprise-wide approach to risk management lends itself to embedding the controls necessary to mitigate risk into every system and every procedure. Thus, all the procedures which cover identification, evaluation and action can transfer into operational systems. Controls need to be built in to systems at the development stage, since to amend systems after they become operational is costly and time consuming. The way to achieve this is to ensure that the risk management system is accepted as part and parcel of the systems development process. That means an acceptance that internal control is a holistic concept and is the bedrock of management control. Thus, a technique such as SPC should not be seen as a separate entity but as an integral part of the overall control system.

Internal control is not just financial control but is all pervasive. Operations require management control just as much as finance does. Accepting that control is a response to a risk, it is clear that if objectives are known, then the interrelationships between every organisational function and unit can be expressed in terms of the risks which may prevent achievement of objectives and the controls put in place to mitigate these risks. SPC is the response to the risk of unacceptable quality just as a bank reconciliation is one of the responses to the risk of fraud in the payments system.

Embedding risk and control into systems is done both from the point of view of addressing management's need to have effective systems but should also include the ability to report on how well the system objectives are being achieved. The most important part of embedding risk and control initiatives is to follow through by introducing them into IT systems and implementing their use. Thereafter, it is essential to take action when things are going wrong. If the report data is not used to take corrective action, there is little point in having a control in the first place.

Feedback on revision question for study session 20

To: Chief Executive

From: J. Bloggs

Date: June

DRAFT REPORT ON DISASTER RECOVERY

1   Introduction

Prevention is better than cure. This philosophy can be applied to the holistic approach to disaster recovery which should cover all contingencies, not only IT recovery. Natural and man-made risks may be reduced through taking a number of preventive measures and, by anticipating potential disaster areas, plans can be put in place which will assist with a speedy recovery.

2   Background

Natural disasters and catastrophic events will happen. The past informs the future in this respect: we know that floods, earthquakes and hurricanes will occur from time to time. Aircraft will crash and terrorist acts will take place. We also know that power and energy supplies will fluctuate and that any number of other events may test our preparedness – and that is the key to disaster recovery: being as prepared as possible for the surprises we know will occur. What we don't know is when, where or how bad these events may be.

This Draft Report aims to highlight areas of our activity for which effective disaster planning can assist in maintaining continuity. The Report will identify the potential impacts of some specific risks that could threaten our business and provide a framework for effective responses.

3 Risks and responses

3.1 The first part of the review should consider our main business activities. The key risks affecting our business come from the potential for loss of systems, loss of people, loss of equipment and loss of buildings. The effect of these on each separate business unit must be reviewed.

3.2 IT recovery is already in place. This report therefore reviews risks in other areas although it should be remembered that IT permeates all our activities and loss of IT constitutes a major risk.

3.3 Risks may come from natural events such as flood or extreme weather while risks created by man may include fire, vandalism, theft and loss of key personnel. The risk response is related more to the effect rather than the cause; in other words it does not matter whether a building is destroyed by fire or aircraft crash, the effect will be the same – although our risk mitigation measures must take into account potential causes and guard against them, eg physical security is a response to the risk of theft.

4 Loss of systems

The main risk to our systems is loss of power. Power backup is covered in the IT recovery plan but we need to consider the effect of a major power loss on our outlying buildings and the operation of equipment other than IT. Where buildings rely on artificial light, there will be a significant effect on productivity if emergency lighting arrangements are not in place quickly. The length of time that mains power is expected to be out will determine our response but it may be that a shortening of the working day to take advantage of daylight hours only will be the best response. Most of our systems are dependent on IT and recovery using paper systems is not a realistic prospect.

5 Loss of people

Loss of people through death or severe injury would have a significant impact on our business if it were to happen on any large scale. Normal risks are more likely to be loss of key personnel through career moves or retirement and we can mitigate this risk by using succession planning for key posts. Continuing development training will allow us to maintain a well-trained workforce ready to take on new responsibilities should the need arise. Good recruitment processes will help us to anticipate vacancies and secure replacements in good time.

6 Loss of equipment

Without the right equipment (and stock) we would be unable to continue in business for long. Each business unit should therefore review the equipment it considers essential for continuity and make plans for the feasibility of holding spare backup equipment or making contractual arrangements for quick replacement. Contractual arrangements reduce our potential costs through not maintaining unutilised equipment and mirror the risk response in IT where we maintain a 'hot start' contract for speedy recovery. JIT stock arrangements should be in place as a matter of course.

7   Loss of buildings

Our business activities are contained within a number of conjoined and separate buildings. We could operate successfully with the loss of one key building by transferring people elsewhere and by shift working to make equipment more available. Loss of several buildings would constitute a significant threat to business continuity and a reasonable response to this threat is difficult to see. It is unrealistic to maintain empty real estate and our only mitigation may be to ensure that our relationships with commercial estate agents are kept up to date and our specific building needs are profiled adequately so that available property can be found quickly.

8   Conclusion

This draft report has not attempted to identify and evaluate all the possible risks which may contribute to a major disaster for our business. Rather, we have looked at generic risk areas where large-scale events could constitute business problems for us. Each business unit should be asked to review its current readiness to face a potential disaster using this Report as a basis for further analysis and action.

References and bibliography

This section contains a complete A-Z listing of all publications, materials or websites referred to in this course book. Books, articles and research are listed under the first author's (or in some cases the editor's) surname. Where no author name has been given, the publication is listed under the name of the organisation that published it. Websites are listed under the name of the organisation providing the website.

Association of Project Managers: http://www.apm.org.

Audit Commission: http://www.audit-commission.gov.uk.

Bernstein, P (1996) *Against the Gods: The remarkable story of risk*. Chichester: Wiley.

Boddy, D (2005) *Management: an Introduction*, 3rd edition. Harlow: Pearson.

British Computer Society: http://www.bcs.org/BCS/Information/Security/disaster.htm.

British Standards Institution: http://www.bsi-global.com.

Business continuity: http://www.continuitycentral.com, http://www.availability.sungard.com.

Business Continuity Institute: http://www.thebci.org.

Business Link: http://www.businesslink.gov.uk.

Canadian Institute of Chartered Accountants: http://www.cica.ca.

Canadian Institute of Chartered Accountants (1995) *Guidance on Control, Control and Governance No 1*.

Chapman, CB, and S Ward (2003) *Project Risk Management*, 2nd edition. Chichester: Wiley.

Committee of Sponsoring Organisations of the Treadway Commission (COSO) (2004) *Enterprise Risk Management*.

COSO: http://www.coso.org.

Cowan, N (2004) *Corporate Governance: that Works!* Singapore: Pearson Prentice Hall.

Cranfield Management Research: http://www.som.cranfield.ac.uk.

Decision Trees: http://www.mindtools.com.

Department for Environment, Food and Rural Affairs: http://www.defra.gov.uk.

Department for Environment, Food and Rural Affairs (2000) *Guidelines for Environmental Risk Assessment and Management.*

Department for Work and Pensions: http://www.ogc.gov.uk. *Change Lifecycle Methodology.* Link from the OGC website Contract Case Studies.

Department of Trade and Industry: http://www.dti.gov.uk.

Department of Trade and Industry (2004) *Resolving Disputes – a new approach in the Workplace* Department of Trade and Industry: http://www.dti.gov.uk.

Department of Trade and Industry. *Standard Terms of Contract* Department of Trade and Industry: http://www.dti.gov.uk/about/procurement/.

Dyson, JR (2004) *Accounting for Non-Accounting Students*, 6th edition. Harlow: FT Prentice Hall.

Eckes, G (2001) *The Six Sigma Revolution.* Chichester: Wiley.

European Foundation for Quality Management: http://www.efqm.org.

Financial Planning Toolkit: http://www.finance.cch.com.

Flowcharts: http://www.startinbusiness.co.uk/flowchart.

Foreign and Commonwealth Office: http://www.fco.gov.uk.

Health and Safety Executive (2004) *Your Health, Your Safety. A Guide for Workers.*

Hillson, D, and R Murray-Webster (2005) *Understanding and Managing Risk Attitude.* Aldershot, UK: Gower.

HM Treasury (2001) *Risk: A Strategic Overview.*

Hofstede, G (2005) *Cultures and Organizations.* London: McGraw-Hill.

Impact Value: http://www.flatstats.co.uk.

Institute of Business Ethics: http://www.ibe.org.uk.

Institute of Chartered Accountants in England and Wales (1999) *Internal Control Guidance for Directors on the Combined Code.*

Institute of Risk Management: http://www.theirm.org, *The Risk Management Standard.*

Intelligent Enterprise: http://www.intelligententerprise.com/040101/701infosc1_2.jhtml

International Chamber of Commerce: http://www.iccwbo.org.

International Labour Organization: http://www.ilo.org.

International Organization for Standardization: http://www.iso.org.

Kocak, NA (2004) Unpublished PhD thesis, University of Westminster, Transport Studies Group.

Kraljic, P (1983) 'Purchasing must become supply management', *Harvard Business Review*, Sept-Oct, pp 109–17.

Krause, DG (1995) *Sun Tzu: The Art of War for Executives.* London: Nicholas Brealey.

Lamming, R, and A Cox (Eds) (1999) *Strategic Procurement Management.* Earlsgate Press.

Lock, D (2003) *Project Management*, 8th edition. Aldershot, UK: Gower.

Lysons, K, and B Farrington (2006) *Purchasing and Supply Chain Management*, 7th edition. Harlow: FT Prentice Hall.

Manifest (ed) (2006) *The Corporate Governance Handbook.* London: Gee and Co.

Monte Carlo Method: http://www.mbrm.com.

Mullins, LJ (1996) *Management and Organisational Behaviour.* London: Pitman Publishing

National Audit Office: http://www.nao.org.uk.

Neverfail: http://www.neverfailgroup.com/.

Oakland, JS (1995) *Total Quality Management.* Oxford: Butterworth-Heinemann.

Office of Government Commerce (2005): http://www.ogc.gov.uk *Management of Risk: Guidance for Practitioners.*

Peters, TJ, and RH Waterman (2004) *In Search of Excellence.* London: Profile.

Pickett, KH, and J Pickett (2002) *Financial Crime Investigation and Control.* Chichester: Wiley.

Porter, ME (1985) *Competitive Strategy.* London: Free Press.

Porter, ME (2004) *Competitive Strategy.* London: Free Press.

Project Management (PRINCE): http://www.concertosupport.co.uk.

Risk Analysis and Disaster Recovery Planning: http://www.eon-commerce.com/riskanalysis/disaster-recovery.htm.

Risk Management Manuals: http://www.ukresilience.info/risk/.

Risk Management Software: http://www.insight.co.uk.

Risk Registers: http://www.dfes.gov.uk.

Robbins, H, and M Finley (2000) *Why Teams Don't Work*. London: Texere.

Sadgrove, K (2005) *The Complete Guide to Business Risk Management*, 2nd edition. Aldershot, UK: Gower.

Saunders, M (1997) *Strategic Purchasing and Supply Chain Management*, 2nd edition. London: Pitman.

Schuyler, J (2001) *Risk and Decision Analysis in Projects*. Philadelphia: Project Management Institute.

Shimell, P (2002) *The Universe of Risk*. Harlow: FT Prentice Hall.

Smith, A (1776) *The Wealth of Nations*. London: Methuen and Co. 5th edition (1904)

Start In Business: http://www.startinbusiness.co.uk/flowchart/8flowchart_ins.htm.

Stationery Office: http://www.tso.co.uk.

SPC Software: http://www.datalyzer.com, http://www.infinityqs.com.

SustainAbility: http://www.sustainability.com/sa-services/stakeholder-engagement.asp

Telegraph: http://www.telegraph.co.uk/money/main.jhtml?xml=/money/exclusions/businessinsurance/bioutline.xml

Transparency International: http://www.transparency.org.

UK Resilience: http://www.ukresilience.info/home.htm.

Waring, AE, and AI Glendon (1998) *Managing Risk*. London: International Thomson Business.

Webb, A (2003) *The Project Manager's Guide to Handling Risk*. Aldershot, UK: Gower.

Wideman, RM (1992) *Project and Program Risk Management*. Upper Darby, PA: Project Management Institute.

Womack, JP, and DT Jones (2003) *Lean Thinking*. London: Simon & Schuster.

Working of Government: http://www.direct.gov.uk.

Index